Lecture Notes in Computer Science 8622

Commenced Publication in 1973
Founding and Former Series Editors:
Gerhard Goos, Juris Hartmanis, and Jan van Leeuwen

More information about this series at http://www.springer.com/series/7410

Emmanuel Prouff (Ed.)

Constructive Side-Channel Analysis and Secure Design

5th International Workshop, COSADE 2014
Paris, France, April 13–15, 2014
Revised Selected Papers

Springer

Editor
Emmanuel Prouff
FNISA
Paris
France

ISBN 978-3-319-10174-3   ISBN 978-3-319-10175-0   (eBook)
DOI 10.1007/978-3-319-10175-0

Library of Congress Control Number: 2014947448

Springer Cham Heidelberg New York Dordrecht London

Printed on acid-free paper

Springer is part of Springer Science+Business Media (www.springer.com)

Preface

The 5th workshop on Constructive Side-Channel Analysis and Secure Design (COSADE 2014), was held in Paris, France, during April 13–15, 2014. The workshop was supported by three golden sponsors (ANSSI, Secure IC, RISCURE) and three silver sponsors (Cryptography Research, INVIA, and SERMA Technologies).

COSADE 2014 received 51 submissions. Each submission was reviewed by at least 3, and on average 4, Program Committee members. The review process was double-blind, and conflicts of interest were carefully handled. The review process was handled through an online review system (Easychair) that supported discussions among Program Committee members. Eventually, the Program Committee selected 20 papers (a 39 % acceptance rate) for publication in the proceedings. The Committee decided to give the Best Paper Award to Mohamed Karroumi, Benjamin Richard, and Marc Joye for their paper "Addition with Blinded Operands," and the Best Student Paper Award to Guilherme Perin for his contribution to the paper "Attacking Randomized Exponentiations Using Unsupervised Learning." The program also included two invited talks, by Dmitry Nedospasov from the Security in Telecommunications (SECT) research group at the Berlin University of Technology (TU Berlin), and by Sebastian Faust from EPFL Lausanne.

Many people contributed to COSADE 2014. I thank the authors for contributing their excellent research. I thank the Program Committee members, and their external reviewers, for making a significant effort over an extended period of time to select the right papers for the program. I particularly thank Jean-luc Danger, the general chair, who took care of many practical details of the event. I also thank Sorin Huss and Werner Schindler for their support and their fruitful advices. I am very grateful to the Telecom Paristech members, and especially Guillaume Duc, for their excellent organization of the event. Finally, I thank our sponsors for supporting COSADE financially: ANSSI, Cryptography Research, Secure IC, Riscure, Invia, and Serma Technologies. COSADE 2014 collects truly exciting results in cryptographic engineering, from concepts to artifacts, from software to hardware, from attack to countermeasure. I feel privileged for the opportunity to develop the COSADE 2014 program. I hope that the papers in this proceedings will continue to inspire, guide, and clarify your academic and professional endeavors.

June 2014   Emmanuel Prouff

Organization

Program Committee

Ray Cheung	City University of Hong Kong, China
Christophe Clavier	University of Limoges, France
Jean-Sebastien Coron	University of Luxembourg, Luxembourg
Jean-Christophe Courrège	THALES Communications and Security S.A, France
Odile Derouet	NXP, Germany
Markus Dichtl	Siemens AG, Germany
Hermann Drexler	Giesecke and Devrient, Germany
Cécile Dumas	CEA, France
Benoit Feix	UL Transaction Security, France
Benedikt Gierlichs	KU Leuven, ESAT-COSIC, Belgium
Christophe Giraud	Oberthur Technologies, France
Sylvain Guilley	GET/ENST, CNRS/LTCI, France
Naofumi Homma	School of Information Sciences, Tohoku University, Japan
Michael Hutter	University of Technology Graz, IAIK, Austria
Eliane Jaulmes	ANSSI, France
Ilya Kizhvatov	RISCURE, The Netherlands
Markus Kuhn	University of Cambridge, UK
Thanh Ha Le	MORPHO, France
Stefan Mangard	Infineon Technologies, Germany
Amir Moradi	Horst Görtz Institute for IT-Security, Ruhr University Bochum, Germany
Debdeep Mukhopadhyay	IIT Kharagpur, India
Axel Poschmann	PACE, Nanyang Technological University, Singapore
Emmanuel Prouff	ANSSI, France
Anand Rajan	Intel, USA
Denis Real	DGA, Germany
Matthieu Rivain	CryptoExperts, France
Kazuo Sakiyama	The University of Electro-Communications, Japan
Patrick Schaumont	Virginia Tech, USA
Joern-Marc Schmidt	University of Technology Graz, IAIK, Austria
Francois-Xavier Standaert	UCL Crypto Group, Belgium
Yannick Teglia	ST Microelectronics, France
David Vigilant	Gemalto, The Netherlands
Carolyn Whitnall	University of Bristol, UK

Additional Reviewers

Agoyan, Michel
Andouard, Philippe
Balasch, Josep
Banciu, Valentina
Basu Roy, Debapriya
Battistello, Alberto
Bhasin, Shivam
Breier, Jakub
Buhan, Ileana
Carbone, Mathieu
Chen, Donald
Dambra, Arnaud
Danger, Jean-Luc
El Mrabet, Nadia
Endo, Sho
Farhady Ghalaty, Nahid
Finiasz, Matthieu
Fontaine, Arnaud
Ghosh, Santosh
Gross, Hannes
Guo, Xiaofei
Hajra, Suvadeep
Heuser, Annelie
Hoffmann, Lars
Jap, Dirmanto
Jessy, Clédière
Korak, Thomas
Kutzner, Sebastian

Li, Yang
Lomné, Victor
Omic, Jasmina
Pan, Jing
Poucheret, François
Razafindralambo, Tiana
Renauld, Mathieu
Reparaz, Oscar
Ricart, Andjy
Roche, Thomas
Rousselet, Mylène
Seysen, Martin
Stöttinger, Marc
Subidh Ali, Sk
Susella, Ruggero
Taha, Mostafa
Therond, Carine
Thierry, Loic
Tordella, Lucille
Unterluggauer, Thomas
van Oldeneel, Loic
Verneuil, Vincent
Villegas, Karine
Wenger, Erich
Witteman, Marc
Wojcik, Marcin
Wurcker, Antoine
Yao, Gavin

Contents

A Note on the Use of Margins to Compare Distinguishers

Oscar Reparaz[✉], Benedikt Gierlichs, and Ingrid Verbauwhede

Department of Electrical Engineering-ESAT/COSIC and iMinds, KU Leuven,
Kasteelpark Arenberg 10, 3001 Leuven-Heverlee, Belgium
{oscar.reparaz,benedikt.gierlichs,ingrid.verbauwhede}@esat.kuleuven.be

Abstract. Relative distinguishing margins are becoming a popular measure for comparing distinguishers. This paper presents some examples that show that this measure, although informative and intuitively sound, should not be taken alone as benchmark of distinguishers.

1 Introduction

Since the introduction of Differential Power Analysis (DPA) in [3], several different statistical tools called distinguishers have been proposed. Some distinguishers claim to be more efficient assuming a leakage model (like CPA [1]) or more generic (MIA [2] and KS [13]). A recurring topic in the literature is the need for establishing fair criteria to compare distinguishers and extract broad conclusions, more generally applicable than the comparison of outcomes in specific empirical experiments.

The notion of success rate is of extended use to evaluate distinguishers, probably due to the accessible interpretation of the measure. One of the first works theoretically analyzing the behavior of several univariate distinguishers is presented by Mangard et al. in [7]. They show that the (asymptotic) efficiency, measured as the success rate, of d;istinguishers based on the correlation coefficient, difference of means and Gaussian templates are essentially the same, given the exact (single-bit) model of the power consumption. This result, however, does not generalize to higher-order attacks as shown by Standaert et al. in [10]. Said work shows that in the context of attacking masked implementations, the choice of distinguisher indeed highly affects the success rate achieved in the attack.

However, measures other than the success rate have also been proposed in previous works. Most notably, Whitnall and Oswald formalized the concept of theoretical margins for a distinguisher in [11,12]. This measure provides an improvement and generalization of several other measures [4,5], and it was shown to be more expressive and informative than the success rate [11]. In short, the relative margin measures to what extent the distinguisher value for the correct key hypothesis stands out over other competing distinguisher values, in a normalized fashion.

© Springer International Publishing Switzerland 2014
E. Prouff (Ed.): COSADE 2014, LNCS 8622, pp. 1–8, 2014.
DOI: 10.1007/978-3-319-10175-0_1

In the same series of papers [8, 11, 12], Whitnall et al. introduce a very interesting idea towards separating the intrinsic distinguishing power of a distinguisher from estimation inaccuracies, both of which affect the success rate. To isolate these two aspects, the distinguisher values are not estimated but directly computed from the probability densities of the simulated leakage via numerical integration. In this approach, the estimation problem (which for some distinguishers is notoriously hard) is worked around. Whitnall et al. apply this technique to theoretically compare several distinguishers and draw the conclusion that MIA and KSA distinguishers have theoretical advantages over CPA and that the underperformance of MIA-like attacks frequently observed in practice is due to estimation errors.

Theoretical margins are receiving an increasing adoption. Recent works have proposed new distinguishers and justified somehow their superiority based on theoretical margin measures [6, 13].

Contribution. This paper presents simple counterexamples of distinguishers that exhibit the exact same success rate, yet their theoretical margins' values can be almost arbitrarily different. Hence, theoretical margins should not be used as the sole measure to compare distinguishers.

Notation. A distinguisher is the statistical tool that is used to compare measurements T to key-dependent predictions Z_k in a standard DPA attack. The *distinguisher vector* $D(k)$ is a vector containing distinguisher values for each subkey k. In the simulations of this paper we assume that the leakage T consists of the Hamming weight of the first DES Sbox output Z with additive Gaussian noise, that is $T = \mathrm{HW}(Z_k) + \epsilon$ with $Z_k = \mathrm{DES\text{-}Sbox1}(p \oplus k)$. The signal-to-noise ratio (SNR) is defined as $\frac{\mathrm{var}\ [\mathrm{HW}(Z_k)]}{\mathrm{var}\ [\epsilon]}$.

Organization. In Sect. 2 we present the main idea: several distinguishers are proposed that serve our purpose of showing that taking only the margins into account can lead to misjudgment. In Sect. 3 we study the behavior of the distinguishers when noise is present.

2   Two Distinguishers

In this section, we present two distinguishers D_1 and D_2 that by construction behave exactly in the same way in practice. That is, the two distinguishers will rank key candidates in exactly the same way: the attack using D_1 will be exactly as successful as the attack using D_2. However, the relative and absolute margins for D_1 and D_2 are different.

2.1   Description

The first distinguisher D_1 is the absolute value of Kocher et al. single bit DPA between measurements T and key-dependent predictions Z_k. That is, for each hypothesis k of the key, the distinguisher computes

$$D_1(k) = \left| \widehat{\mathbf{E}}(T|L(Z_k) = 1) - \widehat{\mathbf{E}}(T|L(Z_k) = 0) \right| \tag{1}$$

where L is a function that extracts one bit from the predictions and $\widehat{\mathbf{E}}$ is the sample mean operator. The second distinguisher D_2 is based on D_1. It computes the squared version of D_1 as

$$D_2(k) = [D_1(k)]^2 \tag{2}$$

$$= \left| \widehat{\mathbf{E}}(T|L(Z_k) = 1) - \widehat{\mathbf{E}}(T|L(Z_k) = 0) \right|^2 . \tag{3}$$

2.2   Properties

It is not hard to see that D_1 and D_2 are in essence the same distinguisher. For any two key hypothesis, D_1 will rank them in the same way as D_2. This means that an attack using D_1 will be exactly as successful as one using D_2. One can see D_2 as the composition of first computing D_1 and then *squaring* every distinguisher value (i.e., applying the map $x \mapsto x^2$), as Fig. 1 (left) shows. Since the map $x \mapsto x^2$ is strictly increasing in $x \geq 0$ (possible values of D_1 will be always $D_1 \geq 0$), it follows from the definition that the order (key ranking) will be preserved. However, as we will see in the next section, D_1 and D_2 have different theoretical relative margins.

2.3   Margins for D_1 and D_2

For a given distinguisher that produces the distinguishing vector D, the *relative distinguishing margin*[1] is defined as

$$\mathrm{RelMargin}(D) = \frac{D(k^*) - \max[D(k)|k \neq k^*]}{\mathrm{std}(D)} \tag{4}$$

where k^* is the correct key and std is the sample standard deviation. The sign of this measure indicates whether an attack using the given distinguisher and a "large enough" number of traces would be successful (or not), and the magnitude of the measure, up to what extend the attack was successful (or not.) In what follows, we computed all relative margins by numerical integration as suggested in [12].

We computed the theoretical relative distinguishing margin for D_1 and D_2 and got, respectively, 0.250 and 0.5176 in a noiseless scenario. Both are positive, which means that the attacks would be successful, given enough traces. The fact that the two magnitudes are different means that the theoretical relative distinguishing margin is, in this situation, measuring something that does not

---

[1] We note that the distinction between *theoretical* distinguishing margins and distinguishing margins is orthogonal to the observations in this paper, and the consequences affect both.

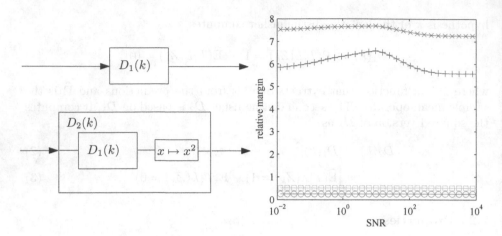

Fig. 1. Left: construction of D_1 and D_2. Right: relative distinguishing margins for D_1 and D_2. Pink $\circ$: margins for D_1. Green $\square$: margins for D_2. Blue $+$: margins for D_1^{MIA}. Red x: margins for D_2^{MIA} (Color figure online).

relate to the intrinsic distinguishing ability of D_1 or D_2, since it is clear that by construction both distinguishers behave identically.

We push further our study by introducing another pair of distinguishers D_1^{MIA} and D_2^{MIA}. The distinguisher D_1^{MIA} is MIA and is defined as

$$D_1^{\mathrm{MIA}} = I(T; L'(Z_k)) \tag{5}$$

where $I(\cdot; \cdot)$ denotes Mutual Information and L' is some leakage model. Analogously, we define D_2^{MIA} as the squared version of D_1^{MIA}:

$$D_2^{\mathrm{MIA}} = \left[D_1^{\mathrm{MIA}}(k)\right]^2 \tag{6}$$
$$= |I(T; L'(Z_k))|^2. \tag{7}$$

We computed theoretical margins for D_1, D_2, D_1^{MIA} and D_2^{MIA} as a function of the SNR and plot them in Fig. 1 (right.) We note that the results of the margin of D_1^{MIA} coincide with those from [12][2]. As expected, the margins for D_1 and D_2 stay constant as the SNR progresses. For the difference of means based distinguishers, noise affects every distinguisher value in the same way, keeping the theoretical distinguishing ability unaffected. For the distinguishers based on MIA the situation is different: margins for D_1^{MIA} and D_2^{MIA} vary as the SNR changes, as [12] pointed out.

From the observation of Fig. 1 it is clear that all distinguishers D_1, D_2, D_1^{MIA} and D_2^{MIA} have distinct margins, albeit D_1 (respectively D_1^{MIA}) is essentially the same as D_2 (respectively D_2^{MIA}). Thus, we see that margins do not necessarily relate to success rate. We would incur a misjudgment if based on Fig. 1 and

---

[2] Up to a typo in the caption of Fig. 2 in [12].

without any more information we assess that distinguisher D_2 has more intrinsic distinguishing abilities than D_1. Furthermore, by the same reasoning, from the observation of Fig. 1 there is not enough information to claim that distinguisher D_2^{MIA} has more intrinsic distinguishing abilities than D_2, which is a different distinguisher not based on MIA. In the next section we elaborate on the applicability of margins to compare distinguishers.

Note that the observation regarding different margins for D_1^{MIA} and D_2^{MIA} will hold in a theoretical scenario (where there are no estimation errors) as well as in a practical scenario (since the estimation errors will affect D_1^{MIA} and D_2^{MIA} in exactly the same way).

3   Discussion

3.1   The Shape of the Margins Is Also Different

Upon the observation of Sect. 2.3, one might ask if the properties of the margin are the same for D_1^{MIA} and D_2^{MIA} as the SNR varies. In other words, whether the relative margin for D_2^{MIA} is just a scaled version of D_1^{MIA}. In this section, we answer this question negatively.

We slightly generalize the construction of D_2^{MIA}. We consider the family of distinguishers $D_{a,b}^{\mathrm{MIA}}$. This family is constructed akin to D_2^{MIA} but substituting the squaring mapping $x \mapsto x^2$ with a different strictly increasing non-linear mapping $x \mapsto (x + a)^b - a^b$ for some $a, b > 0$. Since the mapping is still strictly increasing in $x \geq 0$, all the distinguishers in the family are essentially the same. We further generalize and also consider the family of distinguishers $D_{f(x)}^{\mathrm{MIA}}$ that is constructed similarly to D_2^{MIA} but with a generic strictly increasing non-linear mapping $x \mapsto f(x)$. We note that linear mappings of the form $x \mapsto a \cdot x + b$ would not modify relative margins (and will of course lead to attacks with identical success rates.)

In Fig. 2 we plot the theoretical relative distinguishing margin for some members of the family of distinguishers previously defined. We can see that the evolution of the relative margin as a function of the SNR can be almost arbitrary, even though all the distinguishers in the figure are essentially the same (they relate to the same distinguisher up to a strictly increasing non-linear mapping at their output). Thus, one should also be skeptical about drawing conclusions about the behavior of a specific distinguisher from the observation of the shape of the relative distinguishing margin as the SNR varies. In Fig. 2, one could assert from the curve corresponding to $D_{0,1}^{\mathrm{MIA}}$ (blue, 'x') that there is a stochastic-resonance-like effect around SNR=10 since the margin achieves a maximum. We note that the very same effect does not exhibit itself for the other equivalent distinguisher in the figure (red, '+'; and green, 'o'.) Therefore, margins alone should not be used to assess the properties of a distinguisher as the SNR varies: distinguisher-specific properties may or may not show in the margins.

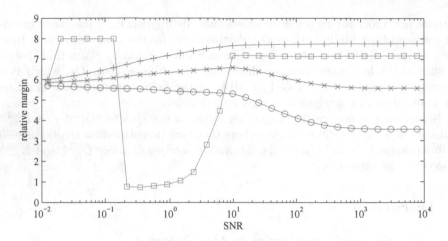

Fig. 2. Red, blue, green: margins for $D_{a,b}^{\mathrm{MIA}}$ for several choices: red, '+': $a = 1.9$, $b = 7$; blue, 'x': $a = 0$, $b = 1$ (this means that $D_{0,1} = D_1$); green, 'o': $a = 0.3$, $b = 0.003$. Pink, $\square$: margins for $D_{f(x)}$ with $f(x) = e^x$ if $x < 0.05$ and $f(x) = 10e^{x+1}$ otherwise $f(x)$ is strictly increasing in $x > 0$ (Color figure online).

3.2 Objection: D_2 is Pathologic

One could argue that the construction of appending a non-linear mapping at the output of a previously proposed distinguisher is pathologic. Although D_2 (and subsequent generalizations) was specifically crafted to show the point in this paper regarding relative distinguishing margins and no reasonable person would think that it is any better (or worse) than D_1, we remark that the derived distinguishers are as sound as the original ones. For example, D_2 is as sound as D_1 and still gives a measure of the degree of the correlation between random variables (only in a different scale than D_1), and is as precise as D_1.

3.3 What is Left to Compare Distinguishers?

The task of comparing in a fair way several distinguishers that work on different scales seems hard. One could resort to the well-known success-rate metric, albeit one should be aware of its limitations. Namely, success rates are highly dependent on the statistical estimator used in the computation of the distinguisher values. Besides, once the signal-to-noise ratio is high enough so that the distinguishers under study behave well (they output the correct key hypothesis with high probability, i.e., their success rates reach values close to 1), it becomes hard to compare distinguishers and rank which one is better, since their success rates are all close to 1. On the bright side, success rates are easily computable in empirical settings and can be used to compare distinguishers that work on different scales. The same observations apply to other metrics that are only sensitive to the ordering of the distinguishing vector, such as guessing entropy [9].

4 Conclusion

We showed in this paper that the theoretical relative distinguishing margin can be a useful measure but is not to be used as the sole measure to compare distinguishers, and to assess properties of a specific distinguisher. Although the measure is intuitively useful, and in many cases it informs of useful properties of distinguishers, there are some counterexamples/corner cases shown in this paper where the measure should not be taken solely to judge the behavior of a distinguisher.

Acknowledgments. We thank the anonymous reviewers for their insightful comments. This work was supported in part by the Research Council of KU Leuven: GOA TENSE (GOA/11/007), by the Flemish Government FWO G.0550.12N and by the Hercules Foundation AKUL/11/19. Oscar Reparaz is funded by a PhD Fellowship of the Fund for Scientific Research - Flanders (FWO). Benedikt Gierlichs is Postdoctoral Fellow of the Fund for Scientific Research - Flanders (FWO).

References

1. Brier, E., Clavier, C., Olivier, F.: Correlation power analysis with a leakage model. In: Joye, M., Quisquater, J.-J. (eds.) CHES 2004. LNCS, vol. 3156, pp. 16–29. Springer, Heidelberg (2004)
2. Gierlichs, B., Batina, L., Tuyls, P., Preneel, B.: Mutual information analysis. In: Oswald, E., Rohatgi, P. (eds.) CHES 2008. LNCS, vol. 5154, pp. 426–442. Springer, Heidelberg (2008)
3. Kocher, P.C., Jaffe, J., Jun, B.: Differential power analysis. In: Wiener, M. (ed.) CRYPTO 1999. LNCS, vol. 1666, pp. 388–397. Springer, Heidelberg (1999)
4. Le, T.-H., Clédière, J., Canovas, C., Robisson, B., Servière, C., Lacoume, J.-L.: A proposition for correlation power analysis enhancement. In: Goubin, L., Matsui, M. (eds.) CHES 2006. LNCS, vol. 4249, pp. 174–186. Springer, Heidelberg (2006)
5. Le, T.-H., Clédière, J., Servière, C., Lacoume, J.-L.: Noise reduction in side channel attack using fourth-order cumulant. IEEE Trans. Inf. Forensics Secur. 2(4), 710–720 (2007)
6. Maghrebi, H., Guilley, S., Rioul, O., Danger, J.-L.: Some results about the distinction of side-channel distinguishers based on distributions. In: 10th International Workshop on Cryptographic Architectures Embedded in Reconfigurable Devices (CryptArchi 2012), Saint-Etienne, France, 19–22 June 2012
7. Mangard, S., Oswald, E., Standaert, F.-X.: One for all - all for one: unifying standard differential power analysis attacks. IET Inf. Secur. 5(2), 100–110 (2011)
8. Oswald, E., Mather, L., Whitnall, C.: Choosing distinguishers for differential power analysis attacks. In: Non-Invasive Attack Testing Workshop, NIST (2011)
9. Standaert, F.-X., Malkin, T.G., Yung, M.: A unified framework for the analysis of side-channel key recovery attacks. In: Joux, A. (ed.) EUROCRYPT 2009. LNCS, vol. 5479, pp. 443–461. Springer, Heidelberg (2009)
10. Standaert, F.-X., Veyrat-Charvillon, N., Oswald, E., Gierlichs, B., Medwed, M., Kasper, M., Mangard, S.: The World Is Not Enough: Another Look on Second-Order DPA. In: Abe, M. (ed.) ASIACRYPT 2010. LNCS, vol. 6477, pp. 112–129. Springer, Heidelberg (2010)

11. Whitnall, C., Oswald, E.: A comprehensive evaluation of mutual information analysis using a fair evaluation framework. In: Rogaway, P. (ed.) CRYPTO 2011. LNCS, vol. 6841, pp. 316–334. Springer, Heidelberg (2011)
12. Whitnall, C., Oswald, E.: A fair evaluation framework for comparing side-channel distinguishers. J. Cryptogr. Eng. 1(2), 145–160 (2011)
13. Whitnall, C., Oswald, E., Mather, L.: An exploration of the Kolmogorov-Smirnov test as a competitor to mutual information analysis. In: Prouff, E. (ed.) CARDIS 2011. LNCS, vol. 7079, pp. 234–251. Springer, Heidelberg (2011)

A Theoretical Study of Kolmogorov-Smirnov Distinguishers

Side-Channel Analysis vs. Differential Cryptanalysis

Annelie Heuser[1](✉), Olivier Rioul[1], and Sylvain Guilley[1,2]

[1] TELECOM-ParisTech, COMELEC, Paris, France
{heuser,rioul,guilley}@enst.fr
[2] Secure-IC S.A.S., Rennes, France

Abstract. In this paper, we carry out a detailed mathematical study of two theoretical distinguishers based on the Kolmogorov-Smirnov (KS) distance. This includes a proof of soundness and the derivation of *closed-form expressions*, which can be split into two factors: one depending only on the *noise* and the other on the *confusion coefficient* of Fei, Luo and Ding. This allows one to have a deeper understanding of the relative influences of the signal-to-noise ratio and the confusion coefficient on the distinguisher's performance. Moreover, one is able to directly compare distinguishers based on their closed-form expressions instead of using evaluation metric that might obscure the actual performance and favor one distinguisher over the other. Furthermore, we formalize the link between the confusion coefficient and differential cryptanalysis, which shows that the stronger an S-box is resistant to differential attacks the weaker it is against side-channel attacks, and *vice versa*.

Keywords: Side-channel distinguisher · Confusion coefficient · Kolmogorov-Smirnov analysis · Closed-form expressions · S-Box differential uniformity · Constrained S-Box search

1 Introduction

Side-channel attacks consist in exploiting leakages in order to extract secrets from any kind of cryptographic devices. Studies of side-channel distinguishers have been initially empirical: they were carried out on real traces, whose characteristics in terms of signal and noise were not exactly known. This allows to compare attacks on a fair setting especially their optimizations, like for instance using the DPA contests measurements [24]. Unfortunately, this does not allow one to understand the role of the different parameters at hand (like the signal-to-noise ratio (SNR) and the impact of the leakage model) and derive conclusions for any kind of data.

Annelie Heuser is Google European fellow in the field of privacy and is partially founded by this fellowship.

© Springer International Publishing Switzerland 2014
E. Prouff (Ed.): COSADE 2014, LNCS 8622, pp. 9–28, 2014.
DOI: 10.1007/978-3-319-10175-0_2

For this reason, another approach consists in generating traces by simulations, according to some archetype leakage signal and noise. The question that now arises is how to compare attacks. Guidelines were given by Standaert et al. in [22], and a formal evaluation framework was presented in [23]. Two metrics were introduced to quantify the efficiency of attacks: *success rate* and *guessing entropy*. In [10] Maghrebi et al. introduced *error bars* on the success rate in order to determine a reliable decision whether one distinguisher is better than another. Another strategy proposed by Whitnall and Oswald in [28] consists in computing various kinds of metrics evaluating theoretical distinguishers, such as the *relative distinguishing margin*. Yet another approach consists in deriving closed-form expressions of the theoretical success rate of distinguishers. Recently, Fei et al. [7] derived a closed-form expression of the theoretical success rate for DPA (difference of means). In order to achieve this they introduced the *confusion coefficient*, which determines the relationship between the sensitive variable of the correct key and any other key hypotheses. Thanks to this concept, Thillard et al. re-derived in [26] the computation of the success rate of CPA given by Rivain in [20] in terms of the confusion coefficient.

Our Contribution. In this paper, we conduct a mathematical study on the Kolmogorov-Smirnov (KS) distinguishers, namely KSA (KS Analysis) and iKSA (interclass KSA). Following the empirical results in [10], we investigate the standard Kolmogorov-Smirnov distinguisher (i.e., KSA), and the interclass KS distinguisher (i.e., iKSA) as it was shown that iKSA outperforms KSA in simulated data using the Hamming weight leakage model [10]. In particular, our study includes the derivation of closed-form expressions as well as a proof of soundness for both KS distinguishers, where we had to focus on the one-bit leakage scenario (as for DPA).

We show that the closed-form expressions of KSA and iKSA depend on two factors: one that is a function only of the noise and another one that is a function only of the confusion coefficient. A closed-form expression having also an independent noise factor has been observed for CPA (and thus also for DPA) by Mangard et al. in [11]. Remarkably, a re-formulation of the formula in [11] in terms of the confusion coefficient shows that the closed-forms of DPA and KSA/ iKSA (in short (i)KSA) only differ in the factor of the noise. As a consequence we show that, in contrast to other distinguishers like mutual information, the relative distinguishing margin of one-bit (i)KSA and DPA does *not* depend on the noise, but only on the confusion coefficients. This behavior for DPA has partially also been observed in [28].

These results highlight the relevance of a theoretical study of distinguishers and the derivation of closed-form expressions, since one is able to exactly determine the impacts of the noise and of the choice of the leakage model (e.g. S-boxes). Moreover, this allows to compare distinguishers among themselves by means of closed-form expressions, instead of using evaluation metrics obscuring relevant factors.

Finally, assuming that the leakage model depends on a substitution box (S-box), we formalize the link between the confusion coefficient and differential cryptanalysis [1] through the cryptanalytic metric called *differential uniformity*. We demonstrate that the stronger the differential resistance, the weaker the side-channel resistance and *vice versa*. This was only implicitly known so far (e.g., results of Prouff in [18]). Furthermore, we show that this behavior is not a direct consequence of the *non-linearity* of the S-box, as it is commonly believed, but rather of its resistance against differential cryptanalysis.

2 Preliminaries

2.1 Notations

Calligraphic letters (e.g., $\mathcal{X}$) denote finite sets, capital letters (e.g., X) denote random variables taking values in these sets, and the corresponding lowercase letters (e.g., x) denote their realizations. We write $\mathbb{P}\{X = x\}$ or $p(x)$ for the probability that $X = x$ and $p(x|y) = \mathbb{P}\{X = x \,|\, Y = y\}$ for conditional probabilities. Let $k^\star$ denote the secret cryptographic key, k any possible key hypothesis from the keyspace $\mathcal{K}$, and let T be the input or cipher text of the cryptographic algorithm. The mapping $g : (\mathcal{T}, \mathcal{K}) \to \mathcal{I}$ maps the input or cipher text and a key hypothesis $k \in \mathcal{K}$ to an internally processed variable in some space $\mathcal{I}$ that is assumed to relate to the leakage X. Usually, $\mathcal{T}, \mathcal{K}, \mathcal{I}$ are taken as $\mathbb{F}_2^n$, where n is the number of bits (for AES $n = 8$).

Generally it is assumed that g is known to the attacker. A common consideration is $g(T, k) = \text{Sbox}[T \oplus k]$ where Sbox is a substitution box. The measured leakage X can then be written as

$$X = \psi(g(T, k^\star)) + N, \tag{1}$$

where N denotes an independent additive noise. The device-specific deterministic function ψ is normally unknown to the attacker, which for this reason is assuming some other function ψ' modeling an exploitable part of ψ. For any key guess $k \in \mathcal{K}$ the attacker computes the *sensitive variable*

$$Y(k) = \psi'(g(T, k)). \tag{2}$$

Without loss of generality we may assume that Y is centered and normalized, i.e., $\mathbb{E}\{Y\} = 0$ and $Var\{Y\} = 1$, and that the values in $\mathcal{Y}$ are regularly spaced with step Δy. For ease of notation, we let $Y^\star = Y(k^\star)$ and $Y = Y(k)$.

2.2 Conditions

First, we assume a basic condition that when looking directly at the leakage distribution (not knowing the message or cipher) we cannot infer any secret.

Condition 1 (Secrecy condition). *The probability distribution of the leakage (see Eq. (1)) does not depend on the actual value of the secret key.*

In other words, the $Y(k)$'s are identically distributed (i.d.) for all $k \in \mathcal{K}$. Second, similarly (but not equivalently) as in [19,30] we require the following condition on the relationship between $Y^\star$ and Y to be able to distinguish between different keys $k \in \mathcal{K}$. This confusion condition will be related to the confusion coefficient later in Proposition 4.

Condition 2 (Confusion condition). *For any $k \neq k^\star$, the correspondence from $Y(k)$ to $Y(k^\star)$ is non-injective, i.e., there does not exist an injective (that is one-to-one) function $\xi : \mathcal{Y} \to \mathcal{Y}$ such that $Y(k^\star) = \xi(Y(k))$ with probability one.*

Lemma 1. *The confusion condition is equivalent to the condition that for all $k \neq k^\star$ there exist $y, y^\star \in \mathcal{Y}$ such that*

$$p(y^\star|y) \text{ is neither } 0 \text{ nor } 1. \tag{3}$$

Proof. Negating the confusion condition, there is a $k \neq k^\star$ such that $\mathbb{P}\{Y(k^\star) = \xi(Y(k))\} = 1$ where ξ is some one-to-one function. This is equivalent to $\mathbb{P}\{Y(k^\star) = \xi(y) \mid Y(k) = y\} = 1$ for all $y \in \mathcal{Y}$, that is, $p(y^\star|y) = 1$ when $y^\star = \xi(y)$ and $p(y^\star|y) = 0$ otherwise. $\square$

Thus, the confusion condition amounts to saying that knowing $Y(k) = y$ (for that particular value y satisfying the condition) does not always permit to conclude for sure about the value of $Y(k^\star)$, which depends on the secret: there is still a nonzero probability that $Y(k^\star)$ has several possible values.

2.3   Multi-bit vs One-bit Leakage Models

The existing literature on KS distinguishers [10,27,29,31] deals with multi-bit leakage models. However, a precise mathematical derivation is very much intricate in the multi-bit case. We therefore present hereafter the scenario where the sensitive variable Y is a binary variable, i.e., $\psi' : \mathcal{I} \to \mathbb{F}_2$.

Note that, we do not make the same restrictions on ψ, for example, let us consider the most common cases for ψ in practice, that have also been investigated in [28]: the Hamming weight (HW) or more generally the (unequal) weighted sum of n bits:

$$X = \sum_{i=1}^{n} \omega_i [g(T, k^\star)]_i + N, \tag{4}$$

with $[\cdot]_i : \mathbb{F}_2^n \to \mathbb{F}_2$ being the projection onto the ith bit, $\omega_i \in \mathbb{R}$ and in case of a HW leakage $\omega_1 = \omega_2 = \ldots = \omega_n = 1$.

Let us assume in the following that $[g(T, k^\star)]_1, \ldots, [g(T, k^\star)]_n$ are independent and uniformly distributed, which is implied when considering a bijective S-box as for example in AES and randomly chosen plaintexts T. Consider that we concentrate on bit $b \in \{1, \ldots, n\}$, so $\psi'(\cdot) = [\cdot]_b$, then we express X in terms of the sensitive variable $Y^\star = [g(T, k^\star)]_b$ as

$$X = \omega_b Y^\star + \underbrace{Z + N}_{N'} \quad \text{with} \quad Z = \sum_{i \neq b} \omega_i [g(T, k^\star)]_i. \tag{5}$$

Remark 1. Note that, when ψ is the HW function ($\omega_i = 1$) Z follows a binomial law of length $n - 1$ and probability $p = \frac{1}{2}$.

In our further analysis, we assume that $N' = Z + N$ is unimodal distributed in the sense of the following definition:

Definition 1 (Unimodal distribution). *A distribution f is called* unimodal *if there exists a mode m such that $f(x)$ is increasing for $x \leq m$ and decreasing for $x \geq m$.*

To verify this assumption empirically, we perform simulations with $N \sim \mathcal{N}(0, \sigma^2)$ for several σ^2, 10000 realisations, and $g(T, k^\star) = \texttt{Sbox}[T \oplus k^\star]$ being the result of the AES S-box (`SubBytes`) operation. Figure 1 shows the conditional distributions of $\{X|Y^\star = y_0\}$ and $\{X|Y^\star = y_1\}$ for (a) the HW model and (b) using weights ω. One can see in Fig. 1(a) that for $\sigma^2 = 0.04$, N' is clearly *not* unimodal distributed[1] , but when $\sigma^2 \geq 0.36$ the unimodality holds. Figure 1(b) illustrates that N' is unimodal distributed for all tested σ^2's. Of course, the bigger σ^2 the closer the distribution of N' will be to N. Note that, observing $\sigma^2 < 1$ is very unrealistic in practice. Moreover, when using an ATMega 163 microcontroller as used in the DPA contest v4 [25], where the signal-to-noise ratio is very high (it is *not* a security product), the condition of unimodality is fulfilled (see Fig. 2), which has also been illustrated for measurements of a microcontroller in [11] (Fig. 4.6). In the rest of the paper, to simplify the notations, we will simply denote by $N \sim \mathcal{N}(0, \sigma^2)$ the noise (sum of *algorithmic* and *measurement* noises).

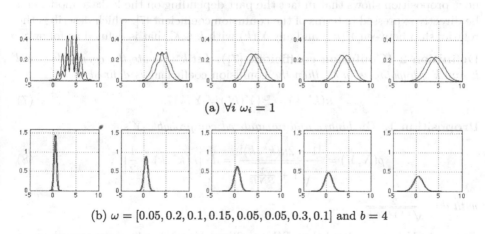

(a) $\forall i \; \omega_i = 1$

(b) $\omega = [0.05, 0.2, 0.1, 0.15, 0.05, 0.05, 0.3, 0.1]$ and $b = 4$

Fig. 1. Estimated conditional distributions $\{X|Y^\star = y_0\}$ and $\{X|Y^\star = y_1\}$ using a noise level of $\sigma^2 = \{0.04, 0.16, 0.36, 0.64, 1\}$.

---

[1] This visual interpretation agrees with several statistical unimodality tests.

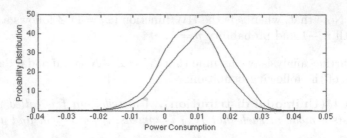

Fig. 2. Estimated conditional leakage distributions $\{X|Y^* = y_0\}$ and $\{X|Y^* = y_1\}$ of measurements from ATMega 163, 2nd AES S-box, 4th bit.

3   Study of Theoretical KS Distinguishers

3.1   A Note on DPA/CPA

In [11] Mangard et al. showed that the theoretical CPA can be expressed as

$$\rho(X,Y) = \frac{\rho(Y^*,Y)}{\sqrt{1 + \frac{1}{SNR}}} \,, \tag{6}$$

where ρ is the *absolute value* of the Pearson correlation coefficient. Thus, $\rho(X,Y)$ can be factored into one part only depending on the leakage model and one depending on the SNR. Note that, CPA using one-bit models is equivalent to DPA [6] (when assuming normalized Y's), thus Eq. (6) also holds for DPA. The next proposition shows that in fact the part depending on the leakage model can be directly expressed in terms of the confusion coefficient [7], which describes the relationship between $Y(k^*)$ and any $Y(k)$ with $k \in \mathcal{K}$ that is defined as follows.

Definition 2 (Confusion coefficient [7]). *Let k^* denote the correct key and k any key hypothesis in $\mathcal{K}$, then the* confusion coefficient *is defined as*

$$\kappa(k^*,k) = \mathbb{P}\{Y(k^*) \neq Y(k)\}. \tag{7}$$

Proposition 1. *For binary and normalized equiprobable Y's*

$$\rho(X,Y) = \frac{|1 - 2\kappa(k^*,k)|}{\sqrt{1 + \frac{1}{SNR}}} = d \cdot \left|\kappa(k^*,k) - \frac{1}{2}\right| \,, \tag{8}$$

with $d = \frac{2}{\sqrt{1+1/SNR}}$.

Proof. As Y is normalized (i.e., $\mathbb{E}(Y) = 0$ and $Var(Y) = 1$) we re-formulate

$$\rho(Y^*,Y) = \frac{|Cov(Y^*,Y)|}{\sqrt{Var(Y^*)Var(Y)}} \tag{9}$$

$$= |1 - 2\kappa(k^*,k)|, \tag{10}$$

since $Cov(Y^*,Y) = \mathbb{E}\{Y^* \cdot Y\} = 1 - 2\mathbb{P}\{Y(k^*) \neq Y(k)\} = 1 - 2\kappa(k^*,k)$. $\square$

3.2   KS Side-Channel Distinguishers

In this subsection we briefly sketch KS distinguishers named after Kolmogorov and Smirnov [9,21]. For more detailed information on their use in the area of side-channel analysis we refer to [27,29] for an evaluation of KS and to [10] for the comparison between KSA and iKSA, which shows that the estimated iKSA is superior to the estimated KSA using simulations for a HW leakage model.

Definition 3 (KS distinguishers). *The (standard) Kolmogorov-Smirnov distinguisher [27] is defined by*

$$\mathsf{KSA}(k) = \mathsf{D}_{\mathsf{KSA}}(X, Y) = \mathbb{E}_Y \{ \|F(x|Y) - F(x)\|_\infty \}, \tag{11}$$

where the expectation is taken over Y's distribution, $\| \cdot \|_\infty$ is the L^∞ norm: $\|\Psi(x)\|_\infty = \sup_{x \in \mathbb{R}} |\Psi(x)|$, and $F(x) = F_X(x)$, $F(x|y) = F_{X|Y=y}(x)$ denote the cumulative distribution functions of X and X given $Y(k) = y$, respectively.
   The inter-class Kolmogorov-Smirnov distinguisher [10] is defined by

$$\mathsf{iKSA}(k) = \mathsf{D}_{\mathsf{iKSA}}(X, Y(k)) = \frac{1}{2} \mathbb{E}_{Y,Y'} \{ \|F(x|Y) - F(x|Y')\|_\infty \}, \tag{12}$$

where Y' is an independent copy of Y, and the expectation is taken over the joint distribution of Y and Y'. The $1/2$ factor makes up for double counts $((Y, Y') \leftrightarrow (Y', Y))$.

   We need the following lemma.

Lemma 2. *With the above notations and assumptions on the leakage model,*

$$\mathsf{KSA}(k) = \sum_{y \in \mathcal{Y}} p(y) \sup_{x \in \mathbb{R}} \left| \sum_{y^\star \in \mathcal{Y}} (p(y^\star|y) - p(y^\star)) \cdot \Phi\left(\frac{x - y^\star}{\sigma}\right) \right| \quad and \tag{13}$$

$$\mathsf{iKSA}(k) = \frac{1}{2} \sum_{\substack{y,y' \in \mathcal{Y} \\ y \neq y'}} p(y)p(y') \sup_{x \in \mathbb{R}} \left| \sum_{y^\star \in \mathcal{Y}} (p(y^\star|y) - p(y^\star|y')) \cdot \Phi\left(\frac{x - y^\star}{\sigma}\right) \right|, \tag{14}$$

where $\Phi(x)$ is the c.d.f. of the standard noise N/σ (of zero mean and unit variance).

Proof. From model Eq. (1), X given $Y(k^\star) = y^\star$ has c.d.f.

$$\mathbb{P}\{X \le x \,|\, Y(k^\star) = y^\star\} = \Phi_N(x - y^\star) = \Phi\left(\frac{x - y^\star}{\sigma}\right), \tag{15}$$

where $\Phi_N(\nu) = \mathbb{P}\{N \le \nu\} = \Phi(\nu/\sigma)$ is the c.d.f. of the noise N. Indeed, we recall our notation: $X = Y(k^\star) + N$. Averaging over $Y(k^\star)$ gives

$$F(x) = \mathbb{P}\{X \le x\} = \sum_{y^\star \in \mathcal{Y}} p(y^\star) \Phi\left(\frac{x - y^\star}{\sigma}\right). \tag{16}$$

Now from Eq. (15) and the formula of total probability, X given $Y(k) = y$ is distributed according to the c.d.f.

$$F(x|y) = \mathbb{P}\{X \le x \,|\, Y(k) = y\} \tag{17}$$

$$= \sum_{y^\star \in \mathcal{Y}} p(y^\star|y) \cdot \mathbb{P}\{X \le x \,|\, Y(k^\star) = y^\star, Y(k) = y\} \tag{18}$$

$$= \sum_{y^\star \in \mathcal{Y}} p(y^\star|y) \cdot \mathbb{P}\{X \le x \,|\, Y(k^\star) = y^\star\} \tag{19}$$

$$= \sum_{y^\star \in \mathcal{Y}} p(y^\star|y) \cdot \Phi\Big(\frac{x - y^\star}{\sigma}\Big). \tag{20}$$

Plugging Eq. (16) and Eq. (20) into Eq. (11) gives Eq. (13); plugging Eq. (20) into Eq. (12) gives Eq. (14) where it should be noted that the terms for which $y = y'$ vanish. □

Remark 2. When the noise is assumed Gaussian, Eq. (20) is the equivalent of the well-known "mixture of Gaussian" as studied in [19].

3.3 Noise Factorization

In the following we consider the scenario highlighted in Subsect. 2.3 where Y is binary and the noise follows a unimodal distribution. The next proposition shows that both KS distinguishers can be factorized as a product of one factor depending only on the noise distribution and another depending only on the sensitive variables, which has also been observed for DPA in [11] (see Subsect. 3.1), but not for any other distinguisher so far.

Proposition 2 (Noise factorization). *One has*

$$\mathsf{KSA}(k) = c \sum_{y \in \mathcal{Y}} p(y)\big|p(y^\star|y) - p(y^\star)\big| \tag{21}$$

$$\mathsf{iKSA}(k) = \frac{c}{2} \sum_{\substack{y,y' \in \mathcal{Y} \\ y \ne y'}} p(y)p(y')\big|p(y^\star|y) - p(y^\star|y')\big| \;, \tag{22}$$

where $y^\star$ denotes any of the two possible values in $\mathcal{Y}$ and where

$$c = 2\Phi\Big(\frac{\Delta y}{2\sigma}\Big) - 1 > 0 \;. \tag{23}$$

Proof. Since $\sum_{y^\star \in \mathcal{Y}}\big(p(y^\star|y) - p(y^\star)\big) = 1 - 1 = 0$, the two coefficients in the inner sum of Eq. (13) are opposite equal. Similarly $\sum_{y^\star}\big(p(y^\star|y) - p(y^\star|y')\big) = 1 - 1 = 0$ and the two coefficients in the inner sum of Eq. (14) are opposite equal. It follows that Eq. (21) and Eq. (22) hold with

$$c = \sup_{x \in \mathbb{R}}\Big|\Phi\Big(\frac{x - y^\star}{\sigma}\Big) - \Phi\Big(\frac{x - \widetilde{y^\star}}{\sigma}\Big)\Big| \;, \tag{24}$$

where $y^\star$ denotes any of the two possible values in $\mathcal{Y}$ and $\widetilde{y^\star}$ denotes the other one. The conclusion now follows from the following lemma. $\square$

Lemma 3. *Let $\Phi(x)$ be the c.d.f. of random variable N/σ having even and unimodal distribution of unit variance. Then for every $y^\star \neq \widetilde{y^\star}$ with $\Delta y = |\widetilde{y^\star} - y^\star|$,*

$$\sup_{x \in \mathbb{R}} \left| \Phi\left(\frac{x - y^\star}{\sigma}\right) - \Phi\left(\frac{x - \widetilde{y^\star}}{\sigma}\right) \right| = 2\Phi\left(\frac{\Delta y}{2\sigma}\right) - 1. \tag{25}$$

Proof. Assume, without loss of generality, that $y^\star < \widetilde{y^\star}$ so that $\Delta y = \widetilde{y^\star} - y^\star$. Since Φ is continuous and nondecreasing, the above supremum is the maximum of $\Phi\left(\frac{x-y^\star}{\sigma}\right) - \Phi\left(\frac{x-\widetilde{y^\star}}{\sigma}\right)$. Since N has even and unimodal density f, the derivative of the latter expression is $f(x - y^\star) - f(x - \widetilde{y^\star})$ which is $= 0$ when $x = \frac{y^\star + \widetilde{y^\star}}{2}$ because f is even, and which is > 0 when $|x - y^\star| < |x - \widetilde{y^\star}|$ and < 0 when $|x - y^\star| > |x - \widetilde{y^\star}|$ because f is unimodal. It follows that the maximum is unique and attained when $x = \frac{y^\star + \widetilde{y^\star}}{2}$. Therefore, the desired maximum equals $\Phi\left(\frac{\widetilde{y^\star} - y^\star}{2\sigma}\right) - \Phi\left(\frac{y^\star - \widetilde{y^\star}}{2\sigma}\right) = \Phi\left(\frac{\Delta y}{2\sigma}\right) - \Phi\left(-\frac{\Delta y}{2\sigma}\right) = 2\Phi\left(\frac{\Delta y}{2\sigma}\right) - 1$. The latter equality holds since f being even, one has $\Phi(-x) = 1 - \Phi(x)$. $\square$

As we shall see, due to this noise factorization, also KS distinguishers are very appealing theoretical objects for formal studies. The quantity $\frac{\Delta y}{2\sigma}$ receives a simple interpretation: since $\mathbb{E}\{Y(k)^2\} = (\Delta y/2)^2$, the square of $\frac{\Delta y}{2\sigma}$ is simply the leakage signal-to-noise ratio (SNR) and we can write $c = 2\Phi\left(\sqrt{\text{SNR}}\right) - 1$. For Gaussian noise[2], this reduces to

$$c = \text{erf}\left(\sqrt{\text{SNR}/2}\right), \tag{26}$$

where $\text{erf} : x \mapsto \frac{2}{\sqrt{\pi}} \int_{-\infty}^{x} \exp\left(-t^2\right)\,dt$ is the standard error function.

3.4   Proof of Soundness

Definition 4 (Soundness). *An attack based on maximizing the values of the distinguisher $D(X, Y(k))$ over k is sound if*

$$D(X, Y(k^\star)) > D(X, Y(k)) \qquad (\forall k \neq k^\star). \tag{27}$$

Several theoretical distinguishers have already been proven sound: DPA, CPA, MIA [14,19]. For KSA and iKSA the soundness conditions read

$$\text{KSA}(k^\star) > \text{KSA}(k) \qquad (\forall k \neq k^\star) \tag{28}$$
$$\text{iKSA}(k^\star) > \text{iKSA}(k) \qquad (\forall k \neq k^\star), \tag{29}$$

respectively. Recall that we assume the secrecy condition (Subsect. 2.2) which amounts to saying that the $Y(k)$'s are identically distributed (i.d.).

---

[2] This assumption holds for sufficiently large values of σ^0 as discussed in Subsect. 2.3, which reflects a practical scenario as illustrated e.g. in Fig. 4.6 of [11].

Proposition 3 (Soundness, i.d. case). *For binary and i.d. $Y(k)$'s, the* KSA *and* iKSA *are sound if and only if the confusion condition holds.*

Proof. Since the $Y(k)$'s are i.d., $p(y)$ does not depend on k. Let $y \neq y'$ be elements of $\mathcal{Y}$. The confusion condition Eq. (3) is equivalent to the strict inequality

$$|p(y^\star|y) - p(y^\star|y')| < 1 \qquad (\forall k \neq k^\star). \qquad (30)$$

Now for $k = k^\star$, $p(y^\star|y)$ is 0 or 1 depending on whether $y = y^\star$ or $y \neq y^\star$, and therefore $|p(y^\star|y) - p(y^\star|y')| = 1$. From Eq. (22) it follows upon multiplying $|p(y^\star|y) - p(y^\star|y')|$ by $p(y)p(y')$ and summing that Eq. (30) is equivalent to Eq. (29), i.e. the soundness of iKSA.

Proving that the KSA is sound is more intricate. Again let $y \neq y'$ be elements of $\mathcal{Y}$. One has $p(y^\star) = p(y)p(y^\star|y) + p(y')p(y^\star|y')$ where $p(y) + p(y') = 1$. It follows that $p(y^\star)$ lies between $p(y^\star|y)$ and $p(y^\star|y')$. Suppose without loss of generality that $p(y^\star|y) \leq p(y^\star) \leq p(y^\star|y')$.

The confusion condition of Eq. (3) states that for any $k \neq k^\star$, one has either

$$|p(y^\star|y) - p(y^\star)| < p(y^\star) \quad \text{or} \quad |p(y^\star|y') - p(y^\star)| < 1 - p(y^\star). \qquad (31)$$

the corresponding non-strict inequalities being always satisfied. It follows from Eq. (21) that this is equivalent to the single strict inequality $\mathsf{KSA}(k) < c \cdot (p(y)p(y^\star) + p(y')(1 - p(y^\star))) = c \cdot (p(y)p(y^\star) + (1 - p(y))(1 - p(y^\star))) = 2c \cdot p(y)p(y^\star)$. Since the expression for $\mathsf{KSA}(k)$ does not depend on the particular value of $y^\star$, the latter upper bound should not either. There are two possibilities:

1. either $y \neq y^\star$ and $\mathsf{KSA}(k) < 2c \cdot (1 - p(y^\star))p(y^\star)$,
2. or $y = y^\star$ and $\mathsf{KSA}(k)$ should be both $< 2c \cdot p(y^\star)^2$ and $< 2c \cdot (1 - p(y^\star))^2$. But since $\min(a, b) \leq \sqrt{ab}$ we obtain $\mathsf{KSA}(k) < 2c \cdot (1 - p(y^\star))p(y^\star)$ in both cases.

Now for $k = k^\star$, equalities hold: $|p(y^\star|y') - p(y^\star)| = 1 - p(y^\star)$ and $|p(y^\star|y) - p(y^\star)| = p(y^\star)$ (since, necessarily, $y \neq y^\star$ and $y' = y^\star$); hence $\mathsf{KSA}(k^\star) = 2c \cdot (1 - p(y^\star))p(y^\star)$. This shows that Eq. (31) is equivalent to Eq. (28). □

As a consequence, provided that the conditions on the sensitive variable in Subsect. 2.2 and 2.3 are met, KSA and iKSA are able to reveal the secret key with arbitrarily high probability as the number of measurements increases indefinitely.

3.5   Simple Closed-Form Expression

In this subsection, we study KSA and iKSA under the assumption introduced by Fei et al. in Theorem 1 of [7], which states that for a *perfectly secret encryption algorithm*, each sensitive variable is equiprobable, i.e., $p(y) = p(y^\star) = 1/2$. This requirement is stronger than our *secrecy condition* (Condition 1). Remarkably, the following proposition shows that the closed-form expressions for DPA and (i)KSA only differ in the part of the noise.

Proposition 4. *For binary and equiprobable Y's, the confusion condition in Eq.* (3) *reduces to the condition that*

$$\kappa(k^\star, k) \quad \text{is neither } 0 \text{ nor } 1 \qquad (\forall k \neq k^\star). \tag{32}$$

Also KSA *and* iKSA *are completely equivalent in this case, with the following closed-form expression*

$$\text{KSA}(k) = 2\,\text{iKSA}(k) = c \cdot \left|\kappa(k^\star, k) - \tfrac{1}{2}\right|. \tag{33}$$

Proof. Since the $Y(k)$'s are binary equiprobable, the joint distribution $\mathbb{P}\{Y(k^\star) = y^\star, Y(k) = y\}$ should be symmetric in $(y^\star, y)$ and, therefore,

$$\begin{aligned}
p(y^\star|y) &= \mathbb{P}\{Y(k^\star) = y^\star | Y(k) = y\} \\
&= 2\mathbb{P}\{Y(k^\star) = y^\star, Y(k) = y\} \\
&= \begin{cases} \kappa(k^\star, k) & \text{if } y \neq y^\star, \\ 1 - \kappa(k^\star, k) & \text{if } y = y^\star. \end{cases}
\end{aligned}$$

This proves Eq. (32). Also, $|p(y^\star|y) - p(y^\star)| = |p(y^\star|y) - 1/2| = |\kappa(k^\star, k) - 1/2|$ and if $y \neq y'$ (whence $y = y^\star$ or $y' = y^\star$), one finds $|p(y^\star|y) - p(y^\star|y')| = |2\kappa(k^\star, k) - 1|$. Plugging these expressions into Eq. (21) and Eq. (22) gives Eq. (33). $\qquad\square$

Remark 3. Using these simple closed-form expressions it is straightforward to recover in the equiprobable case that KSA and iKSA are sound (Proposition 3): Since $\kappa(k^\star) = 0$, the confusion condition Eq. (32) is equivalent to $|\kappa(k^\star, k) - 1/2| < 1/2 = |\kappa(k^\star, k^\star) - 1/2|$ for any $k \neq k^\star$. From Eq. (33), this in turn is equivalent to Eq. (28) or Eq. (29).

Even though KSA and iKSA become equivalent if one insists on having equiprobable bits (in $\mathcal{Y}$), shows the next proposition states that KSA and iKSA are not strictly equivalent in general.

Proposition 5. *For binary $Y(k)$'s,* KSA *and* iKSA *are not equivalent unless the $Y(k)$'s are equiprobable (i.e. the secrecy condition holds).*

Proof. If $y \neq y'$ belong to $\mathcal{Y}$ one has $p(y^\star) = p(y)p(y^\star|y) + p(y')p(y^\star|y')$ where $p(y) + p(y') = 1$. It follows that $p(y^\star)$ lies between $p(y^\star|y)$ and $p(y^\star|y')$. Therefore, $|p(y^\star|y) - p(y^\star|y')| = |p(y^\star|y) - p(y^\star)| + |p(y^\star) - p(y^\star|y')|$ and

$$\sum_{y \neq y'} p(y)p(y')|p(y^\star|y) - p(y^\star|y')| = 2\sum_y p(y)(1 - p(y))|p(y^\star|y) - p(y^\star)| \tag{34}$$

so that

$$\text{iKSA} = c\sum_y p(y)(1 - p(y))|p(y^\star|y) - p(y^\star)|. \tag{35}$$

The equivalence between KSA (Eq. (21)) and iKSA (Eq. (35)) holds only if $p(y)$ and $p(y)(1 - p(y))$ are proportional, which is equivalent to the requirement that $p(y)$ is constant, i.e., the $Y(k)$'s are equiprobable. $\qquad\square$

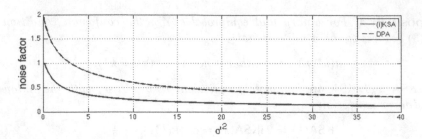

Fig. 3. Noise factor plotted as a function of σ^2.

3.6   Discussion about the Closed-Forms of **DPA** and **(i)KSA**

Note that the equality of the term related to the confusion coefficient in the closed-form expression of DPA and (i)KSA was not obvious before, since DPA distinguishes on a *proportional scale* whereas (i)KSA relies on a *nominal scale* as illustrated in [30]. It can be interpreted as follows: DPA and (i)KSA exploit equivalently the S-Box to discriminate between the correct and the incorrect key guesses.

Figure 3 illustrates the noise factor c of (i)KSA and the noise factor d of DPA as a function of σ^2 where SNR $= \frac{1}{\sigma^2}$. One can see that both factors c and d tend to zero as the noise increases (SNR decreases). However, as c (resp. d) is simply a multiplicative coefficient that applies both to the distinguishers value for the correct and the incorrect key guesses, we can conclude that DPA (resp. (i)KSA) distinguishes hypotheses on the key identically, irrespective of the SNR.

4   Confusion Coefficient Versus Cryptanalytical Metrics

Now we explicitly assume that the sensitive variable Y depends on an S-box through an equation of the form $Y(k) = S(T \oplus k)$, where S is a $\mathbb{F}_2^n \rightarrow \mathbb{F}_2$ Boolean function[3], and $\mathbb{F}_2 = \{0, 1\}$ is the two-element Galois field.

4.1   Relationship between $\kappa(k^\star, k)$ and Differential Metrics

Lemma 4. *The confusion coefficient $\kappa(k^\star, k)$ can be written in terms of the Boolean function S by the following well-known quantity in Boolean functions:*

$$\frac{1}{2} - \kappa(k^\star, k) = \frac{1}{2^{n+1}} \sum_{y \in \mathbb{F}_2^n} (-1)^{S(y) \oplus S(y \oplus (k^\star \oplus k))} \in [-\tfrac{1}{2}, \tfrac{1}{2}]. \qquad (36)$$

---

[3] This Boolean function S is typically *one component* of a substitution box with n output bits. Of course, an attacker could predict the n bits altogether. Still, a mono-bit model has the interest that it reduces the *epistemic noise*, meaning that an assumption on more than one bit certainly deviates from the actual leakage.

Proof. Using the customary interpretation of Booleans $b \in \mathbb{F}_2$ as integers: $b = \frac{1}{2}(1 - (-1)^b) \in \mathbb{Z}$, one has

$$\kappa(k^\star, k) = \mathbb{P}\{Y(k) \neq Y(k^\star)\} = \mathbb{E}\{Y(k) \oplus Y(k^\star)\}$$

$$= \frac{1}{2^n} \sum_{y \in \mathbb{F}_2^n} S(y \oplus k^\star) \oplus S(y \oplus k)$$

$$= \frac{1}{2^n} \sum_y \frac{1}{2} \left(1 - (-1)^{S(y \oplus k^\star) \oplus S(y \oplus k)} \right)$$

$$= \frac{1}{2} - \frac{1}{2^{n+1}} \sum_y (-1)^{S(y) \oplus S(y \oplus (k^\star \oplus k))} \ . \qquad \square$$

S-Boxes are characterized in cryptanalysis by two metrics called *linear* and *differential uniformity* [5,8].

Definition 5 (Linear and differential uniformity). *Let $S : \mathbb{F}_2^n \to \mathbb{F}_2^m$ be an S-Box. The linear (Λ_S) and differential (Δ_S) uniformities of S are defined as:*

$$\Lambda_S = \max_{a \in \mathbb{F}_2^n, \ k \in \mathbb{F}_2^{m*}} \left| \#\{x \in \mathbb{F}_2^n / (a \cdot x) \oplus (k \cdot S(x)) = 0\} - 2^{n-1} \right| \ , \qquad (37)$$

$$\Delta_S = \max_{a \in \mathbb{F}_2^m, \ k \in \mathbb{F}_2^{n*}} \#\{x \in \mathbb{F}_2^n / S(x) \oplus S(x \oplus k) = a\} \ . \qquad (38)$$

The smaller Λ_S and Δ_S, the better the S-Box from a cryptanalytical point of view, respectively against linear [12] and differential [1] cryptanalysis. Note that, in our case $m = 1$ since we restrict ourselves to one-bit of the S-Box output.

Remark 4. Note that *linear uniformity* is related to *nonlinearity*, a well-known notion in the field of vectorial Boolean functions [4]. The nonlinearity of a Boolean function S is defined as $nl(S) = 2^{n-1} - \frac{1}{2} \max_{a \in \mathbb{F}_2^n} \left| \widehat{(-1)^S}(a) \right|$, where $\widehat{f}(a) = \sum_z f(x)(-1)^{a \cdot z}$ is the Fourier transform of f. Again using the customary interpretation of Booleans as integers, $\Lambda_S = \frac{1}{2} \max_{a \in \mathbb{F}_2^n} \left| \sum_{x \in \mathbb{F}_2^n} (-1)^{a \cdot x \oplus S(x)} \right| = 2^{n-1} - nl(S)$. Obviously, the smaller Λ_S, the greater the nonlinearity.

Note that from Eq. (38) one has $2^{n-1} \leq \Delta_S \leq 2^n$ and therefore $0 \leq 2^{-n}\Delta_S - \frac{1}{2} \leq \frac{1}{2}$. Also recall that the confusion coefficient $\kappa(k^\star, k)$ reaches its minimal value $\kappa(k^\star, k^\star) = 0$ for $k = k^\star$, and reaches its maximal value $\kappa(k^\star, k) = 1$ if and only if there exists a key $k \neq k^\star$ such that for all $x \in \mathbb{F}_2^n$, $S(x \oplus k) = \overline{S(x \oplus k^\star)}$. We have the following relationship between Δ_S and $\kappa(k^\star, k)$:

Proposition 6 (Relationship between the differential uniformity and the confusion coefficient). *When considering a Boolean function $S : \mathbb{F}_2^n \to \mathbb{F}_2^m$ with $m = 1$, then*

$$2^{-n}\Delta_S - \frac{1}{2} = \max_{k \neq k^\star} \left| \kappa(k^\star, k) - \frac{1}{2} \right| . \qquad (39)$$

Proof. From Lemma 4,

$$\#\{x \in \mathbb{F}_2^n / S(x) \oplus S(x \oplus k \oplus k^\star) = 1\} = \sum_{y \in \mathbb{F}_2^n} S(y \oplus k^\star) \oplus S(y \oplus k) = 2^n \kappa(k^\star, k)$$

and similarly $\#\{x \in \mathbb{F}_2^n / S(x) \oplus S(x \oplus k \oplus k^\star) = 0\} = 2^n - 2^n \kappa(k^\star, k)$. It follows from Eq. (38) that

$$\begin{aligned}
\Delta_S &= \max_{a \in \mathbb{F}_2, \, k \in \mathbb{F}_2^{n*}} \#\{x \in \mathbb{F}_2^n / S(x) \oplus S(x \oplus k) = a\} \\
&= \max \left\{ \begin{array}{l} \max_{k \in \mathbb{F}_2^{n*}} \#\{x \in \mathbb{F}_2^n / S(x) \oplus S(x \oplus k) = 0\}, \\ \max_{k \in \mathbb{F}_2^{n*}} \#\{x \in \mathbb{F}_2^n / S(x) \oplus S(x \oplus k) = 1\} \end{array} \right\} \\
&= \max \left\{ \begin{array}{l} \max_{k \in \mathbb{F}_2^{n*}} 2^n - \#\{x \in \mathbb{F}_2^n / S(x) \oplus S(x \oplus k) = 1\}, \\ \max_{k \in \mathbb{F}_2^{n*}} \#\{x \in \mathbb{F}_2^n / S(x) \oplus S(x \oplus k) = 1\} \end{array} \right\} \\
&= \max \left\{ \max_{k \neq k^\star} 2^n (1 - \kappa(k^\star, k)), \max_{k \neq k^\star} 2^n \kappa(k^\star, k) \right\} \\
&= 2^n \left(\frac{1}{2} + \max \left\{ \max_{k \neq k^\star} \frac{1}{2} - \kappa(k^\star, k), \max_{k \neq k^\star} \kappa(k^\star, k) - \frac{1}{2} \right\} \right) \\
&= 2^n \left(\frac{1}{2} + \max_{k \neq k^\star} \left| \kappa(k^\star, k) - \frac{1}{2} \right| \right),
\end{aligned} \tag{40}$$

which proves the proposition. □

Therefore, minimizing Δ_S amounts in minimizing the distance between $\kappa(k^\star, k)$ for $k \neq k^\star$ and the factor $\frac{1}{2}$.

Remark 5. There is no direct link between the *linear uniformity* (Eq. (37)) and the confusion coefficient $\kappa(k^\star, k)$.

4.2   Relationship to Closed-Form Expressions

We now relate Eq. (40) to the derived closed-form expression of (i)KSA (see Eq. (33)) and DPA (see Eq. (8)). Let $D(k^\star)$ be the distinguishing value of the correct key and $D(k)$ be the distinguishing value of any incorrect key hypotheses. We consider two metrics, an *extensive* and a *relative* one, which provide us with a theoretical evaluation of the distinguishing power of a distinguisher.

Definition 6 (Distinguishing margin). *The* distinguishing margin DM(D) *is the minimal distance between the distinguisher for the correct key and all incorrect keys. Formally,*

$$DM(D) = D(k^\star) - \max_{k \neq k^\star} D(k). \tag{41}$$

The following definition introduces a normalizing denominator:

Definition 7 (Relative distinguishing margin [28]). *The* relative distinguishing margin RDM(D) *is defined as*

$$RDM(D) = \frac{D(k^\star) - \max_{k \neq k^\star} D(k)}{\sqrt{Var\{D(K)\}}} = \min_{k \neq k^\star} \frac{D(k^\star) - D(k)}{\sqrt{Var\{D(K)\}}}, \tag{42}$$

where K is the uniformly distributed random variable modeling the choice of the key k.

Remark 6. As the noise appears as a multiplicative factor c or d in the closed-form expressions of (i)KSA and DPA, it is eliminated in the relative distinguishing margin. This explains the results of Whitnall et al. in [28] where the relative distinguishing margin of DPA is constant. For KSA we cannot directly compare the results, as in [28] a multi-bit model was used. However, the relative margin of KSA is *almost* independent on the noise (one can observe only a small variation), which motivates for extension of our analysis to the multi-bit case.

Proposition 7 (Distinguishing margin of (i)KSA and DPA under the secrecy condition). *The distance to the nearest rival can be computed exactly as*

$$\mathsf{DM}(\mathsf{D}) = \lambda \cdot \left(\tfrac{1}{2} - \max_{k \neq k^\star} \left| \kappa(k^\star, k) - \tfrac{1}{2} \right| \right) = \lambda \cdot (1 - 2^{-n} \Delta_S). \qquad (43)$$

Proof. Under the secrecy condition, $\mathsf{KSA}(k) = 2\mathsf{iKSA}(k) = c \cdot \left| \kappa(k^\star, k) - \tfrac{1}{2} \right|$ (see Eq. (33)) and $\mathsf{DPA}(k) = d \cdot \left| \kappa(k^\star, k) - \tfrac{1}{2} \right|$ (see Eq. (8)). Plugging this into Eq. (41) with λ being either c or d, and noting that $\kappa(k^\star, k^\star) = 0$ gives

$$\mathsf{D}(k^\star) - \max_{k \neq k^\star} \mathsf{D}(k) = \lambda \cdot \left(\tfrac{1}{2} - \max_{k \neq k^\star} \left| \kappa(k^\star, k) - \tfrac{1}{2} \right| \right), \qquad (44)$$

which yields the required result from Eq. (40). $\qquad \Box$

Proposition 7 shows that if one chooses an S-box that is resistant to differential cryptanalysis (small Δ_S) the side-channel resistance is weak (high DM). Conversely, if the distinguishing margin is minimized, the differential uniformity is maximized. Therefore, there is a trade-off between the security against differential cryptanalyses and side-channel attacks. Note that, contrary to a common belief [4], the easiness to attack an S-box is not directly linked to its *non-linearity*, but rather to its *resistance against differential cryptanalysis*.

Links between cryptanalytic and side-channel metrics were already noted in the literature. However, previously published links (e.g., [3,8,18]) were *inequalities* because the goal was to highlight tendencies, whereas our result of Proposition 7 is an *equality*: the metrics are explicitly and exactly tied.

4.3   Practical Evaluation

We consider in this section three different $\mathbb{F}_{2^8} \to \mathbb{F}_{2^8}$ bijective S-boxes. They can be expressed as affine transforms of power functions [2]:

---

[4] More precisely, as will be made clear in the next Sect. 4.3, the key hypotheses that are the *hardest* to distinguish are those using a *linear* S-box. Indeed, they maximize both Λ_S (i.e. have $nl(S) = 0$) and Δ_S, which could wrongly indicate that the linearity is the relevant criteria.

1. A "bad" Sbox[·], termed S_1, of equation $y \mapsto a \odot y \oplus b$,
2. An "average" Sbox[·], termed S_{101}, of equation $y \mapsto a \odot y^{101} \oplus b$,
3. A "good" Sbox[·], termed S_{254}, of equation $y \mapsto a \odot y^{254} \oplus b$.

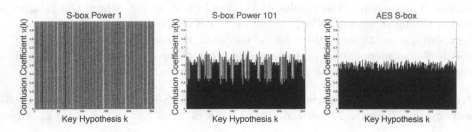

Fig. 4. Confusion coefficients for S_1, S_{101} and S_{254}

In these expressions, the operations $\oplus$ and $\odot$ are respectively the inner addition and multiplication of the Galois field $\mathbb{F}_{2^8}$ of 256 elements. The last S-Box is the one used in the AES, i.e. SubBytes, as $y^{254} = y^{-1}$ in $\mathbb{F}_{2^8}$, by Fermat's little theorem. In all three cases, the 8×8 Boolean matrix a and the 8-bit constant vector b are also those defined in the AES specification [15]; more precisely, we identify $\mathbb{F}_{2^8}$ to $\mathbb{F}_2^8$ when talking about matrices and vectors.

The values of the differential uniformity and the (relative) distinguishing margin are given in Table 1, where DM is computed without additional noise ($\sigma^2 = 0$). Figure 4 displays the confusion coefficients $\kappa(k^\star, k)$ for each S-box. It is obvious from the table and from the figure that when using S_1 (i)KSA and DPA are not able to reveal the key, which can be explained as follows: As S_1 is *linear*, both Λ_{S_1} and Δ_{S_1} are maximal (i.e. attain their upper bounds, respectively $\Lambda_{S_1} = 2^{n-1}$ and $\Delta_{S_1} = 2^n$). Thus, for all key guesses $k = k^\star \oplus \delta k$, S_1 satisfies

$$S_1(T \oplus k) = S_1(T \oplus k^\star \oplus \delta k) = S_1(T \oplus k^\star) \oplus S_1(\delta k)$$

$$= \begin{cases} S_1(T \oplus k^\star) & \text{or} \\ \overline{S_1(T \oplus k^\star)} = 1 - S_1(T \oplus k^\star) \end{cases}.$$

So, either $Y(k) = Y(k^\star)$ or $Y(k) = 1 - Y(k^\star)$, depending on $S_1(\delta k)$. In either case, the confusion condition (see Condition 2) is violated, because there exists an injective correspondence ξ (either the identity or the 1's complement) such that $Y(k^\star) = \xi(Y(k))$ with probability one. Note that, equivalently, Lemma 1 does not apply, since $\kappa(k^\star, k) \in \{0, 1\}$. Hence, (i)KSA and DPA cannot distinguish k from $k^\star$.

Moreover, one can see that the confusion coefficients for S_{254} are close to $1/2$, whereas the coefficients for S_{101} are widely spread. Thus, (i)KSA and DPA are more efficient when using S_{254} instead of S_{101}. The same effect can be seen again in Table 1 when looking at the (relative) distinguishing margin. In contrast,

Table 1. Properties of the studied S-boxes (where $\sigma^2 = 0$ for DM).

S-box	Δ_S	DM (i)KSA/DPA	RDM
S_1	256	0/0	0
S_{101}	184	0.28/0.56	2.58
S_{254}	144	0.44/0.88	9.82

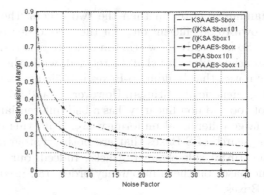

Fig. 5. Distinguishing margin for the studied S-boxes.

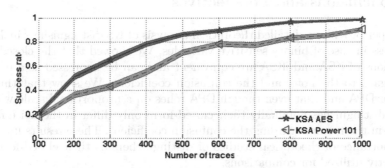

Fig. 6. Empirical success rate for S_{101} and S_{254} and $\sigma^2 = 1$ for (i)KSA.

the resistance against differential attack is less efficient (see the first column). Figure 5 displays the distinguishing margin for several values of σ^2. One can observe that the influence due to the type of S-boxes is still observable even if the noise is very large. Note that, one cannot directly compare the values of the DM of (i)KSA and DPA as it not a relative metric.

Furthermore, we conduct practical experiments using simulations and the estimated (i)KSA as defined in [10] with uniformly distributed T over 100 experiments. Figure 6 shows the empirical success rate when the leakage arises due to the Hamming weight of either S_{101} or S_{254}, where $Y(k) = [S_{101/256}(T \oplus k)]_4$. We additionally highlighted the standard deviation of the success rate by error bars as defined in [10]. As already depicted by the confusion coefficients the side channel resistance is higher for S_{101} than for S_{254}.

4.4 Research of SCA-aware S-Boxes

The traditional way to select S-Boxes is to optimize a bunch of criteria, namely *non-linearity*, *differential uniformity*, and *algebraic degree* (we refer the reader to [4], or [17, Sect. 3.1]). Actually, the algebraic degree can be seen as a less mandatory criterion than the two others: the high-order differential attack is known to be efficient only for the second degree.

So our study shows that in order to also resist SCA, only the criterion on differential uniformity shall be relaxed, while the others can remain stringent. But we notice that building S-Boxes is difficult. One way is via stochastic algorithms (e.g., genetic algorithms). However, a random function, which has (in average) a not too bad non-linearity, has a bad differential spectrum, hence (unfortunately) a large differential uniformity Δ_S. Still, this constraint opens perspectives for the search of S-Boxes that are both cryptographically strong and less prone to the (i)KSA side-channel attacks. Indeed, our criterion is more simple than the one based on the transparency order [18], used for instance in [13,16] to design S-Boxes.

5   Conclusions and Perspectives

This paper provides a detailed theoretical analysis of KS distinguishers including soundness in case of binary sensitive variables. We showed that the closed-form expressions of KSA and iKSA are equivalent and can be expressed as a product with regard to the noise and the confusion coefficient. We show that this also holds for DPA and that even though DPA relies on a proportional scale whereas (i)KSA distinguishes nominally their closed-form only differ in the noise factor, but not in the factor regarding the confusion coefficient. These results underline the importance of theoretical studies of distinguishers as their closed-form can be directly utilized for comparisons.

Moreover, the confusion coefficient is directly related to properties of the S-box, which we further link to a differential cryptanalytic metric. In particular, we highlight that the more an S-box is resistant against side channel attacks the lesser it is secured against cryptanalytic attacks and vice versa. We have noted that the resistance against side-channel attacks is not directly linked to the *non-linearity* of the S-box as commonly believed. In our practical evaluation, we investigated three S-boxes with different power exponents 1, 101 and 254. Interestingly, the S-box of power 1 is resistant against one-bit attacks relying on the confusion coefficient (e.g. KS or DPA), whereas the S-box of power 254 (that is used in AES) is less resistant to side-channel attacks.

For future work we aim to extend our analysis to the multi-bit case and to apply the presented theoretical study as a framework to other side-channel distinguishers. We also expect to extend the study to relate the success probability of (i)KSA to the number of traces and to the S-Box properties. Additionally, the relationship between differential cryptanalytic attacks and side-channel attacks is an interesting field for future work.

Acknowledgements. The authors thank Emmanuel Prouff and Claude Carlet for sharing insights about the criteria for SCA-aware S-Boxes.

References

1. Biham, E., Shamir, A.: Differential cryptanalysis of the full 16-round DES. In: Brickell, E.F. (ed.) CRYPTO 1992. LNCS, vol. 740, pp. 487–496. Springer, Heidelberg (1993)
2. Blondeau, C., Canteaut, A., Charpin, P.: Differential properties of power functions. In: ISIT, pp. 2478–2482. IEEE (2010)
3. Carlet, C.: On highly nonlinear S-Boxes and their inability to thwart DPA attacks. In: Maitra, S., Veni Madhavan, C.E., Venkatesan, R. (eds.) INDOCRYPT 2005. LNCS, vol. 3797, pp. 49–62. Springer, Heidelberg (2005)
4. Carlet, C.: Boolean models and methods in mathematics, computer science, and engineering. In: Crama, Y., Hammer, P. (eds.) Vectorial Boolean Functions for Cryptography, pp. 398–469. Cambridge University Press, Cambridge (2010). (Preliminary version http://www.math.univ-paris13.fr/carlet/pubs.html)
5. Chabaud, F., Vaudenay, S.: Links between differential and linear cryptanalysis. In: De Santis, A. (ed.) EUROCRYPT 1994. LNCS, vol. 950, pp. 356–365. Springer, Heidelberg (1995)
6. Doget, J., Prouff, E., Rivain, M., Standaert, F.-X.: Univariate side channel attacks and leakage modeling. J. Cryptogr. Eng. 1(2), 123–144 (2011)
7. Fei, Y., Luo, Q., Ding, A.A.: A statistical model for DPA with novel algorithmic confusion analysis. In: Prouff, E., Schaumont, P. (eds.) CHES 2012. LNCS, vol. 7428, pp. 233–250. Springer, Heidelberg (2012)
8. Guilley, S., Hoogvorst, P., Pacalet, R.: Differential power analysis model and some results. In: Quisquater, J.-J., Paradinas, Y., Deswarte, Y., Kalam, A. (eds.) Smart Card Research and Advanced Applications VI. IFIP, vol. 153, pp. 127–142. Springer, Heidelberg (2004)
9. Kolmogorov, A.N.: Sulla determinazione empirica di una legge di distribuzione. Giorn. Ist. Ital. Attuari 4, 83–91 (1933)
10. Maghrebi, H., Rioul, O., Guilley, S., Danger, J.-L.: Comparison between side-channel analysis distinguishers. In: Chim, T.W., Yuen, T.H. (eds.) ICICS 2012. LNCS, vol. 7618, pp. 331–340. Springer, Heidelberg (2012)
11. Mangard, S., Oswald, E., Popp, T.: Power analysis attacks: revealing the secrets of smart cards. Springer, December 2006. ISBN: 0-387-30857-1 (2006). http://www.dpabook.org/
12. Matsui, M.: Linear cryptanalysis method for DES cipher. In: Helleseth, T. (ed.) EUROCRYPT 1993. LNCS, vol. 765, pp. 386–397. Springer, Heidelberg (1994)
13. Mazumdar, B., Mukhopadhyay, D., Sengupta, I.: Constrained search for a class of good bijective S-boxes with improved DPA resistivity. IEEE Trans. Inf. Forensics Secur. 8(12), 2154–2163 (2013)
14. Moradi, A., Mousavi, N., Paar, C., Salmasizadeh, M.: A comparative study of mutual information analysis under a gaussian assumption. In: Youm, H.Y., Yung, M. (eds.) WISA 2009. LNCS, vol. 5932, pp. 193–205. Springer, Heidelberg (2009)
15. NIST/ITL/CSD: Advanced Encryption Standard (AES). FIPS PUB 197, Nov 2001. http://csrc.nist.gov/publications/fips/fips197/fips-197.pdf
16. Picek, S., Ege, B., Batina, L., Jakobovic, D., Papagiannopoulos, K.: Optimality and beyond: the case of 4 × 4 S-boxes. In: HOST, Arlington, USA. IEEE Computer Society (2014)
17. Piret, G., Roche, T., Carlet, C.: PICARO – A block cipher allowing efficient higher-order side-channel resistance. In: Bao, F., Samarati, P., Zhou, J. (eds.) ACNS 2012. LNCS, vol. 7341, pp. 311–328. Springer, Heidelberg (2012)

18. Prouff, E.: DPA attacks and S-boxes. In: Gilbert, H., Handschuh, H. (eds.) FSE 2005. LNCS, vol. 3557, pp. 424–441. Springer, Heidelberg (2005)

19. Prouff, E., Matthieu, R.: Theoretical and practical aspects of mutual information-based side channel analysis. Int. J. Appl. Cryptogr. (IJACT) **2**(2), 121–138 (2010)

20. Rivain, M.: On the exact success rate of side channel analysis in the gaussian model. In: Avanzi, R.M., Keliher, L., Sica, F. (eds.) SAC 2008. LNCS, vol. 5381, pp. 165–183. Springer, Heidelberg (2009)

21. Smirnov, N.V.: Tables for estimating the goodness of fit of empirical distributions. Ann. Math. Stat. **19**(2), 279–281 (1948)

22. Standaert, F.-X., Bulens, P., de Meulenaer, G., Veyrat-Charvillon, N.: Improving the rules of the DPA contest. Cryptology ePrint Archive, Report 2008/517, December 8 (2008). http://eprint.iacr.org/2008/517

23. Standaert, F.-X., Malkin, T.G., Yung, M.: A unified framework for the analysis of side-channel key recovery attacks. In: Joux, A. (ed.) EUROCRYPT 2009. LNCS, vol. 5479, pp. 443–461. Springer, Heidelberg (2009)

24. TELECOM ParisTech SEN research group. DPA Contest (1st edn.), 2008–2009. http://www.DPAcontest.org/

25. TELECOM ParisTech SEN research group. DPA Contest (4th edn.), 2013–2014. http://www.DPAcontest.org/v4/

26. Thillard, A., Prouff, E., Roche, T.: Success through confidence: evaluating the effectiveness of a side-channel attack. In: Bertoni, G., Coron, J.-S. (eds.) CHES 2013. LNCS, vol. 8086, pp. 21–36. Springer, Heidelberg (2013)

27. Veyrat-Charvillon, N., Standaert, F.-X.: Mutual information analysis: how, when and why? In: Clavier, C., Gaj, K. (eds.) CHES 2009. LNCS, vol. 5747, pp. 429–443. Springer, Heidelberg (2009)

28. Whitnall, C., Oswald, E.: A fair evaluation framework for comparing side-channel distinguishers. J. Cryptogr. Eng. **1**(2), 145–160 (2011)

29. Whitnall, C., Oswald, E., Mather, L.: An exploration of the kolmogorov-smirnov test as a competitor to mutual information analysis. In: Prouff, E. (ed.) CARDIS 2011. LNCS, vol. 7079, pp. 234–251. Springer, Heidelberg (2011)

30. Whitnall, C., Oswald, E., Standaert, F.-X.: The myth of generic DPA..and the magic of learning. In: Benaloh, J. (ed.) CT-RSA 2014. LNCS, vol. 8366, pp. 183–205. Springer, Heidelberg (2014)

31. Zhao, H., Zhou, Y., Standaert, F.-X., Zhang, H.: Systematic construction and comprehensive evaluation of kolmogorov-smirnov test based side-channel distinguishers. In: Deng, R.H., Feng, T. (eds.) ISPEC 2013. LNCS, vol. 7863, pp. 336–352. Springer, Heidelberg (2013)

Pragmatism vs. Elegance: Comparing Two Approaches to Simple Power Attacks on AES

Valentina Banciu[✉] and Elisabeth Oswald

Department of Computer Science, University of Bristol,
Merchant Venturers Building, Woodland Road, Bristol BS8 1UB, UK
{valentina.banciu,elisabeth.oswald}@bristol.ac.uk

Abstract. Simple side-channel attacks trade off data complexity (i.e. the number of side-channel observations needed for a successful attack) with computational complexity (i.e. the number of operations applied to the side-channel traces). In the specific example of Simple Power Analysis (SPA) attacks on the Advanced Encryption Standard (AES), two approaches can be found in the literature, one which is a pragmatic approach that involves basic techniques such as efficient enumeration of key candidates, and one that is seemingly more elegant and uses algebraic techniques. Both of these different techniques have been used in complementary settings: the pragmatic attacks were solely applied to the key schedule whereas the more elegant methods were only applied to the encryption rounds. In this article, we investigate how these methods compare in what we consider to be a more practical setting in which adversaries gain access to erroneous information about both key schedule and encryption rounds. We conclude that the pragmatic enumeration technique better copes with erroneous information which makes it more interesting in practice.

1 Introduction

Historically, simple side-channel analysis seems an under-researched area in the context of implementations of symmetric schemes: after a short remark by [8], initially only Mangard's article [9] discusses an SPA-style attack on the key schedule of the Advanced Encryption Standard (AES). Thereafter, interest was only revived by the advent of algebraic side-channel analysis (ASCA) (see [13,14,16]). In contrast to Mangard's SPA attack, which used a pragmatic enumeration technique applied to the AES key schedule, ASCA represent the whole block cipher (encryption rounds and key schedule) as a system of equations (in the input, output, and key) that explicitly includes side-channel information. Then some standard solvers (e.g. SAT solver) are employed to (elegantly) solve this system which leads to the extraction of the key.

In these early works little emphasis was put on the fact that, in practice, side-channel information tends to be noisy. Consequently, all early methods implicitly assumed an ideal measurement setup, or some (clever) trace processing, and the use of templates. More recently this shortcoming was picked up in a series of

© Springer International Publishing Switzerland 2014
E. Prouff (Ed.): COSADE 2014, LNCS 8622, pp. 29–40, 2014.
DOI: 10.1007/978-3-319-10175-0_3

papers [10–12,17] which move away from simply using a standard SAT solver to (e.g.) tools that can incorporate probability information about the side-channel observations. This is a step towards making ASCA-style attacks potentially more applicable to practice. However, approaches such as the one in [12] still assume some form of template-based side-channel information extraction so do not move away much from the afore mentioned implications for practice. Other recent contributions in this area [2,10] focus on how the algebraic representation of AES (which can be written in more than one way) influences the computation time/complexity.

By looking at this historical development, one might begin to wonder about the seeming divergence of the 'two' different approaches to SPA. On the one hand, there is the somewhat trivial technique described by Mangard, which only takes key schedule information and extracts the key without much computational effort. On the other hand, there is the elegant technique of algebraic attacks, which only takes round information and extracts the key with considerable computational resources. From a practical perspective (different to the one related to error tolerance above), one can hence wonder why nobody has looked into the strategy of combining key schedule and round information with the aim of using observations concentrated at the beginning or end of AES. This point of staying 'close to' the extremes of AES is motivated by the practical aspect of extracting the side-channel information from the acquired traces: the closer to the beginning (or end) the information is located, the closer one is to the trigger point which can imply a more robust process of finding and extracting the required information. Naturally, practitioners would prefer methods which are robust per se, but also incorporate some error tolerance.

In this article we compare and contrast the two main approaches to SPA on AES in a setting that we consider more practical than what was considered in previous work: we aim to exploit erroneous side-channel information from the beginning of AES (including the key schedule) using an extension of Mangard's simple enumeration technique, as well as using an algebraic method focusing on Hamming weight as leakage model.

Our submission is structured as follows. We briefly review AES in Sect. 2. We explain our extension of Mangard's attack including results in Sect. 3. Thereafter we explain our implementation of algebraic attacks including results in Sect. 4. We conclude in Sect. 5. Appendix A provides results of some more experiments that we performed. These experiments use Hamming distance as power model and show that our conclusion remains valid: the pragmatic approach copes better with erroneous information and hence is more suitable for practice.

2   A Brief Recap of AES

The Advanced Encryption Standard (AES) is a symmetric block cipher, with a fixed block size of 128 bits, and a variable key size of 128, 192, or 256 bits corresponding to 10, 12 and 14 rounds respectively. We use the 128-bit variant as an example in this article, to which we shall refer as simply AES throughout this document. In this section, we give a brief overview of the encryption and key schedule algorithms and explain what intermediate values we assume to be leaking.

2.1 AES Encryption Round

At the start of the encryption process, the 16-byte plaintext block is copied to a 4×4 array called state. The byte elements of the initial plaintext array are copied in column order. Thereafter an encryption round consisting of four round transformations is repeatedly applied to the state. The round transformations are as follows:

1. *AddRoundKey*(state; RK_i) performs a bitwise xor of the current round key and state. One would expect that all memory transfers (i.e. loading of the state as well as key bytes) and the output are leaking, although previous work typically only takes the leakage of the output into account.
2. In the *SubBytes*(state) step, each byte in the state matrix is replaced according to a look-up table. This operation provides *non-linearity*. We only use the leakage of the output (as the input leakage is already being used from the step before).
3. *ShiftRows*(state) operates on the rows of state, performing a cyclical left shift of the bytes in each row by a certain offset: row n is shifted $n - 1$ positions. We assume that this is done implicitly via memory access and so we do not use any leakage.
4. *MixColumns*(state) combines the four bytes of each column of the state. An efficient implementation of this representation on an 8-bit microcontroller is described in the original AES proposal [5], and we list it here to keep our work self contained. Let $in_i, out_i, i = 1 \ldots 4$ be the input, respectively output bytes of a single column, and consider the index i modulo 4. Then, a single column is computed as follows:

$$\begin{aligned} Tmp &= in_1 \oplus in_2 \oplus in_3 \oplus in_4 \\ Tm_i &= in_i \oplus in_{i+1} \\ Tm_i &= \texttt{xtime}(Tm_i) \\ out_i &= in_i \oplus Tm_i \oplus Tmp \end{aligned} \tag{1}$$

where xtime is the multiplication by 02 over $GF(2^8)$. Given the target platform that we have in mind, we would assume that only 2-operand instructions are available on the target platform and hence the exclusive-or of all inputs in_i is done in three steps and the computation of any out_i takes two steps. However, previous work such as [16] set a precedent of only considering leakage of the variables Tmp, Tm_i and out_i and so to keep our work in this respect comparable to theirs we only take 13 out of the 19 leakage points per column.

Adding up the leakage points as explained above amounts to 21 points per column (4 from AddRoundKey, 4 from SubBytes, and 13 from MixColumns).

2.2   AES Key Schedule

For the key expansion, the secret key is represented as 4 concatenated words, $SK = W_1 \parallel W_2 \parallel W_3 \parallel W_4$. Then, subsequent round keys $RK_{1...10}$ are derived in lexicographic order, each key depending on the previous. The operations used the key expansion are as follows:

1. $RotWord(W)$ performs a cyclic shift to the left on a word by one byte. We assume that each byte in the word will leak.
2. $SubWord(W)$ substitutes each of the 4 constituent bytes of W according to the AES S-box, which can be implemented as a 256-bit lookup table. We expect leakage for each S-box look-up.
3. Rcon, which is a predefined round constant, is exclusive-ored to a byte of the key. We expect the result of exclusive-or to leak.

2.3   Further Implementation Aspects

SPA attacks are typically studied in the context of software implementations on simple (i.e. serial) micro-processors. This implies that we expect to observe leakages for all state bytes as and when they are processed. As explained before, we adhere to this by-and-large and only deviate from this principle to keep our work comparable with previous publications.

Typical power models that are found in practice (for small micro-processors) are the Hamming weight (short HW, i.e. the number of non-zero bits) of a byte, or the Hamming distance (short HD, i.e. the number of non-zero bits in the exclusive-or of two bytes). Leakages of this kind are observed mainly because of intermediate values being written to (and read from) memory, which causes bus transfers. Obviously, for HD leakage one then needs to know precisely which two intermediate values are processed in sequence.

Notice that for our attacks we did not use data from an actual device. This is motivated by the fact that we are not interested in the problem of how to find and best extract the available leakage from real traces. Our contribution is with regards to how to best (i.e. mathematically) exploit the extracted leakage. So we use simulations to generate (truly leaked) HW (and HD) values and then 'embed' them in sets of a given size to simulate noise (i.e. the fact that one might not have certainty for the HW (or HD) of correct leakages). These sets are ordered sequences with the correct leakage as centre value, e.g. if the correct leakage for an intermediate value is 5, a set of size three is $\{4, 5, 6\}$. We assume a uniform distribution for the 'incorrect' values within each set in our experiments.

3   Pragmatic Attack on AES

Like [9], we assume that the attacker is able to extract the relevant information from the power traces and assign it to the respective intermediate value in both the encryption round and the key schedule. Differently to [9], we assume, however, that the extracted information is possibly erroneous. Consequently, each

Algorithm 1. An informal description of an enumeration attack aimed at recovering four bytes of the secret key SK using leakages of a single AES round.

1: **for** $i = 1 \to 4$ **do**
2:     generate $KeySet_i$ such that each key in $KeySet_i$ satisfies the observed leaks
       $\mathcal{L}(PT_i \oplus SK_i)$, $\mathcal{L}(SB_i)$ and $\mathcal{L}(SK_i)$.
3: **end for**
4: **for** all $K_1 \in KeySet_1$ **do**
5:     **for** all $K_2 \in KeySet_2$ **do**
6:         **for** all $K_3 \in KeySet_3$ **do**
7:             **for** all $K_4 \in KeySet_4$ **do**
8:                 retain values that also match $\mathcal{L}(Tm_i)$, $\mathcal{L}(Tmp)$, and $\mathcal{L}(out_i)$
9:             **end for**
10:         **end for**
11:     **end for**
12: **end for**
13: **return** four sets $\{K_i\}$ of 8-bit values that simultaneously satisfy all observed leakages

---

leakage point translates into a set of leakage values (rather than a single value). A necessary condition for our attack to produce meaningful results is then that each set includes the correct leakage value.

Whilst we did not aim for the most efficient implementation that is conceivable, we paid some attention to choosing strategies that speed up testing keys against leakages. The basic strategy of an SPA attack such as [9] is that by observing leakages relating to different intermediate (key dependent) values, one learns something about the involved key bytes and hence reduces the overall search space for the key. Illustrating this on a simple example that is the starting point for an SPA attack, we note that by observing leakages on (e.g.) a plaintext byte PT (we denote this with $\mathcal{L}(PT)$) and on the key addition with this byte $PT \oplus SK$ (i.e. we see a leakage $\mathcal{L}(PT \oplus SK)$), we can enumerate and in fact precompute all those values of SK which satisfy the observed leakages (we hence enumerate the set $K_{v,w} = \{k | \mathcal{L}(PT \oplus k) = w, \mathcal{L}(PT) = v\}$). It is in fact sufficient to fix the Hamming weight leakage of the plaintext to an arbitrary value (we chose 0) because $(PT \oplus k) = ((0 \oplus k) \oplus PT)$, which means that the possible key set corresponding to any nonzero plaintext byte can be easily derived by adding PT as offset to the key set corresponding to the null value byte. We hence can optimise and store only one such table for $PT = 0$.

Just observing such a single leak reduces hence the key space and we use this reduced key space to further process and incorporate leakages from our traces, i.e. for each possible key resulting from only looking at the first key addition, we can also check the leakage from the $SubBytes$ operation, which then reduces our key space further. One can again build (precompute) tables that enumerate possible key byte values for given input and output leakages, so this step in a practical attack corresponds to a table lookup.

Advancing further into the AES round means that after *ShiftRows*, which we assumed would give no explicit leakages because it would be done as part of writing the byte back into the state, we work with intermediate values that arise from the *MixColumns* operation. Here, we choose not to attempt further precomputations, but rather took leakages 'on the fly' to further prune the key space, see Algorithm 1 for an informal algorithmic description of this process as applied to a single column in one round.

3.1   Attack Results

We performed all our analysis using noisy Hamming weight leakages, i.e. we chose sets of different sizes that contain the correct leakage (ranging from set size 1, which corresponds to no noise, to set size 5, which corresponds to tolerating 2 bits of noise).

All computations that we now discuss were performed by using a single node on a high-performance computing facility. Such a single node is comprised of two 2.8 GHz 4-core Intel Harpertown E5462 processors, with one GB RAM per core. Our code ran in Matlab on this platform. We terminated attacks after 48 h or if they ran out of RAM memory on the node. We give the percentage of attacks that terminated successfully (i.e. that terminated within the 48 h limit and did not run out of memory) for each experiment. We provide 'indicative execution times' for all experiments: these are mean values taken over the successfully terminated experiments. We want to caution against making any inferences from these times, because although we made some effort to produce 'efficient' attack implementations, we by no means claim any optimality in any respect (recall that we ran the attacks using Matlab). Consequently, these indicative execution times are best understood along the lines of that some attacks terminate within the order of several hours whereas others terminate within the order of seconds, etc. We also note that the timings produced only refer to the effort of reducing the key search space using the side channel information. The overall time required for an attack, i.e. reducing the key search space and the performing the brute-force search, would very much also depend on the brute-force search.

Attack Using Leaks from the First Encryption Round. By referring back to the description of an AES round and the expected leaks that we gave in Sect. 2.1, we note that we have 21 exploitable leakage points to attack 4 bytes of the first round key (which corresponds to one column of the state). Consequently we assume that we have 84 such points available to attack an entire round. The attack strategy that we explained in the previous section, which works on one column, can independently (and hence in parallel) be replicated and applied to all four state bytes.

Table 1a shows that allowing for more noisy leakages increases the computational effort quickly, as one would expect. Clearly for noisy leaks the reduction in key space size renders the attack actually impractical.

Attack Using Leaks from First Encryption Round and Key Schedule. Rather than making more complicated inferences to incorporate more information from the second encryption round, it seems more natural now to incorporate the strategy of [9] and draw on the information that is present in the key schedule. The attack of Mangard requires, depending on how many key hypotheses one wishes to brute force test at the end, 40 up to 81 intermediate values from the key schedule to succeed. We chose, for the sake of consistency, to use leaks from the first round of the key schedule only.

When faced with 'merging' the two attack strategies one has different options. We decided to use the result of the attack on the round as a starting point to the attack on the key schedule. In other words, we start the attack on the key schedule with an already reduced key space.

Table 1c shows the results of the combined attack. The incorporation of the noisy key schedule leakages has had a significant impact especially in the case of set size five (i.e. 2 bits of noise). Now even this case leads to a final key space size that can be searched through and hence leads to a practical attack.

Just for comparison we also give the numbers of Mangard's attack on the key schedule only in Table 1b (re-implemented and adapted to target a single round with possibly noisy leaks). It should be obvious that by itself the strategy does not tolerate noise very well. We can hence conclude that using leaks from both encryption round and key schedule is indeed the most natural and promising attack path.

4 Elegant Attack on AES

The elegant attacks that we now want to consider are essentially algebraic attacks that incorporate additional information about the key bytes because of leakages. The technique is viewed as elegant because one can (in theory) feed the system of equations describing AES into some black box solver which returns the key provided enough side-channel information is supplied.

As mentioned in the introduction, recent research has drawn attention to the fact that it makes a significant difference (to the various black box solvers) how and which equations are fed into them, and hence there is scope to optimise attacks by rewriting the algebraic representation of a cipher—clearly the black box solver is more of a grey box then.

From a practical perspective, anyone implementing an algebraic attack that uses side-channel information needs to hence make two important choices. Firstly, how to represent the cipher and secondly, which sort of solver to use. In our study here we incorporated techniques that were published in previous work to ensure we have a reasonably efficient representation. Of the many available solvers, we used SAT solvers (we use state-of-the-art software, i.e. CryptoMiniSat 2, and did not develop our own tools).

Whilst most side-channel attacks follow a divide-and-conquer strategy, when performing an algebraic attack, the adversary aims for full key recovery in one go and is able to make use of all available side-channel information at once.

Table 1. Summary of results of attack on one round

(a) Encryption round only

Set size	Approximate key space size	Indicative execution time	Successful termination
1	1	0.02 s	100%
2	2^{20}	2.9 s	100%
3	2^{48}	73.9 s	100%
4	2^{64}	27min	100%
5	2^{116}	2.5h	78%

(b) Key schedule only

Set size	Approximate key space size	Indicative execution time	Successful termination
1	2^{58}	0.4 s	100%
2	2^{74}	5 s	100%
3	2^{95}	10 s	72%
4	2^{106}	30 s	40%
5	2^{115}	40 s	22%

(c) Round and key schedule

Set size	Approximate key space size	Indicative execution time	Successful termination
1	1	0.03 s	100%
2	2^{12}	27 s	100%
3	2^{13}	4 min	80%
4	2^{52}	35 min	20%
5	2^{60}	12 h	10%

We assumed that attackers would include leakages corresponding to round operations and, in contrast to previous work, the key schedule.

4.1   Solver-Specific Requirements

To be able to make use of a standard solver, one needs to translate the high-level description of a cipher into a format that the solver can work with. Essentially this translation requires two steps. The first step is to linearise the system of equations that represents the cryptographic algorithm. This can be done by introducing a new variable for each higher degree monomial in the algorithm's representation (monomials might represent (e.g.) bits of intermediate values or bytes). The second step is to translate this linear system into an appropriate format, e.g. conjunctive normal form (CNF) for SAT solvers or a system of Boolean inequalities for Pseudo-Boolean Optimizers.

Linear layers, such as *AddRoundKey* or *MixColumns*, give rise to relatively simple equations. Non-linear layers, i.e. *SubBytes*, lead to fairly complex equations, and there is some scope for optimising them. Based on work by [3], an expression for an 8-bit S-box in polynomials of maximal degree 8 was given in [6]. Still, it was shown in [4] that SAT solvers give best performances when the degree of equations and the size of terms is limited to smaller values. Using some specific algebraic properties of *SubBytes*, Courtois et al. also derive a system of 23 quadratic equations describing it, which is shown to be maximal. We used this approach in our work.

Overall, we thus represented all intermediate values as variables with appropriate equations linking them to each other. An initial count of the expected number of variables is consequently as follows. For the key schedule, 128 variables are required for each round key, and for the secret key. Auxiliary variables can be used for the output of the S-box, but are not needed for xoring with Rcon since this is fixed; this operation can be just as well modelled without introducing any equations, since xoring with 1 is equivalent to negation. Thus, the equations for each round key describe only the S-box (23×4) and the xoring with temp. Additionally, 128 variables are required for each intermediate output state of *AddRoundKey*, *SubBytes* and *MixColumns* during the encryption process, and for the plaintext. The number of equations is calculated as follows: 23×16 for each of the 10 S-box layers, 128 for the 11 key addition layers and the equations corresponding to the 9 rounds of *MixColumns*, which can be represented either as recommended in the Rijndael proposal [5], leading to 13×4 equations per round, or as in [7] as a direct bitslice implementation, leading to 128 equations per round. Of these, the equations corresponding to the S-box are the only non-linear ones. When translating the system to CNF, dummy variables are necessary for linearisation and for keeping the size of each term up to 4 monomials (as recommended by [1,4]), in particular approximately 500 auxiliary variables and 400 equations are required per S-box, which leads to a final form consisting in approximately 100,000 variables and 130,000 equations.

Finally, equations representing side-channel information are added to the system. We adopt the same strategy of [15], to explicitly list all possible values corresponding to each leakage point. However, we do use the pre-computation strategies described in Sect. 3, to build explicit values corresponding to the input and output pairs of each S-box.

4.2   Attack Results

We ran several experiments with our implementation. In these experiments we varied the number of encryption rounds from which we source information as well as the amount of noise that we want to tolerate by varying the set size. Table 2 gives an overview of the results for AES. Remember that our attack (in contrast to previous work on algebraic attacks) uses key schedule information in addition to round information. There is little difference between attacking only one or many rounds (the timings have some variation and the reported means are hence about equal) with regards to timings. We speculate that this is because the complexity of the equations solved stays the same irrespective of how many rounds are used. Obviously, the more rounds one includes the more intermediate values need to by extracted. For each encryption round, 84 intermediate values are used, corresponding to 32 values for the output of *AddRoundKey* and *SubBytes* and 4×13 values corresponding to the intermediate values of

Table 2. Indicative solving time (in seconds) for AES, using encryption and key schedule leakage

Attacked rounds	1 round	2 rounds	3 rounds	4 rounds	5 rounds
set=1	10.39	10.85	11.03	11.10	11.30
set=2	41.24	43.11	43.25	43.49	43.73

MixColumns. Additionally, for each round key at most 21 intermediate values can be exploited, out of which 16 correspond to the key bytes, 4 to the S-box output and 1 to the xoring with the round constant.

As expected the set size is the main factor that influences the overall computation time. We limited any solver run to 48 h (alike previous work). Given this constraint, none of our attempts to solve instances of set size three or larger was successful. However in contrast to previous work we could solve all instances of set size two that terminated within the 48 h cut-off time. Clearly adding some key schedule information helps the solver.

5   Conclusion

The research presented in this paper was based on the question of how elegant (black box) solvers compare with a simple and reasonably efficient extension of Mangard's SPA attack, in a scenario where some erroneous side-channel information is available. In contrast to previous work, we considered the scenario in which an attacker has access to erroneous leakages from both the encryption round and the key schedule (but limited to a single or a few rounds).

Our implementation of a pragmatic SPA attack shows that with very few leakage points (we only use leakage points that occur within the first round of AES and the key schedule) we can reduce the key space even with noisy leakages to a size which can be searched through using today's computing technology. We speculate that with a more efficient implementation, this could be improved further by taking more rounds (of the key schedule and the encryption) into account. Including key schedule information in the elegant ASCA-style approach helps, but we were not able to push beyond set size two. However, all our attacks with set size two were successful, even when limited to using leaks from the first round only, which is some practically relevant progress.

Our conclusion from the performed experiments is that the pragmatic approach seems to be more suited for actual practical attacks because of its ability to better tolerate noisy leakages and its concrete result that allows to actually rule out keys and provide a concrete reduction of the key space. This is in contrast to using algebraic solvers, which either terminate successfully, or leave you with no further information.

Acknowledgments. Valentina Banciu has been supported by EPSRC via grant EP/H049606/1. Elisabeth Oswald has been supported in part by EPSRC via grant EP/I005226/1.

A   More Experimental Results

See Table 3.

Table 3. Summary of results with HD model

(a) Pragmatic attack on one round

Set size	Final key space size	Execution time	Success rate
1	2^{13}	0.03 s	100%
2	2^{48}	7 min	90%
3	2^{58}	4.5 h	32%
4	2^{66}	20 h	8%
5	N/A	>24 h	0%

(b) Algebraic attack up to several rounds

Attacked rounds	1 round	2 rounds	3 rounds	4 rounds	5 rounds
set=1	20.13	20.08	20.13	19.88	19.68
set=2	641.52	601.46	600.33	609.30	640.31

References

1. Bard, G.V., Courtois, N., Jefferson, C.: Efficient methods for conversion and solution of sparse systems of low-degree multivariate polynomials over GF(2) via SAT-solvers. IACR Cryptol. ePrint Arch. **2007**, 24 (2007)
2. Carlet, C., Faugère, J.-C., Goyet, C., Renault, G.: Analysis of the algebraic side channel attack. J. Cryptogr. Eng. **2**(1), 45–62 (2012)
3. Courtois, N., Pieprzyk, J.: Cryptanalysis of block ciphers with overdefined systems of equations. IACR Cryptol. ePrint Arch. **2002**, 44 (2002)
4. Creignou, N., Daude, H.: Satisfiability threshold for random XOR-CNF formulas. Discrete Appl. Math. **96**, 41–53 (1999)
5. Daemen, J., Rijmen, V.: AES proposal: Rijndael. In: First Advanced Encryption Standard (AES) Conference (1998)
6. Gligoroski, D., Moe, M.E.: On deviations of the AES S-box when represented as vector valued Boolean function. Int. J. Comput. Sci. Netw. Secur. **7**(4), 156–163 (2007)
7. Käsper, E., Schwabe, P.: Faster and timing-attack resistant AES-GCM. In: Clavier, C., Gaj, K. (eds.) CHES 2009. LNCS, vol. 5747, pp. 1–17. Springer, Heidelberg (2009)

8. Kocher, P.C., Jaffe, J., Jun, B.: Differential power analysis. In: Wiener, M. (ed.) CRYPTO 1999. LNCS, vol. 1666, pp. 388–397. Springer, Heidelberg (1999)

9. Mangard, S.: A simple power-analysis (SPA) attack on implementations of the AES key expansion. In: Lee, P.J., Lim, C.H. (eds.) ICISC 2002. LNCS, vol. 2587, pp. 343–358. Springer, Heidelberg (2003)

10. Mohamed, M.S.E., Bulygin, S., Zohner, M., Heuser, A., Walter, M., Buchmann, J.: Improved algebraic side-channel attack on AES. In: HOST, pp. 146–151 (2012)

11. Oren, Y., Kirschbaum, M., Popp, T., Wool, A.: Algebraic side-channel analysis in the presence of errors. In: Mangard, S., Standaert, F.-X. (eds.) CHES 2010. LNCS, vol. 6225, pp. 428–442. Springer, Heidelberg (2010)

12. Oren, Y., Renauld, M., Standaert, F.-X., Wool, A.: Algebraic side-channel attacks beyond the hamming weight leakage model. In: Prouff, E., Schaumont, P. (eds.) CHES 2012. LNCS, vol. 7428, pp. 140–154. Springer, Heidelberg (2012)

13. Renauld, M., Standaert, F.-X.: Algebraic side-channel attacks. In: Bao, F., Yung, M., Lin, D., Jing, J. (eds.) Inscrypt 2009. LNCS, vol. 6151, pp. 393–410. Springer, Heidelberg (2010)

14. Renauld, M., Standaert, F.-X.: Combining algebraic and side-channel cryptanalysis against block ciphers. In: 30-th Symposium on Information Theory in the Benelux (2009)

15. Renauld, M., Standaert, F.-X.: Representation-, leakage- and cipher- dependencies in algebraic side-channel attacks. In: Industrial track of ACNS 2010 (2010)

16. Renauld, M., Standaert, F.-X., Veyrat-Charvillon, N.: Algebraic side-channel attacks on the AES: why time also matters in DPA. In: Clavier, C., Gaj, K. (eds.) CHES 2009. LNCS, vol. 5747, pp. 97–111. Springer, Heidelberg (2009)

17. Zhao, X., Zhang, F., Guo, S., Wang, T., Shi, Z., Liu, H., Ji, K.: MDASCA: an enhanced algebraic side-channel attack for error tolerance and new leakage model exploitation. In: Schindler, W., Huss, S.A. (eds.) COSADE 2012. LNCS, vol. 7275, pp. 231–248. Springer, Heidelberg (2012)

Addition with Blinded Operands

Mohamed Karroumi[1]([☒]), Benjamin Richard[1], and Marc Joye[2]

[1] Technicolor, 975 Avenue des Champs Blancs, 35576 Cesson-Sévigné Cedex, France
{mohamed.karroumi,benjamin.richard}@technicolor.com
[2] Technicolor, 735 Emerson Street, Palo Alto, CA 94301, USA
marc.joye@technicolor.com

Abstract. The masking countermeasure is an efficient method to protect cryptographic algorithms against Differential Power Analysis (DPA) and similar attacks. For symmetric cryptosystems, two techniques are commonly used: Boolean masking and arithmetic masking. Conversion methods have been proposed for switching from Boolean masking to arithmetic masking, and conversely. The way conversion is applied depends on the combination of arithmetic and Boolean/logical operations executed by the underlying cryptographic algorithm.

This paper focuses on a combination of one addition with one or more Boolean operations. Building on a secure version of a binary addition algorithm (namely, the AND-XOR-and-double method), we show that conversions from Boolean masking to arithmetic masking can be avoided. We present an application of the new algorithm to the XTEA block-cipher.

Keywords: Masking methods · Differential power analysis (DPA) · Side-channel attacks · Binary addition · Block ciphers · XTEA

1 Introduction

Differential Power Analysis DPA and related attacks, introduced by Kocher *et al.* in [13], exploit side-channel leakage to uncover secret information. During the execution of a cryptographic algorithm, the secret key or some related information may be revealed by monitoring the power consumption of the electronic device executing the cryptographic algorithm. DPA-type attacks potentially apply to all cryptosystems, including popular block ciphers like AES (*e.g.*, [19]). Protection against DPA is achieved thanks to randomization techniques. The commonly suggested way to thwart DPA-type attacks for implementations of block ciphers is random masking [2,3,9]. The idea is to blind sensitive data with a random mask at the beginning of the algorithm execution. The algorithm is then executed as usual. Of course, at some step within a round the value of the mask (or a value derived thereof) must be known in order to correct the corresponding output value. This general technique is referred to as the *duplication method* or the *splitting method*. The *transformed masking method* [1] is a specialized technique wherein the *same* mask is used throughout the computation.

© Springer International Publishing Switzerland 2014
E. Prouff (Ed.): COSADE 2014, LNCS 8622, pp. 41–55, 2014.
DOI: 10.1007/978-3-319-10175-0_4

More specifically, all intermediate values are XORed with a random mask and the inner operations are modified such that the output of a round is masked by the same mask as that of the input. This was for example applied to DES by modifying its non-linear components (namely, the original S-boxes were replaced with modified S-boxes so as to output the correct masked values), which resulted in an implementation shown to be secure against (first-order) DPA attacks.

Masking and Switching Methods. For block ciphers involving different types of operations, two masking techniques must usually be used: a Boolean masking (generally by applying an XOR) and an arithmetic masking. Both techniques were for instance used for protecting the AES finalists against DPA [16]. Further, as shown in [16], it is useful to have efficient and secure methods for switching from Boolean masking to arithmetic masking, and conversely. The algorithm suggested in [16] was however shown to be vulnerable to a 2-bit DPA attack in [3]. A more secure algorithm was later proposed by Goubin in [8]. The algorithm works in both directions. The secure Arithmetic-to-Boolean (A→B) conversion is however less efficient than the secure Boolean-to-arithmetic (B→A) conversion as its complexity depends on the length of the values being masked. This issue was addressed by Coron and Tchulkine in [4] with a method using Look-Up-Tables (LUTs). In [18], an extension to the table-based algorithm of [4] was proposed, reducing the memory footprint. Another improved version can be found in a recent paper by Debraize [5].

TEA Family. The TEA block ciphers [17,21,22] are ciphers designed by Needham and Wheeler, featuring a 128-bit key-size and running over (at least) 64 rounds. They are based on a Feistel structure without use of any S-box, nor any key expansion routines. The ciphers make alternate use of XOR, Shift and modular addition, resulting in simple, efficient, and easy to implement algorithms. The *XTEA cipher* [17] was later proposed as an improvement to TEA to counter the attacks of [10]. The TEA family block-ciphers enjoys several salient features making it attractive for light-weight applications: simplicity, minimal key-setup, no look-up tables, and small footprint.

Our Contribution. The masking problem for (modular) addition can be stated as how to *securely* compute the (modular) addition of k-bit integers x and y from *masked* inputs and the corresponding masks, namely $(\boldsymbol{x}, \boldsymbol{y})$ and (r_x, r_y) where $\boldsymbol{x} = x \oplus r_x$ and $\boldsymbol{y} = y \oplus r_y$, while ensuring that the result, $s = x + y$ (mod 2^k), is still masked with some Boolean mask r_s — 'securely' here has to be understood as in a way resistant against first-order DPA-type attacks.

A classical solution to this problem is to rely on secure mask-switching methods. Blinded values $\boldsymbol{x} = x \oplus r_x$ and $\boldsymbol{y} = y \oplus r_y$ are first converted into values that are *arithmetically* masked, $\boldsymbol{x'} = x - r_x$ and $\boldsymbol{y'} = y - r_y$, using a secure B→A switching algorithm. Next, the resulting values and their masks are separately added:

$$\boldsymbol{s'} = \boldsymbol{x'} + \boldsymbol{y'} \quad \text{and} \quad r_{s'} = r_x + r_y \,.$$

Noticing that $s' = (x + y) - r_{s'}$, the blinded sum $s = (x + y) \oplus r_{s'}$ is obtained through a secure A→B switching algorithm. This is illustrated in Fig. 1b.

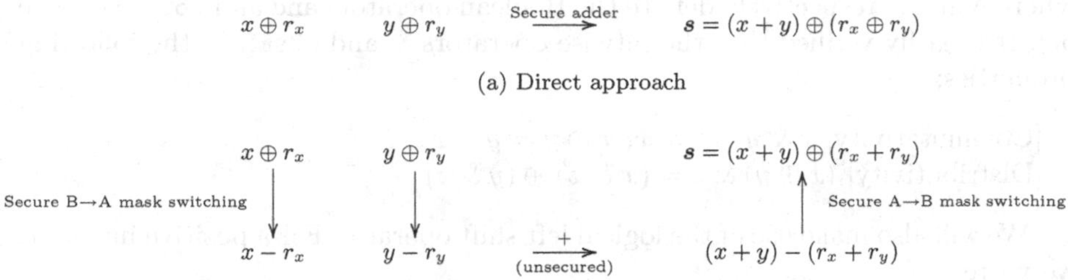

$$x \oplus r_x \qquad y \oplus r_y \qquad \xrightarrow{\text{Secure adder}} \qquad s = (x + y) \oplus (r_x \oplus r_y)$$

(a) Direct approach

$$x \oplus r_x \qquad y \oplus r_y \qquad \qquad s = (x + y) \oplus (r_x + r_y)$$

Secure B→A mask switching $\Big\downarrow$ $\qquad$ $\Big\downarrow$ $\qquad\qquad\qquad$ $\Big\uparrow$ Secure A→B mask switching

$$x - r_x \qquad y - r_y \qquad \xrightarrow[\text{(unsecured)}]{+} \qquad (x + y) - (r_x + r_y)$$

(b) Mask-switching approach

Fig. 1. Solving the masking problem

This paper tackles the masking problem through a more direct approach as described in Fig. 1a. Such an approach was already alluded in [7] where hardware-based solutions using ripple-carry addition methods are presented. These methods are not suited to software implementations and imply dedicated hardware. Dedicated hardware for a specific cryptographic application is in general not available and is expensive to implement. We propose in this paper an example of an algorithm that is *faster* and more *compact* than previous methods—including solutions built on Goubin's method and the table-based methods—for securely adding two blinded operands. The proposed implementation is therefore well adapted to memory-constrained environments. Implementations for securely subtracting two blinded operands and variants thereof are also detailed. We show that the introduced algorithm can be applied to XTEA (and its variants) to protect against DPA-type attacks. The countermeasure advantageously retains the efficiency of the unprotected implementations in terms of memory requirements and speed.

Outline of the Paper. The rest of this paper is organized as follows. In the next section, we introduce the notation that is used throughout. Section 3 is the core of the paper. We review the ADD-XOR-and-double addition algorithm and then derive therefrom an addition algorithm secure against DPA-type attacks. In Sect. 4, we analyze the security of the proposed algorithm. In Sect. 5, we present our approach to thwart DPA on XTEA using various algorithms and evaluate their performance. In Sect. 6, other applications and extensions of our algorithms are proposed. Finally, we conclude in Sect. 7.

2   Notation

This section introduces some notation. Following [12, Section 7.1.3], given three integers in their binary notation, namely $x = (\ldots x_2 x_1 x_0)_2$, $y = (\ldots y_2 y_1 y_0)_2$, and $z = (\ldots z_2 z_1 z_0)_2$, we write

$$x \,\&\, y = z \iff z_i = x_i \wedge y_i, \text{ for all } i \geqslant 0\,;$$
$$x \oplus y = z \iff z_i = x_i \oplus y_i, \text{ for all } i \geqslant 0\,;$$

where $\wedge$ and $\oplus$ respectively denote the Boolean operators and and xor (exclusive or). It is easily verified that the bitwise operators $\&$ and $\oplus$ satisfy the following properties:

- [Commutativity] $x \,\&\, y = y \,\&\, x$, $x \oplus y = y \oplus x$;
- [Distributivity] $(x \oplus y) \,\&\, z = (x \,\&\, z) \oplus (y \,\&\, z)$.

We will also make use of the logical left shift operator. For a positive integer t, we write

$$x \ll t = y \iff y_{i+t} = x_i, \text{ for all } i \geqslant 0, \text{ and } y_0, \ldots, y_{t-1} = 0\,.$$

Notice that $x \ll t = 2^t x$. Hence we will sometimes write $2x$ instead of $x \ll 1$.

Throughout the paper, unless otherwise indicated, we assume that the involved operands are k-bit integers (typically of 8, 16, 32 or 64 bits) and arithmetic operations are performed modulo 2^k. Modular addition and subtraction are noted "+" and "−", respectively. Likewise, unless otherwise indicated, the shifting operations are performed modulo 2^k. To ease the notation, we sometimes omit writing the congruence operation (i.e., (mod 2^k) is implicit). Finally, we will use boldface symbols to represent masked values; for example, $\boldsymbol{x}$ will denote a masked value for x.

3 Boolean Masking and Addition

3.1 Basic Algorithm

Let x and y be two k-bit integers viewed as elements of $\mathbb{Z}_{2^k} = \{0, \ldots, 2^k - 1\}$. The goal is to compute their sum $s = x + y \pmod{2^k}$. Letting $x = \sum_{i=0}^{k-1} x_i 2^i$ and $y = \sum_{i=0}^{k-1} y_i 2^i$ the respective binary expansions of x and y, the pencil-and-paper method to add non-negative integers [11, p. 251] yields $s = \sum_{i=0}^{k-1} s_i 2^i$ in a left-to-right fashion as:

$$c_0 = 0 \quad \text{and} \quad \begin{cases} s_i = (x_i + y_i + c_i) \bmod 2 \\ c_{i+1} = (x_i + y_i + c_i) \operatorname{div} 2 \end{cases}$$

for $0 \leqslant i \leqslant k - 1$. It is readily seen that the carry-out, c_{i+1}, is equal to 1 if and only if at least two of x_i, y_i and c_i are 1. Hence the previous relation can be rewritten using logical operators as

$$c_0 = 0 \quad \text{and} \quad \begin{cases} s_i = x_i \oplus y_i \oplus c_i \\ c_{i+1} = \operatorname{Maj}(x_i, y_i, c_i) \end{cases} \tag{1}$$

using the majority function Maj, given by

$$\mathrm{Maj}\,(x_i, y_i, c_i) := (x_i \,\&\, y_i) \oplus (x_i \,\&\, c_i) \oplus (y_i \,\&\, c_i)$$
$$= (x_i \,\&\, y_i) \oplus \left[(x_i \oplus y_i) \,\&\, c_i\right] = c_i \,\&\, (x_i \oplus y_i) \oplus (x_i \,\&\, y_i)\,.$$

Summing up, given $x, y \in \mathbb{Z}_{2^k}$, their sum (modulo 2^k) can be obtained as

$$s = x \oplus y \oplus c \quad \text{with } c = \sum_{i=1}^{k-1} c_i\, 2^i\,, \tag{2}$$

where $c_0 = 0$ and $c_i = c_{i-1} \,\&\, (x_{i-1} \oplus y_{i-1}) \oplus (x_{i-1} \,\&\, y_{i-1})$ for $1 \leqslant i \leqslant k - 1$.
Since c is defined modulo 2^k, we immediately get from Eqs. (2) and (1)

$$c = \sum_{i=1}^{k-1} c_i\, 2^i = \sum_{i=1}^{k} c_i\, 2^i = 2 \sum_{i=0}^{k-1} c_{i+1}\, 2^i = 2 \sum_{i=0}^{k-1} \left[c_i \,\&\, (x_i \oplus y_i) \oplus (x_i \,\&\, y_i)\right] 2^i$$
$$= 2\left[c \,\&\, (x \oplus y) \oplus (x \,\&\, y)\right] \pmod{2^k}\,.$$

This suggests to obtain the value of c by iterating the relation

$$c \leftarrow 2\left[c \,\&\, (x \oplus y) \oplus (x \,\&\, y)\right] \tag{3}$$

where c is initialized to 0. This yields the following addition algorithm. See
also [14] and [8, Theorem 2].

Algorithm 1. AND-XOR-and-double addition method

Input: $(x, y) \in \mathbb{Z}_{2^k} \times \mathbb{Z}_{2^k}$
Output: $x + y \pmod{2^k}$

1: $A \leftarrow x$; $B \leftarrow y$
2: $C \leftarrow A \,\&\, B$; $A \leftarrow A \oplus B$
3: $B \leftarrow 0$
4: **for** $i = 1$ to $k - 1$ **do**
5: $\quad B \leftarrow B \,\&\, A$; $B \leftarrow B \oplus C$
6: $\quad B \leftarrow B \ll 1$
7: **end for**
8: $A \leftarrow A \oplus B$
9: **return** A

3.2 DPA-Resistant Addition

We now consider the case of masked inputs, namely x and y are blinded as

$$\boldsymbol{x} = x \oplus r_x \quad \text{and} \quad \boldsymbol{y} = y \oplus r_y$$

for some Boolean masks $r_x, r_y \in \mathbb{Z}_{2^k}$. The goal is to securely compute (s, r_s) where $s = (x + y) \oplus r_s$ for some mask $r_s \in \mathbb{Z}_{2^k}$, from (x, r_x) and (y, r_y) and without compromising the values of x or of y through DPA.

We rely on Algorithm 1; an application of Eq. (2) yields

$$\begin{aligned} s &= (x + y) \oplus r_s = (x \oplus y \oplus c) \oplus r_s = (x \oplus r_x) \oplus (y \oplus r_y) \oplus c \oplus r_s \\ &= x \oplus y \oplus c \end{aligned}$$

by setting $r_s = r_x \oplus r_y$. The carry c in the above formula results from the addition of x and y in the clear! As a consequence, if not carefully done, its evaluation might leak information on x or y by mounting a DPA-type attack. In order to solve this issue, in a way analogous to [8], we initialize the value of c with a Boolean mask γ when evaluating Eq. (3). In more detail, letting $c^{(i)}$ the output value of c in Eq. (3) at iteration i and $\boldsymbol{c}^{(i)} = c^{(i)} \oplus 2\gamma$, we have

$$\begin{cases} \boldsymbol{c}^{(0)} = 2\gamma \\ \boldsymbol{c}^{(i)} = 2\left[\boldsymbol{c}^{(i-1)} \,\&\, (x \oplus y) \oplus \Omega\right], & \text{for } 1 \leqslant i \leqslant k - 1 \end{cases} \tag{4}$$

where $\Omega = 2\gamma \,\&\, (x \oplus y) \oplus (x \,\&\, y) \oplus \gamma$.

Proof. We have

$$\begin{aligned} \boldsymbol{c}^{(i)} &= c^{(i)} \oplus 2\gamma = 2\left[c^{(i-1)} \,\&\, (x \oplus y) \oplus (x \,\&\, y)\right] \oplus 2\gamma && \text{by Eq. (3)} \\ &= 2\left[(\boldsymbol{c}^{(i-1)} \oplus 2\gamma) \,\&\, (x \oplus y) \oplus (x \,\&\, y)\right] \oplus 2\gamma \\ &= 2\left[(\boldsymbol{c}^{(i-1)} \,\&\, (x \oplus y)) \oplus (2\gamma \,\&\, (x \oplus y)) \oplus (x \,\&\, y)\right] \oplus 2\gamma \\ &= 2\left[\boldsymbol{c}^{(i-1)} \,\&\, (x \oplus y) \oplus \Omega\right] \end{aligned}$$

as expected. $\square$

Given that $\boldsymbol{c}^{(0)} = 2\gamma$ and the definition of Ω, it is interesting to note that the value of $\boldsymbol{c}^{(1)}$ simplifies to

$$\boldsymbol{c}^{(1)} = 2\left[2\gamma \,\&\, (x \oplus y) \oplus \Omega\right] = 2\left[(x \,\&\, y) \oplus \gamma\right].$$

Hence, letting $\Omega_0 = (x \& y) \oplus \gamma$, we can write $\boldsymbol{c}^{(1)} = 2\Omega_0$ and $\Omega = 2\gamma \& (x \oplus y) \oplus \Omega_0$.

Remark 1. We remark that a similar trick applies to Goubin's arithmetic-to-Boolean conversion. Rearranging the operations leads to a reduced cost, from a total of $5k + 5$ operations down to $\underline{5k + 1}$ operations. This optimized variant is detailed in Appendix A.

It remains to express $\boldsymbol{c}^{(i)}$ and Ω as a function of (x, y, r_x, r_y). From Eq. (4), we have

$$\begin{aligned} \boldsymbol{c}^{(i)} &= 2\left[\boldsymbol{c}^{(i-1)} \,\&\, (x \oplus y \oplus r_x \oplus r_y) \oplus \Omega\right] \\ &= 2\left[(\boldsymbol{c}^{(i-1)} \,\&\, (x \oplus y)) \oplus (\boldsymbol{c}^{(i-1)} \,\&\, (r_x \oplus r_y)) \oplus \Omega\right]. \end{aligned}$$

We also have

$$\Omega = 2\gamma \, \& \, (x \oplus y \oplus r_x \oplus r_y) \oplus \Omega_0 = \left[2\gamma \, \& \, (x \oplus y)\right] \oplus \left[2\gamma \, \& \, (r_x \oplus r_y)\right] \oplus \Omega_0 \, .$$

We need to introduce a useful theorem from [8]:

Theorem 1 (Goubin). *Using previous notations, for any $\delta \in \mathbb{Z}_{2^k}$, function*

$$\Theta_\delta : \mathbb{Z}_{2^k} \to \mathbb{Z}_{2^k}, \gamma \mapsto \left[(2\gamma) \, \& \, \delta\right] \oplus \gamma$$

is bijective.   □

Assume that γ is uniformly distributed over $\mathbb{Z}_{2^k}$. The previous theorem implies that $\left[(2\gamma) \, \& \, (x \oplus y)\right] \oplus \gamma$ is uniformly distributed over $\mathbb{Z}_{2^k}$. In turn, this implies that $\Omega = \left[(2\gamma) \, \& \, (x \oplus y)\right] \oplus \gamma \oplus (x \, \& \, y)$ is uniformly distributed over $\mathbb{Z}_{2^k}$. We exploit this observation and evaluate $c^{(i)}$ as

$$c^{(i)} = 2\left[\left(c^{(i-1)} \, \& \, (x \oplus y)\right) \oplus \Omega \oplus \left(c^{(i-1)} \, \& \, (r_x \oplus r_y)\right)\right] \, .$$

Algorithmically, we implement this as a for-loop using two accumulators, B and T. At the end of the for-loop, accumulator B contains the value of $c = c \oplus 2\gamma$.

```
1: A₀ ← x ⊕ y; A₁ ← rₓ ⊕ r_y
2: B ← c⁽¹⁾; Ω ← Ω
3: for i = 2 to k − 1 do
4:     T ← B & A₀; B ← B & A₁
5:     B ← B ⊕ Ω; B ← B ⊕ T
6:     B ← B ≪ 1
7: end for
```

Similarly, noting that if γ is uniformly distributed over $\mathbb{Z}_{2^k}$ then so is $\Omega_0 = \gamma \oplus (x \, \& \, y)$, we implement the calculation of Ω as:

```
1: A₀ ← x ⊕ y; A₁ ← rₓ ⊕ r_y
2: C ← 2γ; Ω ← Ω₀
3: T ← C & A₀; Ω ← Ω ⊕ T
4: T ← C & A₁; Ω ← Ω ⊕ T
```

The last step is the secure evaluation of Ω_0 (*i.e.*, $\gamma \oplus (x \& y)$) from (x, y, r_x, r_y). We make use of a trick already used in [20]. It exploits the distributive property of the AND over the XOR and evaluates an AND as a series of four AND operations calculated pairwise between masked operands and masks (operations are carried out with masked operands and masks independent from each other). Specifically we implement the calculation of Ω_0 as the left-to-right evaluation of:

$$\Omega_0 = \gamma \oplus (x \, \& \, y) = \gamma \oplus \left[(x \oplus r_x) \, \& \, (y \oplus r_y)\right]$$
$$= \gamma \oplus (x \, \& \, y) \oplus (x \, \& \, r_y) \oplus (y \, \& \, r_x) \oplus (r_x \, \& \, r_y) \, .$$

Putting all together we obtain a DPA-protected addition algorithm. Our secure addition algorithm is depicted in Algorithm 2. It makes use of 3 additional temporary k-bit variables (C, T, and Ω), generates one random mask, and requires $\underline{5k + 8}$ operations:

- $(2k + 6)$ XORs;
- $(2k + 2)$ ANDs;
- k logical shifts.

Algorithm 2. Secure addition with blinded operands

Input: $(x, y, r_x, r_y, \gamma) \in \mathbb{Z}_{2^k}^5$ such that $x = x \oplus r_x$, $y = y \oplus r_y$ and γ a pre-computed random integer

Output: (s, r_s) where $s = (x + y) \oplus r_s \pmod{2^k}$ and $r_s = r_x \oplus r_y$

    /* $\Omega_0 = (x \,\&\, y) \oplus \gamma$ */
1: $\mathsf{C} \leftarrow \gamma$
2: $\mathsf{T} \leftarrow x \,\&\, y;\ \Omega \leftarrow \mathsf{C} \oplus \mathsf{T}$
3: $\mathsf{T} \leftarrow x \,\&\, r_y;\ \Omega \leftarrow \Omega \oplus \mathsf{T}$
4: $\mathsf{T} \leftarrow y \,\&\, r_x;\ \Omega \leftarrow \Omega \oplus \mathsf{T}$
5: $\mathsf{T} \leftarrow r_x \,\&\, r_y;\ \Omega \leftarrow \Omega \oplus \mathsf{T}$ $\triangleright \Omega \leftarrow \Omega_0$

    /* $c^{(1)} = 2\Omega_0$ and $\Omega = 2\gamma \,\&\, (x \oplus y) \oplus \Omega_0$ */
6: $\mathsf{B} \leftarrow \Omega \ll 1;\ \mathsf{C} \leftarrow \mathsf{C} \ll 1$ $\triangleright \mathsf{B} \leftarrow c^{(1)};\ \mathsf{C} \leftarrow 2\gamma$
7: $\mathsf{A}_0 \leftarrow x \oplus y;\ \mathsf{A}_1 \leftarrow r_x \oplus r_y$
8: $\mathsf{T} \leftarrow \mathsf{C} \,\&\, \mathsf{A}_0;\ \Omega \leftarrow \Omega \oplus \mathsf{T}$
9: $\mathsf{T} \leftarrow \mathsf{C} \,\&\, \mathsf{A}_1;\ \Omega \leftarrow \Omega \oplus \mathsf{T}$ $\triangleright \Omega \leftarrow \Omega$

    /* Main loop */
10: **for** $i = 2$ to $k - 1$ **do**
11:    $\mathsf{T} \leftarrow \mathsf{B} \,\&\, \mathsf{A}_0;\ \mathsf{B} \leftarrow \mathsf{B} \,\&\, \mathsf{A}_1$
12:    $\mathsf{B} \leftarrow \mathsf{B} \oplus \Omega$
13:    $\mathsf{B} \leftarrow \mathsf{B} \oplus \mathsf{T}$
14:    $\mathsf{B} \leftarrow \mathsf{B} \ll 1$
15: **end for** $\triangleright \mathsf{B} \leftarrow c \oplus 2\gamma$

    /* Aggregation */
16: $\mathsf{A}_0 \leftarrow \mathsf{A}_0 \oplus \mathsf{B}$
17: $\mathsf{A}_0 \leftarrow \mathsf{A}_0 \oplus \mathsf{C}$
18: **return** $(\mathsf{A}_0, \mathsf{A}_1)$

---

4 Security Analysis

In this section, we study more formally the DPA resistance of the proposed algorithm. An algorithm is *first-order secure* if the intermediate variables do not reveal any information about the sensitive data. To prove first-order DPA resistance, we first list all intermediate variables of the algorithm. We show then that no variable exhibits dependency on the sensitive data. In the sequel, we let V_i denote the values resulting from the intermediate operation performed at Line i in Algorithm 2 (Table 1).

We consider that inputs x and y are respectively masked with r_x and r_y, two random variables uniformly distributed over $\mathbb{Z}_{2^k}$. The sensitive variables and their associated masks are then assumed mutually independent. Furthermore,

Table 1. Intermediate variables

V_i	Values	
V_1	$\mathsf{C} = \gamma$	
V_2	$\mathsf{T} = (x \oplus r_x) \,\&\, (y \oplus r_y)$	$\Omega = (x \oplus r_x) \,\&\, (y \oplus r_y) \oplus \gamma$
V_3	$\mathsf{T} = (x \oplus r_x) \,\&\, r_y$	$\Omega = (x \oplus r_x) \,\&\, y \oplus \gamma$
V_4	$\mathsf{T} = (y \oplus r_y) \,\&\, r_x$	$\Omega = x \,\&\, y \oplus r_x \,\&\, r_y \oplus \gamma$
V_5	$\mathsf{T} = r_x \,\&\, r_y$	$\Omega = x \,\&\, y \oplus \gamma$
V_6	$\mathsf{B} = 2 \cdot (x \,\&\, y \oplus \gamma) = c^{(1)} \oplus 2\gamma$ $\mathsf{C} = 2\gamma$	
V_7	$\mathsf{A}_0 = (x \oplus r_x) \oplus (y \oplus r_y)$	$\mathsf{A}_1 = r_x \oplus r_y$
V_8	$\mathsf{T} = 2\gamma \,\&\, (x \oplus r_x \oplus y \oplus r_y)$	$\Omega = \gamma \oplus 2\gamma \,\&\, (x \oplus y \oplus r_x \oplus r_y) \oplus x \,\&\, y$
V_9	$\mathsf{T} = 2\gamma \,\&\, (r_x \oplus r_y)$	$\Omega = \gamma \oplus 2\gamma \,\&\, (x \oplus y) \oplus x \,\&\, y$
V_{11}	$\mathsf{B}^{(i)} = (c^{(i-1)} \oplus 2\gamma) \,\&\, (r_x \oplus r_y)$ $\mathsf{T} = (c^{(i-1)} \oplus 2\gamma) \,\&\, (x \oplus y \oplus r_x \oplus r_y)$	
V_{12}	$\mathsf{B}^{(i)} = (c^{(i-1)} \oplus 2\gamma) \,\&\, (r_x \oplus r_y) \oplus (\gamma \oplus 2\gamma \,\&\, (x \oplus y) \oplus x \,\&\, y)$	
V_{13}	$\mathsf{B}^{(i)} = \gamma \oplus c^{(i-1)} \,\&\, (x \oplus y) \oplus x \,\&\, y$	
V_{14}	$\mathsf{B} = 2 \cdot (\gamma \oplus c^{(i-1)} \,\&\, (x \oplus y) \oplus x \,\&\, y) = c^{(i)} \oplus 2\gamma$	
V_{16}	$\mathsf{A}_0 = x \oplus y \oplus r_x \oplus r_y \oplus c^{(k-1)} \oplus 2\gamma$	
V_{17}	$\mathsf{A}_0 = (x \oplus y \oplus c^{(k-1)}) \oplus r_x \oplus r_y = (x + y) \oplus r_x \oplus r_y$	

the two random variables r_x and r_y are chosen independently, which gives $r_s = r_x \oplus r_y$ to be also uniform over $\mathbb{Z}_{2^k}$.

A bitwise AND operation between two independent Boolean masked variables does not give a uniformly distributed result. It has however the same distribution as an AND applied to two random variables. Values of T in steps V_2, V_3, V_4, V_5 and values of $\mathsf{T} = (c^{(i-1)} \oplus 2\gamma) \,\&\, (r_s \oplus x \oplus y)$ and $\mathsf{B}^{(i)} = (c^{(i-1)} \oplus 2\gamma) \,\&\, r_s$ in V_{11} are therefore not related to unmasked data (namely x or y). None of these values can act as a mask, and XORing such values would leak through DPA. However, if these are XORed with a random k-bit mask γ, the resulting value retains the uniform distribution of the mask. Consequently, the value of Ω in steps V_2, V_3, V_4 and V_5 and $\mathsf{B}^{(i)} = \gamma \oplus c^{(i-1)} \,\&\, (x \oplus y) \oplus x \,\&\, y$ in V_{13} are all uniformly distributed over $\mathbb{Z}_{2^k}$. The same holds true for Ω in steps V_8 and V_9 because, as already stated in Sect. 3.2, Ω is uniform on $\mathbb{Z}_{2^k}$ when γ is. As Ω is uniform, $\mathsf{B}^{(i)} = (c^{(i-1)} \oplus 2\gamma) \,\&\, r_s \oplus \Omega$ in V_{12} is also uniform on $\mathbb{Z}_{2^k}$.

Calculating an XOR between independent masked values or between random masks has the same distribution as the XOR of two random numbers and so is not related to the unmasked data. The variables $\mathsf{A}_0 = r_s \oplus (x \oplus y)$ and $\mathsf{A}_1 = r_s$ in steps V_7 are therefore not leaking. Likewise, performing an AND between masked values and an independent mask does not reveal anything about unmasked data. Hence, the values of T in steps V_8 and V_9 are not related to unmasked data.

Also, since $2a \bmod 2^k = 2(a \bmod 2^{k-1})$ for any $a \in \mathbb{Z}_{2^k}$, the values of B in V_6 and V_{14} and value of C in V_6 are uniformly distributed over $2\mathbb{Z}_{2^{k-1}}$. Finally, it clearly appears that $\mathsf{A}_0 = 2\gamma \oplus r_s \oplus (x + y)$ and $\mathsf{A}_0 = r_s \oplus (x + y)$, in steps V_{16} and V_{17} respectively do not leak information about unmasked data.

5   Application to XTEA

5.1   XTEA Overview

XTEA is a 64-bit block cipher that has 32 rounds and operates with a key size of 128 bits. It uses similar routines for encryption and decryption module.

Round Function. Let $\mathsf{rk}[2i]$ and $\mathsf{rk}[2i+1]$ be the round keys (for $0 \leqslant i \leqslant 31$). Let also v_0 and v_1 denote the two 32-bit inputs. The outputs are then updated as

$$\begin{cases} v_0 \leftarrow v_0 + (F(v_1) + v_1) \oplus \mathsf{rk}[2i] \\ v_1 \leftarrow v_1 + (F(v_0) + v_0) \oplus \mathsf{rk}[2i+1] \end{cases} \quad \text{where } F(v) = [(v \ll 4) \oplus (v \gg 5)] .$$

The pair (v_0, v_1) is initialized with 64-bit plaintext m, $m = v_0 \| v_1$. The above procedure is run for $i = 0, \ldots, 31$, the ciphertext is the output of round 31.

Key Schedule. The master secret key is a 128-bit value $K = (K[0], K[1], K[2], K[3])$ where $K[j]$'s are 32-bit values ($0 \leqslant j \leqslant 3$). The round keys are defined as

$$\begin{cases} \mathsf{rk}[2i] = K[a_i] + \delta_i \,, \; a_i = \delta_i \,\&\, 3 \\ \mathsf{rk}[2i+1] = K[b_i] + \delta_{i+1} \,, \; b_i = (\delta_{i+1} \gg 11) \,\&\, 3 \end{cases} \quad \text{where } \delta_i = i \cdot \delta \pmod{2^{32}}$$

with $\delta = \mathtt{0x9E3779B9}$.

5.2   Preventing First-Order DPA

A round of XTEA involves Boolean operations (XORs and Shifts) and six additions. Boolean operations are easily masked through an XOR whereas the addition operations are securely evaluated using Algorithm 2. We assume that fresh 32-bit masks w_0, w_1 and Γ are uniformly picked at random for each encryption process. The pair (w_0, w_1) is applied to the input plaintext. The mask Γ is used with the secure addition algorithm. The same masks are then maintained across all rounds, as in the transformed masking method ([1]). At the end of the algorithm the masks (w_0, w_1) are applied to the output data to recover the matching, unmasked ciphertext. For an implementation that is secure against first-order DPA, the round keys do not need to be masked. In such a case, the key schedule is normally implemented. Only 4 additions per round will be then evaluated using Algorithm 2:

– two additions with the evaluation of F,
– two additions when updating the pair (v_0, v_1).

A round of XTEA can be written as

$$v_b \leftarrow v_b + (F(v_{\bar{b}}) + v_{\bar{b}}) \oplus \mathsf{rk}[2i+b] \quad \text{where } F(v_{\bar{b}}) = [(v_{\bar{b}} \ll 4) \oplus (v_{\bar{b}} \gg 5)]$$

for $b \in \{0, 1\}$. Its masked version is implemented as

$$\Gamma \leftarrow \mathtt{random}(2^k)$$
$$(\mathsf{A}_0, \mathsf{A}_1) \leftarrow \big(F(\boldsymbol{v_{\bar{b}}}), F(w_{\bar{b}})\big)$$
$$(\mathsf{A}_0, \mathsf{A}_1) \leftarrow \mathtt{SecADD}(\mathsf{A}_0, v_{\bar{b}}, \mathsf{A}_1, w_{\bar{b}}, \Gamma)$$
$$(\mathsf{A}_0, \mathsf{A}_1) \leftarrow (\mathsf{A}_0 \oplus \mathsf{rk}[2i+b], \mathsf{A}_1 \oplus \mathsf{rk}[2i+b])$$
$$(\mathsf{A}_0, \mathsf{A}_1) \leftarrow \mathtt{SecADD}(\mathsf{A}_0, v_b, \mathsf{A}_1, w_b, \Gamma)$$

where the operations on the masked variables and the masks are processed separately without leaking information about the original variables.

As the two input variables are split into two shares, the number of Boolean operations related to those variables is doubled. This gives 22 basic operations per round plus 4 secure additions. Since the XTEA block-cipher operates on words of size 32 bits, we used the addition algorithm with $k = 32$. Therefore each round requires $4 \times 168 + 22 = 684$ word operations.

5.3 Performance Analysis

We implemented an unmasked version, and a DPA resistant version of XTEA using different addition algorithms. With previous mask-switching methods we implemented the three conversions steps in a row. The addition algorithm includes the two secure B→A conversions (both use the same pre-computed 32-bit random), followed by the secure A→B conversion. The code was written in C and a 32-bit Intel based processor was used for evaluating the implementation. The compilation options were chosen to favor small code size. Optimal code would be possible if written in assembly, but the goal was to determine the relative costs between different secure implementation of XTEA. Details such as the code size, RAM overhead and the cycle count are given in Table 2.

Table 2. Details of various XTEA implementations

Algorithms	ROM [bytes]	RAM [bytes]	Cycles/byte
XTEA	114	16	60
masked XTEA (Algorithm 2)	**379(80)**	**28**	**2410**
masked XTEA ([8] + Algorithm 3)	395(96)	**28**	**2515**
masked XTEA ([18])	620(262)	45	3180
masked XTEA ([5])	664(304)	51	3403

The ROM size represents the complete XTEA code size including the addition algorithm. We also give the size of the addition algorithm inside parenthesis. As the goal is to compare algorithms with smallest memory requirement, for the table-based algorithms we tested the 4-bit nibble size version. The RAM size represents the 16-byte key, the size of the look-up table if any, as well as the size of the random numbers used for masking the inputs, generating the LUTs and computing the secure additions. We assume that a random generator is available to provide the random numbers needed by all algorithms. Although some algorithms need more random numbers, those numbers are only computed once per execution. This is therefore not a determining factor in the comparison. For this reason, the time for their generation was not taken into account.

Table 2 shows that the protected version of XTEA, using the table-based algorithms, requires a ROM space that is almost six times larger than the unprotected version. These versions also have a RAM overhead of at least 45 bytes (*i.e.*, three times bigger than the unprotected version). Our implementation of XTEA requires a ROM space that is only 3.3 times larger than the unprotected version. Remarkably, our method is faster than the methods of [5] and [18] which require a memory space (ROM + RAM) that is at least 1.6 times larger. Goubin's version has a comparable performance especially when considering the improved A→B conversion given in Appendix A, but our algorithm remains better. Indeed, the overall computation cost for one secure addition using Goubin's optimized variant is $5 \cdot k + 1 + 2 \cdot 7 + 2 = \underline{5 \cdot k + 17}$. Our algorithm enables us to save 9 operations per addition, which yields to 1152 operations saved per XTEA execution. Algorithm 2 provides then the best choice regarding the memory versus speed complexity and makes it suitable for resource-constrained devices. This advantage obviously depends on the internal structure of the cryptographic algorithm. If the structure combines additions and Boolean operations such that several additions are performed in a row, the mask-switching methods are then faster. Section 6.1 presents other examples where our addition algorithm presents an advantage over the methods of [8,18] and [5].

6 Further Results

6.1 Other Applications

For larger operands, our algorithm is also applicable to the SKEIN hash function or Threefish block-cipher [6]. These algorithms work with 64-bit variables and make extensive use of the MIX function that combines an XOR, an addition modulo 2^{64} and a rotation by a constant. For smaller k, the gain with our algorithm is even more significant. For instance, one could use our algorithm for protecting SAFER [15]. SAFER encryption alternates between use of a byte-word XORs and additions modulo 256 (*i.e.*, $k = 8$).

6.2 Addition over the Integers

Although described for adding over $\mathbb{Z}_{2^k}$, our secure addition algorithm (Algorithm 2) readily extends to output the result $s = s \oplus r_s$ over the integers. For this purpose, it suffices to run the algorithm by seeing the involved operands as elements in $\mathbb{Z}_{2^{k+1}}$. Indeed, as the input values x and y are smaller than 2^k their sum, $z = x + y$, over the integers is smaller than 2^{k+1} and so is an element of $\mathbb{Z}_{2^{k+1}}$. More generally, our algorithm can accommodate integers x, y of arbitrary length and compute their blinded sum s over $\mathbb{Z}$ by running it over $\mathbb{Z}_{2^{k+1}}$ for any $k \geqslant \max(|x|_2, |y|_2)$ —where $| \cdot |_2$ denotes the binary length.

6.3 Subtraction

Algorithm 2 can also be used for subtraction (which is useful for the XTEA decryption process for example). We use the notation $\overline{x}$ to denote the bitwise complementation of x, namely $\overline{x} = x \oplus (-1)$. From the definition, we immediately get the following identity $\overline{x \oplus y} = x \oplus y \oplus (-1) = x \oplus \overline{y} = \overline{x} \oplus y$.

Our secure subtraction algorithm builds on Algorithm 2 and runs in three steps. The input is $(\boldsymbol{x}, \boldsymbol{y}, r_x, r_y) \in \left(\mathbb{Z}_{2^k}\right)^4$ such that $\boldsymbol{x} = x \oplus r_x$ and $\boldsymbol{y} = y \oplus r_y$ and the output is $(\boldsymbol{w}, r_w)$ where $\boldsymbol{w} = (x - y) \oplus r_w \pmod{2^k}$ and $r_w = r_x \oplus r_y$.

1. Compute $\overline{\boldsymbol{x}}$;
2. Call Algorithm 2 on input $(\overline{\boldsymbol{x}}, \boldsymbol{y}, r_x, r_y)$ and obtain $(\boldsymbol{s}, r_s)$ where $\boldsymbol{s} = (\overline{x}+y) \oplus r_s$ and $r_s = r_x \oplus r_y$;
3. Set $\boldsymbol{w} = \overline{\boldsymbol{s}}$ and $r_w = r_s$, and return $(\boldsymbol{w}, r_w)$.

The correctness follows by observing that $\overline{\boldsymbol{x}} = \overline{x \oplus r_x} = \overline{x} \oplus r_x$. Hence, since $\boldsymbol{y} = y \oplus r_y$, at Step 2, we indeed have $\boldsymbol{s} = (\overline{x} + y) \oplus r_s$ with $r_s = r_x \oplus r_y$. The final step exploits the identity $-x = \overline{x} + 1$; the complementation of $\boldsymbol{s}$ yielding

$$\overline{\boldsymbol{s}} = \overline{(\overline{x} + y)} \oplus r_s = \overline{(-x - 1 + y)} \oplus r_s = \left(-(-x - 1 + y) - 1\right) \oplus r_s = (x - y) \oplus r_s .$$

7   Conclusion

This paper presented a secure addition algorithm for preventing DPA-like attacks in symmetric-key cryptosystems. Remarkably, the developed method involves only Boolean operations (converting to arithmetic masking is not needed) and does not need pre-computed tables. As an illustration, we provided a counter-measure to protect XTEA, which proved well adapted to 32-bit microprocessors.

A   Optimized Variant of Goubin's Method

We show in this appendix how to rearrange the operations in the secure A→B algorithm used for converting $A = x - r$ to $x' = x \oplus r$. As a result, the algorithm cost is slightly reduced.

The carry expansion formula expressed using t_i, $0 \le i \le k - 1$ (see [8, Corollary 2.1]) can be simplified. The idea is to start the recursion with $t_0 = 0$ instead of $t_0 = 2\gamma$. The value of t_1 then simplifies to $t_1 = 2\left[t_0 \& (A \oplus r) \oplus w\right] = 2w$. The recursion formula can so be re-written as

$$t_i = \begin{cases} 2w & \text{if } i = 1, \\ 2\left[t_i \& (A \oplus r) \oplus w\right] & \text{for } 2 \leqslant i \leqslant k - 1 . \end{cases}$$

The main loop within the secure A→B conversion algorithm becomes then:

$\mathsf{T} \leftarrow 2\Omega$

for $i = 2$ **to** $k - 1$ **do**
    $\Gamma \leftarrow \mathsf{T} \ \& \ r; \ \Gamma \leftarrow \Gamma \oplus \Omega; \ \mathsf{T} \leftarrow \mathsf{T} \ \& \ A$
    $\Gamma \leftarrow \Gamma \oplus \mathsf{T}; \ \mathsf{T} \leftarrow 2\Gamma$
end for

We extract the first loop iteration and trade five operations against one logical shift operation. This reduces the algorithm cost to $5k + 1$ operations. This small change has no impact on the security of the algorithm.

Algorithm 3. Improved Goubin's A→B conversion

Input: (A, r), such that $A = x - r \bmod 2^k$
Output: (x', r), such that $x' = x \oplus r$

1: $\Gamma \leftarrow \mathtt{random}(2^k)$
2: $\mathsf{T} \leftarrow 2\Gamma; \; x' \leftarrow \Gamma \oplus r; \; \Omega \leftarrow \Gamma \;\&\; x'; \; x' \leftarrow \mathsf{T} \oplus A; \; \Gamma \leftarrow \Gamma \oplus x'; \; \Gamma \leftarrow \Gamma \;\&\; r; \; \Omega \leftarrow \Omega \oplus \Gamma$
3: $\Gamma \leftarrow \mathsf{T} \;\&\; A; \; \Omega \leftarrow \Omega \oplus \Gamma; \; \mathsf{T} \leftarrow 2\Omega$
4: **for** $i = 2$ **to** $k - 1$ **do**
5:     $\Gamma \leftarrow \mathsf{T} \;\&\; r; \; \Gamma \leftarrow \Gamma \oplus \Omega; \; \mathsf{T} \leftarrow \mathsf{T} \;\&\; A$
6:     $\Gamma \leftarrow \Gamma \oplus \mathsf{T}; \; \mathsf{T} \leftarrow 2\Gamma$
7: **end for**
8: $x' \leftarrow x' \oplus \mathsf{T}$
9: **return** (x', r)

References

1. Akkar, M.-L., Giraud, C.: An implementation of DES and AES, secure against some attacks. In: Koç, Ç.K., Naccache, D., Paar, C. (eds.) CHES 2001. LNCS, vol. 2162, pp. 309–318. Springer, Heidelberg (2001)
2. Chari, S., Jutla, C.S., Rao, J.R., Rohatgi, P.: Towards sound approaches to counteract power-analysis attacks. In: Wiener, M. (ed.) CRYPTO 1999. LNCS, vol. 1666, pp. 398–412. Springer, Heidelberg (1999)
3. Coron, J.-S., Goubin, L.: On boolean and arithmetic masking against differential power analysis. In: Paar, C., Koç, Ç.K. (eds.) CHES 2000. LNCS, vol. 1965, pp. 231–237. Springer, Heidelberg (2000)
4. Coron, J.-S., Tchulkine, A.: A new algorithm for switching from arithmetic to boolean masking. In: Walter, C.D., Koç, Ç.K., Paar, C. (eds.) CHES 2003. LNCS, vol. 2779, pp. 89–97. Springer, Heidelberg (2003)
5. Debraize, B.: Efficient and provably secure methods for switching from arithmetic to boolean masking. In: Prouff, E., Schaumont, P. (eds.) CHES 2012. LNCS, vol. 7428, pp. 107–121. Springer, Heidelberg (2012)
6. Ferguson, N., Lucks, S., Schneier, B., Whiting, D., Bellare, M., Kohno, T., Callas, J., Walker, J.: The Skein hash function family. Submission to NIST (Round 3), October 2010. http://www.skein-hash.info/sites/default/files/skein1.3.pdf
7. Golić, J.D.: Techniques for random masking in hardware. IEEE Trans. Circuits Syst. **54**(2), 291–300 (2007)
8. Goubin, L.: A sound method for switching between boolean and arithmetic masking. In: Koç, Ç.K., Naccache, D., Paar, C. (eds.) CHES 2001. LNCS, vol. 2162, pp. 3–15. Springer, Heidelberg (2001)
9. Goubin, L., Patarin, J.: DES and differential power analysis (The "duplication" method). In: Koç, Ç.K., Paar, C. (eds.) CHES 1999. LNCS, vol. 1717, pp. 158–172. Springer, Heidelberg (1999)

10. Kelsey, J., Schneier, B., Wagner, D.: Related-key cryptanalysis of 3-WAY, Biham-DES, CAST, DES-X, NewDES, RC2, and TEA. In: Han, Y., Quing, S. (eds.) ICICS 1997. LNCS, vol. 1334, pp. 233–246. Springer, Heidelberg (1997)
11. Knuth, D.E.: The Art of Computer Programming, vol. 2, 2nd edn. Addison-Wesley, Readin (1981)
12. Knuth, D.E.: The Art of Computer Programming, vol. 4A. Addison-Wesley, Reading (2011)
13. Kocher, P.C., Jaffe, J., Jun, B.: Differential power analysis. In: Wiener, M. (ed.) CRYPTO 1999. LNCS, vol. 1666, pp. 388–397. Springer, Heidelberg (1999)
14. Lipmaa, H., Moriai, S.: Efficient algorithms for computing differential properties of addition. In: Matsui, M. (ed.) FSE 2001. LNCS, vol. 2355, pp. 336–350. Springer, Heidelberg (2002)
15. Massey, J.L.: SAFER K-64: a byte-oriented block-ciphering algorithm. In: Anderson, R. (ed.) FSE 1993. LNCS, vol. 809, pp. 1–17. Springer, Heidelberg (1994)
16. Messerges, T.S.: Securing the AES finalists against power analysis attacks. In: Schneier, B. (ed.) FSE 2000. LNCS, vol. 1978, pp. 150–164. Springer, Heidelberg (2001)
17. Needham, R.M., Wheeler, D.J.: TEA extensions. Technical report, Computer Laboratory, University of Cambridge, October 1997. http://www.cl.cam.ac.uk/ftp/users/djw3/xtea.ps
18. Neiße, O., Pulkus, J.: Switching blindings with a view towards IDEA. In: Joye, M., Quisquater, J.-J. (eds.) CHES 2004. LNCS, vol. 3156, pp. 230–239. Springer, Heidelberg (2004)
19. Örs, S.B., Gürkaynak, F.K., Oswald, E., Preneel, B.: Power-analysis attack on an ASIC AES implementation. In: International Conference on Information Technology: Coding and Computing (ITCC '04), vol. 2, pp. 546–552. IEEE Computer Society (2004)
20. Trichina, E.: Combinational logic design for AES SubByte transformation on masked data. Cryptology ePrint Archive, Report 2003/236 (2003). http://eprint.iacr.org/2003/236
21. Wheeler, D.J., Needham, R.M.: TEA, a tiny encryption algorithm. In: Preneel, B. (ed.) FSE 1994. LNCS, vol. 1008, pp. 363–366. Springer, Heidelberg (1995)
22. Wheeler, D.J., Needham, R.M.: Corrections to XTEA. Technical report, Computer Laboratory, University of Cambridge, October 1998. http://www.movable-type.co.uk/scripts/xxtea.pdf

On the Use of RSA Public Exponent to Improve Implementation Efficiency and Side-Channel Resistance

Christophe Giraud[✉]

Cryptography and Security Group, Oberthur Technologies,
4, Allée du Doyen Georges Brus, 33600 Pessac, France
c.giraud@oberthur.com

Abstract. Since the end of the nineties, cryptographic developers must not only provide fast implementations but they must also take Side-Channel Analysis and Fault Injection into account. From that time, many side-channel and fault countermeasures have been proposed to reach a double goal: provide a high level of security while having the smallest impact on performance and memory consumption. In the particular case of RSA, the knowledge of the public exponent has been used to propose the most efficient fault countermeasure in terms of security and performance. However so far no study has been published which exploits such a variable to improve RSA efficiency and side-channel resistance.

In this paper, we fill this gap by proposing an original CRT-RSA implementation which makes use of the knowledge of the public exponent. In particular, we investigate an efficient method using only 4 private key parameters out of 5 and we also propose a free message blinding method to reinforce side-channel resistance.

Keywords: CRT-RSA · Efficient implementation · Side-channel countermeasure

1 Introduction

1996 was one of the most amazing years for the Crypto community. Indeed in a few months, two revolutionary attacks called *Side-Channel Analysis* (SCA) [21] and *Fault Injection* (FI) [5] were published. These two attacks definitely affected *practitioners* by changing the way of implementing cryptographic algorithms and they also challenged *theoreticians* to design new cryptosystems meant to resist such threats. The first kind of attack takes advantage of physical interactions between the embedded device and its environment during the execution of the cryptosystem to recover information on the corresponding secret key [24]. Indeed, it was noticed that these interactions, such as the device power consumption [22] or its electromagnetic radiation [15], contain information on the operations and on the variables manipulated by the device. The second kind of attack aims to disturb the correct execution of the algorithm and uses the corresponding

© Springer International Publishing Switzerland 2014
E. Prouff (Ed.): COSADE 2014, LNCS 8622, pp. 56–68, 2014.
DOI: 10.1007/978-3-319-10175-0_5

faulty output to obtain information on the secret key [19]. Of course, numerous countermeasures have been published since 1996 to efficiently counteract these attacks and the fields of SCA and FI are now the most active fields of research in cryptography.

As well as being the first practical public-key cryptosystem, RSA [29] has also been the most widely used for many years, especially in electronic signature schemes. It has thus been a privileged target for cryptologists to mount effective SCA and FI and to propose efficient countermeasures. Concerning FI-resistant RSA implementation, the most efficient method consists in using the public exponent to verify the signature before outputting it. Whereas such an approach has been published more than 15 years ago [6], no publication deals with the exploitation of the public exponent to improve RSA implementation efficiency and side-channel resistance. This article addresses such an open topic.

The rest of this paper is organised as follows. Section 2 briefly presents the state-of-the-art of secure CRT-RSA implementation on embedded devices. In Sect. 3, we present our new approach to implement CRT-RSA by taking advantage of the knowledge of the public exponent. After presenting a functional version of our implementation, we improve its side-channel resistance by proposing a free message blinding method. This new approach is then compared with the state-of-the-art implementation. Finally, we conclude in Sect. 4.

2   State-of-the-Art Secure CRT-RSA Implementation

In this section, we firstly describe RSA before presenting the main SCA and FI countermeasures used nowadays to obtain a secure implementation.

2.1   RSA Presentation

In the following we briefly recall how to compute the RSA signature in both standard and CRT modes.

Let N denote the public modulus being the product of two secret large prime integers p and q. Let d refer to the private exponent and e refer to the public exponent satisfying $d \cdot e \equiv 1 \bmod \varphi(N)$, where φ denotes Euler's totient function. The RSA signature of a message $m \in \mathbb{Z}_N$ is then obtained by computing $S = m^d \bmod N$. To verify the signature, one computes $S^e \bmod N$ and checks if the corresponding result is equal to m.

In embedded systems, most RSA implementations use the Chinese Remainder Theorem (CRT) which yields a speed-up factor of four [13]. By using the CRT, the signature generation is composed of two exponentiations $S_p = m^{d_p} \bmod p$ and $S_q = m^{d_q} \bmod q$, where $d_p = d \bmod (p-1)$ and $d_q = d \bmod (q-1)$. The signature is then obtained by recombining S_p and S_q, which is usually done by using Garner's formula [16]:

$$S - S_q + q \cdot (i_q \cdot (S_p - S_q) \bmod p), \tag{1}$$

where $i_q = q^{-1} \bmod p$.

We depict in Algorithm 1 the algorithmic of a standard CRT-RSA implementation as described above.

Algorithm 1. Standard CRT-RSA signature

INPUTS: The message m and the private key (p, q, d_p, d_q, i_q)
OUTPUT: The signature S of the message m

// First exponentiation
1. $S_p \leftarrow m^{d_p} \bmod p$
// Second exponentiation
2. $S_q \leftarrow m^{d_q} \bmod q$
// Recombination
3. $S \leftarrow S_q + q \cdot (i_q \cdot (S_p - S_q) \bmod p)$
4. **return** S

Although RSA cryptosystem using signature protocol PSS [27] is proved secure against theoretical cryptanalysis, it can be broken if straightforwardly implemented on embedded devices by using Side-Channel Analysis or Fault Injection. In the next sections, we present the main countermeasures which are generally implemented to counteract SCA and FI.

2.2 SCA Countermeasures

When published, SCA was divided into two groups: *Simple Side-Channel Analysis* (SSCA) and *Differential Side-Channel Analysis* (DSCA). The first kind aims at recovering information on the secret key by using the side-channel leakage of only one execution of the algorithm whereas DSCA uses several executions of the algorithm and applies statistical analysis to the corresponding measurements to exhibit information on the secret key.

In the particular case of RSA, the most common countermeasure to prevent SSCA consists in using exponentiation methods where the sequence of modular operations does not depend on the corresponding secret exponent. Example of such exponentiations are the Montgomery Ladder [20] or the Atomic exponentiation [8]. Concerning DSCA countermeasures, most techniques aim at randomizing the message and the exponents. This can be done for instance by applying *additive masking* to these variables [9]. In such a case, one can pick four 64-bit random values k_i, $i \in \{0, \cdots, 3\}$, and compute $S'_p = (m + k_0 \cdot p)^{d_p + k_1 \cdot (p-1)} \bmod 2^{64} \cdot p$ and $S'_q = (m + k_2 \cdot q)^{d_p + k_3 \cdot (q-1)} \bmod 2^{64} \cdot q$ before combining them using the CRT-recombination. The expected signature is finally obtained by performing a final reduction modulo $N = p \cdot q$.

Instead of using additive masking to blind the message, one can apply *multiplicative masking* [24] which consists generally in multiplying the message with $r^e \bmod N$ where r is a non null random value. The blinding is then removed at the end of the computation by multiplying the final result with r^{-1} mod N. However, the inverse computation to obtain r^{-1} mod N is costly in terms of both performance and memory consumption. Such an approach is therefore generally avoided in favor of the traditional additive masking.

When combining both SSCA and DSCA countermeasures, RSA implementations resist most kind of side-channel attacks. However, a third class of SCA called *Horizontal Analysis* (HA) has been published recently and could defeat such implementations by using only one execution of the algorithm [4,10,11,31]. This kind of attack aims generally at distinguishing if each modular operation is a multiplication with the input message or not. To counteract such powerful attacks, one must randomize the order of the single-precision multiplications [4,11] or randomize the blinding of each operand before each long integer multiplication [10].

2.3   FI Countermeasures

RSA has been the first cryptosystem to be analysed versus Fault Injection [6]. In the case of CRT-RSA, only one fault injected during one of the two exponentiations provides a faulty signature which allows the attacker to recover one of the two secret primes p or q. For instance, if a fault is injected during the computation of S_p leading to a faulty signature $\widetilde{S}$ then one can notice that $\widetilde{S} \equiv S$ mod q but $\widetilde{S} \not\equiv S$ mod p. Therefore, the secret parameter q can be easily recovered by computing the gcd of $S - \widetilde{S}$ and N. The other private key parameters can then be straightforwardly deduced.

To protect RSA against such a threat, dozens of countermeasures have been proposed over the last decade. These methods can be divided into four different groups. The first group is based on Shamir's method proposed in [30]. The idea is to perform the two exponentiations over $GF(p \cdot t)$ and $GF(q \cdot t)$ respectively where t is a small random value and then compare both results modulo t. Amongst the numerous variants of Shamir's method, only the improved version of Vigilant's proposal is considered secure against fault injection [12]. The second methodology has been proposed by Giraud in which the fault detection comes from the exponentiation algorithm itself [17]. He pointed out that by using the Montgomery powering ladder [20], both values m^{d-1} mod N and m^d mod N are available at the end of the computation. These values can then be used to verify the integrity of the exponentiation by testing if m times the first value is equal to the second one. This method has then been extended in [7,28]. The third group corresponds to the *infective computation* method which has been introduced by Yen et al. in [32]. The idea of the countermeasure consists in modifying the signature if a fault is detected such that it provides no information to the attacker. Despite several proposals, each and every infective method has been broken [3]. The fourth and last kind of countermeasure consists in verifying the signature by using the public exponent before outputting it [6].

In the rest of this paper we assume that the public exponent is small, typically less than $2^{16}+1$, which is nearly always the case in practice[1]. Therefore the fourth approach presented above is the most efficient way to counteract fault attacks on CRT-RSA in terms of both security and performances.

2.4   Summary

To sum up Sect. 2, we depict in Algorithm 2 the skeleton of a state-of-the-art secure CRT-RSA [2, Sect. 6.1].

Algorithm 2. Secure CRT-RSA signature

INPUTS: A message m, the public exponent e and the private key (p, q, d_p, d_q, i_q)
OUTPUT: The signature S of the message m

---
1. Generate three 64-bit random values k_0, k_1 and k_2
// Message blinding
2. $m' \leftarrow m + k_0 \cdot p \cdot q$
// First secure exponentiation
3. $d'_p \leftarrow d_p + k_1 \cdot (p - 1)$
4. $S'_p \leftarrow m'^{d'_p} \bmod 2^{64} \cdot p$ [Using an SSCA-HA-resistant expo.]
// Second secure exponentiation
5. $d'_q \leftarrow d_q + k_2 \cdot (q - 1)$
6. $S'_q \leftarrow m'^{d'_q} \bmod 2^{64} \cdot q$ [Using an SSCA-HA-resistant expo.]
// Secure recombination
7. $S' \leftarrow S'_q + q \cdot (i_q \cdot (S'_p - S'_q) \bmod (2^{64} \cdot p))$
// Signature verification
8. $N \leftarrow p \cdot q$
9. if $S'^e \bmod N = m$ then
10.   return $S' \bmod N$
11. else
12.   Security action

---

3   A New Approach

Whereas the public exponent has been used for more than 15 years to counteract Fault Injection, no study has been done to investigate how such a value can be used to improve RSA performance and side-channel resistance. This is unfortunate since when setting an RSA private key, the corresponding public exponent e is often known. For example in the case of EMV banking applications [14],

---

[1] According to [23, Table 1], 99.95 % of the RSA public keys which are used nowadays use one of the 15 following values as public exponent: 3, 5, 7, 11, 13, 17, 19, 21, 23, 35, 41, 47, $2^8 + 1$, $2^{16} - 1$ and $2^{16} + 1$. In particular, more than 95 % of the public exponents are equal to $2^{16} + 1$.

there are only 2 different public exponents possible (3 or $2^{16}+1$) and the correct one can be recovered from the private key by using 2 multiplications [18]. It is therefore interesting to investigate an alternative implementation of CRT-RSA taking advantage of the knowledge of the public exponent value.

3.1 Generic Description

In practice, the CRT-recombination is implemented by using Garner's formula as presented in (1) since it is the most efficient formula published so far. However, the CRT-recombination can also be performed by using the Gauss recombination:

$$S = p \cdot i_p \cdot S_q + q \cdot i_q \cdot S_p \bmod N \tag{2}$$

where $S_p = m^{d_p} \bmod p$, $S_q = m^{d_q} \bmod q$, $i_p = p^{-1} \bmod q$ and $i_q = q^{-1} \bmod p$. Of course, such a method requires either to consume extra memory to add the extra private parameter i_p or to perform a costly inverse computation to obtain such a value on-the-fly. However, we explain in the following that CRT-RSA using such a recombination can be more efficient than using Garner's method if the public exponent is known.

Our new method is based on Relation (3):

$$(m \cdot q^e)^{d_p - 1} \cdot m \cdot q^{e-2} \equiv i_q \cdot S_p \bmod p \tag{3}$$

Proof. When expanding the first term of left part of (3), we obtain:

$$(m \cdot q^e)^{d_p - 1} \equiv m^{d_p - 1} \cdot q^{e \cdot (d_p - 1)} \bmod p \tag{4}$$

$$\equiv m^{d_p - 1} \cdot q^{e \cdot d_p - e} \bmod p \tag{5}$$

$$\equiv m^{d_p - 1} \cdot q^{1 - e} \bmod p \tag{6}$$

Therefore

$$(m \cdot q^e)^{d_p - 1} \cdot m \cdot q^{e-2} \equiv m^{d_p - 1} \cdot q^{1-e} \cdot m \cdot q^{e-2} \bmod p \tag{7}$$

$$\equiv m^{d_p} \cdot q^{1-e+e-2} \bmod p \tag{8}$$

This straightforwardly leads to (3). □

Obviously, a similar relation is obtained modulo q:

$$(m \cdot p^e)^{d_q - 1} \cdot m \cdot p^{e-2} \equiv i_p \cdot S_q \bmod q \tag{9}$$

Finally, one may note that (2) is equivalent to the following relation:

$$S = p \cdot (i_p \cdot S_q \bmod q) + q \cdot (i_q \cdot S_p \bmod p) \bmod N \tag{10}$$

Therefore, by combining Relations (3) and (9) with Relation (10), the signature $S = m^d \bmod N$ of a message m can be computed by using the following relation:

$$S = p \cdot S1_q + q \cdot S1_p \bmod N \tag{11}$$

where

$$S1_p = (m \cdot q^e)^{d_p - 1} \cdot m \cdot q^{e-2} \bmod p,$$
$$S1_q = (m \cdot p^e)^{d_q - 1} \cdot m \cdot p^{e-2} \bmod q.$$

We depict in Algorithm 3 the algorithmic of our new method.

Algorithm 3. Our new CRT-RSA signature implementation with e known

---

INPUTS: A message m, the public key e and a subpart of the private key (p, q, d_p, d_q)
OUTPUT: The signature S of the message m

// First exponentiation
1. $q_1 \leftarrow m \cdot q^{e-2} \bmod p$
2. $q_2 \leftarrow q_1 \cdot q^2 \bmod p$ $[q_2 = m \cdot q^e \bmod p]$
3. $S1_p \leftarrow q_2^{d_p-1} \cdot q_1 \bmod p$ $[S1_p = i_q \cdot S_p \bmod p]$
// Second exponentiation
4. $p_1 \leftarrow m \cdot p^{e-2} \bmod q$
5. $p_2 \leftarrow p_1 \cdot p^2 \bmod q$ $[p_2 = m \cdot p^e \bmod q]$
6. $S1_q \leftarrow p_2^{d_q-1} \cdot p_1 \bmod q$ $[S1_q = i_p \cdot S_q \bmod q]$
// Recombination
7. $S \leftarrow p \cdot S1_q + q \cdot S1_p \bmod (p \cdot q)$
8. **return** S

Comparison with the Standard Method. The main advantage of Algorithm 3 over Algorithm 1 consists in a much smaller key since it does not require the private parameter i_q. This leads to a gain of $\log_2(N)/2 - \log_2(e)$ bits of memory to store the key. When using a 2048-bit RSA for instance, we gain 125 bytes when $e = 2^{16} + 1$. Such an improvement is of uttermost importance on embedded devices where the memory space is very limited.

By comparing the complexity of the standard method depicted in Algorithm 1 and of our new proposal depicted in Algorithm 3, one can notice that the performances are very similar for public exponents which are generally used. For instance, if $e = 3$ (resp. $e = 2^{16} + 1$) then we add 8 (resp. 68) modular operations to perform the two exponentiations. In the case of a 2048-bit RSA, this corresponds to a tiny overhead of 0.3 % (resp. 2.2 %) on average in terms of modular operations[2]. Moreover, one may note that the modular reduction of Step 7 of Algorithm 3 can be replaced by a conditional subtraction with N since $p \cdot S1_q + q \cdot S1_p$ is always smaller than $2 \cdot N$.

---

[2] To compute these figures, we assume that a modular exponentiation using d_p, $d_p - 1$, d_q or $d_q - 1$ as exponent requires 1023 squares and 512 multiplications on average, i.e. 1585 modular operations.

One can also notice that the key generation of our method is slightly faster than the traditional one, cf. Algorithms 5 and 6 in Appendix A. Indeed in such a case, the costly inverse computation of $i_q = q^{-1} \bmod p$ is not necessary.

Last but not least, we do not need to change the key structure defined in the Java Card standard [26] to use our method. Indeed, we just need to store the public exponent e instead of the parameter i_q. To do so, the methods setPQ and getPQ, which are meant to set and to output the value of i_q respectively, must be adapted to fit our approach while keeping in line with the Java Card standard functionality. The first method setPQ must compute the public key e from the private key parameters (p, q, d_p, d_q) and store it in the buffer PQ. Most of the time, such a computation can be performed by using the efficient method of [18]. Regarding the method getPQ, it must output $q^{-1} \bmod p$ instead of outputting the content of the buffer PQ. Even if this inverse computation is costly, this is not a problem in practice since this method is almost never used.

3.2   A Free Message Blinding Method

In this section, we take advantage of the new approach previously described to provide a very efficient message blinding method to counteract Side-Channel Analysis.

We notice that by replacing q in Relation (3) by $q' = q \cdot r \bmod p$ where r is a random different from 0 modulo p and modulo q, we obtain:

$$(m \cdot q'^e)^{d_p - 1} \cdot m \cdot q'^{e-2} \equiv i_q \cdot S_p \cdot r^{-1} \bmod p \qquad (12)$$

Similarly, by replacing p with $p' = p \cdot r \bmod q$ in Relation (9), we obtain:

$$(m \cdot p'^e)^{d_q - 1} \cdot m \cdot p'^{e-2} \equiv i_p \cdot S_q \cdot r^{-1} \bmod q \qquad (13)$$

By combining Relations (12) and (13) with Relation (11), we obtain a randomized signature S' which is equal to:

$$S' = p \cdot S1'_q + q \cdot S1'_p \bmod N \qquad (14)$$
$$= r^{-1} \cdot S \bmod N \qquad (15)$$

where

$$S1'_p = (m \cdot q'^e)^{d_p - 1} \cdot m \cdot q'^{e-2} \bmod p,$$
$$S1'_q = (m \cdot p'^e)^{d_q - 1} \cdot m \cdot p'^{e-2} \bmod q.$$

The expected signature S is then obtained by multiplying S' with r modulo N.

To reach a fully secure CRT-RSA, one need also to blind the exponents d_p and d_q, use SSCA-HA-resistant exponentiations and to verify the signature by using the public exponent. We depict in Algorithm 4 such an implementation.

Algorithm 4. Secure CRT-RSA signature using our new approach

INPUTS: The message m, the public key e and a subpart of the private key (p, q, d_p, d_q)
OUTPUT: The signature S of the message m

---

1. Generate a random value r of size $\log_2(N)/2$ such that $r \not\equiv 0 \bmod p$ and $r \not\equiv 0 \bmod q$
2. Generate two 64-bit random values k_0 and k_1
   // First exponentiation
3. $q' \leftarrow q \cdot r \bmod p$
4. $q_1 \leftarrow m \cdot q'^{e-2} \bmod p$
5. $q_2 \leftarrow q_1 \cdot q'^2 \bmod p$ $\hspace{5cm}$ $[q_2 = m \cdot r^e \cdot q^e \bmod p]$
6. $d'_p \leftarrow d_p + k_0 \cdot (p-1)$
7. $S1'_p \leftarrow q_2^{d'_p - 1} \cdot q_1 \bmod p$ $\hspace{3cm}$ [Using an SSCA-HA-resistant expo.]
   // Second exponentiation
8. $p' \leftarrow p \cdot r \bmod q$
9. $p_1 \leftarrow m \cdot p'^{e-2} \bmod q$
10. $p_2 \leftarrow p_1 \cdot p'^2 \bmod q$ $\hspace{4.5cm}$ $[p_2 = m \cdot r^e \cdot p^e \bmod q]$
11. $d'_q \leftarrow d_q + k_1 \cdot (q-1)$
12. $S1'_q \leftarrow p_2^{d'_q - 1} \cdot p_1 \bmod q$ $\hspace{3cm}$ [Using an SSCA-HA-resistant expo.]
   // Recombination
13. $S' \leftarrow p \cdot S1'_q + q \cdot S1'_p \bmod (p \cdot q)$ $\hspace{2cm}$ $[S' = r^{-1} \cdot S \bmod N]$
   // Signature verification
14. $N \leftarrow p \cdot q$
15. **if** $(r \cdot S')^e \equiv m \bmod N$ **then**
16. $\quad$ **return** $r \cdot S' \bmod N$
17. **else**
18. $\quad$ Security action

Comparison with the Standard State-of-the-Art Method. Firstly, Algorithm 4 inherits from the various advantages presented in Sect. 3.1 over the standard Algorithm 2. In particular, it does not require the private key parameter i_q. Since Algorithms 2 and 4 both require the value of the public exponent e, we gain in memory the size of one private key parameter, i.e. $\log_2(N)/2$ bits. Moreover, since Algorithm 2 requires the full private key and the public exponent, the latter must be computed on-the-fly in the context of Java Card environment where the format of the CRT-RSA key is standardized and an extra parameter cannot be added. In such a context, our method simply stores the public exponent e instead of the private parameter i_q.

From a performance point of view, our method keeps the original size of the operands whereas the traditional additive masking used in Algorithm 2 requires to work with 64-bit longer operands and modulus. Since the performance of the crypto-processor is directly linked to the size of the variables which are used, Algorithm 4 is thus expected to be faster than Algorithm 2 since we work with smaller operand length.

Table 1. Performance improvement of Algorithm 4 compared to Algorithm 2 on a smart card providing a 32-bit modular multiplication co-processor.

CRT-RSA key size in bits	Performance improvement of Algorithm 4 compared to Algorithm 2
1024	14.2 %
2048	8.2 %

Table 1 represents our analysis on a smart card providing a 32-bit modular multiplication co-processor. The difference between Algorithms 4 and 2 could be much more significant in some cases, especially with co-processors having a precision of 128 bits.

Moreover, when comparing our method versus the original multiplicative message blinding, one can notice that the costly inverse computation $r^{-1} \bmod N$ is done for free during the exponentiations.

Our approach is not only faster but it also provides various advantages versus Side-Channel Analysis. For instance, since we use Gauss' method to recombine the results of the exponentiations, our method is not vulnerable to specific side-channel attacks on Garner's formula such as the ones presented in [1, 25].

4   Conclusion

Despite the fact that the public exponent has been used for a long time to protect RSA implementation against Fault Injection, no study has been done to investigate the benefit we can obtain from a performance and side-channel point of view. In this paper, we present a novel approach to implement CRT-RSA making use of the knowledge of the public exponent. We show that we can shrink the key length and reach the same level of performance. Moreover, we also show that this new approach can be combined with multiplicative message blinding method without any overhead, leading to the most efficient message blinding scheme published so far.

Acknowledgments. The author would like to thank Guillaume Barbu, Alberto Battistello, Emmanuelle Dottax and Gilles Piret for their comments on the preliminary version of this paper.

A   CRT-RSA Key Generation Algorithms

Algorithm 5 describes the standard CRT-RSA key generation and Algorithm 6 presents the specific CRT-RSA key generation for our new method. One can observe that the costly inverse computation $q^{-1} \bmod p$ is no more necessary. Moreover, since the public exponent is always provided as input for the key generation, we do not need extra-computation to provide such a value.

Algorithm 5. Standard CRT-RSA key generation

INPUTS: The public exponent e and the expected key bit length n
OUTPUT: The private key (p, q, d_p, d_q, i_q)

---

1. Generate a $n/2$-bit random prime p
2. Generate a $n/2$-bit random prime q
3. $d_p \leftarrow e^{-1} \bmod (p-1)$
4. $d_q \leftarrow e^{-1} \bmod (q-1)$
5. $i_q \leftarrow q^{-1} \bmod p$
6. **return** (p, q, d_p, d_q, i_q)

Algorithm 6. CRT-RSA key generation for our new method

INPUTS: The public exponent e and the expected key bit length n
OUTPUT: The private key (p, q, d_p, d_q, e)

---

1. Generate a $n/2$-bit random prime p
2. Generate a $n/2$-bit random prime q
3. $d_p \leftarrow e^{-1} \bmod (p-1)$
4. $d_q \leftarrow e^{-1} \bmod (q-1)$
5. **return** (p, q, d_p, d_q, e)

References

1. Amiel, F., Feix, B., Villegas, K.: Power analysis for secret recovering and reverse engineering of public key algorithms. In: Adams, C., Miri, A., Wiener, M. (eds.) SAC 2007. LNCS, vol. 4876, pp. 110–125. Springer, Heidelberg (2007)
2. Barbu, G., Battistello, A., Dabosville, G., Giraud, C., Renault, G., Renner, S., Zeitoun, R.: Combined attack on CRT-RSA. In: Kurosawa, K., Hanaoka, G. (eds.) PKC 2013. LNCS, vol. 7778, pp. 198–215. Springer, Heidelberg (2013)
3. Battistello, A., Giraud, C.: Fault analysis of infective AES computations. In: Fischer, W., Schmidt, J.-M. (eds.) Fault Diagnosis and Tolerance in Cryptography - FDTC 2014, pp. 101–107. IEEE Computer Society (2014)
4. Bauer, A., Jaulmes, E., Prouff, E., Wild, J.: Horizontal and vertical side-channel attacks against secure RSA implementations. In: Dawson, E. (ed.) CT-RSA 2013. LNCS, vol. 7779, pp. 1–17. Springer, Heidelberg (2013)
5. Bonech, D., DeMillo, R., Lipton, R.: New Threat Model Breaks Crypto Codes. Bellcore Press Release, Morristown (1996)
6. Boneh, D., DeMillo, R.A., Lipton, R.J.: On the importance of checking cryptographic protocols for faults. In: Fumy, W. (ed.) EUROCRYPT 1997. LNCS, vol. 1233, pp. 37–51. Springer, Heidelberg (1997)
7. Boscher, A., Naciri, R., Prouff, E.: CRT RSA algorithm protected against fault attacks. In: Sauveron, D., Markantonakis, K., Bilas, A., Quisquater, J.-J. (eds.) WISTP 2007. LNCS, vol. 4462, pp. 229–243. Springer, Heidelberg (2007)

8. Chevallier-Mames, B., Ciet, M., Joye, M.: Low-cost solutions for preventing simple side-channel analysis: side-channel atomicity. IEEE Trans. Comput. **53**(6), 760–768 (2004)
9. Clavier, C., Feix, B.: Updated recommendations for blinded exponentiation vs. single trace analysis. In: Prouff, E. (ed.) COSADE 2013. LNCS, vol. 7864, pp. 80–98. Springer, Heidelberg (2013)
10. Clavier, C., Feix, B., Gagnerot, G., Giraud, C., Roussellet, M., Verneuil, V.: ROSETTA for single trace analysis. In: Galbraith, S., Nandi, M. (eds.) INDOCRYPT 2012. LNCS, vol. 7668, pp. 140–155. Springer, Heidelberg (2012)
11. Clavier, C., Feix, B., Gagnerot, G., Roussellet, M., Verneuil, V.: Horizontal correlation analysis on exponentiation. In: Soriano, M., Qing, S., López, J. (eds.) ICICS 2010. LNCS, vol. 6476, pp. 46–61. Springer, Heidelberg (2010)
12. Coron, J.-S., Giraud, C., Morin, N., Piret, G., Vigilant, D.: Fault attacks and countermeasures on vigilant's RSA-CRT algorithm. In: Breveglieri, L., Joye, M., Koren, I., Naccache, D., Verbauwhede, I. (eds.) Fault Diagnosis and Tolerance in Cryptography - FDTC 2010, pp. 89–96. IEEE Computer Society (2010)
13. Couvreur, C., Quisquater, J.-J.: Fast decipherment algorithm for RSA public-key cryptosystem. Electron. Lett. **18**(21), 905–907 (1982)
14. EMV. Integrated Circuit Card Specifications for Payment Systems - Book 2 - Security and Key Management, June 2008
15. Gandolfi, K., Mourtel, C., Olivier, F.: Electromagnetic analysis: concrete results. In: Koç, Ç.K., Naccache, D., Paar, C. (eds.) CHES 2001. LNCS, vol. 2162, p. 251. Springer, Heidelberg (2001)
16. Garner, H.: The residue number system. IRE Trans. Electron. Comput. **8**(6), 140–147 (1959)
17. Giraud, C.: An RSA implementation resistant to fault attacks and to simple power analysis. IEEE Trans. Comput. **55**(9), 1116–1120 (2006)
18. Joye, M.: Protecting RSA against fault attacks: the embedding method. In: Breveglieri, L., Gueron, S., Koren, I., Naccache, D., Seifert, J.-P. (eds.) Fault Diagnosis and Tolerance in Cryptography - FDTC 2009, pp. 41–45. IEEE Computer Society (2009)
19. Joye, M., Tunstall, M.: Fault Analysis in Cryptography. Information Security and Cryptography. Springer, Heidelberg (2012)
20. Joye, M., Yen, S.-M.: The Montgomery powering ladder. In: Kaliski Jr., B.S., Koç, Ç.K., Paar, C. (eds.) CHES 2002. LNCS, vol. 2523, pp. 291–302. Springer, Heidelberg (2003)
21. Kocher, P.C.: Timing attacks on implementations of Diffie-Hellman, RSA, DSS, and other systems. In: Koblitz, N. (ed.) CRYPTO 1996. LNCS, vol. 1109, pp. 104–113. Springer, Heidelberg (1996)
22. Kocher, P.C., Jaffe, J., Jun, B.: Differential power analysis. In: Wiener, M. (ed.) CRYPTO 1999. LNCS, vol. 1666, pp. 388–397. Springer, Heidelberg (1999)
23. Lenstra, A.K., Hughes, J.P., Augier, M., Bos, J.W., Kleinjung, T., Wachter, C.: Ron was wrong, Whit is right. Cryptology ePrint Archive, report 2012/064 (2012). http://eprint.iacr.org/
24. Mangard, S., Oswald, E., Popp, T.: Power Analysis Attacks - Revealing the Secrets of Smartcards. Springer, New York (2007)
25. Novak, R.: SPA-based adaptive chosen-ciphertext attack on RSA implementation. In: Naccache, D., Paillier, P. (eds.) PKC 2002. LNCS, vol. 2274, pp. 252–262. Springer, Heidelberg (2002)
26. Oracle Corp. Application Programming Interface, Java Card Platform, Version 3.0.4 Classic Edition (2011)

27. PKCS #1. RSA Cryptography Specifications Version 2.1. RSA Laboratories (2003)
28. Rivain, M.: Securing RSA against fault analysis by double addition chain exponentiation. In: Fischlin, M. (ed.) CT-RSA 2009. LNCS, vol. 5473, pp. 459–480. Springer, Heidelberg (2009)
29. Rivest, R., Shamir, A., Adleman, L.: A method for obtaining digital signatures and public-key cryptosystems. Commun. ACM **21**(2), 120–126 (1978)
30. Shamir, A.: How to check modular exponentiation. In: Eurocrypt'97 rump session (1997)
31. Walter, C.D.: Sliding windows succumbs to Big Mac attack. In: Koç, Ç.K., Naccache, D., Paar, C. (eds.) CHES 2001. LNCS, vol. 2162, pp. 286–299. Springer, Heidelberg (2001)
32. Yen, S.-M., Kim, S., Lim, S., Moon, S.-J.: RSA speedup with residue number system immune against hardware fault cryptanalysis. In: Kim, K. (ed.) ICISC 2001. LNCS, vol. 2288, pp. 397–413. Springer, Heidelberg (2002)

Common Points on Elliptic Curves:
The Achilles' Heel of Fault Attack
Countermeasures

Alberto Battistello[1,2(✉)]

[1] Cryptography and Security Group, Oberthur Technologies,
4, Allée du Doyen Georges Brus, 33600 Pessac, France
[2] Versailles Saint-Quentin-en-Yvelines University, 45 Avenue des Etats-Unis,
78035 Versailles Cedex, France
a.battistello@oberthur.com

Abstract. Elliptic curve cryptosystems offer many advantages over
RSA-like cryptography, such as speed and memory saving. Nonethe-
less the advent of *side-channel* and *fault-injection* attacks mined the
security of such implementations. Several countermeasures have been
devised to thwart these threats, so that simple attacks on state-of-the-
art secured implementations seem unlikely. We took up the challenge
and show that a simple fault attack using a very relaxed fault model
can defeat well known countermeasures. After introducing the notion
of *common points*, we exhibit a new fault-injection attack that breaks
state-of-the-art secured implementations. Our new attack is particularly
dangerous since no control on the injected error is required and only one
fault is sufficient to retrieve the secret.

Keywords: Elliptic curves · Fault attack · Common points

1 Introduction

Elliptic curves cryptosystems (ECC for short) have been introduced independently by Koblitz [13] and Miller [17] in 1985. The advantage of ECC over
other cryptosystems like RSA [19] is that they need smaller keys and parameters size to achieve equivalent security bounds. The reason for such bounds is
that ECC security relies on the elliptic curve discrete-log problem (ECDLP for
short) and no polynomial time algorithm exists to solve it. When implemented
on embedded environments, ECC are also subject to other kind of attacks, such
as *Side-Channel Attacks* [14] (SCA) and *Fault Attacks* [4] (FA). The aim of
these attacks is to retrieve the secret scalar without having to effectively solve
the underlying ECDLP. On the one hand SCA exploit the information leaked
by the physical interactions of the system with its environment, such as the
power consumption or the electromagnetic radiation. Such attacks allowing the
attacker to recover information on the secret by using only one measurement

© Springer International Publishing Switzerland 2014
E. Prouff (Ed.): COSADE 2014, LNCS 8622, pp. 69–81, 2014.
DOI: 10.1007/978-3-319-10175-0_6

are called *Simple Side-Channel Attacks* (SSCA), to be distinguished from *Differential Side-Channel Attacks* (DSCA) [15], where the statistical analysis of multiple execution leakages is used to retrieve information on the manipulated data. On the other hand FA aim at disturbing the computation in order to gain information on the secret values using the erroneous results. For example in [4] the authors observe that if one of the two subfield exponentiations of an RSA-CRT signature is disturbed, the output can be used to produce a secret factor of the public modulus, thus breaking the cryptosystem. Urging for new countermeasures, the cryptographic community started to devise numerous methods to counteract SCA and FA applied on ECC. The basic idea of SSCA countermeasures is to make the algorithm execution independent of the secret scalar. Otherwise, DSCA countermeasures aim at randomizing the manipulated values in order to cancel the correlation of the processed data among different executions. In the context of ECC, faults attacks seem more tricky to thwart as the disturbance of almost any parameter of the curve can lead the attacker to break the system [6]. Among the various countermeasures proposed so far to counteract parameters disturbance, the most intuitive is to test the integrity of each parameter [6]. However, a more efficient way to thwart these attacks is to validate that the used point effectively lies on the curve [2]. Nowadays these two countermeasures are considered equivalent. Other countermeasures aim to thwart faults on the secret scalar, for example by testing the result of two redundant computations.

In this paper we introduce the concept of *common points* to exhibit a new FA on ECC implementations. This new attack allows to retrieve the secret scalar by using a single faulted execution. The main advantage of our attack compared to the other attacks proposed so far is that no control is required on the injected error. Even if our attack does not always recover the full secret scalar, we show that each faulted result provides large amount of information on the secret scalar. With our attack we also prove that the two fault countermeasures presented above are not equivalent since our attack is not detected by one of them. The potential of the attack and its very relaxed fault model makes a serious threat for actual implementations.

The rest of the paper is organized as follows: Sect. 2 introduces elliptic curves cryptography and related fault attacks and countermeasures. Section 3 introduces the concept of common points and presents our new fault attack on state-of-the-art secured implementations. Further analysis of our attack versus known countermeasures is carried out in Sect. 4. Finally Sect. 5 concludes this work.

2   Embedded Elliptic Curve Cryptography

After introducing the required background on elliptic curves, the main attacks and countermeasures against faults on ECC are discussed.

2.1   Elliptic Curves

Let $\mathbb{K}$ be a field with $\mathrm{Char}(\mathbb{K}) \neq 2, 3$, and $a, b \in \mathbb{K}$. The short Weierstraß form of an elliptic curve is defined by the following equation:

$$y^2 = x^3 + ax + b \tag{1}$$

The set of points $(x, y) \in \mathbb{K} \times \mathbb{K}$ satisfying Eq. (1), together with the point at infinity $\mathcal{O}$ is denoted $\mathcal{E}(\mathbb{K})$. For any point $P = (x_p, y_p) \in \mathcal{E}(\mathbb{K})$, the opposite is defined as $-P = (x_p, -y_p)$, and $P + \mathcal{O} = \mathcal{O} + P = P$. For any two points $P = (x_p, y_p)$ and $Q = (x_q, y_q) \in \mathcal{E}(\mathbb{K})$, the sum $R = (x_r, y_r)$ of $P + Q$ is defined as:

- If $P \neq -Q$ then:
$$\begin{cases} x_r = s^2 - x_p - x_q \\ y_r = s(x_p - x_r) - y_p \end{cases}$$

with
$$s = \begin{cases} \frac{(y_q - y_p)}{(x_q - x_p)} & \text{if } P \neq Q \\ \frac{(3x_p^2 + a)}{(2y_p)} & \text{otherwise} \end{cases}$$

- If $P = -Q$ then $P + Q = P - P = \mathcal{O}$

The set $\mathcal{E}(\mathbb{K})$ with the "+" operation defined above form an abelian group of neutral element $\mathcal{O}$. Due to security issues, standard elliptic curves are non supersingular, i.e. $4a^3 + 27b^2 \neq 0$. The cardinality of the elliptic curve is denoted $\#\mathcal{E}(\mathbb{K})$ and for common curves it is often the product of a big prime times a small cofactor. In the following we will drop the explicit field notation when it is implicit or when it is not necessary for the given statement.

Scalar Multiplication and ECDLP. The *scalar multiplication* of the curve point P by the scalar $k \in \mathbb{N}$ is denoted $[k]P$. This is defined as the addition of the point P to himself k times. The interest of scalar multiplication in cryptography is due to its computational *one-wayness*. In fact it is easy to compute the result point $Q = [k]P$ but it is computationally difficult to compute the integer k knowing Q and P. This problem is known as the ECDLP and it is one of the fundamental building blocks used to construct cryptographic protocols on elliptic curves [13,17]. The ECDLP is an interesting problem that challenges mathematicians from decades. For example, by using the Pollard's rho or Shanks "baby-step/giant-step" algorithm, the problem can be solved in time polynomial on the square root of the biggest factor of the order of the base. For example, for a curve of order q prime, the complexity of the aforementioned attacks is $O(q^{0.5})$.

2.2   Fault Attacks on ECC

Before presenting the main fault attacks published so far, we recall that the ECDLP can be efficiently solved if the order of the logarithm base is smooth [16].

This can happen for example if the input point does not lie on the curve, as observed in [1], whose authors suggest that all implementations should verify that the point lies on the curve (PoC for short) before performing the scalar multiplication.

The first DFA on elliptic curves was published in [2]. Similarly to [1], the authors of [2] suggest to fault the input point P after the parameters checking such that the faulted point P' does not lie on the original curve. The attacker may be able to retrieve information on the secret scalar using the corresponding faulty output since the curve on which the computation has been done can have a smooth order. A second attack presented in [2] suggests that by disturbing intermediate values during the scalar multiplication, one may be able to retrieve information on the secret scalar. The idea is to guess the produced error value and a few bits of the secret. The attacker then computes the scalar multiplication backward up to the fault, corrects the error, and recomputes onward to obtain the result. If it is the correct result, then it is likely that the guesses were correct. It is clear that the entropy of the guesses must not be too high in order to exhaustively test them, thus the attack starts with faults near the end of the computation, then steps backward as more bits are known. The authors state that all these attacks can be avoided by PoC testing before and after the scalar multiplication.

In [3], the authors propose another DFA that targets non adjacent form ECC implementations. By disturbing the sign of a point during the scalar multiplication they can retrieve the signed bits of the secret scalar k. As they need several faulty outputs to mount their attack, they focus on implementations that use the same secret scalar for all executions. The countermeasure they suggest is called combined curve check. They build a new curve containing both the given curve and a smaller one, such that scalar multiplication on the small curve is fast. Given the result of the scalar multiplication on the combined curve, with a simple modular reduction they can retrieve the result on both the given curve and the small one. Thus by executing a second scalar multiplication on the small curve they can compare the result with the one obtained from the combined curve and detect faults.

Further analysis of faults on ECC was carried out in [6]. The authors improved the results of [2] by observing that an unknown fault on one of the coordinates of the input point produces a wrong curve parameter b which can be retrieved as a solution of the curve equation with the output point coordinates as known values. The authors also observed that a fault in the prime p defining the field $\mathbb{K}$ produces a curve where the input point will likely have smooth order, thus breaking the security of the cryptosystem. Finally the authors also show that a fault in one of the public parameters (typically a in Eq. (1)) is likely to transfer the elliptic curve on a new one where the ECDLP is easier to solve. They observe that by substituting the input and output point coordinates in Eq. (1) the solution of the obtained system allows the attacker to recover the faulted curve parameters. The authors thus remark that public parameters must be checked for faults prior and after the scalar multiplication. They also claim that performing these checks by using integrity checks or by PoC offer the same security level.

In Sect. 3 we show that this claim is false by exhibiting an attack that can break the cryptosystem if the tests are performed by PoC.

3   Our New Fault Attack

This section introduces the concept of common points, and how we use them in a fault attack to retrieve the secret scalar. The basic idea of our attack is to input a point that lies on a family of curves that includes a weak one (i.e. a smooth one). The attacker then forces the computation on the weak curve by means of a fault injection. She can then use the output to solve the ECDLP and retrieve the secret.

3.1   Common Points

Definition 1 (Common Point). *Let $\mathcal{F}$ be a family of elliptic curves, a point P is a* common point *for the family of curves $\mathcal{F}$, iff $P \in \mathcal{E}, \forall \mathcal{E} \in \mathcal{F}$.*

Example 1 (Common Point). Consider for example Eq. (1) over a field $\mathbb{K}$ with $\text{Char}(\mathbb{K}) \neq 2, 3$, and let $b = g^2 \in \mathbb{K}$:

$$y^2 = x^3 + ax + g^2 \tag{2}$$

The family of curves obtained by varying parameter $a \in \mathbb{K}$ has two common points, namely the points $(0, \pm g)$ satisfy the curve equation for any a.

Among the whole family described in Example 1, most of the curves have composite order. Furthermore some of them have smooth order, allowing an attacker to solve the ECDLP in a reasonable time. Common points are thus contained in any curve whose b is a quadratic residue for the underlying field. Among the curves proposed in FIPS 186-4 [10], only P-224 does not, and four out of eight curves proposed in SECG [21] can be attacked. In the following we present our new fault attack that makes use of these points.

3.2   Fault Attack Using Common Points

In order to apply our attack it is necessary for the attacker to choose the input point of the scalar multiplication and to obtain the corresponding result. The reader will notice that these assumptions are weaker than the ones of [8,12], as we need no leakage hypothesis nor a particular fault model.

Our attack is divided in four steps as detailed below:

- Step 1: the attacker sends a point $P = (0, \pm g)$ to the embedded device, and disturbs the curve parameter a into $\tilde{a}$ at the beginning of the scalar multiplication.
- Step 2: the device performs the scalar multiplication on the faulted curve $\mathcal{E}' : y^2 = x^3 + \tilde{a} \cdot x + g^2$, and return the value $\tilde{Q} = [d]P \in \mathcal{E}'$.

- Step 3: From $\widetilde{Q} = (x_q, y_q)$, the attacker can recover the value $\widetilde{a}$ by solving the equation $y_q^2 = x_q^3 + \widetilde{a} \cdot x_q + g^2$.
- Step 4: the attacker can then solve the ECDLP on the curve $\mathcal{E}'$, which will work if the order o of $\widetilde{Q}$ is smooth.

We remark that in Step 1 the attacker does not need a particular fault model to perform the attack. Furthermore, when the order of $\mathcal{E}'$ is smooth, our attack does involve a single fault, which means that a single, successful execution is sufficient to completely break the cryptosystem. This property is particularly useful for two reasons. First of all our attack does not suffer from the fact that the secret scalar may be freshly regenerated at each execution. Furthermore it works in environments where the number of executions is limited, while other attacks that need to be reiterated a considerable number of times like [3,9] may be thwart.

The simulations carried out in Sect. 3.3 show that the order of $\mathcal{E}'$ is smooth 45 % of the time. We show in the following that the other 55 % of the results also provide very useful information on the secret scalar.

Attack Application on Not-So-Smooth Orders. When the order o of $\widetilde{Q}$ is not smooth enough to use square root attacks [18] for instance, the attacker can still gain information on the secret scalar value. Let us assume that the secret scalar is fixed for multiple executions. For an order o that contains a big factor of ℓ bits, the attacker can use Pohlig-Hellman decomposition [16] and retrieve the secret scalar modulo small factors of size $\log(o) - \ell$ bits on each execution. Thus by performing the attack on $\frac{\log(o)}{\log(o)-\ell}$ executions on average, she can cumulate the information thanks to the Chinese Remainder Theorem and completely reveal the secret scalar.

Comparison with Existing Attacks. In the following, we compare the efficiency of our attack with previously published ones [2,3,6,8]. The attack of [6] uses a fault similar to the one we use to solve the ECDLP, however it is thwarted by simply testing if the point is on the curve after the scalar multiplication. As the authors explain in their work, by faulting parameter a into $\widetilde{a}$, the input point P does not lie on the curve $\widetilde{\mathcal{E}}$ given by the equation:

$$\widetilde{\mathcal{E}} : y^2 = x^3 + \widetilde{a} \cdot x + b$$

There exists instead a value b' such that P lies on the curve $\widetilde{\mathcal{E}}'$ defined by:

$$\widetilde{\mathcal{E}}' : y^2 = x^3 + \widetilde{a} \cdot x + b'$$

As the curve operation formulae do not involve curve parameter b, the scalar multiplication is in fact done on $\widetilde{\mathcal{E}}'$. At the end of the multiplication, the result point will also lie on $\widetilde{\mathcal{E}}'$, and thus not satisfies the equation of curve $\widetilde{\mathcal{E}}$. As b has not been modified, by testing if the result point lies on the curve, the attack is thwarted. On the contrary, due to the use of a common point, our attack is not detected by this countermeasure. Indeed the common point P satisfies the curve equation for any a. In particular the input point lies on the curve $\widetilde{\mathcal{E}}$, thus the scalar multiplication is performed on it. This implies that the result of the multiplication $\widetilde{Q}$ lies on the same curve. Thus our attack is not detected by testing if $\widetilde{P}$ or $\widetilde{Q}$ satisfies the equation for $\widetilde{\mathcal{E}}$ if a is not reloaded before the final PoC test.

The fault attacks of [2,3] need the faulted result of several executions to retrieve the secret scalar value. Hence, implementations using random scalar nonces, or with a limited number of executions may not be vulnerable to them. The PoC countermeasure suggested by [2] does not detect our attack as explained above, and the verification countermeasure suggested in [3] is not effective as we do not disturb the scalar multiplication.

The authors of [8] use a fault to drop the regular input point into a weaker curve (characterized by a wrong b') where the faulted point will leak information by SSCA. However they need strong hypothesis on the fault model and on the leakage for the attack to work. As a common point lies on all curves with the same b, the fault model required by our attack is very relaxed. Indeed, any random fault on the parameter a provides information on the secret scalar. We insist on the fact that our attack needs no SCA hypothesis, which make it work on implementations that do not leak information if the point at infinity is handled during the multiplication, contrary to the attack presented in [8].

Attack Scenario. Unfortunately, to the best of our knowledge the attack scenario that we describe in this paper is not applicable to any protocol. However our context is similar to the one of [2] Sect. 4.1 or [11] Sect. 3 for example, where the attacker can choose the input point P, and get the output Q of the scalar multiplication. While no actual protocol is concerned, we stress that embedded cryptographic developers should choose their countermeasures in order to avoid the attack that we present here, and new cryptographic protocols should be conceived in order to avoid falling into our attack scenario.

3.3   Simulations

In order to validate the efficiency of our attack, simulations have been performed on Pari/gp software [22] by using the standard elliptic curve P-192 proposed in FIPS 186-4 [10].

The attack was mounted by using input point $P = (0, \sqrt{b})$. Afterwards, one byte of the value a was disturbed with an error before the multiplication. For each byte j of a, and for each value e between 1 and $2^8 - 1$, the error was simulated by assigning $a \leftarrow a \oplus 2^{8*j}e$. The scalar multiplication $\widetilde{Q} = [k]P$ was computed for a random value k and the faulty output point $\widetilde{Q}$ was returned. Afterwards for each output point the cardinality o of the new curve was computed by using the Pari/gp implementation of the SEA algorithm [20].

In order to study the probability of revealing the whole secret k with a single fault, the size of the order o was collected for all faulted executions. At most $\log_2(o)$ bits of information can be obtained on the value k for a point Q resulting from a faulted scalar multiplication. Thus the secret k can be fully revealed only

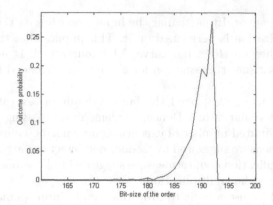

Fig. 1. Outcome probability for each bit-size of the result point order.

if the bit-size of o and k are similar. Figure 1 shows the occurrence probability of the different order sizes obtained during the campaign. From the results it is clear that once the value of k is retrieved with one application of our attack, the remaining secret bits can be obtained by brute force since at most 18 bits are missing.

The second analysis concerns the probability that the resulting ECDLP is smooth enough to be solved by modern computers. For each result we factored the cardinality of the faulted curve to extract the bit-size of its biggest prime factor. Figure 2 displays the probability that the faulted curve cardinality contains a biggest factor of a certain bit-size. To better understand this result we plot in Fig. 3 the cumulative outcome probability of the previous distribution. In other words Fig. 3 shows the probability that the biggest factor of the faulted curve cardinality is smaller than a certain bit-size. We assume that the computation limits of modern parallel Pollard's rho implementations are bound to 112 bits complexity [5], thus as "smooth" orders we consider orders whose biggest prime factor is smaller than 112 bits. From the experiments it can be observed that the probability to obtain sufficiently small sizes for the biggest factor exceeds 45 %.

Finally, in order to obtain information on the time required to solve the logarithm, the attack was mounted on faults that produced a smooth order result. It has been chosen to mount the ECDLP on results whose order biggest factor was 42, 52, and 62 bits. These sizes has been chosen starting by the smallest obtained, in order to speed up the computation time to collect more results. The ECDLP was solved by using Pari/gp library function *elllog* without optimization. The computation times were evaluated on a 3.10 GHz personal computer with 8 GB RAM. The average time was computed over 500 executions for the 42-bit ECDLP, over 205 for the 52-bit, and over 4 for the 62-bit ECDLP. For random values of the secret key k the results are shown in Table 1, for example for a curve whose order biggest factor is 42 bits, the required time is 53 s on average. Thus it is clear that our attack is definitely practical on smooth order curves.

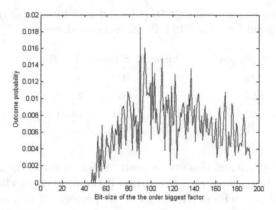

Fig. 2. Outcome probability for the bit-size of each result point order greatest factor.

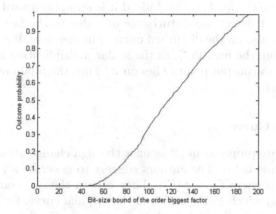

Fig. 3. Cumulative outcome probability for each point order biggest factor bit-size.

4   Countermeasures

Three conditions are necessary for our attack to reveal the secret scalar, namely to control the input point, to know the result of the scalar multiplication, and to have a quadratic residue as parameter b of the curve. In the following, various state-of-the-art countermeasures are analyzed. In addition to standard FA countermeasures we also focus on an SCA countermeasure which provides a good level of resistance against our attack. Finally, Table 2 resumes the results of the countermeasure analysis provided in this section.

4.1   Initial and Final Checks

Intuitively, initial and final parameters checking could thwart our attack, as the curve parameters are disturbed, and thus no more consistent. As already remarked in [8], the initial checks are ineffective if the fault is injected after the

Table 1. Average time to solve the ECDLP for different bit-sizes of the biggest factor of the order of the point by using NIST P-192 as original curve.

Biggest factor bit-size	#Tests	Avg time
42	500	53 s
52	205	20.6 min
62	4	19.21 h

countermeasure application. However for our attack to work, the adversary needs to retrieve the output, which is not returned if the final checks fail. The authors of [6], suggest that parameters checking can be performed by means of integrity check or by PoC testing, and that the two mechanisms offer the same security level. This work shows that this claim is false if parameter a is not reloaded from memory before the final checks. Indeed it is straightforward to see that the initial PoC does not detect the disturbance of a due to the fact that the input common point lies also on the disturbed curve. Furthermore, if a is not reloaded from memory before the final PoC, as the scalar multiplication is performed on the faulted curve, the output point $\widetilde{Q}$ lies on it. Thus the final PoC succeeds and the result is output.

4.2 Combined Curve

The countermeasure proposed in [3] against the sign change attack is applicable to curves over prime fields. The authors suggest to generate a random prime t and a new random curve $\mathcal{E}_t := \mathcal{E}(\mathbb{F}_t)$. They obtain then a "combined" elliptic curve $\mathcal{E}_{pt} := \mathcal{E}(\mathbb{Z}_{pt})$ which contains $\mathcal{E}_t$ and the original curve. By performing the scalar multiplication on $\mathcal{E}_{pt}$ and $\mathcal{E}_t$ they can then verify the result by using a modular reduction. This countermeasure is ineffective against our attack as we do not disturb the scalar multiplication.

4.3 Point Blinding

Intuitively a DSCA countermeasure hardly thwarts a fault attack, however the second countermeasure proposed in [7] performs well against faults, as remarked in [8]. The author of [7] suggests to thwart DSCA by pre-computing $S = [k]R$ for a random point R, then computing $Q = [k](P+R)$ and returning $Q - S$. Then at each execution a random bit b is generated and the random points are updated with $R \leftarrow (-1)^b[2]R$ and $S \leftarrow (-1)^b[2]S$. Such a countermeasure counteracts efficiently our attack if the attacker has no control on the fault. However, if she can inject the same error twice, such a countermeasure can be bypassed. Indeed, let us assume that for two consecutive executions the bit b equals 0 (the case $b = 1$ is similar). For the same fault injected in the two executions she will thus obtain two results: $Q_1 = [k](P + 2R) - [2]S$ and $Q_2 = [k](P + 4R) - [4]S$. As the value S is pre-computed, the scalar multiplications $[2]S$ and $[4]S$ are done over $\mathcal{E}$, while the computation of $[k](P + [j]R)$ for $j = 1, 2$ is done over $\widetilde{\mathcal{E}}$. Furthermore if the fault is injected before the update of R and S, the doubling of these two values is also done over $\widetilde{\mathcal{E}}$. The attacker thus computes over $\widetilde{\mathcal{E}}$, the value $Q_2 - [2]Q_1 = [k]P + [4k]R - [4]S - [2k]P - [4k]R + [4]S$, by simplifying she obtains $Q_2 - [2]Q_1 = [k](P - [2]P)$, and thus she can mount the ECDLP on the faulted curve as the result is independent of R.

Table 2. Countermeasures effectiveness against our new attack. For the point blinding countermeasure we assume that the same fault can be injected in two executions.

Countermeasure	Result
PoC before multiplication	Ineffective
Integrity check before multiplication	Ineffective
PoC after multiplication	Ineffective
Integrity check after multiplication	Effective
Combined curve	Ineffective
Point blinding	Ineffective

5 Conclusion

In this paper we introduce the concept of common points, i.e. points that lie on a whole family of curves, which have never been remarked before. Then we show how to exploit their properties in our new attack to thwart state-of-the-art secure implementations with a single fault. By forcing the computation to be performed on another curve of the family, an attacker can try to solve the ECDLP on this new curve which is expected to be weaker than the standard one. The use of common points overcome the drawbacks of other known attacks, such as the need for high accuracy on the injected error. Furthermore it was claimed that one of the most complete still less expensive solutions to thwart fault attacks is to test that the used point lies on the curve. Our new attack shows that implementations relying on this countermeasure are in fact in a great danger. Simulations of our attack show that it is practical on most standard curves, and that the probability of success for a single execution exceeds 45 %. By analyzing state-of-the-art SCA, DSCA and FA countermeasures, we show that our attack is thwart only by verifying the integrity of the curve parameter a at the end of the scalar multiplication. Last but not least, we exploited common points to mount a very efficient fault attack but one should wonder if there is no other way to make the most of these points by producing other kind of attacks or countermeasures.

Acknowledgment. I am grateful to Christophe Giraud for the many fruitful discussions and the time he spent to help me writing this paper. I would also like to thank

Guillaume Barbu, Laurie Genelle, Emmanuelle Dottax, Franck Rondepierre and the anonymous reviewers of COSADE 2014 for their helpful comments.

References

1. Antipa, A., Brown, D., Menezes, A., Struik, R., Vanstone, S.: Validation of elliptic curve public keys. In: Desmedt, Y.G. (ed.) PKC 2003. LNCS, vol. 2567, pp. 211–223. Springer, Heidelberg (2002)
2. Biehl, I., Meyer, B., Müller, V.: Differential fault attacks on elliptic curve cryptosystems. In: Bellare, M. (ed.) CRYPTO 2000. LNCS, vol. 1880, pp. 131–146. Springer, Heidelberg (2000)
3. Blömer, J., Otto, M., Seifert, J.-P.: Sign change fault attacks on elliptic curve cryptosystems. In: Breveglieri, L., Koren, I., Naccache, D., Seifert, J.-P. (eds.) FDTC 2006. LNCS, vol. 4236, pp. 36–52. Springer, Heidelberg (2006)
4. Boneh, D., DeMillo, R.A., Lipton, R.J.: On the importance of checking cryptographic protocols for faults. In: Fumy, W. (ed.) EUROCRYPT 1997. LNCS, vol. 1233, pp. 37–51. Springer, Heidelberg (1997)
5. Bos, J.W., Kaihara, M.E., Kleinjung, T., Lenstra, A.K., Montgomery, P.L.: Solving a 112-bit prime elliptic curve discrete logarithm problem on game consoles using sloppy reduction. IJACT 2(3), 212–228 (2012)
6. Ciet, M., Joye, M.: Elliptic curve cryptosystems in the presence of permanent and transient faults. Des. Codes Crypt. 36(1), 33–43 (2005)
7. Coron, J.-S.: Resistance against differential power analysis for elliptic curve cryptosystems. In: Koç, Ç.K., Paar, C. (eds.) CHES 1999. LNCS, vol. 1717, pp. 292–302. Springer, Heidelberg (1999)
8. Fan, J., Gierlichs, B., Vercauteren, F.: To infinity and beyond: combined attack on ECC using points of low order. In: Preneel, B., Takagi, T. (eds.) CHES 2011. LNCS, vol. 6917, pp. 143–159. Springer, Heidelberg (2011)
9. Faugère, J.-C., Goyet, C., Renault, G.: Attacking (EC)DSA given only an implicit hint. In: Knudsen, L.R., Wu, H. (eds.) SAC 2012. LNCS, vol. 7707, pp. 252–274. Springer, Heidelberg (2013)
10. FIPS PUB 186-4. Digital Signature Standard. National Institute of Standards and Technology, July 2013
11. Fouque, P., Lercier, R., Réal, D., Valette, F.: Fault attack on elliptic curve montgomery ladder implementation. In: Breveglieri, L., Gueron, S., Koren, I., Naccache, D., Seifert, J.-P. (eds.) Fault Diagnosis and Tolerance in Cryptography - FDTC 2008, pp. 92–98. IEEE Computer Society (2008)
12. Goubin, L.: A refined power-analysis attack on elliptic curve cryptosystem. In: Desmedt, Y.G. (ed.) PKC 2003. LNCS, vol. 2567, pp. 199–211. Springer, Heidelberg (2002)
13. Koblitz, N.: Elliptic curve cryptosystems. Math. Comput. 48(177), 203–209 (1987)
14. Kocher, P., Jaffe, J., Jun, B.: Introduction to differential power analysis and related attacks. Technical report, Cryptography Research Inc. (1998)
15. Kocher, P.C., Jaffe, J., Jun, B.: Differential power analysis. In: Wiener, M. (ed.) CRYPTO 1999. LNCS, vol. 1666, pp. 388–397. Springer, Heidelberg (1999)
16. Lim, C.H., Lee, P.J.: A key recovery attack on discrete log-based schemes using a prime order subgroup. In: Kaliski Jr., B.S. (ed.) CRYPTO 1997. LNCS, vol. 1294, pp. 249–263. Springer, Heidelberg (1997)
17. Miller, V.S.: Use of elliptic curves in cryptography. In: Williams, H.C. (ed.) CRYPTO 1985. LNCS, vol. 218, pp. 417–426. Springer, Heidelberg (1986)

18. Pollard, J.: Monte Carlo methods for index computation (mod p). Math. Comput. **32**, 918–924 (1978)
19. Rivest, R., Shamir, A., Adleman, L.: A method for obtaining digital signatures and public-key cryptosystems. Commun. ACM **21**(2), 120–126 (1978)
20. Schoof, R., Schoof, P.R.E.: Counting points on elliptic curves over finite fields. J. Théor. Nombres Bordeaux **7**(1), 219–254 (1995)
21. Standards for Efficient Cryptography Group (SECG). SEC 2 Ver 2.0 : Recommended Elliptic Curve Domain Parameters. Certicom Research, January 2010
22. The PARI-Group. Pari/gp, version 2.5.3, Bordeaux (2013). http://pari.math. u-bordeaux.fr/

On Adaptive Bandwidth Selection
for Efficient MIA

Mathieu Carbone[1,2]([✉]), Sébastien Tiran[2], Sébastien Ordas[2], Michel Agoyan[1],
Yannick Teglia[1], Gilles R. Ducharme[3], and Philippe Maurine[2,4]

[1] ST Microelectronics - Advanced System Technology,
Avenue Célestin Coq, 13790 Rousset, France
{mathieu.carbone,michel.agoyan,yannick.teglia}@st.com
[2] LIRMM - Laboratoire d'Informatique de Robotique et de Microélectronique
de Montpellier, 161, Rue Ada, 34090 Montpellier Cedex 5, France
{sebastien.tiran,sebastien.ordas}@lirmm.fr
[3] EPS - Institut de Mathématiques et de Modélisation de Montpellier 2, Place
Eugène Bataillon, Université Montpellier 2, 34095 Montpellier Cedex 5, France
gilles.ducharme@univ-montp2.fr
[4] CEA - Centre Microélectronique de Provence Georges Charpak,
880, Route de Mimet, 13541 Gardanne, France
philippe.maurine@cea.fr

Abstract. Recently, a generic DPA attack using the mutual information index as the side channel distinguisher has been introduced. Mutual Information Analysis's (MIA) main interest is its claimed genericity. However, it requires the estimation of various probability density functions (PDF), which is a task that involves the complicated problem of selecting tuning parameters. This problem could be the cause of the lower efficiency of MIA that has been reported. In this paper, we introduce an approach that selects the tuning parameters with the goal of optimizing the performance of MIA. Our approach differs from previous works in that it maximizes the ability of MIA to discriminate one key among all guesses rather than optimizing the accuracy of PDF estimates. Application of this approach to various leakage traces confirms the soundness of our proposal.

1 Introduction

Adversaries aim at disclosing secret information contained in integrated systems which are currently the main vector of data exchanges. One approach is Side Channel Analysis (SCA), which tries to reveal cryptographic keys by exploiting the information in one or several physical leakages of cryptographic devices, especially power consumption and electromagnetic emanations. In the seminal paper of [1], the difference of means was used as a distinguisher to identify from power consumption leakage the information about the key. Since then, more efficient distinguishers have been considered, notably Pearson's correlation coefficient [2], leading to a SCA referred to as CPA, and the Mutual Information

© Springer International Publishing Switzerland 2014
E. Prouff (Ed.): COSADE 2014, LNCS 8622, pp. 82–97, 2014.
DOI: 10.1007/978-3-319-10175-0_7

(MI) index, which appears as a promising alternative because it is capable of capturing any type of association. Mutual Information Analysis (MIA) in SCA was introduced in [3,4] and much work has been devoted to investigate its potential in attacking cryptographic implementations, featuring various countermeasures and background noises in leakage traces [5,6]. To summarize, MI was shown generally less efficient than Pearson's coefficient when the leakage function is nearly linear, as is usually the case in unprotected devices [4,7]. However, MIA appears promising when an adequate leakage profiling is a priori challenging [8,9] or for attacking some protected devices [5,6,9,10].

The main difficulty in implementing a MIA is that, in contrast to Pearson's coefficient which is easily estimated via sample moments, the estimation of the MI index requires the estimation of a number of probability distribution functions (PDF) and this task is, both theoretically and practically, a difficult statistical problem. Further, it has been stated [6,11,12] that the choice of a good PDF estimator is crucial for the efficiency of a MIA. Thus, a variety of parametric (cumulant [9] or copula [13]) and nonparametric estimators (histograms [4], splines [14] and kernels [3,8]) have been explored. Among the nonparametric methods, Kernel Density Estimators (KDE) [15,16] have emerged in the statistical literature as one of the most popular approaches, in view of their many appealing theoretical properties. However, KDE involves a major technical difficulty because it requires the choice of a crucial tuning parameter, referred to as the bandwidth (see Sect. 3). There exists formulas for choosing in some optimal fashion this bandwidth for the problem of estimating a PDF. Unfortunately, formulas for the problem of estimating the MI index have not yet been developed. Thus, most MIA based on KDE (i.e. KDE-MIA) have taken the route of estimating the PDF using these formulas, the logic being that if all PDF are well estimated, plugging these estimates in the expression of the MI index should yield a good estimator. But these formulas, beside being based on an asymptotic argument (optimizing the trade-off between asymptotic bias and variance), are averages over the whole range of the PDF. Moreover they involve unknown quantities that in turn must be estimated. In practical situations, there is no guarantee that such average estimated values will yield globally good PDF estimators and it is often recommended that they be used as starting points in the estimation process. Thus, applying them in an automatic fashion amounts to using an unsharpened tool. All this is further compounded by the fact that in computing the MI index, many different PDF need to be simultaneously estimated and integrated over their range. As stated by [12], this may help inexplaining the often lower efficiency of a standard MIA, as compared to CPA.

In this paper, we develop a new approach that selects the bandwidth in KDE-MIA from the point of view of optimizing the quality of the attack regarding two criteria, namely efficiency and genericity, instead of aiming at the quality of the PDF estimates. Applying our approach to some data sets, the new MIA, referred to as ABS-MIA (ABS for Adaptive Bandwidth Selection), is much better than the standard MIA and can even compete favorably with CPA.

The paper is organized as follows. Section 2 briefly recalls the modus operandi of SCA attacks and introduces the basics of MIA. Section 3 presents the KDE. Section 4 motivates and presents our proposal. This is then applied in Sect. 5 to some data. Section 6 concludes the paper and discusses some extensions.

2 Side Channel Analysis: An Overview

SCA is based on the fact that the physical leakage emanating from secure devices contains information on secret keys, and that an adversary can retrieve such keys by relating this information to the known course of the cryptographic device. In practice, this is done by relating the leakage to intermediate values computed by the target device which depend on parts (e.g. sub-keys) of the secret key. The set $\mathcal{K}$ of all candidate sub-keys k is assumed known and not too large. The secret sub-key targeted is noted κ. The relation is typically achieved in three steps.

2.1 Device Observation

To implement a SCA, an adversary first observes the target device by feeding it with known messages m in a set $\mathcal{M}$, while collecting the corresponding leakage traces $\{o(m) = (o_1(m), \ldots, o_T(m))\}$ as vectors representing the evolution of the physical leakage at T time points. Thus, the adversary first observes $\mathcal{O} = \{o(m), m \in \mathcal{M}\}$.

2.2 Device Activity Modeling

Then the adversary measures a proxy for the electrical activity of the device. A target intermediate value of w bits manipulated by the device is chosen and its values are recorded for each possible combination of candidate sub-keys k and messages m.

Then, for each candidate sub-key $k \in \mathcal{K}$, the adversary splits the intermediate values into several clusters with similar electrical activity, using a selection function $L(m, k) = v \in \mathcal{V}$ (typically the Hamming Weight (HW) or Hamming Distance (HD)). For each $v \in \mathcal{V}$, the groups $\mathcal{G}_k(v) = \{(m, o(m)) \in \mathcal{M} \times \mathcal{O} \mid L(m, k) = v\}$ are formed and collected to give a partition $\mathcal{P}(k) = \{\mathcal{G}_k(v), v \in \mathcal{V}\}$ of $\mathcal{M} \times \mathcal{O}$.

Note that there are several ways to manipulate the intermediate values. For example, one could work at the word level or at the bit level. For details, see Appendix A.

2.3 Estimation of κ

The final step of a SCA consists in processing the $\mathcal{P}(k)$ to get an estimate $\hat{\kappa}$ of κ. This is done through a distinguisher. In CPA, the distinguisher is Pearson's correlation coefficient: at each time point $t \in \{1, \ldots, T\}$ and for each candidate sub-key $k \in \mathcal{K}$, its value $r_k(t)$ for the data in $\{(L(m,k), o_t(m)), m \in \mathcal{M}\}$ is computed. Setting $R_k = \max_{t \in \{1,\ldots,T\}} r_k(t)$, κ is estimated by $\hat{\kappa} = \arg\max_{k \in \mathcal{K}} R_k$. The rationale is that when $k = \kappa$, the grouping of the traces induced by $L(\cdot, k)$ could show a strong enough linear association to allow distinguishing the correct sub-key from incorrect candidates. CPA is most fruitful when the data points $\{(L(m,\kappa), o_t(m)), m \in \mathcal{M}\}$ exhibit a linear trend.

In MIA, the MI index is used. In the context considered here, where the random vector (X, Y) is hybrid, that is X is discrete while Y is continuous with support S_Y, the theoretical version of this index is defined as

$$MI = \sum_x l(x) \int_{S_Y} f(y|x) \log \frac{f(y|x)}{g(y)} \, dy, \tag{1}$$

where $f(y|x)$ is the conditional (on X) PDF of Y while $g(y)$ (resp. $l(x)$) is the marginal PDF of Y (resp. X)[1] and the symbol $\sum_x$ refers to a sum taken over values x of X such that $l(x) > 0$. We have $MI \geq 0$ and $= 0$ if and only if X and Y are statistically independent. There are other equivalent formulas defining the MI index, notably

$$MI = H(Y) - \sum_x l(x) H(Y|x) \tag{2}$$

$$= H(Y) - H(Y|X), \tag{3}$$

where $H(Y) = -\int_{S_Y} g(y) \log g(y) dy$ is the (differential) entropy of random variable Y and similarly $H(Y|x) = -\int_{S_Y} f(y|x) \log f(y|x) \, dy$.

Specializing formula (3), MIA can be expressed as computing at each time point $t \in \{1, \ldots, T\}$ and for each sub-key $k \in \mathcal{K}$, the quantity

$$MI_k(t) = H(o_t(m)) - H(o_t(m)|L(m,k)). \tag{4}$$

The correct sub-key κ should satisfy

$$\kappa = \arg\max_{k \in \mathcal{K}} \left\{ \max_{t \in \{1,\ldots,T\}} MI_k(t) \right\}, \tag{5}$$

and if $\widehat{MI_k(t)}$ is an estimate of $MI_k(t)$, an estimate $\hat{\kappa}$ of κ is obtained as

$$\hat{\kappa} = \arg\max_{k \in \mathcal{K}} \left\{ \max_{t \in \{1,\ldots,T\}} \widehat{MI_k(t)} \right\}. \tag{6}$$

The main difficulty in implementing a MIA is in estimating the values $MI_k(t)$.

---

[1] Formally $l(x)$ is a probability mass function (PMF) because X is discrete. To simplify notation, we use the generic acronym PDF.

3   Estimating a PDF

Suppose a sample of independent copies $\{(X_n, Y_n), n = 1, ..., N\}$ of (X, Y) is at disposal. The problem of estimating the MI index (2) requires estimators of the entropies $H(Y)$ and $H(Y \mid x)$, which in turn requires estimators of the PDF $g(y)$ and $f(y|x)$. As stated earlier, estimation of these underlying PDF is a difficult statistical problem.

In general, a PDF estimator must offer a good trade-off between accuracy (bias) and variability (variance). In this section, we present the KDE. For the interested reader, details about other nonparametric methods (histogram or B-spline) can be found in [4,14]. Note that, for simplicity, we restrict attention to the case of univariate PDF.

The kernel method uses a function $K(\cdot)$, referred to as the kernel, in conjunction with a bandwidth $h > 0$. The KDE of $g(y)$ is then

$$\hat{g}_{KDE}(y) = \frac{1}{N} \sum_{n=1}^{N} K_h(y - Y_n), \tag{7}$$

where $K_h(y) = h^{-1}K(y/h)$. Regarding the kernel, classical choices are the Gaussian function: $K(y) = \frac{1}{\sqrt{2\pi}} e^{-y^2/2}$ or the Epanechnikov function: $K(y) = \frac{3}{4}(1 - y^2)$ for $|y| \leq 1$, but in general, this choice has less impact on the estimator than the bandwidth, which is critical in controlling the trade-off between bias and variance. A huge literature, over-viewed in [17], has been devoted to choosing this tuning parameter, and the expression of an optimal (in an asymptotic and global mathematical sense) bandwidth has been obtained. A relatively good estimator of this optimal bandwidth is obtained by Silverman's rule [18], which, for Epanechnikov's kernel, is

$$h_S = 2.34 \, \hat{\sigma} N^{-1/5}, \tag{8}$$

where $\hat{\sigma}$ the sample standard deviation of the data $\{Y_n, n = 1, ..., N\}$. From (2), $H(Y)$ can be estimated by

$$H_{KDE}(Y) = -\int_{S_Y} \hat{g}_{KDE}(y) \log \hat{g}_{KDE}(y) \, dy, \tag{9}$$

and similarly

$$H_{KDE}(Y|x) = -\int_{S_Y} \hat{f}_{KDE}(y|x) \log \hat{f}_{KDE}(y|x) \, dy, \tag{10}$$

while $l(x)$ can be estimated by N_x/N where $N_x = \sum_{n=1}^{N} \mathbb{I}\{X_n = x\}$ where $\mathbb{I}\{A\} = 1$ if event A is realized and 0 otherwise.

At this stage, another hurdle is encountered because the above computations require integration. To reduce the computational cost, one can choose points $\mathcal{Q} = \{q_0 < \ldots < q_B\}$ (referred to as query points) and estimate $H(Y)$ by

$$H^*_{KDE}(Y) = -\sum_{b=1}^{B} \hat{g}_{KDE}(q_b) \log \hat{g}_{KDE}(q_b)(q_b - q_{b-1}), \tag{11}$$

and similarly with $H^*_{KDE}(Y|x)$ in place of (10). If there exists computational constraints, a small number of query points in Q will be preferred, but then they be properly chosen to provide mathematical accuracy of the integral, a problem for which various solutions exist, for example via the rectangular method of (11) or more sophisticated quadrature formulas. Accuracy also depends on the number of these query points B and can be made arbitrarily good by increasing B, at the expense of computational cost. We have taken the strategy of choosing these query points systematically, along a grid covering all the sample points, whose coarseness is chosen depending on the available computing power.

We stress that Silverman's rule has been developed with the view of getting a globally good estimate of a PDF. There are no guarantees however that the formula yields a good bandwidth for estimation of complex functionals as the MI index, and this is a problem that requires further theoretical work in mathematical statistics. In the next section, we present our proposal to address this problem in the context of a SCA, where subject matter information allows another solution.

4 Setting the Tuning Parameters of KDE-MIA: Bandwidth and Query Points

To show the effect of various choices of bandwidth and query points on KDE-MIA, a small simulation study with synthetic data was conducted.

Ten thousand pairs (HW, L) were drawn from the following non-linear leakage function with probability 0.5 either $-0.9017 + 0.009 \cdot HW - 0.0022 \cdot HW^2 + \epsilon$ or $-0.9017 + \epsilon$, where $\epsilon \sim N(0, 0.005)$. The values of HW were independently computed from intermediate values of four independent binary (i.e. with range $\{0, 1\}$) random variables. We used here synthetic data so that the exact value of the MI index ($= 0.0312$) could be computed. This leakage model is inspired from the actual EM data considered in Sect. 5.

Figure 1 shows the results of estimating the MI index as the bandwidth h and the number of equispaced query points are changed. As expected, Silverman's rule yields a good estimate of the actual MI index when Q contains a reasonable number of points (e.g. ≥ 16).

Note also that as the bandwidth is increased, the bias of the MI estimator increases (hence its variance decreases) as the estimator (i.e. MI) decays to zero. This is explained by the fact that, as h increases, all KDE get oversmoothed and converge to the same function that resemble the initial kernel spread over S_Y, with the entropies converging to the same value and the MI index vanishing.

All this dovetails nicely with intuition and the admonishments in almost all publications on MIA that, in order to have a good estimator of the MI index, one should use adequate PDF estimators.

However, this does not guarantee maximal efficiency of the MIA. Based on real data, Fig. 2 shows surprisingly that increasing the bandwidth results in better attacks, in terms of partial Success Rate (pSR). This behavior was replicated

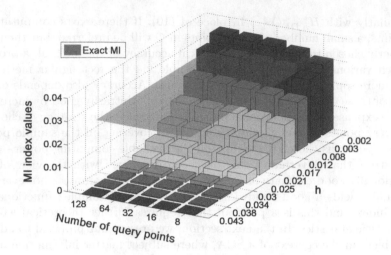

Fig. 1. Behavior of the estimator of the MI index as a function of the number of query points and with bandwidth values h. ($h_S = 0.003$)

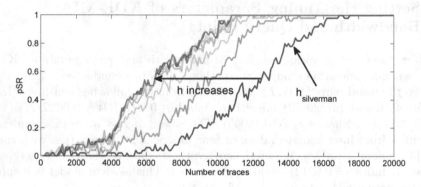

Fig. 2. Partial Success Rate on 1st Sbox at the last round of AES from the publicly available traces of DPAContestV2 [19] using the HD model at the word level.

with other data sets and suggests that good PDF estimation does not necessarily translate in efficiency of the attack, where larger bandwidths, and smoother PDF estimators, seem to yield better results.

It is this counterintuitive behavior that has led to the realization that the bandwidth could be seen, not as a nuisance parameter to be dealt with in a statistical estimation procedure, but more profitably as a lever that could be used to fine-tune a SCA. Note that such a lever does not exist in standard CPA and arises only with more complex distinguisher.

Our Adaptive Bandwidth Selection (ABS) procedure explicitly exploits the fact that there exists exactly one correct sub-key κ. For all other $k \in \mathcal{K}$, there should be statistical independence between the intermediate value and the leakage, so that $MI_k = 0$ when $k \neq \kappa$ while $MI_\kappa > 0$ (for simplicity, we suppress the time point $t \in \{1, \ldots, T\}$ from the notation because we consider only one point of leakage). We consider the average distance to the rivals instead of the second best rival to eliminate ghost peak effects. Thus, an alternate expression to (5) is

$$\kappa = \arg\max_{k \in \mathcal{K}} \left\{ MI_k - \overline{MI_{-k}} \right\}, \tag{12}$$

where $\overline{MI_{-k}}$ denotes the mean of all the MI values except MI_k.

Now, using KDE, let $\widehat{MI_k}(h)$ be an estimator of MI_k using the bandwidth h in all PDF involved in (2). The empirical version of (12) leads to the first estimator

$$\hat{\kappa} = \arg\max_{k \in \mathcal{K}} \left\{ \widehat{MI_k}(h) - \overline{\widehat{MI_{-k}}(h)} \right\}, \tag{13}$$

where $\overline{\widehat{MI_{-k}}(h)}$ stands for the mean of all estimators except $\widehat{MI_k}(h)$. At this stage, the value h is still unused. The above suggests choosing this value to facilitate the identification of κ. But, as noted earlier, when h increases all PDF in (2) are oversmoothed (so that all $\widehat{MI_k}(h)$ decay to zero, albeit at a different rate for $\widehat{MI_\kappa}(h)$). This suggests normalizing expression (13) and leads to the consideration of

$$\hat{\kappa} = \arg\max_{k \in \mathcal{K}} \left\{ \max_{h > 0} \left[\frac{\widehat{MI_k}(h) - \overline{\widehat{MI_{-k}}(h)}}{\overline{MI_{-k}}(h)} \right] \right\} \tag{14}$$

as an estimator of κ. The value of h where the inner max operator is attained will be noted h_{ABS}.

Some computational and statistical comments are in order at this stage. First, even when $MI_k = 0$, $\widehat{MI_k}(h) \geq 0$ (e.g. is upwardly biased) so that the denominator $\overline{\widehat{MI_{-k}}(h)}$ is almost surely >0; this eliminates the risk of indeterminacy. Second, the estimator $\widehat{MI_\kappa}(h)$ will tend to be greater than $\widehat{MI_k}(h)$ when $k \neq \kappa$, in the sense that $Prob(\widehat{MI_\kappa}(h) > \widehat{MI_k}(h))$ will be high. Simple algebra shows that the term in bracket in (14) should then be in the interval $[-1, 0]$ with high probability, whereas when $k = \kappa$, this term should tend to be positive, thus allowing a good probability of discrimination for κ. The following maximization on h aims at making this discrimination independent of the choice of h and is an automatic bandwidth selection procedure targeting the goal of getting a good estimate of κ, in contrast to Silverman's rule that aims at getting good estimates of the PDF involved in MI_k. The maximization also has the side effect of smoothing the quirks that could occur in the individuals estimated PDF, and thus in the resulting MI_k, with a single value of h. Finally, the smoothness of $\widehat{MI_k}(h)$ as a function of h allows to evaluate the max operator over a (finite to avoid trivial problems) grid of properly chosen h values ranging from some point in the neighbourhood of the value h_S to some large multiple of this value, and this accelerates the computation of $\hat{\kappa}$. In practice, (14) is implemented as

$$\hat{\kappa} = \arg\max_{k \in \mathcal{K}} \left\{ \max_{h \in \mathcal{I}} \left[\frac{\widehat{MI_k}(h) - \widehat{MI_{-k}}(h)}{\widehat{MI_{-k}}(h)} \right] \right\}, \tag{15}$$

where $\mathcal{I} = \{h_i\}_{1 \le i \le H}$ a set of $H \ge 2$ bandwidths.

From an engineering point of view, we can see the action (via the value of h) of (14) as a focus adjustment to visualize a set of K pixels (i.e. $K = 256$ in the case of the MI index associated with each of the 256 key assumptions in the case of AES). The numerator allows to highlight a single pixel (a single key guess) while the denominator makes uniform the background of the picture, i.e. standardizing the estimated MI values associated with the remaining guesses.

To get some feeling about the behavior of our approach, we illustrate its action with real data. We consider the 1st Sbox at the last round of AES from the publicly available traces of the DPAContestV2 [19] with a HD model at the word level. It turns out that $h_{ABS} = 1.8 > h_S = 0.17$ (Volt), so that our PDF estimators are smoother.

Figure 3 shows the action of our ABS criterion. The top panel gives the term in brackets of (14) for the 256 key guesses using h_S. The bottom panel shows the same with h_{ABS}. In both cases, the correct sub-key value ($\kappa = 83$), is disclosed by MIA after the processing of all traces. However, for h_S, the margin with the second sub-key guess is relatively small while being much larger using h_{ABS}.

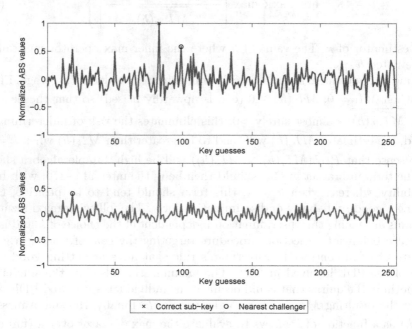

Fig. 3. Values of the term in brackets in (14) for h_S (top panel) and h_{ABS} (bottom panel) for the 256 key guesses after processing all DPAContestV2 traces with HD model at word level.

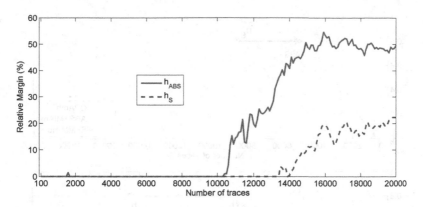

Fig. 4. Evolution of the relative margins (%) for h_S and h_{ABS} with the number of processed DPAContestV2 traces with HD model at word level.

Thus, the maximizing step over h reduces the impact of ghost peaks and allows a better discrimination of the correct sub-key.

Figure 4 presents another view sustaining this behavior. It reports the relative margin (%) of the best (correct) sub-key with respect to the second (wrong) best sub-key guess, i.e. the difference between the estimated MI for the correct sub-key and the highest MI value among wrong sub-keys, during each step of the attack for h_{ABS} and h_S. Again, the approach based on h_{ABS} is more effective at reducing ghost peaks.

We close this section by noting that the principle embodied in (14) is consonant with the idea mentioned in [13] who suggest detecting outlier behavior of the correct key to perform successful recoveries. Also, when analysing a set of traces over many time points $t \in \{1, \ldots, T\}$, in (15), the $\max_{t \in \{1,\ldots,T\}}$ operation should be computed after $\max_{h \in H}$ (to optimize the extraction of information at each leakage point), with the result being the operand of $\arg \max_{k \in \mathcal{K}}$.

5   Experimental Results

In this section, we further compare the performance of our ABS-MIA, to MIA using h_S, referred to as S-MIA. During this evaluation, CPA was also computed and used as a benchmark regarding three main criteria:

1. Efficiency, as measured by the number of traces to reach a target success rate [20].
2. Genericity, the ability of a SCA to be more or less successful under a unknown leakage model.
3. Computational burden.

Comparisons were conducted according to two scenarii

1. Bit level (multi-bit).
2. Word level.

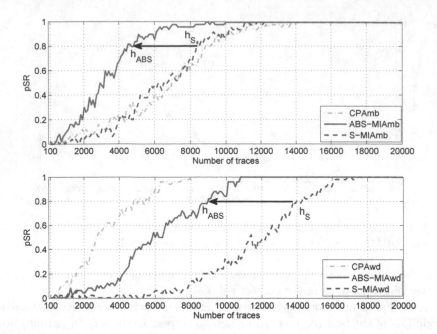

Fig. 5. Partial Success Rates (pSR) evaluated on the 1st Sbox at the last round of the AES with the DPAContestV2 traces over two scenarii: 'mb' (top) and 'wd' (bottom). The HD model was considered.

To distinguish between these scenarii, 'mb' and 'wd' suffixes are used in the remainder of the paper (see Appendix A for details).

5.1   ABS-MIA Efficiency

The attacks were conducted with the traces of the DPAContestV2 [19] at the same fixed time point chosen in Sect. 4. Again, we focused on the 1st Sbox at the last round of the AES. We used both the Gaussian and the Epanechnikov kernel but report only on the latter as both give very similar results. For the estimation of the MI index, a grid of 128 equidistant query points was taken to cover the peak-to-peak amplitude of traces (fixed by the choice of caliber and sensitivity during measurements) of the analog-to-digital converter of the oscilloscope (with a 8-bit resolution). Efficiency was measured by Success Rate (SR) following the framework in [20]. This metric has been sampled over 50 independent attacks to obtain an average partial Success Rate (pSR). The attacks were conducted with the HD model. Figure 5 illustrates the promising features of our approach. In all scenarii, ABS-MIA requires smaller number of measurements than S-MIA, demonstrating the improvement. More importantly, we observe that ABS-MIAmb compares favorably with the very efficient CPAwd. To sustain these results, we carried out CPA, ABS-MIA and S-MIA on a different data set of 10000 EM traces collected above a hardware AES block, mapped into an

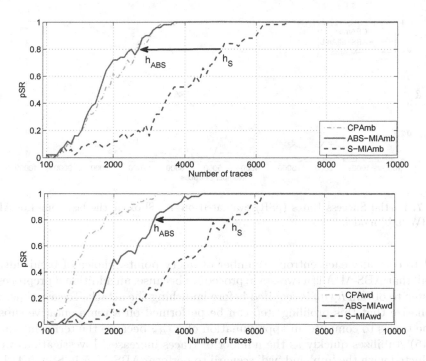

Fig. 6. Partial Success Rates (pSR) evaluated on 4th Sbox at the last round of AES with our EM traces over two scenarii: 'mb' (left top) and 'wd' (left bottom). The HD model was considered.

FPGA, operating at 50 MHz with a RF2 probe and 48 dB low noise amplifier. We concentrated on the 4th Sbox at the last round. The HD linear model was once again considered. Figure 6 shows results similar to those obtained with the DPAContestV2 data above, with ABS-MIA showing again a large improvement over S-MIA while staying competitive with CPA.

5.2 ABS-MIA Genericity

To investigate genericity, the evaluations were performed using the second set of traces in the previous section under the unknown HW leakage model. As the pSR of the attacks using the 'wd' scenario never reached 10 % after processing the 10000 traces, we excluded it for further considerations. Interestingly, ABS-MIAmb is the only successful HW-based attack, with a pSR of 80 % after processing 7400 traces (see Fig. 7). Besides, all the variants of CPA (i.e. CPAmb and CPAwd) fail in this case.

5.3 ABS-MIA Computational Burden

Regarding runtime, the computational cost of MIA is related to the number of entropies to be computed (17 for 'mb' and 10 for 'wd') and on the parameters

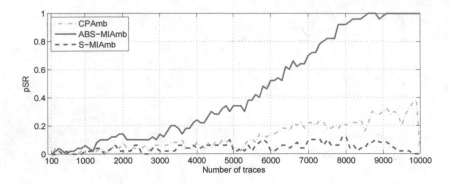

Fig. 7. Partial Success Rates (pSR) evaluated on 4th Sbox at the last round of AES for HW 'mb' model.

used to compute each entropy (number of query points, choice of bandwidth). Recall that ABS-MIA is a two-stage procedure because, an additional preprocessing step to obtain h_{ABS} is required before launching the attack. To save time, we emphasize that this profiling step can be performed on a representative subset of the traces to compute an approximation of h_{ABS} because the terms in braces in (15) stabilizes quickly as the number of traces increases. Investigations were conducted with the 'mb' and 'wd' scenarii to perform ABS-MIA in Sect. 5.4. The time spent for this preprocessing for each Sbox is approximately one twentieth of the time required for S-MIA. However, this time is partly recovered by the reduction in the number of query points required for good behavior of ABS-MIA (16 compared to at least 96 for S-MIA; because the PDF are smoother in ABS-MIA, the integrals in (9), (10) are more easily approximated). This significantly reduces the number of computations involved in getting $\widehat{MI_k(h)}$.

5.4 ABS-MIA: Global Success Rate for the DPAContestV2

Finally, we applied S-MIA and ABS-MIA to the DPAContestV2 traces and considered the global Success Rate (gSR) using the HD model. We also launched CPAwd and CPAmb as benchmarks. As in Sect. 5.1, 50 trace orders were considered. The evolutions of gSR are shown in Fig. 8. We observe that ABS-MIAmb dominates with, in particular, 15200 traces for the gSR to be stable above 80 %. On the other hand, S-MIA fails in recovering the key. Thirty minutes (resp. two hours) were necessary to complete both the preprocessing and the ABS-MIAwd (resp. ABS-MIAmb) on a personal computer.

6 Conclusions

MIA was motivated by its ability to capture all structures of dependencies between leakage and intermediate values. But the cost of this attractive feature is the difficulty in choosing adequately some tuning parameters. By focusing on

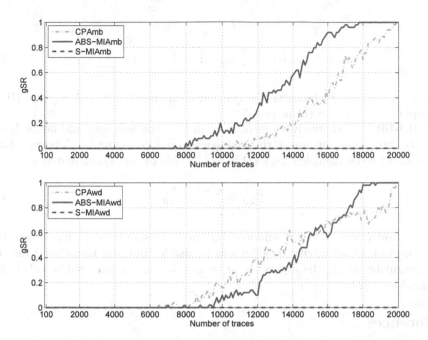

Fig. 8. Global Success Rates (gSR) evaluated at the last round of AES available traces of the DPAContestV2. The HD model was considered.

the goal of optimizing the KDE-based MIA instead of the auxiliary task of estimating PDF, we have obtained an efficient bandwidth selection procedure. The resulting bandwidths are usually larger than the commonly used h_S (obtained by Silverman's rule) and give better results in terms of attack efficiency across various experiments. We have shown that MIA driven by this method is comparable to the variant of CPA [2]. Additionally, we have reported that our MIA could succeed when CPA failed (see Sect. 5.2). Our approach could be applied to select the tuning parameters in other SCA involving nonparametric estimators, namely histograms and splines. We feel the present work shows there can be some benefits in adapting the principles of statistical methods to the task at end: SCA in the present case.

A Appendix

From Sect. 2, modeling leakage consists essentially in choosing a selection function L to classify the leakage samples $o(m)$, based on the predictions $v_{m,k}$ according to $m \in \mathcal{M}$ and $k \in \mathcal{K}$, either at the word level or at the bit level (Multi-bit).

- **Word.** In view of the additive property of the power consumption in CMOS technologies, traditional leakage models inspired are based on works in [2,21], aims at mapping activities of components using intermediate values to the physical observations by equal summation of w bits

$$L : \mathbb{F}_2^w \to [0; w]$$

$$v_{m,k} = ([v_{m,k}]_1, \ldots, [v_{m,k}]_w) \to L(v_{m,k}) = \sum_{b=1}^{w} [v_{m,k}]_b. \tag{16}$$

with $[.]_b : \mathbb{F}_2^w \to \mathbb{F}_2$ being the projection onto the ith bit. (AES (resp. DES) output Sbox : $w = 8$ (resp. $w = 5$))

- **Multi-bit.** Alternatively, as mentioned in [22], the leakage could be analyzed bit by bit, summing up at the end each equal contribution. The multi-bit version of a distinguisher $\mathcal{D}_{k,t}$ ($\mathcal{D} \equiv MI$ in this paper) is calculated as

$$\mathcal{D}_{k,t} = \sum_{b=1}^{w} |[\mathcal{D}_{k,t}]_b|. \tag{17}$$

This model seems better adapted to the EM side-channel for which the assumption of additivity may be less plausible. Initially introduced for the distinguisher using the *difference of means*, it can be extended to other distinguishers [23].

References

1. Kocher, P.C., Jaffe, J., Jun, B.: Differential power analysis. In: Wiener, M. (ed.) CRYPTO 1999. LNCS, vol. 1666, pp. 388–397. Springer, Heidelberg (1999)
2. Brier, E., Clavier, C., Olivier, F.: Correlation power analysis with a leakage model. In: Joye, M., Quisquater, J.-J. (eds.) CHES 2004. LNCS, vol. 3156, pp. 16–29. Springer, Heidelberg (2004)
3. Aumonier, S.: Generalized correlation power analysis. In: ECRYPT Workshop on Tools For Cryptanalysis, Kraków, Poland, September 2007
4. Gierlichs, B., Batina, L., Tuyls, P., Preneel, B.: Mutual information analysis. In: Oswald, E., Rohatgi, P. (eds.) CHES 2008. LNCS, vol. 5154, pp. 426–442. Springer, Heidelberg (2008)
5. Batina, L., Gierlichs, B., Prouff, E., Rivain, M., Standaert, F.X., Veyrat-Charvillon, N.: Mutual information analysis: a comprehensive study. Cryptol. J. **24**, 269–291 (2001). Springer, New York
6. Prouff, E., Rivain, M.: Theoretical and practical aspects of mutual information-based side channel analysis. Int. J. Adv. Comput. Technol. (IJACT) **2**(2), 121–138 (2010)
7. Moradi, A., Mousavi, N., Paar, C., Salmasizadeh, M.: A comparative study of mutual information analysis under a Gaussian assumption. In: Youm, H.Y., Yung, M. (eds.) WISA 2009. LNCS, vol. 5932, pp. 193–205. Springer, Heidelberg (2009)
8. Veyrat-Charvillon, N., Standaert, F.-X.: Mutual information analysis: how, when and why? In: Clavier, C., Gaj, K. (eds.) CHES 2009. LNCS, vol. 5747, pp. 429–443. Springer, Heidelberg (2009)
9. Le, T.-H., Berthier, M.: Mutual information analysis under the view of higher-order statistics. In: Echizen, I., Kunihiro, N., Sasaki, R. (eds.) IWSEC 2010. LNCS, vol. 6434, pp. 285–300. Springer, Heidelberg (2010)
10. Gierlichs, B., Batina, L., Preneel, B., Verbauwhede, I.: Revisiting higher-order DPA attacks: multivariate mutual information analysis. In: Pieprzyk, J. (ed.) CT-RSA 2010. LNCS, vol. 5985, pp. 221–234. Springer, Heidelberg (2010)

11. Flament, F., Guilley, S., Danger, J.L., Elaabid, M.A., Maghrebi, H., Sauvage, L.: About probability density function estimation for side channel analysis. In: Proceedings of International Workshop on Constructive Side-Channel Analysis and Secure Design (COSADE), pp. 15–23 (2010)
12. Whitnall, C., Oswald, E.: A comprehensive evaluation of mutual information analysis using a fair evaluation framework. In: Rogaway, P. (ed.) CRYPTO 2011. LNCS, vol. 6841, pp. 316–334. Springer, Heidelberg (2011)
13. Veyrat-Charvillon, N., Standaert, F.-X.: Generic side-channel distinguishers: improvements and limitations. In: Rogaway, P. (ed.) CRYPTO 2011. LNCS, vol. 6841, pp. 354–372. Springer, Heidelberg (2011)
14. Venelli, A.: Efficient entropy estimation for mutual information analysis using B-splines. In: Samarati, P., Tunstall, M., Posegga, J., Markantonakis, K., Sauveron, D. (eds.) WISTP 2010. LNCS, vol. 6033, pp. 17–30. Springer, Heidelberg (2010)
15. Rosenblatt, M.: Remark on some nonparametric estimates of a density function. Ann. Math. Stat. **27**, 832–837 (1956)
16. Parzen, E.: On the estimation of a probability density function and the mode. Ann. Math. Stat. **33**, 1065–1076 (1962)
17. Sheather, S.J.: Density estimation. Stat. Sci. **19**(4), 588–597 (2004)
18. Silverman, B.W., Green, P.J.: Density Estimation for Statistics and Data Analysis. Chapman and Hall, London (1986)
19. VLSI Research Group and TELECOM ParisTech: The DPA contest (2008/2009)
20. Standaert, F.-X., Gierlichs, B., Verbauwhede, I.: Partition *vs.* comparison side-channel distinguishers: an empirical evaluation of statistical tests for Univariate side-channel attacks against two unprotected CMOS devices. In: Lee, P.J., Cheon, J.H. (eds.) ICISC 2008. LNCS, vol. 5461, pp. 253–267. Springer, Heidelberg (2009)
21. Messerges, T.S., Dabbish, E.A., Sloan, R.H., Messerges, T.S., Dabbish, E.A., Sloan, R.H.: Investigations of power analysis attacks on smartcards. In: Proceedings of the USENIX Workshop on Smartcard Technology, pp. 151–162 (1999)
22. Bévan, R., Knudsen, E.W.: Ways to enhance differential power analysis. In: Lee, P.J., Lim, C.H. (eds.) ICISC 2002. LNCS, vol. 2587, pp. 327–342. Springer, Heidelberg (2003)
23. Tiran, S., Maurine, P.: SCA with magnitude squared coherence. In: Mangard, S. (ed.) CARDIS 2012. LNCS, vol. 7771, pp. 234–247. Springer, Heidelberg (2013)

Generic DPA Attacks: Curse or Blessing?

Oscar Reparaz[✉], Benedikt Gierlichs, and Ingrid Verbauwhede

Department of Electrical Engineering-ESAT/COSIC, KU Leuven and iMinds,
Kasteelpark Arenberg 10, B-3001 Leuven-Heverlee, Belgium
{oscar.reparaz,benedikt.gierlichs,ingrid.verbauwhede}@esat.kuleuven.be

Abstract. Generic DPA attacks, such as MIA, have been recently proposed as a method to mount DPA attacks without the need for possibly restrictive assumptions on the leakage behaviour. Previous work identified some shortcomings of generic DPA attacks when attacking injective targets (such as the AES Sbox output). In this paper, we focus on that particular property of generic DPA attacks and explain limitations, workarounds and advantages. Firstly we show that the original fix to address this issue (consisting of dropping bits on predictions to destroy the injectivity) works in practice. Secondly, we describe how a determined attacker can circumvent the issue of attacking injective targets and mount a generic attack on the AES using previously mentioned non-injective targets. Thirdly, we explain important and attractive properties of generic attacks, such as being effective under any leakage behaviour. Consequently, we are able to recover keys even if the attacker only observes an encrypted version of the leakage, for instance when a device is using bus encryption with a constant key. The same property also allows to mount attacks on later rounds of the AES with a reduced number of key hypotheses compared to classical DPA. All main observations are supported by experimental results, when possible on real measurements.

Keywords: DPA · Generic DPA · MIA · KSA

1 Introduction

Side-channel attacks pose nowadays a significant threat for the security of cryptographic embedded devices. Since the first publication [8] in 1996, a respectable body of academic research on side-channel attacks and countermeasures has been produced. Besides, side-channel attacks are not only a topic of academic research but also relevant to industry. Present embedded security devices, such as bank cards, phone SIMs and electronic passports normally feature some kind of protection against side-channel attacks.

An important class of side-channel attacks are Differential Power Analysis (DPA) attacks, introduced in [9] by Kocher et al. They showed that cryptographic keys could be extracted from embedded devices by first measuring their instantaneous power consumption while performing cryptographic operations and subsequently performing a statistical analysis of the power consumption

© Springer International Publishing Switzerland 2014
E. Prouff (Ed.): COSADE 2014, LNCS 8622, pp. 98–111, 2014.
DOI: 10.1007/978-3-319-10175-0_8

measurements. The relatively inexpensive equipment needed for performing DPA attacks greatly increases the threat of this family of attacks.

Since [9], a substantial work on the so-called distinguisher in DPA attacks has been carried out [2,4,6,10,13]. In a nutshell, this trend tries to optimize the performance of a DPA attack, measured in the number of traces needed for a successful attack, under the assumption that the device leaks information in a specific manner, usually Hamming weight (HW) or Hamming distance (HD). Pearson's sample correlation coefficient distinguisher is a popular choice when mounting DPA attacks (also known as CPA attacks) on devices whose behaviour can be linearly approximated by some leakage model (usually HD or HW) given beforehand (essentially, acquired based on previous knowledge of the chip and its implementation).

The choice of leakage model when attacking a device is crucial. In fact, there must be some correspondence between the leakage behaviour of the device and the leakage model for the attack to succeed. An example of this requirement is shown in [18], where CPA is shown to fail if the model is sufficiently wrong. Actually, there is a whole family of countermeasures that try to alter the leakage signal such that it becomes more difficult to model, and thus make the attack harder. One example of a countermeasure belonging to this family is balanced circuits, such as dual-rail logic (for instance WDDL [15]). While in theory dual-rail logic aims at producing data independent leakage, in practice, imperfectly-balanced dual-rail implementations produce a leakage behaviour that is difficult to model, rendering DPA attacks that employ inexact, non-corresponding leakage models ineffective [15] (although in practice regression-based approaches that perform a leakage modeling on the fly [19] can provide good results).

An important enhancement of power analysis are profiled attacks, such as [5,14]. These attacks do not require a leakage model previously known to the practitioner, but instead derive the leakage model itself in a profiling step that characterizes the device. The attack step is usually based on Maximum Likelihood classification and can be shown to be optimal if the derived model is sound. During the profiling step, the attacker has virtually unlimited access to a device identical to the device under attack. This access might be difficult to obtain in reality. In short, profiled attacks are a powerful attack strategy that is carried out by a strong adversary.

Recently, several (non-profiled) DPA strategies have been proposed that try to bring the best from both worlds: on the one hand, they do not require a leakage model of the device given beforehand, and thus they could be potentially applied against any device; on the other hand, these generic strategies do not require a profiling step, so that even a weak adversary can perform them. Typically these generic strategies work with measurements in a nominal scale. Exemplary generic DPA strategies are based on Mutual Information [7], on the Kolmogorov-Smirnov distance [16], on the Cramér-von-Mises test [16] or on copulas [17]. We will use MIA in this paper but results apply to all of them.

Despite the attractive properties of generic DPA attacks, earlier papers have identified some theoretical shortcomings of these attacks regarding injective targets [7,17–19]. This paper addresses the practical relevance of these theoretical shortcomings and explores limitations, workarounds and advantages of generic DPA attacks.

Contribution. The contribution of this paper is threefold. Firstly, we present experimental evidence confirming that the "bit drop" trick already proposed in [7] to attack injective targets works even in realistic environments with high, but not infinite, signal-to-noise ratio (SNR). Secondly, we show that by carefully redefining the non-injective targets of the attack, it is indeed possible to launch a fully generic MIA attack on the AES. Thirdly, we demonstrate that precisely the same apparently unappealing property that causes MIA to fail against injective targets enables an attacker to launch MIA attacks exploiting the leakage from an encrypted bus, or from later rounds of AES at reduced number of key hypotheses compared to a traditional DPA attack. The experimental results we provide do not contradict any theoretical result from [17–19], but clarify the practical relevance of the issues.

Organization. The remainder of this paper is organised as follows. Section 2 reviews previous work. Section 3 presents some practical experiments regarding the practical applicability of the "bit drop" trick. Section 4 elaborates on a generic MIA attack against the AES. Section 5 studies some properties of MIA that can be exploited to mount MIA attacks on later rounds, and Sect. 6 concludes the paper.

2   Previous Work

In this section we recall the fundamental concepts for MIA attacks and we state the issues that arise when performing MIA attacks on injective targets.

2.1   Notation

Capital letters in bold face, e.g. $\mathbf{X}$, denote random variables. Lower-case letters, e.g. x, denote a specific realization of $\mathbf{X}$, e.g. $\mathbf{X} = x$. The plaintext byte number i is denoted by p_i. The i-th key byte is denoted by k_i. The function drop_i drops i least significant bits of its argument. The expression $I(\mathbf{X}; \mathbf{Y})$ denotes Mutual Information between $\mathbf{X}$ and $\mathbf{Y}$, and is defined [7] as

$$I(\mathbf{X}; \mathbf{Y}) = H(\mathbf{X}) - H(\mathbf{X}|\mathbf{Y}) \tag{1}$$

where $H(\cdot)$ denotes Shannon entropy. S denotes some operation within the computation of a cryptographic primitive. In particular, we denote the AES Sbox by S_{AES}. $\mathbf{L}_{\text{device}}$ denotes the leakage behaviour of the cryptographic device. $\mathbf{L}_{\text{model}}$ denotes a leakage model. Id is the identity function. HW denotes the Hamming weight function. ϵ denotes a Gaussian noise process, its standard deviation is clear from the context.

2.2   Original MIA

MIA was originally introduced in [7] as a new information-theoretic distinguisher that aims at detecting any kind of dependency between observed measurements and predicted power consumption. MIA was different from previous distinguisher flavours in the sense that it is a generic tool suitable for attacking a wide variety of target devices without a priori knowledge, instead of an efficient tool that does require a priori assumptions about the target device. In this respect, MIA neither requires specific knowledge about the exact relation between processed data and observed measurements (leakage behaviour) nor requires to model such behaviour under a leakage model.

More precisely, to target some intermediate value $\mathbf{Z} = S(\mathbf{P} \oplus k)$, MIA uses as distinguisher the value of the Mutual Information between the observed measurements $\mathbf{O} = \mathbf{L}_{\text{device}}(\mathbf{Z})$ and the predicted power consumption $\mathbf{H} = \mathbf{L}_{\text{model}}(\mathbf{Z}_k)$ based on a key guess,

$$I(\mathbf{O}; \mathbf{H}). \tag{2}$$

MIA computes the value of Eq. (2) for each key hypothesis k, ranks the key candidates according to decreasing values of $I(\mathbf{O}; \mathbf{H})$ and selects the key candidate as the one that maximizes the Mutual Information value.

In contrast to other previous distinguishers, such as Pearson's sample correlation coefficient, the Mutual Information value between two random variables expresses the degree of statistical dependency between these two variables, independently of the specific form that the potential dependency between variables may take. This powerful property allows the attacker to skip modelling the leakage behaviour $\mathbf{L}_{\text{device}}$. As a matter of fact, in [7] it was mentioned that the attacker can directly plug in Eq. (2) the hypothesized values handled by the device as the predicted power consumption by setting $\mathbf{H} = \text{Id}(\mathbf{Z})$. By doing so, the attacker does not place any restrictive assumption on the leakage behaviour and thus the attack is expected to work against any device that leaks "somehow".

Moreover, should some information about the leakage behaviour be available beforehand, then that can be used to improve the efficiency of the MIA attack [7], but this is not required for an attack to succeed.

2.3   Issues with Injective Targets

In several references [7,19] it was noted that for injective targets S (for instance, $S = S_{\text{AES}}(\mathbf{P} \oplus k)$) a straightforward application of Eq. (2) with a generic leakage model by setting $\mathbf{H} = \text{Id}(\mathbf{Z})$ would result in an ineffective attack. Actually, different key hypotheses just imply a permutation of the values $\mathbf{H}$, and thus result in equally meaningful partitions of the observed measurements. This, in turn, leads to the same value for the Mutual Information of Eq. (2) for each key hypothesis, and therefore renders the discrimination of the correct key impossible. Note that this result is not exclusive to MIA, but it extends to a broad set of carefully defined generic attacks, as Whitnall et al. formally reason in [19].

In [7], the authors proposed a fix to solve this issue. They suggested dropping one bit in the predictions, $\mathbf{H} = \mathrm{drop}_1(\mathbf{Z})$, effectively destroying the phenomenon of different keys causing equivalent (up to a permutation) values of $\mathbf{H}$, yet preserving the generic nature of the attack. This fix is called the "bit drop trick" throughout this paper. They provided empirical evidence of the correctness of this method against one AES Sbox output byte $S = S_{\mathrm{AES}}(p \oplus k)$ with real power measurements using three bits of the prediction, $\mathbf{H} = \mathrm{drop}_5(\mathbf{Z})$.

The bit drop trick has been studied more thoroughly in [17,18]. First, in [17], Veyrat-Charvillon and Standaert provide experiments in a noiseless simulated scenario where the device leaks exactly Hamming weights $\mathbf{L}_{\mathrm{device}}(\mathbf{Z}) = \mathrm{HW}(\mathbf{Z})$ and the target is the AES Sbox output $\mathbf{Z} = S_{\mathrm{AES}}(p \oplus k)$. The predictions consist of the intermediate value $\mathbf{Z}$ when a variable amount of bits are dropped: $\mathbf{H} = \mathrm{drop}_i(\mathbf{Z})$ for $i \in \{1, 2, \ldots, 7\}$. In this situation, they show that although a MIA attack that uses $\mathbf{H} = \mathrm{drop}_i(\mathbf{Z})$ for $i \in \{7, 6, 5, 4, 3, 2\}$ works, a MIA attack that uses $\mathbf{H} = \mathrm{drop}_1(\mathbf{Z})$ unexpectedly fails.

In addition, in [18], Whitnall et al. further study this effect by taking the environmental noise into account with $\mathbf{L}_{\mathrm{device}}(\mathbf{Z}) = \mathrm{HW}(\mathbf{Z}) + \epsilon$. They conclude, from simulations, that a MIA attack on the AES Sbox output using $\mathbf{H} = \mathrm{drop}_1(\mathbf{Z})$ as predictions will fail for large values of the signal-to-noise ratio (that is, when the noise ϵ has small variance). On the other hand, when the signal-to-noise is below a certain threshold, MIA attacks with $\mathbf{H} = \mathrm{drop}_1(\mathbf{Z})$ will eventually succeed. Hence, it was shown that there are high-SNR scenarios where the bit drop trick does not work.

3   Practical Relevance of the Bit Drop Trick

In this section, we experimentally verify the practical relevance of the negative results regarding dropping some bits in the predictions.

We performed all the experiments for this paper on an 8-bit micro controller from Atmel's AVR family running an unprotected implementation of AES-128. We obtained 10, 000 power traces from encryptions of randomly chosen plaintexts covering the first one and a half rounds. The card is clocked at 4 MHz and the sampling frequency is 10 MS/s. The device leakage behaviour is known to be close to Hamming weight, however, in what follows we do not make use of this fact and proceed as if the leakage behaviour were unknown to us.

3.1   Dropping One Bit

We performed a MIA attack targeting the first Sbox output, by setting as targeted intermediate value the byte $\mathbf{Z} = S_{\mathrm{AES}}(\mathbf{P}_1 \oplus k_1)$ and dropping one bit on the predictions $\mathbf{H} = \mathrm{drop}_1(\mathbf{Z})$. The (non-parametric) density estimation process was performed without placing any hypotheses on the leakage behaviour of the device. Thus, densities were estimated with histograms with 256 bins, since measurement samples have a resolution of 8 bits.

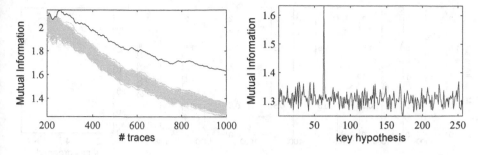

Fig. 1. Left: evolution of the MIA attack targeting the intermediate value $z = S_{AES}(p \oplus k)$ dropping one bit in the predictions, $\mathbf{H} = \mathrm{drop}_1(\mathbf{Z})$, as the number of traces increases. Correct key in black, incorrect key hypothesis in grey. Right: outcome of the attack using 1,000 traces.

Figure 1 shows the result this attack when using 1,000 traces at time sample 485. It can be observed that the attack is successful, the correct key clearly stands out over all other competing key hypotheses. We confirmed that around time sample 485 the implementation performs the Sbox lookups from the first round.

The experiment highlights the limited impact of the negative results in [17, 18] regarding the drop$_1$ trick. We can hardly conceive a practical scenario with a higher SNR than ours, since our platform (AVR) has relatively high leakage for industry standards. Furthermore, in reality implementations will feature some countermeasures that will only degrade the SNR. Thus, the negative results of [18] regarding the bit drop trick in strong-signal settings are of theoretical relevance but we conclude that the bit drop trick works in practical, high yet finite SNR scenarios. In other words, the high SNR of our measurements is "low enough" for the bit drop trick to work.

3.2 Dropping More than One Bit

The experiment from Sect. 3.1 was repeated for a different amount of least significant bits dropped, ranging from 1 to 7, following the spirit of [17]. All the other parameters of the attack are kept constant: we focus on the same time sample 485 and use the same Mutual Information estimation procedure with histograms of 256 bins in order not to place any assumption about the leakage behaviour during the density estimation process.

Figure 2, left, shows 7 plots for 7 different attacks. Each attack drops a different number of bits (leftmost drops 1 bit, rightmost drops 7 bits). Each subplot shows the evolution of the corresponding attack as the number of traces increases.

The attacks are, in every case, successful. Note that the mutual information decreases as the number of bits dropped increases. This is natural and can be easily explained by expanding Eq. 2 as Eq. 1 and noting that $H(\mathbf{U}|\mathbf{H})$ will only increase as $\mathbf{H}$ considers fewer bits of $\mathbf{Z}$.

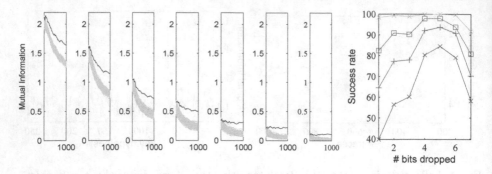

Fig. 2. Left: evolution of the performance of the attack from Fig. 1 for 1, 2, ..., 7 dropped bits. For each sub plot the X axis is number of traces and ranges from 200 to 1000. Correct key hypothesis is in black, incorrect key hypotheses are in grey. Right: success rate of the same attacks as in left. Each line represents a fixed number of traces. Bottommost line is 200 curves, next lines correspond to increments of 40 traces.

Albeit the attacks are eventually successful for any number of dropped bits, the distinguishing capabilities are not the same. Figure 2, right, studies the effect of different number of bits dropped on the success rate. Each line corresponds to a fixed amount of power traces, starting with 200 curves for the line at the bottom. All the parameters in the estimation process (number of bins) were kept constant, allowing for a fair comparison.

We can see two main tendencies in Fig. 2. First, as the number of dropped bits increases, from 1 to 5, the success rate also increases, for a given number of traces. Second, if the number of dropped bits continues increasing to 6 and 7, the success rate drops. Thus, for this particular target and this particular attack, the optimum number of bits to drop to maximize the success rate of this attack is 5. We believe that this fact is the result of the superposition of two opposite effects. As the number of dropped bits increases, the target becomes "more non-injective" and thus the attack works better. This is true until a certain threshold (in our case, 5 bits), from where the effect of the algorithmic noise introduced by the dropped, unmodelled bits is predominant. Note that this observation fits nicely with the classic result of Messerges in [11,12], who found that in the context of d-bit DPA, modelling only 3 bits from an 8-bit bus gave the best SNR for a fixed number of traces.

4   Non-injective Targets on AES

There are situations, however, in which an attacker might not be able to use the bit drop trick. As pointed out in the experiments in [18], if the leakage behaviour of the device consists only of higher order terms, the bit drop trick will fail. In this section, we note that an attacker who wishes to recover the key from an AES implementation is not restricted to only performing attacks against the Sbox output. Thus, he is not forced to employ the bit drop trick. Although we focus on the AES, we expect that any reasonable block cipher contains non-injective target functions.

In the rest of this section, we give an example of such a non-injective target that enables generic MIA attacks. This target was briefly mentioned in [1], in the following we provide a detailed study and show its attractive properties.

4.1 Suitable Targets

There are suitable non-injective targets for an attack in AES. Intuitively speaking, we want to find some intermediate value $\mathbf{Z}$ that results from the *compression* of public and secret data. One such value $\mathbf{Z}$ suitable for generic MIA attacks naturally arises as follows.

Let us take a closer look at the computation of the MixColumns transformation that is applied to the first column of the state during the first round. Name (u, v, w, x) the 4-byte input column to this MixColumns transformation. These 4 input bytes correspond to 4 output bytes of ShiftRows in the first round. Suppose that during the computation of the first output byte $2u \oplus 3v \oplus w \oplus x$ of this MixColumns invocation, the implementation handles the partial intermediate value $z = 2u \oplus 3v = 2S_{AES}(p_1 \oplus k_1) \oplus 3S_{AES}(p_6 \oplus k_6)$[1]. The target $z = 2u \oplus 3v$ is obviously non-injective (since it maps 16 bits of public input and 16 bits of secret input to 8 bits) and suitable for a generic MIA attack. Below we provide results of such an attack against our unprotected AES software implementation.

4.2 Practical Results

Since we are attacking a non-injective target, we can use directly $\mathbf{Z}$ as the predicted power consumption (without the bit drop trick), and proceed with a generic MIA attack on the 16 key bits (corresponding to key bytes 1 and 6). That is, we use the identity leakage model $\mathbf{H} = \mathrm{Id}(\mathbf{Z}) = \mathbf{Z}$.

To perform the attack without placing any assumption on the leakage behaviour, Mutual Information was estimated using histograms with 256 bins. In Fig. 3 we can see that the attack works correctly: the correct key stands out and the attack has a unique solution. Note also that the magnitude of the Mutual Information values is different than in the previous section, this is because we are targeting a different time sample, 523, corresponding to the computation of MixColumns.

4.3 Different Leakage Behaviours

The bit drop trick is known not to work against devices with highly non-linear leakage behaviours. However, a generic MIA attack against a non-injective target does not suffer from this limitation and can be used in such cases.

Unfortunately, we do not have access to a chip with highly non-linear leakage behaviour. For this reason, we resort to simulations to give an example of an attack against $z = 2u \oplus 3v$ on an hypothetical device that leaks as

---

[1] Note that the sixth Sbox output of the first round will be in state byte 5 after first round ShiftRows.

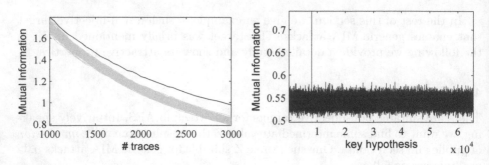

Fig. 3. Left: evolution of the generic MIA attack targeting the intermediate value $z = 2S_{\text{AES}}(p_1 \oplus k_1) \oplus 3S_{\text{AES}}(p_6 \oplus k_6)$. Correct key in black, incorrect keys in grey. Time sample index 523. Right: outcome of the attack using 3,000 traces.

$\mathbf{L}_{\text{device}}(\mathbf{Z}) = S_{\text{AES}}(\mathbf{Z})$ (resembling a highly non-linear leakage behaviour) and as $\mathbf{L}_{\text{device}}(\mathbf{Z}) = \text{HW}(S_{\text{AES}}(\mathbf{Z}))$ (resembling an encrypted bus scenario as explained in the following section).

Figure 4 shows the outcomes of these attacks when the simulated curves include Gaussian additive noise with standard deviation $\sigma = 1$. The attacks are successful in both cases $\mathbf{L}_{\text{device}}(\mathbf{Z}) = S_{\text{AES}}(\mathbf{Z})$ and $\mathbf{L}_{\text{device}}(\mathbf{Z}) = \text{HW}(S_{\text{AES}}(\mathbf{Z}))$. Mutual Information was estimated, as in previous cases, using histograms and 256 bins. The attacks are successful also when there is no noise $\sigma = 0$ in the simulated traces.

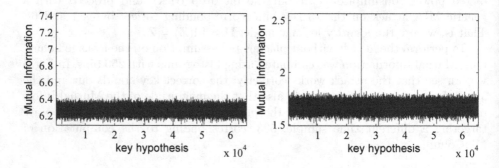

Fig. 4. Left: Simulation of the attack from Section under leakage behaviour $\mathbf{L}_{\text{device}} = S_{\text{AES}}$. Right: idem, under $\mathbf{L}_{\text{device}} = \text{HW}(S_{\text{AES}})$

To sum up, unlike the drop$_1$ strategy on the AES Sbox output, generic MIA attacks against non-injective target functions work under any leakage condition, any SNR level at the expense of a slightly more costly computational effort of 2^{16} key hypotheses.

5 Discussion

In this section we elaborate on the notable properties of the previous attack that are of practical relevance when attacking devices with encrypted buses. In addition, we comment on the possibility of mounting MIA attacks on later rounds and discuss the implications of a parallel implementation of the AES.

5.1 Arbitrary Leakage Model and Bus Encryption

As already stated in Sect. 4.3, generic MIA attacks against non-injective targets in AES will work with any leakage behaviour. This fact has important consequences for real-world devices that employ bus encryption (also called *bus scrambling*.) We can successfully apply the attack of Sect. 4.1 even if the attacker has only access to the leakage of some "encrypted" version of the intermediate value (under a constant key), instead of the leakage of the actual intermediate value. An advantage of this attack is that the adversary does not need to know the exact details of the "encryption" function (for example, the key might be unknown). The attacker launches the generic attack of Sect. 4.1 using as predictions the "unencrypted" values for the intermediate sensitive variable, disregarding the exact details of the encryption function. In what follows we explain why this attack returns the correct key.

For instance, consider a smart-card that "encrypts" the values before sending them over its bus[2]. Let $\mathbf{Y}$ be the "encrypted" value of $\mathbf{Z}$, that is, $\mathbf{Y} = \mathrm{enc}(\mathbf{Z})$ for some bus "encryption" function enc (which is a permutation). We claim that the following two attacks are equivalent (that is, have equal success rate):

1. A MIA attack against a device that handles the values in clear, $\mathbf{O} = \mathbf{L}_{\mathrm{device}}(\mathbf{Z})$ and the attacker predictions correspond to the values in clear, $\mathbf{H} = \mathbf{Z}$.
2. A MIA attack against a device that handles the intermediate values encrypted, $\mathbf{O} = \mathbf{L}_{\mathrm{device}}(\mathbf{Y})$ and the attacker uses as predictions the values in clear, $\mathbf{H} = \mathbf{Z}$.

We will show that both attacks produce the same values of mutual information, $I(\mathbf{L}_{\mathrm{device}}(\mathbf{Y}); \mathbf{L}_{\mathrm{model}}(\mathbf{Z})) = I(\mathbf{L}_{\mathrm{device}}(\mathbf{Z}); \mathbf{L}_{\mathrm{model}}(\mathbf{Z}))$, and thus have the same behaviour. We can develop Eq. (2) as

$$I(\mathbf{L}_{\mathrm{device}}(\mathbf{Y}); \mathbf{L}_{\mathrm{model}}(\mathbf{Z})) = I(\mathbf{L}_{\mathrm{device}}(\mathbf{Y}); \mathbf{L}_{\mathrm{model}}(\mathbf{Y}))$$
$$= I(\mathbf{L}_{\mathrm{device}}(\mathbf{Z}); \mathbf{L}_{\mathrm{model}}(\mathbf{Z})) \qquad (3)$$

where the first line results from $\mathbf{Y}$ and $\mathbf{Z}$ being related by a permutation (note that the attack from Sect. 4.1 uses $\mathbf{L}_{\mathrm{model}} = \mathrm{Id}$) and the second line results from $\mathbf{Y}$ and $\mathbf{Z}$ being identically (uniformly) distributed (thus, due to symmetry of

---

[2] Here we are assuming without loss of generality that the most leaking component of the smart-card is the bus. This assumption is just for illustration purposes and the following discussion is orthogonal to this assumption.

H, the value of $H(\mathbf{Z}) - H(\mathbf{Z}|\mathbf{L}_{\text{device}}(\mathbf{Z}))$ does not change if the events of $\mathbf{Z}$ are reordered).

Therefore, the previous result shows that the bus encryption has no effect on generic DPA attacks and is transparent to them. The attacker can recover the key observing leakage of the encrypted intermediate values, even if he ignores the exact details of the bus encryption mechanism and the exact leakage behaviour of the device.

5.2   Arbitrary Leakage Model and Absorbing Next Round Keys

The very same property used in the previous Subsect. 5.1 can be exploited to mount MIA attacks that use observations of intermediate values from the second round at a reduced number of key hypotheses. The rationale is similar: Suppose that the attacker chooses one output byte of MixColumns as the target, $z'' = 2u \oplus 3v \oplus w \oplus x$. Assume that the value z'' is later transformed into z''' through AddRoundKey and further into z^{IV} through SubBytes of the second round, $z''' = \text{AK}(z'')$ and $z^{IV} = \text{SB}(z''')$ as shown in Fig. 5. These operations merely permute z'' (they do not introduce any other "variable" data), and thus the result from Subsect. 5.1 can be applied. The attacker can perform the attack placing hypotheses on $\mathbf{Z}''$ as $\mathbf{L}_{\text{model}}(\mathbf{Z}'') = \text{Id}(\mathbf{Z}'')$ but he can use the observations $\mathbf{O}$ corresponding to the handling of the intermediate value from the second round such as z^{IV} with a 2^{32} work load. This is not possible with standard DPA, unless the attacker places 8 additional bits on the key hypothesis corresponding to one key byte from the second round, resulting in an attack with 2^{40} work load.

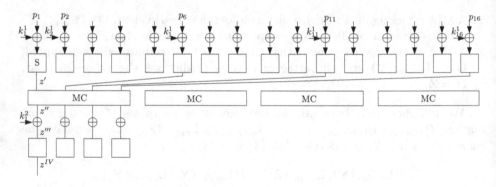

Fig. 5. A schematic representation of the computation of the first 1.5 rounds of AES. As explained in Sect. 5.2, the attacker can use the leakage coming from later in the computation, for instance, z''' after the next key addition or even z^{IV} after the Sbox lookup, without placing extra key hypotheses on the second round key k_1^2.

This means that the attacker can easily bypass the protections in the first round and exploit directly leakage from the second round to recover first round keys. This is helpful for the attacker if only the first round is protected with, for example, the masking countermeasure and highlights, again, the importance of not only masking the outer rounds, as e.g. discussed in [3].

5.3   What Happens if MixColumns Leaks in Parallel?

In Sect. 4.1, we assumed that the implementation computes MixColumns in a serial fashion. In this section, we analyse the case when this no longer holds, i.e., the implementation computes and leaks in parallel (for example, a hardware implementation using a 32-bit or 128-bit data path). In what follows we will work with a reduced exemplary data path of 16 bits (2 bytes). (The implications of the study can be extrapolated to any other bit width.)

Suppose that the observations O available to the attacker correspond to the simultaneous leakage $O = L_{\text{device}}(Z, N)$ of two output bytes z and n from first round MixColumns. Suppose the attacker sets z as target (and therefore n will be considered as "algorithmic noise") and executes the attack of Sect. 4.1. We can distinguish two cases:

1. The leakage contribution of Z can be "decoupled" from that of N. For instance, $L_{\text{device}}(Z, N) = HW(Z) + HW(N)$. Here the attacker can eventually cancel the algorithmic noise induced by the term $HW(N)$ (note that Z and N are statistically independent) and the attack will succeed. Another example of L_{device} that falls in this category is $L_{\text{device}}(Z, N) = HW(S_{\text{AES}}(Z)) + HW(S_{\text{AES}}(N))$.
2. The leakage contribution of Z cannot be "decoupled" from that of N. For instance, $L_{\text{device}}(Z, N) = HW(Z \oplus N)$. Here the attacker cannot cancel the algorithmic noise (the signal from Z is effectively "masked" with N, which by assumption is unknown to the attacker). Hence, the attack of Sect. 4.1 will not work. Another example that falls in this category is $L_{\text{device}}(Z, N) = HW(SHA(Z \| N))$ where $\|$ is concatenation and SHA is a cryptographic hash function.

The requirement for a leakage behaviour to belong to the first category is that the distribution of $L_{\text{device}}(Z, N)$ should still be informative about Z when the effect of N is marginalized, that is,

$$I(Z; \mathbb{E}_N[L_{\text{device}}(Z, N)]) > 0. \tag{4}$$

In fact we can also use the example of a MIA attack against an injective Sbox to illustrate the restriction of Eq. 4. We can rewrite $L_{\text{device}}(Z, N) = L_0(L_1(Z), L_2(N))$ where Z are 7 bits of the Sbox output and N is the other bit of the Sbox output. If L_0 is such that Eq. 4 holds, the trick of using drop_1 will work. On the other hand, if L_0 is such that Eq. 4 does not hold, the attack will fail.

Hence, in the case of a parallel MixColumns implementation, if L_0 is such that Eq. 4 does not hold, we would have to redefine the target value as $Z' = (Z, N)$, and we find ourselves in the same situation as if we were attacking a (large) injective Sbox. Hence, we would need to choose another suitable non-injective target, deeper in the algorithm, at the cost of more key hypotheses.

What does it mean to impose constraints on L_0? We point out that these restrictions on L_0 are easily met in practice. For example, the restrictions mean that we can allow arbitrary cross-talk between the wires that represent **Z**, and also arbitrary cross-talk between the wires that represent **N**, but there should not be only significant cross-talk between wires from both variables. Or, equivalently, leakage of **Z** can be "encrypted", and also that of **N**, but not jointly "encrypted". Intuitively, we allow arbitrary leakage of **Z** and of **N**, but impose some mild restrictions on how these individual leakages are combined (through L_0).

6   Conclusion

In this work, we elaborated on the practical properties of the bit drop trick, pointed out how generic DPA attacks can be mounted on the AES and showed their appealing properties when attacking devices with encrypted leakage or exploiting leakage from inner rounds. Echoing the title, generic attacks are certainly endowed with two-sided properties - curse or blessing depending on the concrete situation.

Acknowledgments. We thank the anonymous reviewers for their thorough evaluation. This work was supported in part by the Research Council of KU Leuven: GOA TENSE (GOA/11/007), by the Flemish Government FWO G.0550.12N and by the Hercules Foundation AKUL/11/19. Oscar Reparaz is funded by a PhD Fellowship of the Fund for Scientific Research - Flanders (FWO). Benedikt Gierlichs is Postdoctoral Fellow of the Fund for Scientific Research - Flanders (FWO).

References

1. Batina, L., Gierlichs, B., Prouff, E., Rivain, M., Standaert, F.-X., Veyrat-Charvillon, N.: Mutual information analysis: a comprehensive study. J. Cryptol. **24**, 269–291 (2011)
2. Bévan, R., Knudsen, E.W.: Ways to enhance differential power analysis. In: Lee, P.J., Lim, C.H. (eds.) ICISC 2002. LNCS, vol. 2587, pp. 327–342. Springer, Heidelberg (2003)
3. Biryukov, A., Khovratovich, D.: Two new techniques of side-channel cryptanalysis. In: Paillier, P., Verbauwhede, I. (eds.) CHES 2007. LNCS, vol. 4727, pp. 195–208. Springer, Heidelberg (2007)
4. Brier, E., Clavier, C., Olivier, F.: Correlation power analysis with a leakage model. In: Joye, M., Quisquater, J.-J. (eds.) CHES 2004. LNCS, vol. 3156, pp. 16–29. Springer, Heidelberg (2004)
5. Chari, S., Rao, J., Rohatgi, P.: Template attacks. In: Kaliski Jr., B.S., Koç, Ç.K., Paar, C. (eds.) CHES 2002. LNCS, vol. 2523, pp. 13–28. Springer, Heidelberg (2003)
6. Coron, J.-S., Kocher, P.C., Naccache, D.: Statistics and secret leakage. In: Frankel, Y. (ed.) FC 2000. LNCS, vol. 1962, pp. 157–173. Springer, Heidelberg (2001)
7. Gierlichs, B., Batina, L., Tuyls, P., Preneel, B.: Mutual information analysis. In: Oswald, E., Rohatgi, P. (eds.) CHES 2008. LNCS, vol. 5154, pp. 426–442. Springer, Heidelberg (2008)

8. Kocher, P.C.: Timing attacks on implementations of Diffie-Hellman, RSA, DSS, and other systems. In: Koblitz, N. (ed.) CRYPTO 1996. LNCS, vol. 1109, pp. 104–113. Springer, Heidelberg (1996)

9. Kocher, P.C., Jaffe, J., Jun, B.: Differential power analysis. In: Wiener, M. (ed.) CRYPTO 1999. LNCS, vol. 1666, pp. 388–397. Springer, Heidelberg (1999)

10. Mayer-Sommer, R.: Smartly analyzing the simplicity and the power of simple power analysis on smartcards. In: Paar, C., Koç, Ç.K. (eds.) CHES 2000. LNCS, vol. 1965, pp. 78–92. Springer, Heidelberg (2000)

11. Messerges, T.S., Dabbish, E.A., Sloan, R.H.: Investigations of power analysis attacks on smartcards. In: Proceedings of the USENIX Workshop on Smartcard Technology on USENIX Workshop on Smartcard Technology, WOST'99, Berkeley, CA, USA, p. 17. USENIX Association (1999)

12. Messerges, T.S., Dabbish, E.A., Sloan, R.H., Member, S.: Examining smart-card security under the threat of power analysis attacks. IEEE Trans. Comput. 51, 541–552 (2002)

13. Oswald, E.: On side-channel attacks and the application of algorithmic countermeasures. Ph.D thesis, Graz University of Technology (2003)

14. Schindler, W., Lemke, K., Paar, C.: A stochastic model for differential side channel cryptanalysis. In: Rao, J.R., Sunar, B. (eds.) CHES 2005. LNCS, vol. 3659, pp. 30–46. Springer, Heidelberg (2005)

15. Tiri, K., Hwang, D., Hodjat, A., Lai, B.-C., Yang, S., Schaumont, P., Verbauwhede, I.: Prototype IC with WDDL and differential routing – DPA resistance assessment. In: Rao, J.R., Sunar, B. (eds.) CHES 2005. LNCS, vol. 3659, pp. 354–365. Springer, Heidelberg (2005)

16. Veyrat-Charvillon, N., Standaert, F.-X.: Mutual information analysis: how, when and why? In: Clavier, C., Gaj, K. (eds.) CHES 2009. LNCS, vol. 5747, pp. 429–443. Springer, Heidelberg (2009)

17. Veyrat-Charvillon, N., Standaert, F.-X.: Generic side-channel distinguishers: improvements and limitations. In: Rogaway, P. (ed.) CRYPTO 2011. LNCS, vol. 6841, pp. 354–372. Springer, Heidelberg (2011)

18. Whitnall, C., Oswald, E.: A fair evaluation framework for comparing side-channel distinguishers. J. Cryptogr. Eng. 1(2), 145–160 (2011)

19. Whitnall, C., Oswald, E., Standaert, F.-X.: The myth of generic DPA.. and the magic of learning. In: Benaloh, J. (ed.) CT-RSA 2014. LNCS, vol. 8366, pp. 183–205. Springer, Heidelberg (2014). http://eprint.iacr.org/

Support Vector Machines for Improved IP Detection with Soft Physical Hash Functions

Ludovic-Henri Gustin[1,2], François Durvaux[1], Stéphanie Kerckhof[1(✉)],
François-Xavier Standaert[1], and Michel Verleysen[2]

[1] Crypto Group - ICTEAM, Université catholique de Louvain,
Louvain-la-Neuve, Belgium
{francois.durvaux,stephanie.kerckhof,fstandae}@uclouvain.be
[2] Machine Learning Group - ICTEAM, Université catholique de Louvain,
Louvain-la-Neuve, Belgium
michel.verleysen@uclouvain.be, lg.gustin@gmail.com

Abstract. Side-channel analysis is a powerful tool to extract secret information from microelectronic devices. Its most frequently considered application is destructive, i.e. key recovery attacks against cryptographic implementations. More recently, it has also been considered constructively, in the context of intellectual property protection/detection, e.g. through the use of side-channel based watermarks or soft physical hash functions. The latter solution is interesting from the application point-of-view, because it does not require any modification of the designs to protect (hence it implies no performance losses). Previous works in this direction have exploited simple (correlation-based) statistical tools in different (more or less challenging) scenarios. In this paper, we investigate the use of support vector machines for this purpose. We first argue that their single-class extension is naturally suited to the problem of intellectual property detection. We then show experimentally that they allow dealing with more complex scenarios than previously published, hence extending the relevance and applicability of soft physical hash functions.

1 Introduction

Protecting Intellectual Property (IP) from illegal use is an important issue for the development of markets based on third party designs (next referred to as IP cores). Different solutions have been proposed to mitigate this problem, among which permission-based and watermarking-based techniques are usual candidates. The first one consists in checking whether the system has the right permission before performing any operation (i.e. works *a priori*). Most common solutions are implemented with an enhanced security chip or a Physically Unclonable Function (PUF) that contain some secret [4,16,27,37]. If the IP gets the right answer to a defined challenge, it means that it is used properly and can start processing. The second family (i.e. watermarking-based protections) consists in hiding a piece a information for authentication or identification inside the IP, which will be recovered by its owner(s) if needed [3,21,22,26]. The inserted

E. Prouff (Ed.): COSADE 2014, LNCS 8622, pp. 112–128, 2014.
DOI: 10.1007/978-3-319-10175-0_9

information must be robust to noise and to slight transformations that may occur in the IP manipulation. It must also be invisible to the adversary. Recently, it has been proposed to place the mark in physical features such as the temperature, power consumption, ... of the device on which the IP is executed [6,40]. In opposition to the permission-based mechanism, which prevents illegally used IPs from running, watermarks can only detect this illegal use (i.e. they work *a posteriori*).

As an alternative to these proposals, Soft Physical Hash (SPH) functions are an *a posteriori* solution that also exploits information extracted from the physical features of a target circuit. The difference with the watermarking-based solution lies in the fact that the information extracted comes from the very characteristics of the implementation, and is not inserted by the IP owner. Therefore, and in contrast with both previous families, this solution does not need any piece of hardware to be added, and it cannot be removed or altered as it depends on the IP itself. SPH functions have been formalized together with IP detection infrastructures in [14], where the requirements for this solution to be effective (namely perceptual robustness and content sensitivity) have also been defined. They have first been applied in a simple case study of 8-bit software implementations, and next in the more challenging context of FPGA implementations [23].

While these previous works can be seen as encouraging proofs-of-concept, and validate the idea that SPH can be useful components in the detection of IP theft, the main question naturally remains to know how robust it is against challenging adversarial conditions. For example, can it be effective without knowing the inputs/outputs of the IP to detect?, how does it resist against re-compiled/re-synthesized IPs?, and (in the most interesting case of hardware IP) how does it react to other parasitic IPs running in parallel (i.e. when included in a larger system combining several proprietary designs)? In particular, the work in [23] suggested that simple instances of SPH (where the detection procedure is based on Pearson's correlation-based statistics) start to encounter some failures in the context of re-synthesized FPGA designs with a parasitic IP running in parallel. In this work, we aim to complement these first results, and consider Support Vector Machines (SVM) to enhance IP detection in such complex scenarios. For comparison purposes, we consider the same case study as [23] (i.e. six FPGA implementations of block ciphers) and show experimentally that SVM lead to significant (perceptual robustness and content sensitivity) improvements.

Why SVM? As IP detection infrastructures based on SPH functions exploit standard techniques from side-channel analysis, one can wonder why SVM are preferred to other more standard tools that usually improve over correlation-based statistics (e.g. templates [11] or stochastic approaches [34]). Before entering the core of the paper, we provide a brief argument in this respect. First, one can notice that SVM have been shown to provide an interesting alternative to such tools (see, e.g. [5,17,19,25]). So while it is unclear that they generally provide significant advantages over other distinguishers (especially in the context of "standard" first-order side-channel attacks where many statistics are equivalent to some extent [29]), they are at least expected to work reasonably in this context too. Second and more importantly, the problem of IP detection differs from the one of key recovery in one important aspect. Namely, the number of classes in key recovery is usually well identified (e.g. 256 when targeting the AES S-box output), while it is not enumerable in IP detection. Indeed, the IP owner can only characterize his own design, and the number and shape of suspicious IPs is a priori unknown. As a result, the single-class extension of SVM appears to be naturally suited to this context (since it only requires the knowledge of the reference IP during its characterization). Eventually, SVM are particularly interesting for dealing with large dimensionalities (e.g. large measurement traces in side-channel attacks), which contrasts with templates and stochastic approaches that work best if good points-of-interest have been identified. But the selection of such points-of-interest usually relies on criteria such as the signal-to-noise ratio, that (ideally) requires the knowledge of the different classes to discriminate (since they define the signal). So the fact that we do not need to find points-of-interest in SVM is appealing in our context. Summarizing, while we certainly do not rule out the possibility that other standard side-channel distinguishers provide further improvements to our results under certain heuristic assumptions, we believe SVM are natural candidates to investigate for enhanced IP detection.

The rest of the paper is structured as follows. Section 2 introduces the necessary background regarding the IP detection infrastructure, its underlying definitions, and the SVM classification tool. Section 3 instantiates our IP detection infrastructure. Experimental results in different contexts are presented and discussed in Sect. 4 and a conclusion is eventually given in Sect. 5.

2   Background

2.1   IP Detection Infrastructure

We take advantage of the IP detection infrastructure introduced in [14] and represented in Fig. 1. It essentially makes use of soft hash functions [24]. By contrast to cryptographic hash functions, for which the output string is highly sensitive to small perturbations of the input, soft hash functions are such that similar objects should return highly correlated digests (i.e. be *perceptually robust*), while different objects should produce uncorrelated ones (i.e. be *content-sensitive*). The SPH used in this paper are a variation of soft hash function, where we additionally extract a physical feature from the objects to protect. The resulting IP detection infrastructure embeds the following elements:

- *Object to protect:* this can be any type of IP (source code, netlist, layout).
- *Physical feature vector evaluation:* this process outputs an intermediate response that is expected to represent the object to characterize in the most accurate manner. In other words, this intermediate string must be very content-sensitive. It can correspond to any physical emanation of the device running the IP (e.g. power consumption, electromagnetic radiation, ...).
- *Extraction:* this (optional) process essentially applies some signal processing and summarizes the feature vector into a (usually smaller) output hash value,

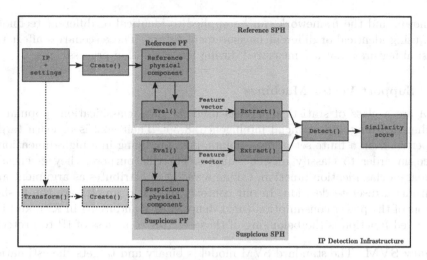

Fig. 1. Generic framework for IP detection.

that best trades content sensitivity for perceptual robustness (e.g. by selecting the "points of interest" in a side-channel measurement).

- *Detection:* this can be any statistical tool that allows determining the level of similarity between two hash values. Most side-channel distinguishers can be used for this purpose (e.g. Pearson's correlation coefficient in [14,23]).

As the detection of counterfeited IPs essentially works by comparing hash values, it is assumed that the IP owner has characterized the SPH function of his design. Note that this characterization process does not have to be done during development time, but may also be done after the product has been released. As indicated by the dotted part on Fig. 1, the suspicious IP may directly correspond to counterfeited designs, or slightly transformed ones. In the following, we will consider the re-synthesis of a design under a different set of constraints and the addition of a parasitic IP running in parallel as IP-preserving transformations. By contrast, a change of block cipher is naturally considered as non IP-preserving. In this context, the detection performances are measured with the content sensitivity and perceptual robustness properties defined as:

- *Perceptual robustness*: probability that two implementations that only differ by IP-preserving transformations lead to a similarity score higher than τ_r.
- *Content sensitivity*: probability that two implementations that differ by non-IP-preserving transformations lead to a similarity score lower than τ_s.

For the detection process to be successful, the condition $\tau_r \geq \tau_s$ must always be satisfied. Otherwise, a legitimate IP could be mistaken for a fraudulent one (or conversely). Eventually, such a generic framework can be run in different scenarios that make the detection more or less easy to perform. For example, the inputs/outputs of the design to protect and its source code can be known or unknown, and the framework can be applied to identical or different technologies, using identical or different measurement setups. These scenarios affect the physical features that are measured during the evaluation process.

2.2 Support Vector Machines

SVM are a class of statistical models used for data classification, popular in machine learning and artificial intelligence [8,39]. Their goal is to learn target properties from a finite set of data points, possibly living in a high-dimensional space, in order to classify unseen samples. For this purpose, they essentially estimate a classification function, taking a vector of attributes as argument and returning a discrete decision. In our context, the data samples are the hashed vectors of the power consumption (next denoted as $\mathbf{x}$ and living in $\mathbb{R}^n$), and the estimated function is the belonging of those vectors to a class of IP to protect.

Binary SVM. The standard SVM model is binary and targets the estimation of Boolean functions. It requires a supervised (i.e. profiled) learning with labels $\{-1, +1\}$, annotating each sample of the training dataset. Its goal it to output a correct label for the samples of an independent test set. Let us assume that the training set is composed of m samples $\mathbf{x_i} \in \mathbb{R}^n$, with $i = 1, .., m$. For each sample $\mathbf{x_i}$, let $y_i \in \{-1, +1\}$ be the associated label. The binary SVM will estimate a decision function g whose sign defines the binary outcome of the classifier. This function g is based on the construction of an hyperplane, separating the two classes with the largest possible margin, in the geometrical space of the vectors. The margin represents the distance between the hyperplane and the closest member(s) of both distributions, identical for both sides. Maximizing this quantity leads to a better discrimination ability on unseen samples. These concepts are illustrated in Fig. 2, handling a simple 2D classification task (diamonds vs. circles) where dashed lines are margin borders around the hyperplane.

Let $b \in \mathbb{R}$ and $\mathbf{w} \in \mathbb{R}^n$ be the parameters of the hyperplane, and $\mathbf{x}$ a data vector such that we have the following decision function:

$$g(\mathbf{x}) = \mathbf{w}^t \phi(\mathbf{x}) + b = \mathbf{w} \cdot \phi(\mathbf{x}) + b. \tag{1}$$

Here ϕ denotes a projection function that maps the data vectors into a higher (sometimes infinite) dimensional space. If ϕ is not defined as the trivial identity function (as in the figure), the hyperplane will be built in the projected space, usually called feature space (as opposed to the original data space). This allows to find non-linear boundaries in the data space, fitting to more complex observations. Equation (1) returns a quantity proportional with the analytical distance of a sample from the frontier ($d_{\mathbf{x_i}}$ in Fig. 2): the further the point, the more robust the classification. When further referring to the distance from the hyperplane, we will always mean an evaluation of the g function. Parameters b and $\mathbf{w}$ are obtained by solving the following constrained quadratic program:

$$\min_{\mathbf{w}, b} \quad \tfrac{1}{2} \mathbf{w}^t \mathbf{w}$$
$$\text{subject to } y_i * g(\mathbf{x_i}) \geq 1 \quad \forall i = 1, ..., m. \tag{2}$$

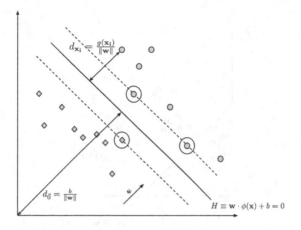

Fig. 2. Binary SVM with a 2D classification problem (the analytical distances from the hyperplane H to the origin and a datapoint $\mathbf{x_i}$ are given by d_0 and $d_{\mathbf{x_i}}$, respectively).

When the problem is feasible with respect to the constraints, the data is said to be linearly separable in the feature space. As the problem is convex, there is a guarantee to find a unique global minimum. Usually, solvers compute the solution of the associated dual problem, with dual variables α_i, $i = 1, .., m$. This leads to an alternative formulation of the decision function g, whose sign provides the outcome of the classification of a new data vector $\mathbf{x}$:

$$f_{classify}(x) = sign \left(\sum_{\mathbf{x_i} \in SV} \alpha_i y_i \, \mathbf{K}(\mathbf{x_i}, \mathbf{x}) + b \right). \tag{3}$$

Here, SV denotes a subset of the original training set called the support vectors. They are solely needed to define the hyperplane associated with non-zero dual variables ($\alpha_i \neq 0$), and represent the closest points to the hyperplane living on the margin (circled in Fig. 2). The symmetric kernel function $\mathbf{K}$ implicitly takes into account the projection ϕ in the dual problem: $\mathbf{K}(\mathbf{x_i}, \mathbf{x_j}) \equiv \phi(\mathbf{x_i})^T \phi(\mathbf{x_j})$. It substitutes the dot product appearing in Eq. (1). This *kernel trick* allows the usage of complex projections without explicitly computing ϕ, which can be computational intensive (or even impossible) in high dimensions (e.g. using a Gaussian Kernel as we did in our experiments - see next - is equivalent to using an infinite-dimensional feature space).

The Single Class Extension. Binary SVM require both positive and negative samples in the training set. In the context of IP detection, this is not directly applicable since the negative distribution is unknown (i.e. we cannot expect to obtain samples for all the IP that have been developed by third parties). For this reason, we will use a slightly more complex version of SVM called "unsupervised One-class SVM" (OSVM). It allows getting rid of any hypothesis made about the distribution of the negative class, by working with unlabeled data. This extension

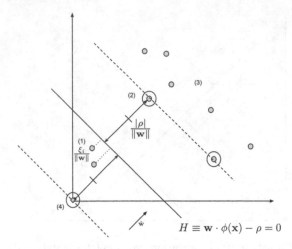

Fig. 3. OSVM with a 2-dimensional classification problem in which we distinguish four classes of points: (1) outliers with their penalty cost ξ_i, (2) support vectors, (3) other points, (4) the origin (the analytical half margin size is given by $\frac{|\rho|}{\|\mathbf{w}\|}$).

was derived from the binary case thanks to the work of B. Schölkopf et al. in the early 2000's [35, 36]. The main underlying idea is to estimate the geometrical region concentrating most points of the distribution, by building a separating hyperplane having a maximum margin from the origin. For this purpose, OSVM rely on the assumption that the dataset contains a small fraction of outliers that will be considered as rejected samples. They associate these rejected samples with a penalty cost, that depends on their distance from the hyperplane (cfr. Fig. 3), and is added to the original SVM objective function (adjusted with a new parameter $\nu \in]0, 1]$). Let $\rho \in \mathbb{R}$ and $\mathbf{w} \in \mathbb{R}^n$ be the parameters of the hyperplane and $\xi_i \in \mathbb{R}^+$ a penalty cost associated with $\mathbf{x_i}$ ($i = 1, .., m$), it leads to the following quadratic problem:

$$\min_{\mathbf{w}, \rho, \xi_i} \quad \tfrac{1}{2}\mathbf{w}^T\mathbf{w} + \tfrac{1}{\nu m}\sum_{i=1}^{m}\xi_i - \rho$$
$$\text{subject to } \mathbf{w} \cdot \phi(\mathbf{x_i}) \geq \rho - \xi_i \qquad \xi_i \geq 0, \forall i = 1, ..., m, \tag{4}$$

with the classification function according to dual variables α_i given by:

$$f_{classify}(\mathbf{x}) = sign\left(\sum_{\mathbf{x_i} \in SV} \alpha_i \, K(\mathbf{x_i}, \mathbf{x}) - \rho\right). \tag{5}$$

Instantiation. In this work, we use a Gaussian Radial Basis Function (RBF) kernel within the OSVM model:

$$K(\mathbf{x_i}, \mathbf{x_j}) = \exp\left(\frac{-\|\mathbf{x_i} - \mathbf{x_j}\|}{2\sigma^2}\right) = \exp(-\gamma\|\mathbf{x_i} - \mathbf{x_j}\|), \quad \gamma, \sigma > 0. \tag{6}$$

Such a kernel has been proven to work well for a wide range of application data. Moreover, it can be shown that this RBF-OSVM model guarantees to find a solution (i.e. any dataset $x_1, x_2, ..., x_m$ is separable under a Gaussian kernel [35]). We also observed that the computational overhead of using that kernel instead of the linear one was negligible in our case. Eventually, building a model requires the setting of the parameters γ and ν. We selected them thanks to a grid-search, by optimizing the true positive rate TPR, defined as:

$$TPR = \frac{\#TP}{\#TP + \#FN}, \tag{7}$$

where $\#TP$ represents the frequency of vectors from the validation set correctly detected, while $\#FN$ is the frequency of vectors wrongly rejected by the model. This function has been evaluated on a dataset independent of the training set (the validation set) to avoid overfitting the parameters with the data used to train the model itself. Our choice of objective function is admittedly heuristic. As will be clear next, it was sufficient to obtain good experimental results (and in particular, we verified that it improved over randomly selected parameters).

3   Specification of the IP Detection Infrastructure

Given the tools presented in Sect. 2, we now need to incorporate SVM in the generic IP detection infrastructure of Fig. 1. In this work we use the same datasets as in the earlier studies exposed in [23], leading to an identical evaluation phase. This section will briefly recall our measurement setup, valid for both reference and suspicious traces, then describes what the construction of the OSVM model implies in the extraction and detection phases. The LibSVM library suite was used to process the data, train and evaluate models, as it supports OSVM and many more features related to SVM classification tasks (see [10] for the details).

Object to Protect. We investigated an FPGA case-study and took the netlists of five lightweight ciphers (HIGHT [18], ICEBERG [38], KATAN [9], NOEKEON [13] and PRESENT [7]), together with the one of the AES Rijndael, as objects to protect. These netlists were synthesized for a Xilinx Virtex-II Pro FPGA. We built only one reference model per protected IP, from its measurement obtained in a standalone context (i.e. with no parasitic IP in parallel), loaded and synthesized under standard options. Conversely, suspicious traces were measured in three different contexts corresponding to increasingly difficult detection challenges, namely identical standalone IPs, re-synthesized (still standalone) designs, and re-synthesized designs with parasitic IP running in parallel.

Evaluation Phase. We used the FPGA power consumption as physical feature vector. Measurement traces were obtained by measuring the voltage variations around a shunt resistor on the Sasebo-G board [1]. The device was running at 24 MHz, and the oscilloscope sampling frequency was set to 2.5 GHz.

Extraction Phase. This step slightly differs from the one in previous papers, since we consider profiled side-channel distinguishers. Hence, while the extraction procedure applied to the reference IP (at the top of Fig. 1) and the suspicious IP (at the bottom of the figure) was the same when using Pearson's correlation as detection tool, it has to differ in the case of SVM. Namely, the reference IP extraction outputs the parameters of the hyperplane that define the IP to protect, and the physical feature vectors of the suspicious IP will be compared to this model (rather than to other feature vectors). Besides and as usual, the extraction could include additional signal processing and selection of points-of-interest (e.g. some dimensionality reduction can be used to speed up computations). In our experiments, these optional steps were usually ignored and we manipulated the full measurement traces directly. As mentioned in introduction, it is an interesting feature of SVM to allow dealing with such large dimensionalities efficiently. The only exception is our last case-study, where averaging was performed on the traces, to reduce the noise and improve detection capabilities.

As a technical remark, note that the OSVM require to work with vectors having identical dimension, both for the training and the evaluation of the model. Since different IPs were processed, a common length had to be fixed. We choose to work with the shortest iteration length among our 6 IPs (i.e. $n = 1251$ dimensions for the AES). This implicitly assumes that the traces can be synchronized, i.e. starting all their encryption cycle at t_0. This can be achieved by different means, e.g. computing the correlation over a sliding window. In our experiments, we observed that these cropped physical feature vectors were sufficiently specific to their generating IP for making effective detections. Both reference and suspicious extraction processes include this cropping operation as a preliminary step.

Detection Phase. Each suspicious hash value is evaluated in the reference model. For this purpose, the OSVM simply outputs a value that is proportional to the distance of this hash from the decision boundary (i.e. the SVM hyperplane), whose sign indicates the classification outcome. As previously mentioned, we will call it a "distance" for simplicity, and it can be interpreted as a similarity score lying on an open scale, whose expression is given by Eq. (5).

4   Case Studies

In this section, we analyze our RBF-OSVM model applied in four detection scenarios of increasing complexity. First we tackled the basic case of suspicious traces emitted by a standalone design for each of the 6 IPs. Secondly, we evaluated the case where each design was re-synthesized under a different set of constraints. We then moved to a more challenging context, by including a parasitic IP running in parallel of the tested design (which is aimed to emulate a complex system). Eventually, we considered a combination of all these cases (which turned out to be more challenging, as we will explain). In practice, we made use of 2000 measurements per IP in each context. Two thirds were used for building the reference model (i.e. 1333 traces) and the remaining third was used as suspicious IP traces for validating the detection (i.e. 667 traces). We only present results for the case where PRESENT is the IP to protect since it was shown previously (and confirmed in our experiments) that it is the one leading to the most ambiguities (hence the most challenging to detect). Unless specified otherwise, the context in which the IP-detection is performed in the next subsections is the following: the inputs provided to the IP are unknown, we do not have access to the source code, and the same device and measurement setup was used for all the tests.

Before describing our experimental results in details, it is important to note a difference between (i) the classification outcome provided by the OSVM and (ii) the detection outcomes resulting from the use of the OSVM distance as a similarity score. In the first case, classification returns whether a sample has been properly labeled (belonging or not to the reference set) according to its relative position to the hyperplane. In the second case, detection is successful if the perceptual robustness threshold is higher than the content sensitivity one (we further call the difference the disambiguation gap). In theory (and, as it turns out, in practice too), it may of course happen that the classification fails while still giving rise to a sufficient disambiguation gap. This possibility essentially follows from the fact that the IP detection infrastructure can rely on carefully chosen thresholds for the content sensitivity and perceptual robustness.

4.1   Standalone FPGA Designs

The results of the IP detection infrastructure applied to the standalone case are presented in Fig. 4. Each column contains the similarity scores corresponding to one particular suspicious IP. The black dashed line corresponds to the decision threshold used for classification. The solid green line and red dashed line respectively correspond to the perceptual robustness threshold (i.e. the PRESENT trace having the lowest similarity score), and the content sensitivity threshold (i.e. the highest similarity score among all the non-PRESENT traces). Having positive similarity scores for the PRESENT IP implies that the classification outcome is correct. Having the perceptual robustness threshold higher than the content sensitivity one implies that the detection is successful. Note that the figure is in fact a zoom of the region of interest of Fig. 8 available in appendix. In this zoomed version, we omitted the AES IP which is (as expected) quite different from other IPs, and is therefore strongly rejected by the OSVM model. More precisely, we measured a voltage swing about 5 times larger in intensity, explaining this distance. This observation remains valid for the other detection scenarios and the AES was therefore left out of all the figures, for readability reasons. We observe from Fig. 4 that all non-PRESENT IPs are correctly rejected by the OSVM classification since their scores lie below the decision threshold. PRESENT traces expose mostly positive scores, which was expected. A few outliers have however been rejected by the classification (<2.1 %). This is mainly a consequence of the construction properties of the OSVM model. Still, the detection is successful in all our standalone experiments, as a disambiguation gap separates PRESENT traces from non-PRESENT ones. In [23], this case required to work with 10 times averaged traces (both for suspicious and reference traces) to get a similar result.

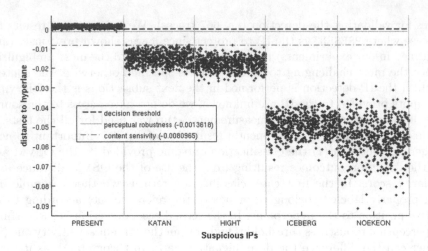

Fig. 4. Similarity scores for single suspicious standalone traces with unknown inputs.

4.2 Re-Synthesized FPGA Designs

In this second (more challenging) scenario, we consider the application of a first IP-preserving transformation by a potential counterfeiter. Namely, we evaluate the impact of a placement and routing of our different block cipher implementations under a different set of constraints (i.e. with parameters to optimize the area of the layout instead of its timing). This reconfiguration does not modify the IP, which lies one abstraction layer above (source code or netlist).

Our experiments are summarized in Fig. 5. We notice a slight increase of suspicious PRESENT wrongly rejected by the classification, as the model was originally trained to recognize traces corresponding to another set of synthesis parameters. Yet, the re-synthesis does not significantly affect the mean similarity scores of the other IPs, which still guarantees a safe disambiguation gap. This result is interesting since in the previous work [23], such a detection was not possible in an unknown-plaintext scenario and the authors further had to average their traces to reach good IP detection probabilities. So it already suggests a useful improvement of our OSVM-based approach. Note that the set of synthesis options that we used in this section could equally stand as reference. We observed that the results are roughly identical independent of this a priori choice.

4.3 Parasitic IP Running in Parallel

We now study a practically-important case-study, where not only the suspicious IP would run on the target platform but also a parasitic one. As previously mentioned, the goal is to emulate a more realistic system where the IP is inserted in a neighborhood made of other running IPs, hence altering the measured signal. As a first step in this direction, we investigated the case of a Linear Feedback

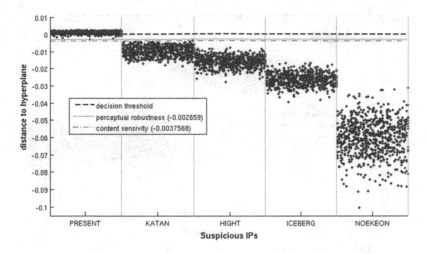

Fig. 5. Similarity scores for single suspicious re-synthesized traces, unknown inputs.

Shift Register (LFSR) generating an "algorithmic noise" essentially proportional to its size (and studied sizes of up to 2018 bits). Figure 6 illustrates the results of our IP detection infrastructure in the most challenging (2048-bit) context. This time, we observe that the OSVM classification clearly fails at detecting the IP-preserving transformation applied on PRESENT, as their traces lie below the decision threshold. However, there still exists a disambiguation gap that ensures a perfect detection. So at this stage, the interest of the OSVM-based detection is clearly exhibited. Indeed, [23] provided an efficient detection until a 1024-bit LFSR, while our method allows us to detect IP with a 2048-bit LFSR. Moreover, this previous work had to harness data dependencies (i.e. known inputs) and averaging on selected points-of-interest for lowering the noise in the extraction phase, conversely to our work that considers unknown inputs and raw traces.

4.4   Advanced Detection Scenario

We finally investigated an advanced scenario where we combined the suspicious traces from all the previous contexts in a single experiment. This choice was mainly motivated by the observation of Figs. 5 and 6, where we can see that the content sensitivity threshold in the parasitic IP scenario is higher than the perceptual robustness threshold in the re-synthesized one. It means that when these scenarios are mixed together, false detection or false non-detection may occur whatever detection threshold is chosen. Such pathological cases typically happen with the most challenging detection of PRESENT with parasitic IP from a re-synthesized KATAN, and required two modifications/improvements.

First, we had to move to a known input context (i.e. we kept the key and plaintext constant during the experiments), allowing us to take advantage of data dependencies in the traces. Intuitively, this is because the information

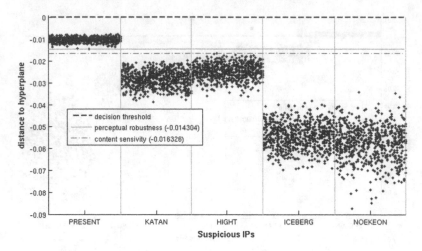

Fig. 6. Similarity scores for single suspicious traces with parasitic IP, unknown inputs.

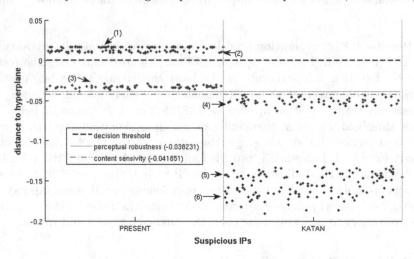

Fig. 7. Similarity scores for 10 times averaged suspicious traces in a combined setting with known inputs: (1) standalone PRESENT, (2) re-synthesized PRESENT, (3) PRESENT with paras. IP, (4) standalone KATAN, (5) re-synthesized KATAN, (6) KATAN with paras. IP.

exploited in the feature vectors captured in an unknown input scenario essentially corresponds to a correlation between the operations performed by the IP and its measured power consumption. The known input context adds a correlation between the data being manipulated and the measurements. Hence, a new (data-dependent) reference model was built for PRESENT. Secondly, and in order to get rid of a part of the algorithmic noise, we worked with averaged suspicious traces rather than single ones. This implies a slight change in the definition of the extraction phase, which now includes this 10 times averaging step.

The corresponding results are reported in Fig. 7. This time, only PRESENT and KATAN are considered as suspicious IPs, since they are the most challenging ones. Combining averaging with a characterization of the data dependencies naturally gave rise to more detailed profiles for the reference IP, as can be observed in this zoomed figure. First, we can now distinguish the different PRESENT IPs, even after IP-preserving transformations. For example the similarity scores of standalone (1) and re-synthesized (2) designs are nicely separated (even though the latter ones have the right classification label, as expected). Next, we observe that the classification outcome for PRESENT with parasitic IP is even worse than before (moving from -0.01 to -0.04, roughly). However, this new model strongly rejects the different variants of KATAN (4,5,6). So the tweaked IP detection returns a positive disambiguation gap that makes these two implementations distinguishable. It is interesting to note that in this last combined context, we required both an improvement of the signal (i.e. data dependencies) and a reduction of the noise (i.e. averaging) to obtain successful detections.

5 Conclusion

Our results further validate SPH functions as a useful ingredient in the detection of IP theft. They also suggest a context in which SVM (and their single-class extension) seem an appealing side-channel distinguisher. Of course, IP protection is an extremely challenging (and sometimes hard to define) problem. So the tools in this work should only be seen as one part of the solution. In particular, determined adversaries could envision more complex IP-preserving transformations than the ones we analyzed, and evaluating a change of technology between the reference and suspicious IP is an interesting scope for further research. Hopefully, there also remains tracks for improving the detection results, either by advanced statistical tools, or by improved (e.g. localized electromagnetic) measurements. In other words, there is a wide range of tradeoffs, between the complete reverse engineering of a chip and the characterization of its power consumption, that can be used by designers to protect their IP. As the cheapest and most flexible solution for this purpose, we believe SPH functions can at least be used as a first step in this direction, prior to more expensive approaches.

Acknowledgements. This work has been funded in parts by the Walloon region WIST program project MIPSs and by the European Commission through the ERC project 280141 (acronym CRASH). François-Xavier Standaert is an Associate Researcher of the Belgian Fund for Scientific Research (FNRS-F.R.S.). Stéphanie Kerckhof is a PhD student funded by a FRIA grant, Belgium.

A   Stand-Alone FPGA Designs: Complete Results

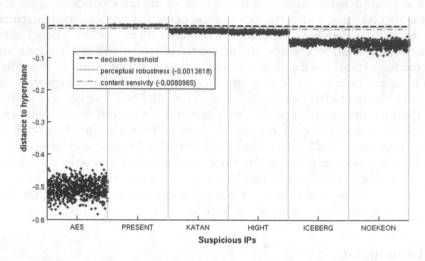

Fig. 8. Similarity scores for single suspicious standalone traces with unknown inputs.

References

1. Sasebo-G measurement board. http://www.rcis.aist.go.jp/special/SASEBO/ SASEBO-G-en.html
2. 32nd IEEE Symposium on Security and Privacy, S&P 2011, 22–25 May 2011, Berkeley, California, USA. IEEE Computer Society (2011)
3. Abdel-Hamid, A.T., Tahar, S., Aboulhamid, E.M.: A survey on IP watermarking techniques. Des. Autom. Emb. Sys. **9**(3), 211–227 (2004)
4. Baetoniu, C.: FPGA IFF copy protection using Dallas semiconductor/Maxim DS2432 secure EEPROMs. XAPP780, May 28 (2010)
5. Bartkewitz, T., Lemke-Rust, K.: Efficient template attacks based on probabilistic multi-class support vector machines. In: Mangard [29], pp. 263–276
6. Becker, G.T., Kasper, M., Moradi, A., Paar, C.: Side-channel based watermarks for integrated circuits. In: HOST, pp. 30–35 (2010)
7. Bogdanov, A., Knudsen, L.R., Leander, G., Paar, C., Poschmann, A., Robshaw, M.J.B., Seurin, Y., Vikkelsoe, C.: PRESENT: An ultra-lightweight block cipher. In: Paillier and Verbauwhede [31], pp. 450–466
8. Boser, B.E., Guyon, I.M., Vapnik, V.N.: A training algorithm for optimal margin classifiers. In: Proceedings of the 5th Annual Workshop on Computational Learning Theory, COLT '92, pp. 144–152, New York, NY, USA, 1992. ACM (1992)
9. De Cannière, C., Dunkelman, O., Knezevic, M.: KATAN and KTANTAN - a family of small and efficient hardware-oriented block ciphers. In: Clavier and Gaj [13], pp. 272–288
10. Chang, C.-C., Lin, C.-J.: LIBSVM: A library for support vector machines. ACM Trans. Intell. Syst. Technol. **2**, 27:1–27:27 (2011). (Software. http://www.csie.ntu.edu.tw/cjlin/libsvm)

11. Chari, S., Rao, J.R., Rohatgi, P.: Template attacks. In: Jr. et al. [21], pp. 13–28
12. Clavier, C., Gaj, K. (eds.): CHES 2009. LNCS, vol. 5747. Springer, Heidelberg (2009)
13. Daemen, J., Peeters, M., Assche, G.V., Rijmen, V.: Nessie proposal: NOEKEON. http://gro.noekeon.org/
14. Durvaux, F., Gérard, B., Kerckhof, S., Koeune, F., Standaert, F.-X.: Intellectual property protection for integrated systems using soft physical hash functions. In: Lee, D.H., Yung, M. (eds.) WISA 2012. LNCS, vol. 7690, pp. 208–225. Springer, Heidelberg (2012)
15. Goubin, L., Matsui, M. (eds.): CHES 2006. LNCS, vol. 4249. Springer, Heidelberg (2006)
16. Guajardo, J., Kumar, S.S., Schrijen, G.-J., Tuyls, P.: FPGA intrinsic PUFs and their use for IP protection. In: Paillier, P., Verbauwhede, I. (eds.) CHES 2007. LNCS, vol. 4727, pp. 63–80. Springer, Heidelberg (2007)
17. Heuser, A., Zohner, M.: Intelligent machine homicide - breaking cryptographic devices using support vector machines. In: Schindler and Huss [34], pp. 249–264
18. Hong, D., Sung, J., Hong, S., Lim, J., Lee, S., Koo, B., Lee, C., Chang, D., Lee, J., Jeong, K., Kim, H., Kim, J., Chee, S.: HIGHT: A new block cipher suitable for low-resource device. In: Goubin and Matsui [16], pp. 46–59
19. Hospodar, G., Gierlichs, B., De Mulder, E., Verbauwhede, I., Vandewalle, J.: Machine learning in side-channel analysis: a first study. J. Cryptogr. Eng. 1(4), 293–302 (2011)
20. Kaliski Jr., B.S., Koç, Ç.K., Paar, C. (eds.): CHES 2002. LNCS, vol. 2523. Springer, Heidelberg (2003)
21. Kahng, A.B., Lach, J., Mangione-Smith, W.H., Mantik, S., Markov, I.L., Potkonjak, M., Tucker, P., Wang, H., Wolfe, G.: Watermarking techniques for intellectual property protection. In: DAC, pp. 776–781 (1998)
22. Kahng, A.B., Mantik, S., Markov, I.L., Potkonjak, M., Tucker, P., Wang, H., Wolfe, G.: Robust IP watermarking methodologies for physical design. In: DAC, pp. 782–787 (1998)
23. Kerckhof, S., Durvaux, F., Standaert, F.-X., Gérard, B.: Intellectual property protection for FPGA designs with soft physical hash functions: First experimental results. In: HOST, pp. 7–12 (2013)
24. Lefèbvre, F., Czyz, J., Macq, B.M.: A robust soft hash algorithm for digital image signature. ICIP 2, 495–498 (2003)
25. Lerman, L., Bontempi, G., Markowitch, O.: Side channel attack: an approach based on machine learning. In: Constructive Side-Channel Analysis and Secure Design, COSADE (2011)
26. Lewandowski, M., Meana, R., Morrison, M., Katkoori, S.: A novel method for watermarking sequential circuits. In: HOST, pp. 21–24 (2012)
27. Linke, B.: Xilinx FPGA IFF copy protection with 1-wire SHA-1 secure memories. XAPP3826, July 21 (2006)
28. Mangard, S. (ed.): CARDIS 2012. LNCS, vol. 7771. Springer, Heidelberg (2013)
29. Mangard, S., Oswald, E., Standaert, F.-X.: One for all - all for one: unifying standard differential power analysis attacks. IET Inf. Secur. 5(2), 100–110 (2011)
30. Paillier, P., Verbauwhede, I. (eds.): CHES 2007. LNCS, vol. 4727. Springer, Heidelberg (2007)
31. Rao, J.R., Sunar, B. (eds.): CHES 2005. LNCS, vol. 3659. Springer, Heidelberg (2005)
32. Roy, B., Meier, W. (eds.): FSE 2004. LNCS, vol. 3017. Springer, Heidelberg (2004)

33. Schindler, W., Huss, S.A. (eds.): COSADE 2012. LNCS, vol. 7275. Springer, Heidelberg (2012)
34. Schindler, W., Lemke, K., Paar, C.: A stochastic model for differential side channel cryptanalysis. In: Rao and Sunar [32], pp. 30–46
35. Schölkopf, B., Platt, J.C., Shawe-Taylor, J.C., Smola, A.J., Williamson, R.C.: Estimating the support of a high-dimensional distribution. Neural Comput. 13(7), 1443–1471 (2001)
36. Schölkopf, B., Smola, A.J., Williamson, R.C., Bartlett, P.L.: New support vector algorithms. Neural Comput. 12(5), 1207–1245 (2000)
37. Simpson, E., Schaumont, P.: Offline hardware/software authentication for reconfigurable platforms. In: Goubin, L., Matsui, M. (eds.) CHES 2006. LNCS, vol. 4249, pp. 311–323. Springer, Heidelberg (2006)
38. Standaert, F.-X., Piret, G., Rouvroy, G., Quisquater, J.-J., Legat, J.-D.: ICEBERG : An involutional cipher efficient for block encryption in reconfigurable hardware. In: Roy and Meier [33], pp. 279–299
39. Vapnik, V.N.: The Nature of Statistical Learning Theory. Springer, New York (1995)
40. Ziener, D., Teich, J.: Power signature watermarking of IP cores for FPGAs. Sig. Process. Syst. 51(1), 123–136 (2008)

Collision-Correlation Attack
Against a First-Order Masking Scheme
for MAC Based on SHA-3

Luk Bettale[(⊠)], Emmanuelle Dottax, Laurie Genelle, and Gilles Piret

Oberthur Technologies, 420 Rue D'Estienne D'Orves, 92700 Colombes, France
{l.bettale,e.dottax,g.piret}@oberthur.com,
laurie.genelle.p@gmail.com

Abstract. In 2012, KECCAK has been selected as the SHA-3 competition winner, and NIST recently announced the standardization of a keyed version for message authentication codes. In this paper, we consider an implementation of this keyed function, protected against first-order side-channel analysis with an efficient masking scheme proposed by the designers. We show that this masking scheme is vulnerable to a non-linear collision-correlation attack. Our attack advantageously needs no assumption on device-depending parameters, and hence constitutes an interesting alternative to second-order differential analysis.

Keywords: SHA-3 · Side-channel analysis · Collision attack · Masking scheme

1 Introduction

Hash functions are part of the foundations of information security. When the security of existing standards SHA-1 and SHA-2 has been questioned, the National Institute of Standards and Technology (NIST) announced a hash function competition for a new standard SHA-3. On October 2012, KECCAK [5] was selected as the winner of this competition. This hash function can naturally be used in a keyed version to build a Message Authentication Code (MAC) algorithm. As KECCAK uses the sponge construction [4], a cryptographically secure MAC can be obtained by simply hashing the concatenation of the secret key and the message. NIST recently announced that the standardization of this mechanism is planned as well [20]. As any algorithm manipulating secret data, such a keyed function might be vulnerable to Side-Channel Analysis (SCA).

The principle of SCA is to exploit dependencies that exist between a physical leakage (*e.g.*, power consumption, electromagnetic emanations) produced during the execution of a cryptographic algorithm and the value of the manipulated secrets. The variety of attacks ranges from *Simple* SCA (*e.g.*, [21,29]) to the

---

Laurie Genelle - This work was done while this author was a member of the Cryptography Group of Oberthur Technologies.

E. Prouff (Ed.): COSADE 2014, LNCS 8622, pp. 129–143, 2014.
DOI: 10.1007/978-3-319-10175-0_10

more advanced *Differential* SCA (DSCA) (*e.g.,* [12, 22]) or *Template Attacks* [14]. To prevent these attacks, *masking* is an appropriate countermeasure [13]. The principle is to inject randomness in the cryptographic algorithm computations, so that the leakage observed at a given time does not depend on the secret anymore. To do so, each *sensitive variable x* is split into several shares, by means of random *masks*. For instance, a Boolean *first-order* masking scheme involves one random mask r and the masked value $x \oplus r$. *Second-order* DSCA (2O-DSCA) can then be used to defeat the masking (*e.g.,* [24, 25, 27]). Their principle is to combine leakages related to the manipulation of two variables that are jointly dependent on the sensitive variable (*e.g.,* r and $x \oplus r$). However, 2O-DSCA require a significantly higher number of leakage observations.

A specific type of SCA is *collision-based* SCA. The principle is to detect collisions between internal values. The idea has been used for the first time against a DES implementation [32]. An attack against AES has been later proposed [31], and several improvements have followed [8–10]. Interestingly, this kind of attack can naturally be extended against some masked implementations [15]. The advantage of these attacks when compared to classical DSCA is that they do not rely on a leakage model, and hence do not require an *a priori* knowledge of the device leakage function. This can be of particular interest, for instance when no information on the device under attack is available, or for some leakage models (*e.g.,* [1, 16]).

In this paper, we focus on the KECCAK-based MAC [4] considered by NIST for standardization, protected against first-order DSCA with an efficient masking scheme introduced in [6]. We notice that the same mask is used on both the input and the output of the non-linear step, and exploit it with a collision detection based on correlation computation similar to [15]. It allows us to gather equations involving secret bits. We show how to build a system of non-linear equations that can be solved efficiently to recover the full key. To assess the feasibility of the attack, we also give the results of some experiments done with simulations.

As already mentioned, a collision-based attack advantageously does not require any knowledge on the leakage function of the target device. Moreover, our attack does not rely on any other device dependent parameters either, contrary to previous collision-based SCA (*e.g.,* [15] fixes a correlation threshold to distinguish collisions, which implies a profiling step). Hence this attack can be used in a non-profiled setting.

The rest of the paper is organized as follows. Section 2 sums up the previous works in the field of collision-based SCA. Section 3 briefly introduces KECCAK and notations, and summarizes existing results regarding SCA. Section 4 is devoted to the description of our new attack, while Sect. 5 exhibits the results of our experiments for the correlation attack. Eventually, Sect. 6 concludes this paper.

2   Collision-Correlation SCA

The principle of collision-correlation attacks is to detect collisions (*i.e.* identical state at two different times) using side-channel leakage during a cryptographic computation, and to use them in order to retrieve the key. The first premise of the idea can be found in the BigMac attack [35]. Several results on asymmetric implementations came afterwards, which we do not discuss further as our concern is symmetric implementations.

The first application of collision attacks to a symmetric implementation has been suggested by Schramm et al.in an attack on DES [32], and improved by Ledig et al. [23]. One year later it was applied on AES [31]. The idea of these papers was to use collision detection in conjunction with a differential crypt-analysis style attack; as a consequence these attacks are chosen plaintext ones (contrary to classical DSCA). As the collisions that are exploited are related to the encryption of different messages, one can efficiently protect against them by using a masking countermeasure (as masks change from one encryption to another, collisions are no longer meaningful).

On the contrary the so-called *linear collision attack* presented in [15] and [26] can be used to attack masked implementations as well. It applies to the first round of a SPN (Substitution-Permutation Network) block cipher with bijective S-boxes (like AES). The principle is to detect collisions at the output of two S-boxes: that is, we try to obtain equations of type $S(p_i \oplus k_i) = S(p_j \oplus k_j)$. They imply $p_i \oplus k_i = p_j \oplus k_j$ (by bijectivity of the S-box) and thus $k_i \oplus k_j = p_i \oplus p_j$. In [15] a masked implementation is attacked, but with the masks being identical for all S-boxes. In [26] masks are different, but the authors acknowledge that the attack is made possible because of a flaw in the hardware implementation.

The seminal papers [32] and [31] made the hypothesis that collisions are easy to detect. However in noisy environments it is a challenge in itself. To this end a few papers elaborate on using statistical tools. Bogdanov [10] proposes the use of binary and ternary votings. The drawback of these tools is that a threshold has to be fixed *a priori* to decide whether a given pair of traces corresponds to a collision or not. Gérard and Standaert [18] and Roche and Lomné [30] use a different technique to overcome this problem: still in the context of linear collision attacks, they derive a complete probability distribution for all differences of pairs of key bytes $\Delta_{a,b} = k_a \oplus k_b$, and consider the word $(\Delta_{1,1}, \Delta_{1,2}, \dots, \Delta_{15,16})$ as a noisy version of a codeword corresponding to the key. Then they use decoding techniques to retrieve it.

The attacks aforementioned only consider linear equations, which imposes to be very restrictive on the location of the bytes that are expected to collide. In [11] Bogdanov et al. go one step further by exploiting several different types of collisions; each such collision transposes into a non-linear equation. Collisions between bytes in the first and in the second round of AES are considered, as well as collisions between bytes in the first round and bytes in the last round. Faugère's F4 algorithm [17] is then used to solve the system of non-linear equa-tions.

This technique results in a reduction of the number of measurements needed for successful key recovery. However it applies to non masked implementations.

3   Side-Channel Analysis of KECCAK

3.1   Introduction to KECCAK

We here briefly present KECCAK as specified in [5] and introduce notations for
the rest of the paper.

KECCAK is a family of functions with a variable-length input M and a fixed-
length output Z, based on a sponge construction which iterates a permutation
f on an internal state. The input is first padded and split in r-bit blocks, which
are *absorbed* sequentially into an internal state by a bitwise XOR operation. The
output is *squeezed* from the state. The overall hashing process is depicted in
Fig. 1: r is called the *bit-rate*, and c the *capacity*. The value b = r + c is the
width of the permutation.

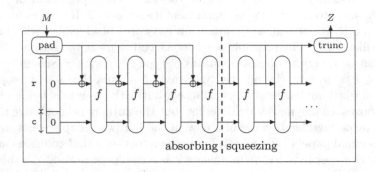

Fig. 1. KECCAK

Seven variants of the permutation are defined, with parameter $\mathtt{b} = 25w$
ranging from 25 to 1600 ($w = 2^i, i \in \{0, \dots, 6\}$); however $\mathtt{b} = 1600$ ($w = 64$)
is the only value that has been submitted to the competition. The state A is
organized as a set of $5 \times 5 \times w$ bits with (x, y, z) coordinates. $A[x][y][z]$ denotes
the bit at position (x, y, z), with indexes starting from 0, where x, y coordinates
are taken modulo 5, and z coordinate is taken modulo w.

The function f is an iterated permutation over $\mathbb{Z}_2^b$ consisting in the repetition
24 times of a round function which is the composition of five primitives: $\iota \circ \chi \circ
\pi \circ \rho \circ \theta$. At round i, they are defined as follows:

- $\theta : A[x][y][z] \leftarrow A[x][y][z] + \sum_{y'=0}^{4} A[x-1][y'][z] + \sum_{y'=0}^{4} A[x+1][y'][z-1]$;
- $\rho : A[x][y][z] \leftarrow A[x][y][z - (t+1)(t+2)/2]$, where t depends on x and y;
- $\pi : A[x][y][z] \leftarrow A[x'][y'][z]$, with $\begin{pmatrix} x \\ y \end{pmatrix} = \begin{pmatrix} 0 & 1 \\ 2 & 3 \end{pmatrix} \begin{pmatrix} x' \\ y' \end{pmatrix}$;
- $\chi : A[x][y][z] \leftarrow A[x][y][z] + (A[x+1][y][z] + 1) \cdot A[x+2][y][z]$;
- $\iota : A \leftarrow A + \mathrm{RC}[i]$;

where additions and multiplications are performed in GF(2), and RC[i] is a
round constant.

It is possible to build a MAC based on this function by simply taking as input the concatenation of a secret key K and a message M and truncating the output to p bits, with p < c: $\text{KECCAK}_K(M) = \lfloor \text{KECCAK}(K \| M) \rfloor_p$. Thanks to the sponge construction, this MAC function is secure [4].

3.2   Side-Channel Analysis of KECCAK

Considerations about side-channel analysis of keyed versions of KECCAK have been first presented by the designers at the SHA-3 conference [3]. They look at keyed versions of KECCAK in general and focus on the security evaluation of countermeasures. They propose to use a classical first-order masking scheme for software implementations, where each sensitive variable is split into two shares. Let R and S denote the two shares of the state A: $A = R \oplus S$. Secure evaluation of a linear function is easy to implement: let λ denotes the linear layer $\lambda = \pi \circ \rho \circ \theta$, one has just to compute $\lambda(R)$ and $\lambda(S)$. The non-linear function χ can be computed on the shares without manipulating the sensitive variables. To ease reading, we will omit y and z indexes and simply note a_x for $A[x][y][z]$ (the same holds for R and S). If the sensitive bits a_x, a_{x+1}, a_{x+2} are represented by the shares r_x, r_{x+1}, r_{x+2} and s_x, s_{x+1}, s_{x+2} (i.e. $a_x = r_x + s_x$ and so on), the authors propose to implement the χ operation

$$a_x \leftarrow a_x + (a_{x+1} + 1) \cdot a_{x+2}$$

as follows:

$$r_x \leftarrow r_x + (r_{x+1} + 1) \cdot r_{x+2} + r_{x+1} \cdot s_{x+2}$$
$$s_x \leftarrow s_x + (s_{x+1} + 1) \cdot s_{x+2} + s_{x+1} \cdot r_{x+2} \, . \tag{1}$$

This masking scheme has been improved in [6]. The idea is to fix one of the shares during one execution, say share S, so that (1) can be rewritten as:

$$r_x \leftarrow r_x + (r_{x+1} + 1) \cdot r_{x+2} + r_{x+1} \cdot s_{x+2} + (s_{x+1} + 1) \cdot s_{x+2} + s_{x+1} \cdot r_{x+2}$$
$$s_x \leftarrow s_x \, . \tag{2}$$

Doing so, the processing of S through the linear part λ can be saved by pre-computing the value $Y = S \oplus \lambda(S)$. The linear part can then be implemented as:

$$R \leftarrow \lambda(R) \oplus Y$$
$$S \leftarrow S \, .$$

The designers also propose in [3] a hardware architecture protected against first-order attacks, based on a threshold implementation with three shares. The same subject has been further studied in [2], and the masking scheme has been improved recently by [7]. We do not detail these works here as we are interested in software implementations.

Additionally, some papers deal with side-channel analysis of unprotected implementations of the KECCAK-based MAC. In [37] and [34], the authors consider classical DSCA and exhibit the different algorithm steps that can be targeted in order to recover the full key: the absorbing phase, the θ and the χ

operations. Depending on the key length, different attack paths are identified. Only a short section of [37] is devoted to KECCAK, hence scenarios for all possible key lengths are not presented. This is done in [34], and some of these attacks are put into practice on an FPGA implementation. The classical first-order Boolean masking schemes introduced in [3,6] are adequate countermeasures against these attacks.

In the next section, we show how one can mount a collision attack on the optimized version of the masking scheme.

4   A Collision-Correlation Attack on Masked Keyed KECCAK

When the enhanced masking scheme (2) is implemented, the same value is used to mask both the input and the output of χ. This setting can be used to efficiently detect collisions between these variables. In this section, we first present an overview of the attack principle in a non-masked setting, then we focus on the algebraic aspects and finally we explain how the masking scheme allows to detect collisions.

4.1   Attack Principle

As already said, we consider the keyed function that consists in hashing the concatenation of a key and a message (in this order). Without loss of generality and as proposed in [4], we assume that the key is first padded to a complete input block, so that the state value obtained after absorbing the key can be precomputed. The goal of our attack is to retrieve this secret state, which is called the key in the following.

The attack focuses on the χ operation in the first round of the f function. We denote by M the $\mathbf{r}$-bit input message and K the 25 w-bit key. Both M and K can be viewed as a 3-dimensional state. Let $M[x, y, z] = 0$ when $(5\,x + y)\,w + z > r$. In the first round of f, the following operations are performed:

1. $A \leftarrow M \oplus K$
2. $A \leftarrow \lambda(A) = \pi \circ \rho \circ \theta(A)$
3. $A \leftarrow \chi(A)$
4. $A \leftarrow \iota(A)$.

More specifically, at bit level for χ operation, we have

$$A[x, y, z] \leftarrow A[x, y, z] + (A[x + 1, y, z] + 1) \cdot A[x + 2, y, z],$$

for each x, y, z, $0 \leqslant x < 5$, $0 \leqslant y < 5$, $0 \leqslant z < w$. Let us assume that a collision is found during the χ step, that is, it exists x, y, z such that

$$A[x, y, z] + (A[x + 1, y, z] + 1) \cdot A[x + 2, y, z] = A[x, y, z]$$
$$\iff (A[x + 1, y, z] + 1) \cdot A[x + 2, y, z] = 0. \tag{3}$$

Such a collision gives valuable information on the secret. Indeed, let $M' = \lambda(M)$ and $K' = \lambda(K)$. As λ is a linear transformation, it holds that $\lambda(M \oplus K) = \lambda(M) \oplus \lambda(K) = M' \oplus K'$. Equation (3) becomes

$$(M'[x+1,y,z] + K'[x+1,y,z] + 1) \cdot (M'[x+2,y,z] + K'[x+2,y,z]) = 0. \quad (4)$$

All bits $M'[x,y,z]$ can be known by computing $\lambda(M)$. Thus, (4) is a quadratic equation in 2 variables representing the bits of K'. If an attacker succeeds in recovering all bits of K', she just has to compute $\lambda^{-1}(K')$ to recover K.

The attack is split in two steps: the collision detection which allows to recover equations, and the algebraic system solving which allows to recover the key from the equations. In the following, we show that if an attacker is able to recover enough equations, she is able to recover the secret key K. In the next section we first assume that collisions have been reliably detected on any bit of the state and focus on the resulting algebraic system. Afterward in Sect. 4.3, we address the problem of detecting such collisions on a masked implementation.

4.2 Algebraic Collision Attack

To present our attack, we first suppose that during the execution of a keyed KECCAK, an attacker is able to detect a collision between an input bit and an output bit of the first round χ for any input message M. Say that an attacker detects collisions when processing n messages $M^{(1)}, \ldots, M^{(n)}$. We denote by t_i the number of collisions obtained with the message $M^{(i)}$, $1 \leqslant i \leqslant n$. We denote by $(x_{i,j}, y_{i,j}, z_{i,j})$ the position of the j-th bit collision found with message $M^{(i)}$, $1 \leqslant j \leqslant t_i$. Finally, let $M'^{(i)} = \lambda(M^{(i)})$. The attacker obtains several equations similar to (4) as follows:

$$((M'^{(i)} \oplus K')[x_{i,1}+1, y_{i,1}, z_{i,1}] + 1) \cdot ((M'^{(i)} \oplus K')[x_{i,1}+2, y_{i,1}, z_{i,1}]) = 0,$$

$$\vdots \qquad\qquad (5)$$

$$((M'^{(i)} \oplus K')[x_{i,t_i}+1, y_{i,t_i}, z_{i,t_i}] + 1) \cdot ((M'^{(i)} \oplus K')[x_{i,t_i}+2, y_{i,t_i}, z_{i,t_i}]) = 0,$$

for each i, $1 \leqslant i \leqslant n$. Note that each equation involves only 2 variables. If these equations are gathered according to y and z, one obtains smaller independent systems in only 5 variables. Let $m_{y,z}$ be the number of gathered equations, we denote by $f_1^{(y,z)}, \ldots, f_{m_{y,z}}^{(y,z)}$ the polynomials composing one such small system:

$$\mathcal{F}_{y,z} = \begin{cases} f_1^{(y,z)}(K'[0,y,z], \ldots, K'[4,y,z]) = 0 \\ \qquad\qquad \vdots \\ f_{m_{y,z}}^{(y,z)}(K'[0,y,z], \ldots, K'[4,y,z]) = 0, \end{cases} \quad (6)$$

for each y, $0 \leqslant y < 5$, z, $0 \leqslant z < w$. The equations of each subsystem depend on the messages $M^{(1)}, \ldots, M^{(n)}$ that have been chosen. The number $m_{y,z}$ of equations is also related to the input messages and their number.

Proposition 1. *For a given key K, there are at most 15 different equations in each system $\mathcal{F}_{y,z}$.*

Proof. When a message M is known, each equation (4) involves only 2 unknown variables $K'[x+1,y,z]$ and $K'[x+2,y,z]$. For each value x, $0 \leqslant x < 5$, Eq. (4) holds if and only if one of the following equations holds:

(i) $M'[x+1,y,z] = K'[x+1,y,z] + 1$ and $M'[x+2,y,z] = K'[x+2,y,z] + 1$
(ii) $M'[x+1,y,z] = K'[x+1,y,z]$ and $M'[x+2,y,z] = K'[x+2,y,z]$
(iii) $M'[x+1,y,z] = K'[x+1,y,z] + 1$ and $M'[x+2,y,z] = K'[x+2,y,z]$.

So we have 3 possible equations for each x, $0 \leqslant x < 5$.   □

With enough detected collisions, one would obtain a total of $5 \times w$ small systems (6) of at most 15 equations in 5 variables. Solving each system independently gives 5 secret bits $K'[0,y,z], \ldots, K'[4,y,z]$. Algebraic systems (6) can be solved by exhaustive search (only 2^5 possibilities). If a small system does not contain enough equations, several solutions may exist, which will leave us at the end with a set of candidates for K to be exhaustively tested. To summarize, the overall attack process is as follows.

1. Detect collisions coming from n different messages.
2. Build the $5 \times w$ small systems $\mathcal{F}_{y,z}$ for $0 \leqslant y < 5$, $0 \leqslant z < w$.
3. Solve each system $\mathcal{F}_{y,z}$. Let $\mathcal{V}_{y,z}$ be the set of solutions of $\mathcal{F}_{y,z}$.
4. Build all candidates K' from the $\mathcal{V}_{y,z}$ (there are $\prod_{y,z} \#\mathcal{V}_{y,z}$ candidates).
5. Compute $K = \lambda^{-1}(K')$ for all K'. Exhaustively search the correct key.

It has to be emphasized that the number of solutions of the small systems (6) may be a blocking factor in the attack. The more collisions are detected, the more the small systems are determined, and the better the attack is in terms of efficiency. Figure 2 illustrates the overall process.

4.3   Collision Detection

The success of the above algebraic collision attack depends on the ability to detect a collision between the input and the output of the χ function (*i.e.*, in the same execution). As explained in Sect. 2, collision detection from side-channel leakage has been widely studied lately, mostly on the AES block cipher. The problem in KECCAK is a bit different.

The collision detection on AES generally targets two outputs of an S-box, and hence can advantageously correlate the traces during the whole S-box computations. In our attack, we need to detect collisions between two intermediate values that collide in two different sequences of instructions. Often, this means narrowing the compared traces to a few instructions. The main difficulty is that, depending on the leakage of the device, two different values could have a similar leakage. Let L be the device's leakage function, in general $(\mathrm{L}(a) = \mathrm{L}(b)) \not\Rightarrow (a = b)$. This is the case for instance if L is the Hamming weight. Hence in general, detecting such collisions may not be possible.

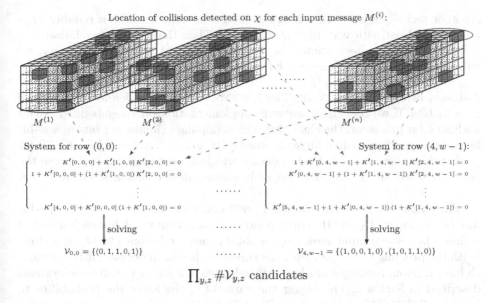

Fig. 2. General view of the attack: collisions detected on several input messages are modeled as algebraic equations and gathered in small systems according to the corresponding row. Each system is solved independently. We obtain candidates for $\lambda(K)$. The correct key K is finally found by inverting λ.

Interestingly, the masking scheme presented in Sect. 3 will help to detect collisions. Indeed, suppose that one looks for a collision between two variables a and b which are masked with the same mask r: let $\widetilde{a} = a \oplus r$ and $\widetilde{b} = b \oplus r$ be the masked values. When $a = b$, it holds that $\widetilde{a} = \widetilde{b}$ for any value of r. Thus the correlation between the leakages related to $\widetilde{a}$ and $\widetilde{b}$ is an adequate tool to detect the desired collision, as for classical leakage functions, it also holds that

$$(\forall r, \mathrm{L}(a \oplus r) = \mathrm{L}(b \oplus r)) \Rightarrow (a = b).$$

We can hence use the collision-correlation analysis technique [15] to take advantage of the fact that the implementation is masked.

As stated in [15,26], one advantage of the collision-correlation is that the attacker does not need to make an assumption on the leakage model[1]. Contrary to a classical DSCA, we do not correlate the leakages against a prediction function, but against other leakages supposed to leak exactly in the same way. The main drawback is that we need to detect a *high enough* correlation, that is, to decide whether a correlation corresponds to a collision. At least two approaches are possible. Either the device has been profiled beforehand, in which case the correlation value for a collision can be known in advance. This assumption is made in [15] where the authors use a threshold to detect collisions.

---

[1] But of course, we need to find where the sensitive variables are manipulated. We will not describe this process and assume it has already been done.

Another technique is to use enough messages so that a collision reliably happens (or at least with very high probability). Then the highest correlations are collisions. This has been studied in [30] in the case of AES. In this paper, we will consider both approaches for KECCAK.

Collision detection in KECCAK. The KECCAK algorithm is defined on words of $w = 64$ bits. If we consider a software implementation on an embedded device with an ℓ-bit processor, the algorithm will manipulate chunks of ℓ bits of a w-bit lane, corresponding to an ℓ-bit state word $(A[x, y, k\,\ell], \dots, A[x, y, k\,\ell + \ell - 1])$ for given values of x, y and k. Such a device will leak on ℓ-bit data, and hence the correlation will detect collisions on ℓ-bit values. Most common sizes are $\ell = 8$, $\ell = 16$ or $\ell = 32$.

From now on, the term "collision" will denote a collision between an ℓ-bit word of the input of χ and the corresponding ℓ-bit output word. For each detected collision in a single input message, we obtain then ℓ relations like (4) at a time. With the profiling technique, after the threshold has been decided, it is sufficient to hash random messages until enough relations are found to solve the systems described in Sect. 4.2. The bigger the value of ℓ, the lower the probability to have a collision. This probability will determine the number of messages needed to reach the necessary amount of equations. In the non-profiled approach, ℓ also determines the number of messages required to be able to probabilistically detect a collision. In both cases (profiled and non-profiled), the value ℓ is an important parameter for the success of our attack. In what follows, we study the probability for a collision to happen.

Collision probability of KECCAK. The probability to obtain a collision on a word depends on the probability of collision for one bit (*i.e.*, the probability that (4) is satisfied), and on the word size ℓ.

Proposition 2. *In* KECCAK, *given a size ℓ, if the bits of the internal state A are uniformly distributed, then for any values x, y, k, $0 \leqslant x < 5$, $0 \leqslant y < 5$, $0 \leqslant k < \frac{w}{\ell}$, the probability that $(A[x, y][k\,\ell], \dots, A[x, y][(k + 1)\,\ell - 1])$ is equal to $(\chi(A)[x, y][k\,\ell], \dots, \chi(A)[x, y][(k + 1)\,\ell - 1])$ is $\left(\frac{3}{4}\right)^{\ell}$.*

Proof. For a given triplet (x, y, z), the bit collision $A[x, y, z] = \chi(A)[x, y, z]$ is equivalent to have Eq. (3) satisfied. Equation (3) is false only when $A[x+1, y, z] = 0$ and $A[x + 2, y, z] = 1$ (1 case among 4), and true otherwise (3 cases among 4). If A is uniformly distributed, (3) is then true with probability $\left(\frac{3}{4}\right)$. Equations for $A[x, y, z]$ and $A[x, y, z']$ with $z' \neq z$ are independent from one another. Then the probability to have an ℓ-bit collision is $\left(\frac{3}{4}\right)^{\ell}$.   □

We recall that the input of χ is $A = \lambda(M \oplus K)$. If the input M of keyed KECCAK is uniformly chosen, we may suppose that the input of the χ function in the first round is also uniform. During a single execution of the χ function, each word has a probability $p = \left(\frac{3}{4}\right)^{\ell}$ to collide. The whole KECCAK state is composed of $25 \times \frac{w}{\ell}$ words. Having at least one collision during a single execution of KECCAK is the complementary event of having no collision in any of the $25 \times \frac{w}{\ell}$ words. The probability to have at least one collision is then $1 - (1 - p)^{25 \times \frac{w}{\ell}}$. This value is given in Table 1 for several usual values of ℓ.

Table 1. Probability to have at least one collision during a single KECCAK execution.

Bit-size ℓ	8	16	32
prob. collision	$(1 - 10^{-9})$	0.635	0.005

According to Table 1, for $\ell = 8$ or $\ell = 16$, the probability to have at least one collision is quite high, contrary to the attacks on the AES. A profiling step is then not necessary to detect a collision. The higher correlations obtained from the $\frac{25\,w}{\ell}$ correlations are collisions with high probability.

Remark 1. As in the attacks on the AES, it is possible to build a set of messages such that for any ℓ-bit word of the state, a collision occurs for at least one of these messages. In the case of KECCAK, as the collision probability is high, using random messages is a better strategy (less messages are needed).

5   Experiments

In this section we give some experiments regarding the algebraic collision attack. We consider the setting $\ell = 8$ and we try to determine the feasibility of the attack depending on the number of available messages. Even when the considered set of messages allows to have one collision equation for each bit of the state, the system may have too many valid solutions. More messages are needed for the system to have one unique solution, or at least a sufficiently low number of solutions so that an exhaustive search is possible. We summarize in Table 2 the number of collisions, obtained equations and solutions observed in average.

According to Table 2, 70 messages are enough to mount the algebraic attack with an extra exhaustive search on 2^{20} key candidates. For all messages,

Table 2. Algebraic attack behavior depending on the number of messages for $\ell = 8$ bits leakages. The table shows the number of collisions $\#C$, the number of equations $\#\mathcal{F}_{y,z}$ and the number of solutions $\#\mathcal{V}$ of the attack. The values are averaged over 20 executions of the attack.

n	0	1	20	50	60	70	80	90	140	170
$\#C$ (avg.)	0	20.4	177.3	199.0	199.7	199.8	199.9	200	200	200
$\#\mathcal{F}_{y,z}$ (avg.)	0	0.5	7.4	12.2	13.1	13.6	14.0	14.3	14.9	15.0
$\#\mathcal{V}$ (avg.)	2^{1600}	2^{1558}	2^{589}	2^{78}	2^{38}	2^{20}	379.0	19.4	1.1	1

the collisions have to be reliably found (no false collisions). The success rate of the attack depends on the success rate of the collision detection, which is related to the attacked device and the detection technique.

As a proof of concept, we simulated our attack in the following framework: we consider a device whose leakage on an $\ell = 8$ bits variable is the sum between the Hamming weight of this variable and an independent noise. The latter is modeled with a Gaussian distribution centered in zero and with a standard deviation σ. We give in Fig. 3 an example of the correlations obtained for various numbers of executions for a fixed input message. The traces in black correspond to the 8-bit words that are actually colliding. It can be seen that these are the more correlated.

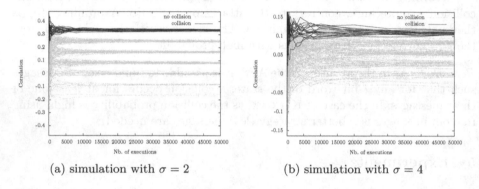

(a) simulation with $\sigma = 2$ (b) simulation with $\sigma = 4$

Fig. 3. Correlations obtained for 8-bit leakages according to the number of executions.

We consider the collision detection step of our attack to be successful when the highest correlation obtained for a non-collision is significantly above the lowest correlation obtained for a collision. The success rate of this step can be experimentally computed according to the number of executions for different σ. For instance, when $\sigma = 2$ (Fig. 3a), only 4 500 executions are needed to have 100 % of correct collisions (averaged over 100 trials). This value has to be multiplied by the number of messages needed to succeed in the algebraic solving part. This amounts to 315 000 total executions to reach a 100 % success rate. For $\sigma = 4$ (Fig. 3b), a total of 3 500 000 executions are needed. Experiments with other leakage models and comparison to second order DSCA are available in Appendix A.

6   Conclusion

In this paper, we have presented the first collision-correlation attack on an implementation of a MAC based on SHA-3, secure against first-order DSCA. This attack builds an algebraic system from the detected collisions. We have given a full description of this system, and we have studied in detail the feasibility of the attack. As any collision-based SCA, our attack does not require knowledge of the leakage function. Moreover, the collision detection of our attack requires no knowledge of any other characteristic of the component. Thus this attack can advantageously be used in a non-profiled setting, when no information on the device is available.

A   Comparison with Second-Order DSCA

We compare our new attack to second-order DSCA for different leakage models studied in the literature [16]. For the 2O-DSCA, we make predictions in the HW model and we use Pearson's linear correlation coefficient as a distinguisher [12]. We use the normalized product as a combination function [28,33]. The considered leakage models for our simulations are the Hamming Weight of the byte (HW), a polynomial combination of the bits of degree two (*quad*), and a polynomial combination of the bits not bounded on the degree (*full*). For the HW leakage model, we used the same noise level as the simulations in [30]. We have adapted the noise level to keep the same signal-to-noise ratio for the two other leakage functions. The number of executions needed are given in Table 3.

Table 3. Number of executions needed to perform our attack and a 2O-DSCA according to the leakage model (simulations).

	HW	*quad*	*full*
This attack	315 000 × 70	200 000 × 70	5 000 × 70
2O-DSCA	600 000	>1 500 000	>1 500 000

We observe that for both the *quad* and *full* leakage functions, the 2O-DSCA proves to be less efficient than our attack (more traces are needed). This is due to the fact that the predicted and actual leakage functions are no more linearly related. In such cases, we conclude that a collision-correlation attack is a valuable alternative to 2O-DSCA.

References

1. Akkar, M.-L., Bévan, R., Dischamp, P., Moyart, D.: Power analysis, what is now possible. In: Okamoto, T. (ed.) ASIACRYPT 2000. LNCS, vol. 1976, pp. 489–502. Springer, Heidelberg (2000)
2. Bertoni, G., Daemen, J., Debande, N., Le, T.H., Peeters, M., Van Assche, G.: Power analysis of hardware implementations protected with secret sharing. In: 45th Annual IEEE/ACM International Symposium on Microarchitecture Workshops (MICROW), pp. 9–16. IEEE Computer Society (2012)
3. Bertoni, G., Daemen, J., Peeters, M., Van Assche, G.: Building power analysis resistant implementations of Keccak. In: Second SHA-3 Candidate Conference (2010)

4. Bertoni, G., Daemen, J., Peeters, M., Van Assche, G.: Cryptographic Sponge Functions, Version 0.1 (2011)
5. Bertoni, G., Daemen, J., Peeters, M., Van Assche, G.: The Keccak Reference, Version 3.0 (2013)
6. Bertoni, G., Daemen, J., Peeters, M., Van Assche, G., Van Keer, R.: Keccak implementation overview, Version 3.2 (2012)
7. Bilgin, B., Daemen, J., Nikov, V., Nikova, S., Rijmen, V., Van Assche, G.: Efficient and first-order DPA resistant implementations of Keccak. In: Francillon, A., Rohatgi, P. (eds.) Smart Card Research and Advanced Applications. LNCS, vol. 8419, pp. 187–199. Springer, Heidelberg (2014)
8. Biryukov, A., Khovratovich, D.: Two new techniques of side-channel cryptanalysis. In: Paillier, P., Verbauwhede, I. (eds.) CHES 2007. LNCS, vol. 4727, pp. 195–208. Springer, Heidelberg (2007)
9. Bogdanov, A.: Improved side-channel collision attacks on AES. In: Adams, C., Miri, A., Wiener, M. (eds.) SAC 2007. LNCS, vol. 4876, pp. 84–95. Springer, Heidelberg (2007)
10. Bogdanov, A.: Multiple-differential side-channel collision attacks on AES. In: Oswald, E., Rohatgi, P. (eds.) CHES 2008. LNCS, vol. 5154, pp. 30–44. Springer, Heidelberg (2008)
11. Bogdanov, A., Kizhvatov, I., Pyshkin, A.: Algebraic methods in side-channel collision attacks and practical collision detection. In: Chowdhury, D.R., Rijmen, V., Das, A. (eds.) INDOCRYPT 2008. LNCS, vol. 5365, pp. 251–265. Springer, Heidelberg (2008)
12. Brier, E., Clavier, C., Olivier, F.: Correlation power analysis with a leakage model. In: Joye and Quisquater [19], pp. 16–29
13. Chari, S., Jutla, C., Rao, J., Rohatgi, P.: Towards sound approaches to counteract power-analysis attacks. In: Wiener [36], pp. 398–412
14. Chari, S., Rao, J., Rohatgi, P.: Template attacks. In: Kaliski Jr., B.S., Koç, Ç.K., Paar, C. (eds.) CHES 2002. LNCS, vol. 2523, pp. 13–29. Springer, Heidelberg (2003)
15. Clavier, C., Feix, B., Gagnerot, G., Roussellet, M., Verneuil, V.: Improved collision-correlation power analysis on first order protected AES. In: Preneel, B., Takagi, T. (eds.) CHES 2011. LNCS, vol. 6917, pp. 49–62. Springer, Heidelberg (2011)
16. Dabosville, G., Doget, J., Prouff, E.: A new second-order side channel attack based on linear regression. IEEE Trans. Comput. 62(8), 1629–1640 (2013)
17. Faugère, J.C.: A new efficient algorithm for computing Gröbner bases (F4). J. Pure Appl. Algebra 139(1–3), 61–88 (1999). (http://www-salsa.lip6.fr/jcf/Papers/F99a.pdf)
18. Briais, S., et al.: 3D hardware canaries. In: Prouff, E., Schaumont, P. (eds.) CHES 2012. LNCS, vol. 7428, pp. 1–22. Springer, Heidelberg (2012)
19. Joye, M., Quisquater, J.-J. (eds.): CHES 2004. LNCS, vol. 3156. Springer, Heidelberg (2004)
20. Kelsey, J.: SHA3 - past, present, and future. In: Presented at the rump session of CHES 2013 (2013)
21. Kocher, P.C.: Timing attacks on implementations of Diffie-Hellman, RSA, DSS, and other systems. In: Koblitz, N. (ed.) CRYPTO 1996. LNCS, vol. 1109, pp. 104–113. Springer, Heidelberg (1996)
22. Kocher, P., Jaffe, J., Jun, B.: Differential power analysis. In: Wiener [36], pp. 388–397
23. Ledig, H., Muller, F., Valette, F.: Enhancing collision attacks. In: Joye and Quisquater [19], pp. 176–190

24. Mangard, S., Pramstaller, N., Oswald, E.: Successfully attacking masked AES hardware implementations. In: Rao, J.R., Sunar, B. (eds.) CHES 2005. LNCS, vol. 3659, pp. 157–171. Springer, Heidelberg (2005)
25. Messerges, T.S.: Using second-order power analysis to attack DPA resistant software. In: Paar, C., Koç, Ç.K. (eds.) CHES 2000. LNCS, vol. 1965, pp. 238–251. Springer, Heidelberg (2000)
26. Moradi, A., Mischke, O., Eisenbarth, T.: Correlation-enhanced power analysis collision attack. In: Mangard, S., Standaert, F.-X. (eds.) CHES 2010. LNCS, vol. 6225, pp. 125–139. Springer, Heidelberg (2010)
27. Oswald, E., Mangard, S., Herbst, C., Tillich, S.: Practical second-order DPA attacks for masked smart card implementations of block ciphers. In: Pointcheval, D. (ed.) CT-RSA 2006. LNCS, vol. 3860, pp. 192–207. Springer, Heidelberg (2006)
28. Prouff, E., Rivain, M., Bévan, R.: Statistical analysis of second order differential power analysis. IEEE Trans. Comput. **58**(6), 799–811 (2009)
29. Quisquater, J.J., Samyde, D.: A new tool for non-intrusive analysis of smart cards based on electro-magnetic emissions, the SEMA and DEMA methods. In: Presented during EUROCRYPT'00 Rump Session (2000)
30. Roche, T., Lomné, V.: Collision-correlation attack against some 1st-order boolean masking schemes in the context of secure devices. In: Prouff, E. (ed.) COSADE 2013. LNCS, vol. 7864, pp. 114–136. Springer, Heidelberg (2013)
31. Schramm, K., Leander, G., Felke, P., Paar, C.: A collision-attack on AES (Combining Side Channel and Differential-Attack). In: Joye and Quisquater [19], pp. 163–175
32. Schramm, K., Wollinger, T., Paar, C.: A new class of collision attacks and its application to DES. In: Johansson, T. (ed.) FSE 2003. LNCS, vol. 2887, pp. 206–222. Springer, Heidelberg (2003)
33. Standaert, F.-X., Veyrat-Charvillon, N., Oswald, E., Gierlichs, B., Medwed, M., Kasper, M., Mangard, S.: The world is not enough: another look on second-order DPA. In: Abe, M. (ed.) ASIACRYPT 2010. LNCS, vol. 6477, pp. 112–129. Springer, Heidelberg (2010)
34. Taha, M., Schaumont, P.: Side-channel analysis of MAC-Keccak. In: IEEE International Symposium on Hardware-Oriented Security and Trust - HOST 2013. IEEE Computer Society (2013)
35. Walter, C.D.: Sliding windows succumbs to big mac attack. In: Koç, Ç.K., Naccache, D., Paar, C. (eds.) CHES 2001. LNCS, vol. 2162, pp. 286–299. Springer, Heidelberg (2001)
36. Wiener, M. (ed.): CRYPTO 1999. LNCS, vol. 1666. Springer, Heidelberg (1999)
37. Zohner, M., Kasper, M., Stöttinger, M., Huss, S.A.: Side channel analysis of the SHA-3 finalists. In: Rosenstiel, W., Thiele, L. (eds.) Design, Automation and Test in Europe Conference & Exhibition, DATE 2012, pp. 1012–1017. IEEE Computer Society (2012)

Attacking Randomized Exponentiations Using Unsupervised Learning

Guilherme Perin[1](✉), Laurent Imbert[1](✉), Lionel Torres[1],
and Philippe Maurine[1,2]

[1] LIRMM/UM2, 161, Rue Ada, 34095 Montpellier, France
{perin,laurent.imbert}@lirmm.fr
[2] CEA-TECH LSAS Laboratory, 880 Avenue de Mimet, 13541 Gardanne, France

Abstract. Countermeasures to defeat most of side-channel attacks on exponentiations are based on randomization of processed data. The exponent and the message blinding are particular techniques to thwart simple, collisions, differential and correlation analyses. Attacks based on a single (trace) execution of exponentiations, like horizontal correlation analysis and profiled template attacks, have shown to be efficient against most of popular countermeasures. In this paper we show how an unsupervised learning can explore the remaining leakages caused by conditional control tests and memory addressing in a RNS-based implementation of the RSA. The device under attack is protected with the exponent blinding and the leak resistant arithmetic. The developed attack combines the leakage of several samples over the segments of the exponentiation in order to recover the entire exponent. We demonstrate how to find the points of interest using trace pre-processing and clustering algorithms. This attack can recover the exponent using a single trace.

Keywords: RSA · Randomized exponentiation · Electromagnetic analysis · Unsupervised learning · Clustering algorithms · Single-execution attacks

1 Introduction

Not only designers of cryptographic devices have to implement the algorithms efficiently, they also have to ensure that sensible information that leaks through several side-channels (time, temperature, power consumption, electromagnetic emanations, etc.) during the execution of an algorithm, remains unexploited by an attacker. If not sufficiently protected, both symmetric and asymmetric cryptographic implementations are vulnerable to these so-called side-channel attacks (SCA). For public-key algorithms such as RSA, the main operation to be armoured consists of a multi-digit exponentiation over a finite ring. In this paper, we present an improved single-execution attack on a randomized implementation of RSA. However, the ideas and tools that we exploit would also apply in the context of CRT-RSA and (hyper)elliptic curves.

© Springer International Publishing Switzerland 2014
E. Prouff (Ed.): COSADE 2014, LNCS 8622, pp. 144–160, 2014.
DOI: 10.1007/978-3-319-10175-0_11

Attacking an exponentiation consists of identifying the bits of the exponent, a value that is often to be kept secret (it is either a secret key or a random secret value). Simple side-channel attacks [2], which uses a single trace of execution, are easily protected using so-called constant-time algorithms such as square-and-multiply-always [4], the Montgomery ladder [7] or atomicity [23].

However, these constant-time algorithms are not sufficient to defeat the more powerful differential [3] and correlation attacks [5]. Although very efficient on not sufficiently protected implementations, these attacks suffer from the very large number of traces to be collected in order to recover (part of) the secret. Collision attacks proposed by Fouque in 2003 [6] are very efficient; they only require two traces of execution on well chosen inputs. All these attacks are generally protected using exponent and/or message blinding using elementary algebraic manipulations. For example, randomization of an RSA exponent relies on the fact that $m^d \equiv m^{d+r\phi(n)} \mod n$ for any (random) value r (see Sect. 5). Apart from these well known tricks, randomization can also take place at the arithmetic level. The LRA concept [9], based on the Residue Number System, seems to be a robust, yet efficient [24,25] alternative to more expensive (hardware) countermeasures.

Novel attacks [14–17] have recently emerged. Unlike the well studied family of differential [3] and correlation attacks [5], these so-called horizontal correlation attacks (HCA), aim at correlating the Hamming Weight $HW(m)$ of a known message m, with a set of well-chosen sample points t_i from one single trace. Some of them [15,17] are indeed efficient in the presence of message blinding. They exploit the very high regularity of multi-digit exponentiation algorithms and represent a very serious threat against classical randomization countermeasures. A major advantage of single-trace-based attacks is their natural immunity to exponent blinding, since, in many cases, recovering a random exponent is sufficient to break the cryptosystem (see Sect. 5).

Profiled template attacks can recover the exponent using few traces. As the original template attack [11] suggests, the attacker must have full control of the device. In particular, he must be able to send plain-texts of his choice to a known key device. In the case of public-key algorithms, the public-key is known and also can be used in the profiling phase. In this case, the pre-computations whose objective is to build the template set is refereed to as supervised learning. In [13] supervised template attacks are successfully applied on modular exponentiations in order to differentiate squarings from multiplications. More recently, a template attack on constant-time exponentiation algorithms was presented in [12], while [19] suggests a technique to attack the exponent blinding. A template attack targeting the memory addressing was presented in [22]. All those methods fall into the class of supervised attacks, i.e., a learning phase is required during which the adversary constructs templates by exploring the statistical characteristics of various types of operations.

When the adversary does not have a full control of the device, unsupervised methods are necessary. In [18], unsupervised learning has been presented to demonstrate the efficiency of localized EM attacks on exponentiations using a

k-means clustering algorithm to differentiate the attacked samples. Their attack is performed on an ECC [27] implementation over a binary field using Lopez-Dahab coordinates [26]. The scalar is recovered using leakages collected during the execution of a single scalar multiplication ($k \in \mathbb{Z}, P \in E(\mathbb{F}_{2^m}) \longrightarrow [k]P \in E(\mathbb{F}_{2^m})$. However, their attack relies on the ability to acquire several simultaneous EM traces from different probe positions[1]. The leakages obtained from these multi-measurement sources are then combined together in order to reduce the signal-to-noise ratio. By doing so, they managed to classify the sampled points into two distinct sets which correspond to the zero bits (resp. non-zero bits) of the scalar k.

In this paper, we present a single-trace, single-probe unsupervised attack, i.e. the side-channel data is collected from one EM probe only. In the next sections, we present the setting and statistical tools that we used to recover the entire exponent of a constant-time, randomized RSA implementation. Our attack is unsupervised because it does not require any a priori knowledge of the device, in particular we did not use the public key or send any chosen messages in order to learn the characteristics of the device. The chip under attack is a constant-time, RNS-based FPGA implementation of RSA protected with the Leak Resistant Arithmetic [9] and exponent blinding. Since all manipulated data is randomized, we explore the remaining leakages due to control instructions and memory activities. As previously demonstrated in the literature [20], memory and register addresses leak information related to the secret key. Instead of using simultaneous measurements as in [18], we combine the cluster classifications of several samples from each bit of the exponent. We thus process the probabilities obtained from this first phase to recover the entire exponent. Our attack requires four phases: trace pre-processing, points of interest identification, fuzzy k-means clustering, and exponent recovery. For this final phase, we present results obtained with three different statistical techniques (majority rule, normal probability density function and Bayesian classifier).

The paper is organized as follows: Sect. 2 gives details about the randomized exponentiation and the device under attack. The unsupervised learning based on clustering algorithms is detailed in Sect. 3. Section 4 presents the attack in details and the results that we obtained with the three statistical tools mentioned above. Possible countermeasures are suggested in Sect. 6.

2   The Randomized Exponentiation and the Device Under Test

The device under attack is a RNS-based implementation of RSA mapped onto a Spartan-3E xc3s1600 FPGA. For demonstration purposes, we considered a very weak 512-bit RSA. The modular exponentiation is computed with the regular and SPA-protected Montgomery ladder [8] using two sets of RNS bases

---

[1] Their setting simulates the use of 9 probes uniformly positioned over the chip under attack.

$\mathcal{A}$ and $\mathcal{B}$ [10]. The atomic square-and-multiply [23] is also a regular and faster exponentiation. However as proposed in [15], randomized exponentiations can be explored through horizontal correlation attacks (HCA) if one of the intermediate operands, in the case the randomized input message, is used in several modular multiplications.

According to the leak resistant arithmetic (LRA) concepts [9], the RNS moduli can be randomized before each exponentiation. This countermeasure acts as a message blinding technique because it offers a high degree of randomization to the data. Furthermore, HCA exploits the regularity of long-integer multiplication (or squaring). The parallel RNS arithmetic is then a very limiting factor for this attack. Moreover, our hardware is protected with exponent blinding. Algorithm 1 shows the randomized exponentiation.

Algorithm 1. LRA-RNS Montgomery Powering Ladder [9]

Data: x in $\mathcal{A} \cup \mathcal{B}$, where $\mathcal{A} = (a_1, a_2, ..., a_k)$, $\mathcal{B} = (b_1, b_2, ..., b_k)$, $A = \prod_{i=1}^{k} a_i$,
$B = \prod_{i=1}^{k} b_i$, $\gcd(A, B) = 1$, $\gcd(B, N) = 1$ and $d = (d_\ell...d_2 d_1)_2$.

Result: $z = x^d \bmod N$ in $\mathcal{A} \cup \mathcal{B}$

1 **Pre-Computations:** $|AB \bmod N|_{\mathcal{A} \cup \mathcal{B}}$
2 $randomize(\mathcal{A}, \mathcal{B})$
3 $d_r = d + r.\phi(N)$
4 $A_0 = MM(1, AB \bmod N, N, \mathcal{A}, \mathcal{B})$ (in $\mathcal{A} \cup \mathcal{B}$)
5 $A_1 = MM(x, AB \bmod N, N, \mathcal{A}, \mathcal{B})$ (in $\mathcal{A} \cup \mathcal{B}$)
6 **for** $i = \ell$ **to** 1 **do**
7     $A_{\overline{d_{r_i}}} = MM(A_{\overline{d_{r_i}}}, A_{d_{r_i}}, N, \mathcal{B}, \mathcal{A})$ (in $\mathcal{A} \cup \mathcal{B}$)
8     $A_{d_{r_i}} = MM(A_{d_{r_i}}, A_{d_{r_i}}, N, \mathcal{B}, \mathcal{A})$ (in $\mathcal{A} \cup \mathcal{B}$)
9 **end**
10 $A_0 = MM(A_0, 1, N, \mathcal{B}, \mathcal{A})$ (in $\mathcal{A} \cup \mathcal{B}$)

The operation $MM(x, y, N, \mathcal{B}, \mathcal{A})$ returns $xyB^{-1} \bmod N$ in the two RNS bases $\mathcal{A}$ and $\mathcal{B}$. Both squarings and multiplications are computed with the same number of clock cycles.

First, as the exponent is randomized, single-trace attack was the only option. Further, because the manipulated data is randomized with LRA, the target information of our unsupervised attack is not the data contribution in the EM traces. By data, we mean the intermediate variables which depend on the randomly selected RNS bases and the input message. Exponent-dependent decisions are taken by the architecture's control in order to determine the memory address for reading or writing operands before, during and after the modular multiplications. These conditional tests, as well as the accessed memory addresses, cause subtle leakages of information. These are the only sources of leakages that we exploit in the present unsupervised attack. We present the details of our attack in the next sections.

3   Unsupervised Learning and the Clustering Algorithms

Clustering is one of the most frequently used data mining techniques, which is an unsupervised learning process for partitioning a data set into sub-groups so that the instances within a group are similar to each other and are very dissimilar to the instances of other groups. That is, we shall see what can be done when the collected samples are unlabelled and must be grouped in homogeneous clusters. Two different clustering methods are used in this work: the k-means and the fuzzy k-means algorithms [28].

The k-means algorithm is a geometric procedure for finding c means or centers $(\mu_1, \ldots, \mu_c)$ considering a set of n samples x_j, where $1 \leq j \leq n$. The initialization phase consists in defining the number of clusters c and setting a random sample to each mean μ_i. Thereafter, the algorithm computes the Euclidean distances $ED_{i,j} = \parallel x_j - \mu_i \parallel^2$ for all n samples to obtain the maximum-likelihood estimation of the means μ_i. The k-means algorithm is shown in Algorithm 2.

Algorithm 2. K-Means Clustering Algorithm

1 **begin initialize** $\mathbf{x}, n, c, \mu_1, \ldots, \mu_c$
2   **do** classify n samples x_j according to nearest μ_i by computing $ED_{i,j}$
3   recompute μ_i
4   **until** no change in μ_i
5 **return** $\mu_1, \ldots, \mu_c$
6 **end**

The k-means algorithm iterates until no changes in μ_i are verified. In all iterations each sample is assumed to be in exactly one cluster. The fuzzy k-means algorithm relaxes this condition and assumes that each sample x_j has some membership with different clusters ω_i, rather than belonging completely to just one cluster.

Initially, the probabilities of cluster membership for each point x_j of a n sample vector $\mathbf{x}$ are normalized according to all clusters ω_i as:

$$\sum_{i=1}^{c} P(\omega_i | x_j) = 1 \tag{1}$$

where $P(\omega_i | x_j)$ is the probability that the sample x_j is in the cluster ω_i. At each iteration of the fuzzy k-means algorithm, the means (or centers) μ_i are recomputed according to the following equation:

$$\mu_j = \frac{\sum_{j=1}^{n} [P(\omega_i | x_j)]^b x_j}{\sum_{j=1}^{n} [P(\omega_i | x_j)]^b} \tag{2}$$

and the new probabilities are recomputed:

$$P(\omega_i | x_j) = \frac{(1/ED_{ij})^{1/(b-1)}}{\sum_{r=1}^{c} (1/ED_{rj})^{1/(b-1)}}, \quad ED_{ij} = \parallel x_j - \mu_i \parallel^2 \tag{3}$$

where $b > 1$ is a free parameter chosen to adjust the "blending" of different clusters. Its appropriate choice can improve the cluster classification if the analyzed

---

Algorithm 3. Fuzzy K-Means Clustering Algorithm

1 **begin initialize** $n, c, \mu_1, \ldots, \mu_c, P(\omega_i|x_j)$
2   normalize probabilities of cluster memberships by Eq. 1
3   **do** classify n samples according to nearest μ_i
4   recompute μ_i by Eq. 2
5   recompute $P(\omega_i|x_j)$ by Eq. 3
6   **until** no change in μ_i and $P(\omega_i|x_j)$
7   **return** $\mu_1, \ldots, \mu_c$
8 **end**

---

data set is too much noisy. In this work, this parameter is set to 2. Algorithm 3 shows the fuzzy k-means algorithm.

The next section describes the unsupervised attack in four phases. The k-means algorithm is used in the search for the points of interest. The fuzzy k-means is employed in the cluster classification after having selected the points of interest.

4 The Unsupervised Attack

In a realistic assumption for single-execution attacks on exponentiations, the adversary works in a noisy environment and, as already stated in [19], *"single bits are never known with certainty [...] and an SPA attacker [...] can only give a probability that any particular operation is a squaring or a multiplication"*, if the attacked device executes the square-and-multiply algorithm. If a single-execution attack is able of recovering 98 % of the 1024 exponent bits and the adversary does not know the wrong bit positions inside the exponent, a brute force attack requires $\sum_{j=0}^{21} C_j^{1024} = 2^{144}$ steps to retrieve the incorrect bits. Therefore, the number of wrong bits in the recovered exponent must be at least very low, otherwise a single-execution attack is impracticable.

When applying non-profiled attacks on a single trace of an exponentiation, the adversary has no knowledge about the operation features (mean μ, variance σ^2). All information must be recovered in a unsupervised manner. Regular binary algorithms [8, 23] compute the exponentiation iteratively and for each bit of the exponent (or segment) same operations are performed. Thus, a initial partitioning step is applied to the measured electromagnetic exponentiation trace in order to have ℓ segments, each one representing one exponent bit interpretation. The segments are aligned and compressed to reduce the noise and clock jitter effects. Thereafter, as proposed in this attack, several points of interest are identified in each segment by computing an estimated and approximated difference of means. The cluster classification using the fuzzy k-means algorithm is applied in each set of compressed samples, each set representing a selected point of interest and providing an estimated exponent. The last step consists in retrieving the randomized exponent using all estimated exponents obtained

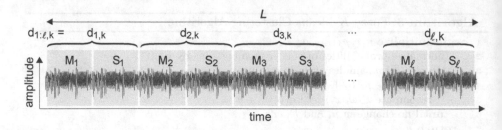

Fig. 1. Exponentiation trace and the segmentation in multiplications and squarings.

with the cluster classification. The proposed attack, divided in four phases, is detailed below.

4.1   Phase 1: Trace Pre-processings

The attack starts by acquiring a single execution exponentiation trace from the device. Let us consider that the randomized exponent is $d_{1:\ell,k}$, where ℓ is the length of the exponent and k is index of the exponentiation trace. In our case, the exponentiation is computed using the regular Montgomery ladder algorithm. The EM trace, with size L, is sliced in ℓ operations of multiplications and ℓ operations of squarings, as depicted in Fig. 1.

Each multiplication (M_i) or squaring (S_i) in the acquired EM trace contains 74 clock cycles. The oscilloscope sampling rate was set to $20\,\mathrm{GS/s}$ during the acquisition step and the hardware computes the exponentiation at a clock frequency of $50\,\mathrm{MHz}$, resulting in 59200 samples per exponent bit interpretation (M_iS_i). The device under attack does not feature any hardware countermeasure, e.g., time disarrangement, dummy cycles or frequency dividers. Therefore, the ℓ segments of multiplication-squarings M_iS_i, can be easily identified and combined to explore the leakage of information. However, the clock jitter effect is still present in the acquired EM trace and must be suppressed using a trace alignment procedure.

Another important role in unsupervised single-execution attacks is to identify the points of interest which present greater leakages. A simple solution consists in averaging the 400 samples of one clock cycle into 1 sample and taking each averaged sample as a point of interest. Here, in order to preserve the information over smaller windows, the trace is compressed by averaging 100 samples into 1 sample. Then, this allows reducing the amount of data from 59200 to 592 compressed samples during an exponent bit interpretation $d_{i,k}$ (denoted by operation $\langle MS \rangle_i$ in the sequel).

Now, the ℓ operations are represented by a matrix T:

$$T = \begin{bmatrix} \langle MS \rangle_1 \\ \langle MS \rangle_2 \\ \vdots \\ \langle MS \rangle_\ell \end{bmatrix} = \begin{bmatrix} t_{1,1} & t_{1,2} & \cdots & t_{1,592} \\ t_{2,1} & t_{2,2} & \cdots & t_{2,592} \\ \vdots & \vdots & \ddots & \vdots \\ t_{\ell,1} & t_{\ell,2} & \cdots & t_{\ell,592} \end{bmatrix} \tag{4}$$

Each row of the matrix T is a set of compressed samples $\langle \text{MS} \rangle_i = \{t_{i,j}\}$ representing an exponent bit interpretation $d_{i,k}$. The term ℓ is the exponent bit length and, of course, is the iterations number in the Algorithm 1 (steps 6–9). After the trace pre-processing, the attack enters in the second phase that consists in finding the points of interest.

4.2   Phase 2: Finding the Points of Interest

The success of the attack depends on the choice of the points of interest. With profiling or supervised attacks, these points can be found by computing a difference of means and observing the highest peaks of amplitude. In such a case, the adversary has a known key d and computes averaged traces Tr_0 and Tr_1 representing the truncated windows of sampled points when the exponent bit is zero and one, respectively and according to:

$$\text{Tr}_0 = \sum_i \langle \text{MS} \rangle_{d_i=0} \qquad\qquad \text{Tr}_1 = \sum_i \langle \text{MS} \rangle_{d_i=1} \qquad (5)$$

Because the presented attack aims at revealing the exponent through an unsupervised manner, the attacker should be considered as having minimal knowledge about the target implementation to identify the points of interest. Because all data are randomized, the remaining leakage is related to addressing and control executions. Therefore, by observing and studying the collected EM trace, the attacker can, for instance, localize the time points where the device performs such operations and discard the points that clearly show no compromising information.

Our unsupervised analysis needs a set of points of interest in each segment $\langle \text{MS} \rangle_i$ to retrieve the exponent. A basic idea is to initially apply a clustering algorithm over each set of compressed samples $\{t_{1:\ell,j}\}$ (each column of matrix T) and find 592 approximated exponents $\widehat{d_{1:\ell,j}}$, for $1 \leq j \leq 592$. In our practical experiments, this leads to the recovery of around 93 % of the entire exponent on the most leaking set of compressed samples $\{t_{1:\ell,j}\}$. It is insufficient. However, this result can be used for calculating approximated and averaged traces $\widehat{\text{Tr}_0}$ and $\widehat{\text{Tr}_1}$ from the approximated exponent $\widehat{d_{1:\ell,j}}$. For this initial step, we considered the k-means clustering algorithm because it is a simple and fast technique. Figure 2(a) shows the relation between the percentage of success recovery of the exponent and the analyzed set of compressed samples $\{t_{1:\ell,j}\}$, for $1 \leq j \leq 592$.

If the adversary selects the most likely exponent (in the case the set $\{t_{1:\ell,465}\}$) he computes the averaged traces $\widehat{\text{Tr}_0}$ and $\widehat{\text{Tr}_1}$. Figure 2(b) shows the approximated difference of mean traces $\widehat{D} = \widehat{\text{Tr}_0} - \widehat{\text{Tr}_1}$. The difference of means $D = \text{Tr}_0 - \text{Tr}_1$, for the real randomized exponent running in the device, is depicted in Fig. 2(c).

Note that the results in Fig. 2(b) and (c) are quite similar and the adversary can select points of interest observing the highest peaks of amplitude in D. In a worst case, the adversary would try to compute approximated difference of mean

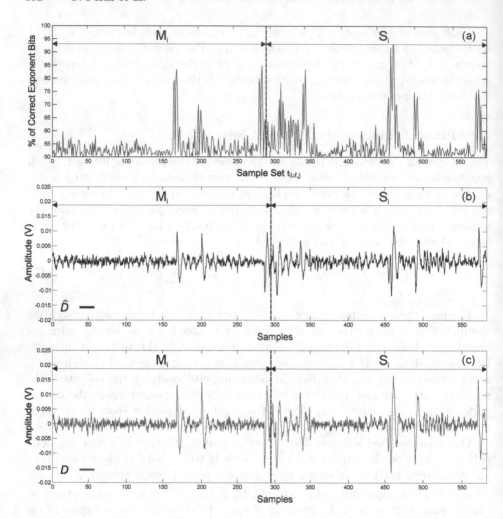

Fig. 2. (a) Percentage of correct exponent bits. (b) Approximated difference of mean traces $\widehat{D} = \widehat{\mathrm{Tr}_0} - \widehat{\mathrm{Tr}_1}$ (c) Difference of mean traces $D = \mathrm{Tr}_0 - \mathrm{Tr}_1$.

traces, and selecting points of interest, from each one of the 592 possibilities. It is clear that the selection of the most leaking point of interest reduces the computational time of the unsupervised attack. Besides, we observed (see Fig. 2) that the highest percentages of correct exponent recovery match with the highest peaks of amplitude in the approximated difference of means $\widehat{D}$. We used this observation as a heuristic in order to select the points of interest.

4.3   Phase 3: Cluster Classification

After computing the approximated difference of mean traces from the set of compressed samples $\{t_{1:\ell,465}\}$, let us suppose the selection of u points of interest

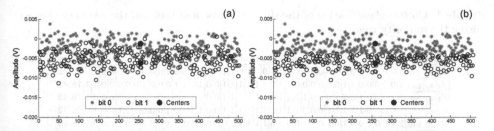

Fig. 3. Errors of cluster classification: (a) Correct classification. (b) Fuzzy k-means classification.

$P = \{p_j\}$, for $1 \le j \le u$, among the 592 possibilities. Observing the approximated difference of means $\widehat{D}$ in Fig. 2(b), 17 points of interest were selected ($p_j = 165, 166, 169, 281, 282, 284, 285, 342, 461, 462, 464, 465, 497, 498, 577, 580, 581$), which evidently are the most leaking points.

A clustering is computed for all set of compressed samples $\{t_{1:\ell,p_j}\}$, for $1 \le j \le u$ by applying the fuzzy k-means algorithm. Thus, a classification for these samples in two classes (bits zeros and ones), which leads to one estimated exponent $\widehat{d_{1:\ell,p_j}}$ per set of samples $\{t_{1:\ell,p_j}\}$, is obtained. Because real attacks work on noisy environments, the clustering over each point of interest p_j contains errors of classification. Figure 3 illustrates the cluster classification error for the set of compressed samples $\{t_{1:\ell,169}\}$. Figure 3(a) shows the correct classification according to the real randomized exponent $d_{1:\ell,k}$ and the Fig. 3(b) presents the cluster classification returned by the fuzzy k-means algorithm.

For each point of interest p_j, the fuzzy k-means clustering algorithm returns two centers μ_1 and mu_2 and two groups of clustered samples. A common problem would be to identify what class or operation (exponent bit zero or one) each cluster center represents. With $u = 17$ cluster classifications into two classes, there will be $2^{17} = 131072$ different possibilities. The identification of the classes can be performed in two different ways:

1. Instead of selecting random samples to initialize the values μ_1 and μ_2 in the Algorithm 3, we select the minimum and maximum samples from the set $\{t_{1:\ell,p_j}\}$ according to their amplitudes. The initialization in Algorithm 3 is done by assigning $\mu_1 = min\{t_{1:\ell,p_j}\}$ and $\mu_2 = max\{t_{1:\ell,p_j}\}$. It ensures that $\mu_1 < \mu_2$ after the clustering. Then, comparing the resulting cluster means μ_1 and μ_2 with the amplitude of the approximated difference of means $\widehat{D}$, and also $\widehat{Tr_0}$ and $\widehat{Tr_1}$, it is straightforward to identify the classes.
2. As all selected leaking points may lead to more than 50 % of exponent recovery, we take one recovered exponent $\widehat{d_{1:\ell,v}}$ from one point of interest v, $v \in \{p_j\}$, and compute the bitwise XOR between this exponent and the other estimated exponent values. Let ℓ be the size of the exponent, $\widehat{d_{1:\ell,p_j}}$ all the recovered exponents for $1 \le j \le u$, $p_j \ne v$, and the bitwise results

Table 1. Cluster classification of the (first 40) exponent bits and the recovery of $\widehat{d_{1:\ell,k}}$ using the majority rule.

exponent	classified exponent bits $\widehat{d_{i,k}}$	correct
$\widehat{d_{1:40,497}}$	1 0 0 0 0 0 0 1 0 0 0 0 1 0 1 1 1 0 0 1 0 1 1 0 0 0 1 0 0 1 0 0 0 0 0 0 0 0 1 0	76.02%
$\widehat{d_{1:40,498}}$	1 0 0 0 0 0 1 1 0 0 0 0 0 0 1 1 0 1 1 1 1 1 1 0 0 1 0 1 1 0 0 0 1 0 0 0 0 0 1 1	76.42%
$\widehat{d_{1:40,166}}$	1 1 0 0 0 1 0 1 1 0 0 0 1 0 1 1 1 1 1 1 1 1 0 0 1 1 1 0 1 0 0 1 1 0 0 0 0 0 1	76.42%
$\widehat{d_{1:40,462}}$	1 0 0 0 0 1 1 1 1 1 0 0 0 1 1 1 0 1 1 1 1 1 1 0 0 1 1 1 0 1 0 0 1 1 1 1 0 0 1 0	76.42%
$\widehat{d_{1:40,580}}$	1 1 0 0 0 0 0 1 0 1 0 1 1 0 0 1 0 1 1 1 1 1 0 0 0 1 1 1 1 1 0 0 1 0 0 1 0 0 0 1	78.86%
$\widehat{d_{1:40,342}}$	1 0 1 1 0 0 0 0 1 0 0 0 1 0 1 1 0 0 0 1 1 0 1 0 1 0 1 1 0 1 0 0 1 0 1 0 0 1 0 1	79.27%
$\widehat{d_{1:40,282}}$	1 0 0 0 0 0 0 1 0 0 0 1 1 0 1 1 0 1 1 1 1 1 1 0 0 1 1 1 0 1 0 0 1 0 0 1 0 0 0 1	78.86%
$\widehat{d_{1:40,281}}$	1 1 0 1 0 0 0 1 0 0 0 0 1 0 1 1 0 1 1 1 0 1 1 0 1 1 1 1 0 1 1 1 1 0 0 0 0 0 0 1	80.08%
$\widehat{d_{1:40,169}}$	1 0 0 0 0 0 1 1 0 1 0 0 1 1 1 1 0 0 1 1 0 1 1 0 1 1 0 1 0 0 0 0 1 0 0 0 1 0 0 0	80.08%
$\widehat{d_{1:40,165}}$	1 0 0 0 0 0 0 1 0 0 0 0 0 1 0 0 1 0 0 1 1 1 1 1 0 0 1 1 1 0 1 1 0 0 1 0 0 0 1 1	80.89%
$\widehat{d_{1:40,581}}$	1 0 1 0 0 0 0 1 1 0 1 0 1 0 1 1 1 1 1 1 0 1 0 1 1 1 1 1 0 0 1 0 0 0 0 0 0 0 1	82.52%
$\widehat{d_{1:40,577}}$	1 0 0 0 0 0 0 1 0 0 0 0 1 0 1 0 0 1 0 1 1 1 0 0 1 1 1 0 1 1 0 1 1 0 0 0 0 0 1	82.52%
$\widehat{d_{1:40,284}}$	1 0 0 0 0 0 0 0 1 0 0 0 1 1 1 0 0 1 1 1 1 1 1 0 1 1 1 1 1 1 0 0 1 0 0 0 0 1 0 1	83.74%
$\widehat{d_{1:40,285}}$	1 0 0 0 0 1 0 1 0 0 0 0 1 0 1 1 0 1 0 1 1 1 1 1 1 1 1 1 0 0 0 1 0 0 0 0 0 0 1	89.43%
$\widehat{d_{1:40,465}}$	1 0 0 0 0 0 0 0 0 0 0 0 1 0 1 1 0 1 1 0 1 1 0 1 1 1 0 1 0 0 1 0 0 0 0 0 0 0 1	90.65%
$\widehat{d_{1:40,461}}$	1 0 0 0 0 0 0 1 0 0 0 0 1 0 1 0 0 1 1 1 1 1 1 0 1 1 1 1 0 1 0 1 1 0 0 0 0 0 0 1	91.25%
$\widehat{d_{1:40,464}}$	1 0 0 0 0 0 0 1 0 0 0 0 1 0 1 1 0 0 1 1 1 1 1 0 1 1 1 0 0 1 0 0 1 0 0 0 0 0 0 1	93.06%
$\widehat{d_{1:40,k}}$	1 0 0 0 0 0 0 1 0 0 0 0 1 0 1 1 0 1 1 1 1 1 1 0 1 1 1 0 1 0 0 1 0 0 0 1 0 0 0 0 1	100%
$d_{1:40,k}$	1 0 0 0 0 0 0 1 0 0 0 0 1 0 1 1 0 1 1 1 1 1 1 0 1 1 1 0 1 0 0 1 0 0 0 1 0 0 0 0 1	100%

$h_{1:\ell} = \mathrm{XOR}(\widehat{d_{1:\ell,p_j}}, \widehat{d_{1:\ell,v}})$ for $p_i \neq v$. If $\sum_{i=1}^{\ell} h_i < \ell/2$ then returns NOT $(\widehat{d_{1:\ell,p_j}})$, otherwise keep unchanged.

After the cluster classifications and respective association of the classes, the attack enters in the last step in order to combine all estimated exponents into one final exponent.

4.4   Phase 4: Exponent Recovery

The recovery of the final randomized exponent is computed through three different statistical techniques: majority decision, probability density function (pdf) and Bayesian classifier.

Majority Decision. Table 1 shows the cluster classification results for the first 40 bits of each estimated exponent $\widehat{d_{1:\ell,p_j}}$ considering the $u = 17$ points of interest. Using the majority decision we can retrieve a randomized exponent $\widehat{d_{1:\ell,k}}$.

Because the majority rule is a simple statistical procedure, it requires more points of interest for achieving the correct exponent if compared to the next two adopted techniques, as will be demonstrated at the end of this section.

Probability Density Function. In [19], the probability density function, which is based on the normal distributions parameters $\mathcal{N}(\mu_0, \sigma_0)$ and $\mathcal{N}(\mu_1, \sigma_1)$, where μ and σ are the mean and the standard deviation, returns the likelihood that a sample $t_{i,j}$ is the operation when the exponent bit $d_{i,k} = 0$. As the presented analysis is unsupervised, we do not know μ_0 and μ_1. However, the fuzzy k-means cluster classification returns two means or centers μ_1 and μ_2 for each set of compressed samples $\{t_{1:\ell,p_j}\}$ which can be used in place of the means. The standard deviation σ is computed from all the set of samples $\{t_{1:\ell,p_j}\}$, considering the evaluated point of interest p_i. Then, the likelihood that a sample t_{i,p_j} is an operation when $d_{i,k} = 0$ is given by the equation below:

$$p(t_{i,p_j},\mu_1) = \frac{e^{-\frac{1}{2}(t_{i,p_j}-\mu_1)^2/2\sigma^2}}{e^{-\frac{1}{2}(t_{i,p_j}-\mu_1)^2/2\sigma^2} + e^{-\frac{1}{2}(t_{i,p_j}-\mu_2)^2/2\sigma^2}}, \quad 1 \le i \le \ell, 1 \le j \le u \quad (6)$$

Following, the defined sum of probabilities gives the likelihood that a set of points of interest $\{t_{i,p_{1:u}}\}$, representing the operation $\langle MS \rangle_i$, is an operation performed when the randomized exponent bit $d_{i,k} = 0$ and is computed by:

$$S_{0,1:u} = \frac{1}{u} \sum_{j=1}^{u} p(t_{i,p_j},\mu_1) \quad 1 \le i \le \ell \quad (7)$$

Then, for $1 \le i \le \ell$, the following decision returns the estimated randomized exponent bit $\widehat{d_{i,k}}$:

$$\widehat{d_{i,k}} = \begin{cases} 0, & \text{if } S_{0,1:u} \ge 0.5) \\ 1, & \text{if } S_{0,1:u} < 0.5) \end{cases} \quad (8)$$

Table 2 shows the final sum of probabilities $S_{0,1:u}$ and the exponent decision from Eq. 8 considering the 20 first exponent bits $\widehat{d_{1:20,k}}$ (for space in Table 2) and $u = 17$ points of interest.

Bayesian Classifier. The Bayesian decision theory makes the assumption that the decision problem is posed in probability terms. The classifier lies on the computation of the posterior probabilities $P(\mu_c|t_{i,p_j})$ which is computed from the prior probabilities $P(\mu_c)$ and the probability density function for normal distributions $p(t_{i,p_j},\mu_c)$, where $c = \{0,1\}$ and $p(t_{i,p_j},\mu_c) \in [0,1]$. Thus, the classification starts by obtaining the pdf estimation for each point of interest t_{i,p_j} of each operation i. Again, this analysis considers the two cluster centers μ_1 and μ_2 in the place of means and the standard deviation is computed from all the set of compressed samples $\{t_{1:\ell,p_j}\}$:

$$p(t_{i,p_j},\mu_1) = \frac{1}{\sigma\sqrt{2\pi}} e^{-\frac{(t_{i,p_j}-\mu_1)^2}{2\sigma^2}} \quad (9)$$

$$p(t_{i,p_j},\mu_2) = \frac{1}{\sigma\sqrt{2\pi}} e^{-\frac{(t_{i,p_j}-\mu_2)^2}{2\sigma^2}} \quad (10)$$

The probability density functions $p(t_{i,p_j},\mu_1)$ and $p(t_{i,p_j},\mu_2)$ are obtained for $1 \le i \le \ell$ and $1 \le j \le u$. Considering $P(\mu_c)$ as the prior probabilities for

Table 2. Cluster classification of the (first 20) exponent bits and the recovery of $\widehat{d_{1:\ell,k}}$ using the probability density function for normal distributions.

point	probabilities $p(t_{i,p_j}, \mu_1)$																				correct
$d_{1:20,p_1}$	0.1	1.0	0.5	0.6	0.7	0.9	0.9	0.4	1.0	0.7	0.6	0.9	0.0	0.8	0.0	0.2	0.3	0.7	0.5	0.1	76.02%
$d_{1:20,p_2}$	0.3	1.0	0.8	0.6	0.8	0.5	0.4	0.1	0.9	0.7	0.9	0.5	0.7	0.9	0.5	0.2	0.8	0.4	0.1	0.2	76.42%
$d_{1:20,p_3}$	0.5	0.5	0.5	0.5	0.5	0.5	0.5	0.5	0.5	0.5	0.5	0.5	0.5	0.5	0.5	0.5	0.5	0.5	0.5	0.5	76.83%
$d_{1:20,p_4}$	0.2	0.9	0.9	0.8	0.6	0.3	0.5	0.2	0.5	0.3	0.7	0.9	0.6	0.2	0.1	0.2	0.8	0.2	0.1	0.1	76.42%
$d_{1:20,p_5}$	0.5	0.5	0.9	0.9	0.9	0.6	0.8	0.3	0.9	0.1	0.8	0.3	0.2	0.6	0.7	0.1	0.8	0.0	0.3	0.3	78.86%
$d_{1:20,p_6}$	0.1	0.7	0.5	0.4	0.8	0.7	0.7	0.9	0.5	1.0	0.8	0.6	0.2	0.9	0.5	0.3	0.9	0.6	0.7	0.4	78.86%
$d_{1:20,p_7}$	0.5	0.8	0.9	0.8	0.9	0.8	0.8	0.0	0.9	0.6	0.9	0.5	0.1	0.6	0.2	0.1	0.9	0.0	0.3	0.1	78.86%
$d_{1:20,p_8}$	0.3	0.4	0.8	0.5	0.6	0.9	0.7	0.0	0.7	0.5	1.0	0.8	0.2	0.8	0.4	0.1	0.8	0.3	0.0	0.2	80.08%
$d_{1:20,p_9}$	0.4	0.7	1.0	0.9	0.9	0.5	0.4	0.1	0.8	0.2	1.0	0.8	0.1	0.4	0.3	0.1	0.7	0.7	0.1	0.4	80.08%
$d_{1:20,p_{10}}$	0.2	0.9	0.8	0.5	0.7	0.8	1.0	0.4	0.7	1.0	0.8	0.7	0.2	0.5	0.8	0.3	0.6	0.5	0.4	0.1	80.89%
$d_{1:20,p_{11}}$	0.1	0.7	0.3	0.9	0.7	0.7	0.7	0.2	0.5	0.9	0.3	0.8	0.1	0.5	0.0	0.2	0.2	0.3	0.0	0.2	82.52%
$d_{1:20,p_{12}}$	0.1	0.6	1.0	0.8	0.6	0.9	0.8	0.2	0.8	0.9	0.9	0.8	0.1	0.9	0.3	0.6	0.8	0.2	0.5	0.1	82.52%
$d_{1:20,p_{13}}$	0.1	0.8	0.7	1.0	0.7	0.9	0.8	0.7	0.5	0.8	0.9	1.0	0.1	0.2	0.2	0.6	0.6	0.3	0.2	0.3	83.74%
$d_{1:20,p_{14}}$	0.3	0.7	0.7	1.0	0.9	0.3	0.8	0.2	0.9	0.7	0.9	0.6	0.2	0.6	0.4	0.1	0.9	0.1	0.6	0.2	89.43%
$d_{1:20,p_{15}}$	0.1	0.7	0.7	0.9	0.7	0.7	0.7	0.6	0.7	0.9	0.6	0.9	0.2	0.9	0.2	0.4	0.8	0.4	0.2	0.7	89.43%
$d_{1:20,p_{16}}$	0.2	0.8	1.0	0.8	1.0	0.9	0.9	0.3	0.5	0.9	0.7	0.7	0.0	0.8	0.1	0.7	0.8	0.2	0.0	0.2	90.65%
$d_{1:20,p_{17}}$	0.3	0.7	0.6	0.6	1.0	0.7	1.0	0.1	0.8	1.0	0.8	0.7	0.3	0.8	0.3	0.1	0.6	0.5	0.3	0.1	93.06%
$S_{0,1:17}$	0.3	0.6	0.6	0.6	0.7	0.6	0.6	0.3	0.7	0.7	0.7	0.6	0.2	0.6	0.3	0.3	0.7	0.3	0.2	0.3	100%
$\widetilde{d_{1:20,k}}$	1	0	0	0	0	0	0	1	0	0	0	0	1	0	1	1	0	1	1	1	100%
$d_{1:20,k}$	1	0	0	0	0	0	0	1	0	0	0	0	1	0	1	1	0	1	1	1	100%

the points of interest p_{j-1}, where $c = \{0, 1\}$, by Bayes's formula we obtain the posterior probabilities $P(\mu_c | t_{i,p_j})$ for the operations i and points of interest p_j:

$$P(\mu_1 | t_{i,p_j}) = \frac{p(t_{i,p_j}, \mu_1) P(\mu_1)}{p(t_{i,p_j}, \mu_1) P(\mu_1) + p(t_{i,p_j}, \mu_2) P(\mu_2)} \tag{11}$$

$$P(\mu_2 | t_{i,p_j}) = \frac{p(t_{i,p_j}, \mu_2) P(\mu_2)}{p(t_{i,p_j}, \mu_1) P(\mu_1) + p(t_{i,p_j}, \mu_2) P(\mu_2)} \tag{12}$$

The Bayes's formula is repeated for all points of interest p_j over the same operation i. At the end, this estimation returns the probabilities that a certain operation $\langle MS \rangle_i$ is being executed when the exponent bit $d_{i,k} = 0$. Table 3 shows the evolution of posterior probabilities $P(\mu_1 | t_{i,p_j})$ over all points of interest t_{i,p_j}, for $1 \leq j \leq u$, and the respective percentage of correct exponent bits. Again, in this example we consider the first 20 exponent bits.

For the three presented methods, we showed the cluster classification results for $u = 17$ points of interest. Figure 4 demonstrates the evolution of the exponent recovery related to the number of points. In Fig. 4(a), it was considered the evolution from the least to the most leaking point. Note that using the Bayesian classifier 11 points are necessary to recover the entire exponent. The same result can be observed in Table 3. On the other hand, in Fig. 4(b), if the evolution is from the most to the least leaking point, the Bayesian classifier achieves 100 % of the exponent using only 4 points of interest per exponentiation segment.

Table 3. Cluster classification of the (first 20) exponent bits and the recovery of $\widehat{d_{i:\ell,k}}$ using the Bayesian classifier.

point	probabilities $P(\mu_1|t_{1:20,p_j})$																				correct
$P(\mu_1|t_{1:20,p_1})$	0.7	0.4	0.6	0.8	0.7	0.8	0.6	0.4	0.8	0.8	0.9	0.8	0.4	0.7	0.4	0.3	0.6	0.2	0.4	0.6	75.23%
$P(\mu_1|t_{1:20,p_2})$	0.5	1.0	0.8	0.9	0.7	0.9	0.4	0.2	1.0	1.0	0.9	0.8	0.2	0.9	0.0	0.0	0.8	0.2	0.1	0.6	82.89%
$P(\mu_1|t_{1:20,p_3})$	0.5	1.0	0.8	0.9	0.7	1.0	0.5	0.1	1.0	1.0	0.9	0.8	0.1	0.9	0.0	0.1	0.9	0.3	0.1	0.6	89.02%
$P(\mu_1|t_{1:20,p_4})$	0.1	1.0	0.9	1.0	0.7	0.9	0.9	0.0	1.0	1.0	1.0	0.8	0.0	1.0	0.0	0.0	1.0	0.1	0.0	0.1	93.45%
$P(\mu_1|t_{1:20,p_5})$	0.4	1.0	1.0	1.0	0.9	1.0	0.8	0.0	0.9	1.0	1.0	0.6	0.0	1.0	0.0	0.0	1.0	0.0	0.0	0.3	96.34%
$P(\mu_1|t_{1:20,p_6})$	0.4	1.0	1.0	1.0	0.9	1.0	0.8	0.0	0.9	1.0	1.0	0.6	0.0	1.0	0.0	0.0	1.0	0.0	0.0	0.3	97.56%
$P(\mu_1|t_{1:20,p_7})$	0.4	1.0	0.9	1.0	1.0	1.0	0.7	0.0	1.0	1.0	1.0	1.0	0.0	1.0	0.0	0.0	1.0	0.0	0.0	0.3	99.59%
$P(\mu_1|t_{1:20,p_8})$	0.0	1.0	1.0	1.0	1.0	1.0	0.7	0.0	1.0	1.0	1.0	1.0	0.0	1.0	0.0	0.0	1.0	0.0	0.0	0.0	99.59%
$P(\mu_1|t_{1:20,p_9})$	0.0	1.0	1.0	1.0	1.0	1.0	0.8	0.0	1.0	1.0	1.0	1.0	0.0	1.0	0.0	0.0	1.0	0.0	0.0	0.0	99.59%
$P(\mu_1|t_{1:20,p_{10}})$	0.0	1.0	1.0	1.0	1.0	1.0	0.9	0.0	1.0	1.0	1.0	1.0	0.0	1.0	0.0	0.0	1.0	0.0	0.0	0.0	99.18%
$P(\mu_1|t_{1:20,p_{11}})$	0.0	1.0	1.0	1.0	1.0	1.0	1.0	0.0	1.0	1.0	1.0	1.0	0.0	1.0	0.0	0.0	1.0	0.0	0.0	0.0	100.00%
$P(\mu_1|t_{1:20,p_{12}})$	0.0	1.0	1.0	1.0	1.0	1.0	1.0	0.0	1.0	1.0	1.0	1.0	0.0	1.0	0.0	0.0	1.0	0.0	0.0	0.0	100.00%
$P(\mu_1|t_{1:20,p_{13}})$	0.0	1.0	1.0	1.0	1.0	1.0	1.0	0.0	1.0	1.0	1.0	1.0	0.0	1.0	0.0	0.0	1.0	0.0	0.0	0.0	100.00%
$P(\mu_1|t_{1:20,p_{14}})$	0.0	1.0	1.0	1.0	1.0	1.0	1.0	0.0	1.0	1.0	1.0	1.0	0.0	1.0	0.0	0.0	1.0	0.0	0.0	0.0	100.00%
$P(\mu_1|t_{1:20,p_{15}})$	0.0	1.0	1.0	1.0	1.0	1.0	1.0	0.0	1.0	1.0	1.0	1.0	0.0	1.0	0.0	0.0	1.0	0.0	0.0	0.0	100.00%
$P(\mu_1|t_{1:20,p_{16}})$	0.0	1.0	1.0	1.0	1.0	1.0	1.0	0.0	1.0	1.0	1.0	1.0	0.0	1.0	0.0	0.0	1.0	0.0	0.0	0.0	100.00%
$P(\mu_1|t_{1:20,p_{17}})$	0.0	1.0	1.0	1.0	1.0	1.0	1.0	0.0	1.0	1.0	1.0	1.0	0.0	1.0	0.0	0.0	1.0	0.0	0.0	0.0	100.00%
$\widehat{d_{1:20,k}}$	1	0	0	0	0	0	0	1	0	0	0	0	1	0	1	1	0	1	1	1	100%
$d_{1:20,k}$	1	0	0	0	0	0	0	1	0	0	0	0	1	0	1	1	0	1	1	1	100%

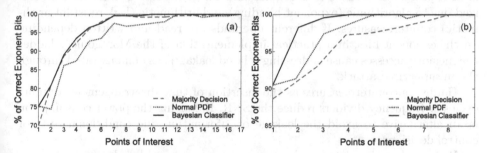

Fig. 4. Relation between the exponent recovery and the number of points of interest: (a) from the least to the most leaking point and (b) from the most to the least leaking point (this Figure is represented in a different scale).

5   Obtaining the Private Key from Randomized Exponents

For decryption and message signing, the retrieval of the randomized exponent $d_r = d + r.\phi(N)$ is the same as retrieving d. Therefore, a single-execution attack is sufficient to break the target device. However, for non-CRT implementations of RSA and in the case when the recovered randomized exponents present few error bits, the adversary can also improve the procedure using a step-by-step attack, as proposed in [19]. In this case, the recovering of several blinding factors r in the exponent randomization is used to derive the exponent d.

Approximately the $\ell/2$ most significant bits of the exponent d are exposed when the public key e is small (3, 17 or $2^{16} + 1$). In this procedure, the term $\phi(N)$ is approximated by N and the approximated exponent is given by, $k \in \mathbb{Z}$:

$$\tilde{d} = \left\lfloor \frac{1 + kN}{e} \right\rfloor$$

Consequently, the adversary can obtain the $\ell/2$ most significant bits of all the possible randomized exponents by computing $\tilde{d_{r_i}} = \tilde{d} + r_i.N$, for all i and $r_i \in [0, 2^{32} - 1]$. Considering λ as being the bit length of the blinding factor r, the λ most significant bits of $d + r.\phi(N)$ are equivalent to the most significant bits of $\tilde{d} + r.N$. Then, the adversary can compute all possible values for r and by observing the recovered randomized exponent d_r, he can deduce r. Finally, he constructs the attack on exponentiation traces containing possibly known blinding factors.

6 Countermeasures

The efficiency of single-execution attacks on exponentiations are related to the signal-to-noise ratio (SNR) of acquired traces. Theoretically, the Algorithm 1 is SPA-protected because it is regular and all manipulated data are randomized due to algorithmic (exponent blinding) and arithmetic (leak resistant arithmetic) countermeasures. If different operands are read and written depending on the exponent bits, in a practical implementation of the Montgomery ladder the memory accesses cause addressing related leakages, as demonstrated through the unsupervised attack.

Hardware countermeasures as the insertion of time disarrangement, dummy cycles or frequency dividers reduce the SNR. Balancing the power consumption is an alternative to avoid the leakage of information due conditional tests or control decisions.

If the leakage is related to memory accesses, a possible solution is the randomization of the RAM addresses during the exponentiation. By doing so, the unsupervised attack was unable to entirely recover the randomized exponent. By selecting the same points of interest $P = \{p_j\}$, we applied the fuzzy k-means clustering algorithm and recovered approximately 80 % of the exponent using the Bayesian classifier technique.

7 Conclusions

This paper presented an unsupervised attack on randomized exponentiations. The explored leakages are based on control executions and memory addressing. We proposed to combine the cluster classification for several points of interest over each exponent bit interpretation in order to derive the randomized exponent using a single EM trace. The results were presented through three different statistical techniques and specifically for the probability density function and Bayesian Classifier techniques, we showed the likelihood for the randomized exponent bits.

The presented unsupervised attack demonstrated the efficiency of clustering algorithms against single execution of exponentiations even in the presence of algorithmic and arithmetic countermeasures. The obtained results show the importance of employing hardware countermeasures in public-key architectures.

References

1. Rivest, R., Shamir, A., Adleman, L.: A method for obtaining digital signatures and public key cryptosystems. Commun. ACM **21**(2), 120–126 (1978)
2. Kocher, P.C.: Timing attacks on implementations of Diffie-Hellman, RSA, DSS, and other systems. In: Koblitz, N. (ed.) CRYPTO 1996. LNCS, vol. 1109, pp. 104–113. Springer, Heidelberg (1996)
3. Kocher, P.C., Jaffe, J., Jun, B.: Differential power analysis. In: Wiener, M. (ed.) CRYPTO 1999. LNCS, vol. 1666, p. 388. Springer, Heidelberg (1999)
4. Coron, J.-S.: Resistance against differential power analysis for elliptic curve cryptosystems. In: Koç, Ç.K., Paar, C. (eds.) CHES 1999. LNCS, vol. 1717, pp. 292–302. Springer, Heidelberg (1999)
5. Brier, E., Clavier, C., Olivier, F.: Correlation power analysis with a leakage model. In: Joye, M., Quisquater, J.-J. (eds.) CHES 2004. LNCS, vol. 3156, pp. 16–29. Springer, Heidelberg (2004)
6. Fouque, P.-A., Valette, F.: The doubling attack – *why upwards is better than downwards*. In: Walter, C.D., Koç, Ç.K., Paar, C. (eds.) CHES 2003. LNCS, vol. 2779, pp. 269–280. Springer, Heidelberg (2003)
7. Montgomery, P.L.: Speeding the Pollard and elliptic curve methods of factorization. Math. Comput. **48**(177), 243–264 (1987)
8. Joye, M., Yen, S.-M.: The Montgomery powering ladder. In: Kaliski, B.S., Koç, Ç.K., Paar, C. (eds.) CHES 2002. LNCS, vol. 2523, pp. 291–302. Springer, Heidelberg (2003)
9. Bajard, J.-C., Imbert, L., Liardet, P.-Y., Teglia, Y.: Leak resistant arithmetic. In: Joye, M., Quisquater, J.-J. (eds.) CHES 2004. LNCS, vol. 3156, pp. 62–75. Springer, Heidelberg (2004)
10. Bajard, J.-C., Didier, L.-S., Kornerup, P.: An RNS Montgomery modular multiplication algorithm. IEEE Trans. Comput. **47**(7), 766–776 (1998)
11. Chari, S., Rao, J.R., Rohatgi, P.: Template attacks. In: Kaliski, B.S., Koç, Ç.K., Paar, C. (eds.) CHES 2002. LNCS, vol. 2523, pp. 13–28. Springer, Heidelberg (2003)
12. Herbst, C., Medwed, M.: Using templates to attack masked Montgomery ladder implementations of modular exponentiation. In: Chung, K.-I., Sohn, K., Yung, M. (eds.) WISA 2008. LNCS, vol. 5379, pp. 1–13. Springer, Heidelberg (2009)
13. Hanley, N., Tunstall, M., Marnane, W.P.: Using templates to distinguish multiplications from squaring operations. IJIS **10**(4), 255–266 (2011)
14. Clavier, C., Feix, B., Gagnerot, G., Roussellet, M., Verneuil, V.: Horizontal correlation analysis on exponentiation. In: Soriano, M., Qing, S., López, J. (eds.) ICICS 2010. LNCS, vol. 6476, pp. 46–61. Springer, Heidelberg (2010)
15. Clavier, C., Feix, B., Gagnerot, G., Giraud, C., Roussellet, M., Verneuil, V.: ROSETTA for single trace analysis. In: Galbraith, S., Nandi, M. (eds.) INDOCRYPT 2012. LNCS, vol. 7668, pp. 140–155. Springer, Heidelberg (2012)
16. Bauer, A., Jaulmes, E., Prouff, E., Wild, J.: Horizontal and vertical side-channel attacks against secure RSA implementations. In: Dawson, E. (ed.) CT-RSA 2013. LNCS, vol. 7779, pp. 1–17. Springer, Heidelberg (2013)

17. Bauer, A., Jaulmes, É.: Correlation analysis against protected SFM implementations of RSA. In: Paul, G., Vaudenay, S. (eds.) INDOCRYPT 2013. LNCS, vol. 8250, pp. 98–115. Springer, Heidelberg (2013)
18. Heyszl, J., Ibing, A., Mangard, S., Santis, F., Sigl, G.: Clustering algorithms for non-profiled single-execution attacks on exponentiations. In: Francillon, A., Rohatgi, P. (eds.) CARDIS 2013. LNCS, pp. 79–93. Springer, Heidelberg (2014)
19. Bauer, S.: Attacking exponent blinding in RSA without CRT. In: Schindler, W., Huss, S.A. (eds.) COSADE 2012. LNCS, vol. 7275, pp. 82–88. Springer, Heidelberg (2012)
20. Itoh, K., Izu, T., Takenaka, M.: Address-bit differential power analysis of cryptographic schemes OK-ECDH and OK-ECDSA. In: Kaliski, B.S., Koç, Ç.K., Paar, C. (eds.) CHES 2002. LNCS, vol. 2523, pp. 129–143. Springer, Heidelberg (2003)
21. Walter, C.D.: Sliding windows succumbs to Big Mac attack. In: Koç, Ç.K., Naccache, D., Paar, C. (eds.) CHES 2001. LNCS, vol. 2162, p. 286. Springer, Heidelberg (2001)
22. Dyrkolbotn, G.O., Snekkenes, E.: Modified template attack detecting address bus signals of equal hamming weight. In: The Norwegian Information Security Conference (NISK), pp. 43–56 (2009)
23. Chevallier-Mames, B., Ciet, M., Joye, M.: Low-cost solutions for preventing simple side-channel analysis: side-channel atomicity. IEEE Trans. Comput. 51(6), 760–768 (2004)
24. Guillermin, N.: A coprocessor for secure and high speed modular arithmetic, Cryptology ePrint Archive, report 2011/354 (2011). http://eprint.iacr.org/
25. Perin, G., Imbert, L., Torres, L., Maurine, P.: Electromagnetic analysis on RSA algorithm based on RNS. In: Proceedings of 16th Euromicro Conference on Digital System Design (DSD), pp. 345–352. IEEE, September 2013
26. Lopez, L., Dahab, R.: Fast multiplication on elliptic curves over $GF(2^m)$ without precomputation. In: Koç, Ç.K., Paar, C. (eds.) CHES'99. LNCS, vol. 1717, pp. 316–327. Springer, Heidelberg (1999)
27. Hankerson, D., Menezes, A.J., Vanstone, S.: Guide to Elliptic Curve Cryptography, Springer Professional Computing (2004)
28. Duda, R.O., Hart, P.E., Stork, D.G.: Pattern Classification, 2nd edn. Wiley, Boston (2001)

On the Optimal Pre-processing for Non-profiling Differential Power Analysis

Suvadeep Hajra[✉] and Debdeep Mukhopadhyay

Department of Computer Science and Engineering,
Indian Institute of Technology Kharagpur, Kharagpur, India
{suvadeep.hajra,debdeep.mukhopadhyay}@gmail.com

Abstract. Differential Power Analysis (DPA) is often preceded by various noise reduction techniques. Digital Signal Processing (DSP) and Principal Component Analysis (PCA) have found their numerous applications in this area. However, most of them either require explicit profiling/semi-profiling step or depend on some heuristically chosen parameters. In this paper, we propose optimal pre-processing of power traces in non-profiling setup using an *optimum* linear filter and an *approximate optimum* linear filter. We have also empirically evaluated the proposed filters in several noisy scenarios which show significant improvements in the results of Correlation Power Analysis (CPA) over the existing pre-processing techniques. We have further investigated the optimality of the one proposed pre-processing technique by comparing it with a profiling attack.

1 Introduction

The success rate of the DPA [1,2] attacks is largely influenced by the noise present in the power traces. Thus, in many of the existing works, various pre-processing techniques have been introduced to reduce the amount of noise in the power traces. Most of these pre-processing techniques are inspired by well-known Digital Signal Processing (DSP) techniques.

First use of DSP in power analysis attack has been reported in [3] where matched filter was used to increase the Signal-to-Noise Ratio (SNR) of the power traces. In [4], comb filter has been used to attack a device protected with random process interrupts. Subsequently, Fast Fourier Transform (FFT) has been introduced as a new domain for performing power analysis attack in [5,6]. Later, several works have been published which employed various frequency domain filters like low-pass filter, band-pass filter or band-stop filter [7–9] for reducing noise in the power traces. However, those filters are only useful when there is less overlapping of signal and noise in the frequency domain. In [10,11], Principal Component Analysis (PCA) has been used for reducing noise in non-profiling DPA attacks. The authors of [11] have further noticed that PCA performs suboptimally for noisy traces.

Though these techniques are useful for some specific applications, they are mostly heuristic in nature. Moreover, optimality of these techniques have been

© Springer International Publishing Switzerland 2014
E. Prouff (Ed.): COSADE 2014, LNCS 8622, pp. 161–178, 2014.
DOI: 10.1007/978-3-319-10175-0_12

rarely studied. Recently in [12], linear Finite Impulse Response (FIR) filter has been used for the optimal pre-processing of power traces. However, their method requires a semi-profiling setup. In this paper, we try to find an optimal linear filter in a non-profiling setup. In signal processing, matched filters are widely used for optimizing the SNR of a noisy signal. We explore the applicability of matched filter for optimal pre-processing of the power traces.

In DSP, matched filter is used to maximize the SNR of a noisy signal. Designing a matched filter for the traces affected by non-white noise requires to know the autocorrelation function of the noise, thus is not feasible in non-profiling DPA attacks. In this paper, we propose an *optimum* linear filter which also maximizes the SNR of the power traces. Besides, when the power traces follow the *multivariate leakage model* introduced (for Xilinx Virtex-5 FPGA) in [13], the proposed filter can be derived without knowing the secret key. Thus, it can be applicable to non-profiling DPA also. We have further proposed an approximation of the proposed filter to make it computationally more efficient. The approximate optimum filter is also more resistant to the estimation error which can be significantly high when the number of power traces used in the attack are less. Pre-processing using the proposed filters have been experimentally verified on various noisy scenarios. The results show significant improvements in the performance of CPA using the introduced pre-processing techniques over the existing ones. We have further verified the optimality of one proposed pre-processing technique by comparing its results with profiling Stochastic attack.

Rest of the paper is organized as follows. Section 2 describes the background of DPA along with the necessary notations used in the work. In Sect. 3, the multivariate leakage model for Xilinx Virtex-5 FPGA has been described. Section 4 derives an expression for the impulse response of the optimum linear filter. The proposed optimum linear filter has been further approximated to make it robust against estimation error and computationally efficient. In Sect. 5, the improvements in the performance of CPA using the proposed filtering techniques are experimentally verified for various noisy scenarios. Section 6 verifies the optimality of one proposed pre-processing technique. Finally, conclusion has been drawn in Sect. 7.

2   Preliminaries

2.1   Notations

For the rest of the paper, we will use a calligraphic letter like $\mathcal{X}$ to denote a finite set. The corresponding capital and small letter, X and x, are used to denote a random variable over the set and a particular element of it respectively. $E[X]$, σ_X and $Var(X)$ are used to denote mean, standard deviation and variance of the random variable X respectively. We also denote by $Cov(X, Y)$ the covariance between the random variables X and Y. The vector $\{x_0, \cdots, x_k\}$ is denoted by $\{x_i\}_{0 \le i \le k}$. Alternatively, it is also denoted by a letter in bold face like $\mathbf{x}$. For convenience, sometimes we use μ_X to denote the mean of the random variable X. Gaussian distribution with mean m and standard deviation σ is represented by $N(m, \sigma)$. $\mathbf{x}'$ and $\mathbf{X}'$ respectively denote the transpose of the vector $\mathbf{x}$ and matrix $\mathbf{X}$.

2.2 Differential Power Analysis

In [14], Standaert et al. has formalized the notion of side-channel key recovery attack. However in this paper, we will only consider standard non-profiling DPA. It can be described by the following steps:

1. An intermediate key-dependent variable $S = F_{k^*}(X)$ is identified as the *target* of the attack. The variable k^* is a small part of the correct key commonly referred to as subkey and $F_{k^*} : \mathcal{X} \to \mathcal{S}$ is a function of a known part $x \in \mathcal{X}$ of the plaintext which is determined by both the algorithm and the correct subkey k^*.
2. The attacker executes the Device Under Attack repeatedly, say q times, for different plaintexts. At the end, the attacker collects q measurement curves or power traces $\{\mathbf{l}^0, \cdots, \mathbf{l}^{q-1}\}$ for the plaintext vector $\{x_0, \cdots, x_{q-1}\}$. Depending upon the measurement setup, each power trace $\mathbf{l}^j$ is a vector of T power measurements i.e. $\{l_0^j, \cdots, l_{T-1}^j\}$ where l_t^j is the power measurement for the tth time instant or sample point and T is the total number of sample points measured during each encryption. Let us denote the leakage by the vector of random variables $\mathbf{L} = \{L_0, \cdots, L_{T-1}\}$ whose t^{th} element L_t represents the leakage of sample point t for $0 \leq t < T$.
3. The collection of traces is followed by an optional pre-processing step such as trace compression, filtering, averaging etc.
4. For all possible key guess $k \in \mathcal{K}$, the target intermediate variable S_k is predicted using $S_k = F_k(X)$ for each value of X from the vector $\{x_0, \cdots, x_{q-1}\}$.
5. Next, the attacker chooses a suitable prediction model $\Psi : \mathcal{S} \to \mathbb{R}$ depending on the hardware leakage behavior of the device and computes the predicted leakage P_k for key guess k as $P_k = \Psi(S_k)$. For CMOS device, Hamming weight and Hamming distance are commonly used as the prediction model.
6. For each key guess k, a statistical tool D, commonly known as distinguisher, is employed to detect the dependency between the predicted leakage P_k and actual leakage L. In *univariate* DPA attacks, the distinguisher D is applied on the leakage of a single time instant t^* which is referred to as point of interest. In most of the practical DPA attacks, the point of interest t^* is not known before hand. Thus, D is applied on each of the sample points independently and the best result is chosen among those.
7. At the end of Step 6, a vector $\mathbf{D} = \{d_k\}_{k \in \mathcal{K}} = \{\mathrm{D}(P_k, \mathbf{L})\}_{k \in \mathcal{K}}$ is generated. The attack is said to be sound if for enough number of traces $k^* = argmax_{k \in \mathcal{K}} d_k$ holds with some non-negligible probability.

Throughout the literature, many distinguishers such as Difference of Mean (DoM [1]), Partition Power Analysis (PPA [15]), Correlation Power Analysis (CPA [16]) have been introduced. Among those, CPA is one of the widely used DPA attack which uses Pearson's correlation coefficient as the distinguisher to detect the linearity between the leakages of some sample points with the pre-dicted leakage for the correct key P_{k^*}. Interestingly, [17] has shown that most of the univariate DPA attacks can be expressed as CPA using a different prediction model. Thus, in this paper, all the experimental verification has been done with respect to CPA.

In practice, a large number of sample points may contain information about the target S. In noisy scenarios, the SNR of the power traces can be increased sig-nificantly by accumulating the signal energy over the sample points. Let leakages of two sample points, L_{t_1} and L_{t_2}, follow $L_{t_1} = \Psi(S) + N_1$ and $L_{t_2} = \Psi(S) + N_2$ where N_1 and N_2 are the independent Gaussian noises with variance σ^2. Then by taking the average of the two leakages, one can reduce the noise variance of the resultant leakage to $\sigma^2/2$, thus can double the effective SNR. However, such kinds of leakage combining may not always lead to higher SNR. In profiling attacks, leakage can be combined in an optimal way since it can compute the distribution of the leakages using the secret key. In this paper, our objective is to optimally extract information from multiple sample points by combining their leakages in a non-profiling setup where the secret key is not known.

3   Extending the Leakage Model over Multiple Time Samples

It is common in the literature to assume a linear relationship of the leakage to the Hamming weight of the target (in Hamming weight model) or to the Hamming distance between the target and a known value (in Hamming distance model) [16,18,19]. In other words, the leakage of some sample point L_{t^*} is assumed to follow:

$$L_{t^*} = a\Psi(S) + N = aP + N \tag{1}$$

where a is some real, $P = \Psi(S)$ and N be a random variable representing Gaussian noise. Recently, [13] has extended this relationship for all the leakages of a window of sample points as

$$L_t = a_t P + N_t, \qquad\qquad t_0 \leq t < t_0 + \tau$$

where a_t belongs to the set of real numbers. They have further incorporated the algorithmic noise into the above equation as:

$$L_t = a_t(P + U + c) + N_t = a_t(I + c) + N_t, \qquad t_0 \leq t < t_0 + \tau \tag{2}$$

where U represents the leakage due to the algorithmic noise, c be the leakage due to key scheduling algorithm and control bits. The random variable $I = P + U$ and τ-dimensional random variable $\mathbf{N} = \{N_{t_0}, \cdots, N_{t_0+\tau-1}\}$ follows a multivariate Gaussian distribution with zero mean vector and covariance matrix $\mathbf{\Sigma_N}$. The time window $\{t_0, \cdots, t_0+\tau-1\}$ is broadly determined by the clock cycle in which the target operation is being performed (please refer to the next paragraph). We denote this time window by $\{0, \cdots, \tau-1\}$ and in the rest of the paper, the power traces are referred by the leakages of this time window only.

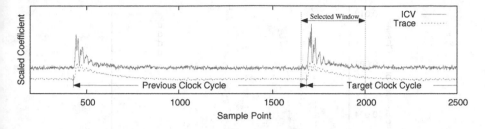

Fig. 1. The dashed line plots a trace for the last two clock cycles of an AES encryption. The solid line is the plot for ICV computed for the two rounds using $1,000$ traces. The figure shows higher peak in the ICV curve for the target clock cycle.

Selection of the Time Window. The model is valid only in the clock cycle in which the target operation is being performed (called the *target clock cycle*). In [20], the authors suggested to use Inter-Class Variance (ICV), $Var(E[L_t|X])$, for the selection of correct time-window in collision attack. Recently in [21], Normalized Inter-Class Variance (NICV) has been introduced as a metric for window selection. NICV takes the ratio of Inter-Class Variance, $Var(E[L_t|X])$, and the leakage variance, $Var(L_t)$, to determine the relevant sample points. We have found better result using ICV. Figure 1 shows the ICV computed at each of the sample points of the last two rounds of an AES encryptions using 1000 traces. For the target clock cycle, ICV shows a higher peak. Once the target clock cycle has been identified using the ICV, an window of sample points around the peaks of the target clock cycle can be selected as the target window.

In the next subsection, we provide the experimental validation of Eq. (2) in our setup.

3.1   Experimental Validation

To validate Eq. (2), we first classify all the traces according to the values of I which has been computed using the correct key. Then we estimate the deterministic leakage $\mathbf{d}^i = \{E[L_t|I = i]\}_{t_0 \le t < t_0 + \tau}$ for all $i \in \mathcal{I}$ by computing the mean leakage curve of each class. Lastly, we verify the linear equation $E[L_t|I = i] - E[L_t|I = 0] = a_t \cdot i$ for all $i \in \mathcal{I} \setminus \{0\}$ and $t_0 \le t < t_0 + \tau$ using linear regression. However, we do not know the values of $a_t, t_0 \le t < t_0 + \tau$. Thus, we start with correlating $\mathbf{d}^{i_1}$ and $\mathbf{d}^{i_2}$ for all $i_1, i_2 \in \mathcal{I}$ and then use the high correlation among those to estimate $\mathbf{a} = \{a_t\}_{t_0 \le t < t_0 + \tau}$.

We implemented an iterative structure of 32 parallel 10×4 S-boxes using distributed ROM in the setup described in Appendix A. All of the S-boxes were connected to the same input to increase the SNR of the power traces by the synchronous computations of the S-boxes. It should be noted that though the duplication of a single S-box increases the SNR of all the sample points, their relative SNR remains same. We collected $1,600$ power traces each having 200 sample points with random inputs. The values of the target variable S is taken to be the output of the S-box. We have also considered the Hamming distance model

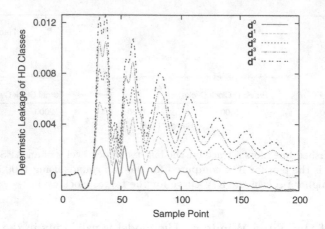

Fig. 2. Mean Leakage for the five Hamming distance classes.

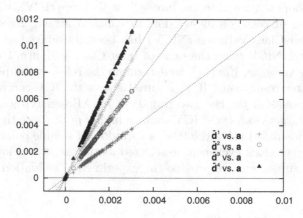

Fig. 3. Scatter Plots of $\bar{\mathbf{d}}^1$, $\bar{\mathbf{d}}^2$, $\bar{\mathbf{d}}^3$ and $\bar{\mathbf{d}}^4$ against $\mathbf{a}$.

i.e. $\Psi(s)$ is taken to be the Hamming distance between s and the least significant 4 bit of the S-box input for all $s \in S$. Since all the parallel S-boxes have the same input and the output, the algorithmic noise U is zero i.e. $I = P = \Psi(S)$.

The classification involves partitioning all the 1,600 traces into five HD classes for $I = 0$ to 4. Figure 2 shows the deterministic leakage curve $\mathbf{d}^i = \{E[L_t|I = i]\}_{t_0 \leq t < t_0+\tau}$ for $0 \leq i \leq 4$ i.e. for each of the five classes. It is seen in the figure that the deterministic leakage for different HD classes i.e. different values of I are following almost same pattern. However, the non-zero leakage for HD class 0 is caused by the switching activities of the control bits and the DC power consumption which is also present in the leakages of all other classes. To remove this factor, we computed absolute deterministic leakage curves as $\bar{\mathbf{d}}^i = \mathbf{d}^i - \mathbf{d}^0 = \{E[L_t|I = i] - E[L_t|I = 0]\}_{t=t_0}^{t_0+\tau-1} = \{a_t \cdot i\}_{t=t_0}^{t_0+\tau-1}$ (from Eq. (2)) for $i = 1, \cdots, 4$. Table 1 shows the correlation between $\bar{\mathbf{d}}^{i_1}$ and $\bar{\mathbf{d}}^{i_2}$ for all $i_1, i_2 \in \mathcal{I} \setminus \{0\}$. The values of these correlations are close to one which ensure

Table 1. Pearson's correlation between absolute deterministic leakage curves of different pairs of HD classes.

Correlation	$\bar{\mathbf{d}}^1$	$\bar{\mathbf{d}}^2$	$\bar{\mathbf{d}}^3$	$\bar{\mathbf{d}}^4$
$\bar{\mathbf{d}}^1$	1	0.9991	0.9981	0.9978
$\bar{\mathbf{d}}^2$	0.9991	1	0.9995	0.9992
$\bar{\mathbf{d}}^3$	0.9981	0.9995	1	0.9997

Table 2. Relations of $\bar{\mathbf{d}}_1$, $\bar{\mathbf{d}}_2$, $\bar{\mathbf{d}}_3$ and $\bar{\mathbf{d}}_4$ with $\mathbf{a} = \{a_t\}_{t=0}^{\tau-1}$.

Variable	Obtained relation	Expected relation
$E[L_t|I=1] - E[L_t|I=0]$	$a_t \times 1.23 - 1.60 \times 10^{-5}$	$a_t \times 1$
$E[L_t|I=2] - E[L_t|I=0]$	$a_t \times 2.17 - 7.26 \times 10^{-8}$	$a_t \times 2$
$E[L_t|I=3] - E[L_t|I=0]$	$a_t \times 2.95 - 1.41 \times 10^{-6}$	$a_t \times 3$
$E[L_t|I=4] - E[L_t|I=0]$	$a_t \times 3.65 - 1.75 \times 10^{-5}$	$a_t \times 4$

that all of these vectors follow linear relations with a common vector namely $\mathbf{a} = \{a_{t_0}, \cdots, a_{t_0+\tau-1}\}$. We estimate $\mathbf{a}$ by $\frac{\sum_{i=1}^{4} \bar{\mathbf{d}}^i}{\sum_{i=1}^{4} i}$.

Next, we plot the vectors $\bar{\mathbf{d}}^i$ for all $i \in \mathcal{I} \setminus \{0\}$ against the estimated $\mathbf{a}$. The plot is shown in Fig. 3. The figure shows the linear relationships of $\bar{\mathbf{d}}^i$'s with the estimated $\mathbf{a}$. So, we have further used linear regression to find the closest linear models of the relation between each of $\bar{\mathbf{d}}_1$, $\bar{\mathbf{d}}_2$, $\bar{\mathbf{d}}_3$ and $\bar{\mathbf{d}}_4$ and the estimated $\mathbf{a} = \{a_t\}_{t=0}^{\tau-1}$. The relations obtained using linear regression are sufficiently close to the expected relation which are shown in Table 2. This provides an evidence of the validity of Eq. (2).

4   Optimum Linear Filter

A linear Finite Impulse Response (FIR) filter of order ν is defined by the impulse response represented by the vector $\{h_0, \cdots, h_{\nu-1}\}$. The response $f_{\text{out}}(t)$ of the filter for the input signal $f_{\text{in}}(t)$ is given by the convolution of the input signal with the impulse response, i.e. $f_{\text{out}}(t) = \sum_{j=0}^{\nu-1} h_j f_{\text{in}}(t-j)$. The input signal $f_{\text{in}}(t)$ is a time-shifted version of a known signal $f_s(t)$ corrupted by some additive noise. The filter coefficients are derived to maximize the SNR of the output signal $f_{\text{out}}(t)$. Thus, it detects the presence of the known signal $f_s(t)$ in the input signal $f_{\text{in}}(t)$ by maximizing the output signal $f_{\text{out}}(t)$ at some time index. The time index is later used to find the shifted position of the known signal $f_s(t)$ in the input signal $f_{\text{in}}(t)$. Such a filter is called matched filter.

In side-channel attack, a trace following Eq. (2) can be represented as $\mathbf{l} = \{l_0, \cdots, l_{\tau-1}\} = \{a_0(i+c)+n_0, \cdots, a_{\tau-1}(i+c)+n_{\tau-1}\}$ where i and $\{n_0, \cdots, n_{\tau-1}\}$ be the instants of the random variables I and $\mathbf{N} = \{N_0, \cdots, N_{\tau-1}\}$ respectively. Thus, it is a sum of deterministic signal $\{a_0(i+c), \cdots, a_{\tau-1}(i+c)\}$ and the noise $\{n_0, \cdots, n_{\tau-1}\}$. Consequently, a matched filter with impulse response

$\mathbf{h} = \{h_0, \cdots, h_{\tau-1}\}$ can be used to maximize the SNR of the trace by integrating energy of the signal (deterministic leakage) over time. Since there is no time shift of the deterministic signal $\{a_0(i+c), \cdots, a_{\tau-1}(i+c)\}$ in the trace l, we do not need to compute the time shift in this application. Consequently, it is enough to compute the impulse response of the matched filter at $t = \tau - 1$ given by $\sum_{j=0}^{\tau-1} h_j l_{(\tau-j-1)}$. However for convenience, we re-write this expression using inner product form

$$l_o = \sum_{t=0}^{\tau-1} h_t l_t = \mathbf{h}'\mathbf{l} \tag{3}$$

Since $\mathbf{l} = \{l_0, \cdots, l_{\tau-1}\} = \{a_0(i+c)+n_0, \cdots, a_{\tau-1}(i+c)+n_{\tau-1}\}$, we re-write Eq. (3) as

$$l_o = \sum_{t=0}^{\tau-1}(h_t a_t \cdot (i+c) + h_t n_t) = (i+c)\mathbf{h}'\mathbf{a} + \mathbf{h}'\mathbf{n} \tag{4}$$

where $\mathbf{a} = \{a_0, \cdots, a_{\tau-1}\}$ and $\mathbf{n} = \{n_0, \cdots, n_{\tau-1}\}$. Without loss of generality, we assume that the output leakage is centered to zero with respect to its mean over all the traces i.e.

$$\tilde{l}_o = \mathbf{h}'(\mathbf{l} - E[\mathbf{L}]) \tag{5}$$
$$= (i - E[I])\mathbf{h}'\mathbf{a} + \mathbf{h}'\mathbf{n}$$
$$= \tilde{i}\mathbf{h}'\mathbf{a} + \mathbf{h}'\mathbf{n} \tag{6}$$

where $\tilde{i} = i - E[I]$.

Our goal is to derive an expression for $\mathbf{h}$. To start with, we formally define *Signal to Noise Ratio* (SNR) of the output leakage as the ratio of the power of the deterministic leakage and the average power of the noise in the centered output leakage $\tilde{l}_o$:

$$SNR = \frac{|\tilde{i}\mathbf{h}'\mathbf{a}|^2}{E[|\mathbf{h}'\mathbf{n}|^2]} = \tilde{i}^2 \times \frac{|\mathbf{h}'\mathbf{a}|^2}{E[(\mathbf{h}'\mathbf{n})(\mathbf{h}'\mathbf{n})']} = \tilde{i}^2 \times \frac{|\mathbf{h}'\mathbf{a}|^2}{\mathbf{h}'\Sigma_{\mathbf{N}}\mathbf{h}} \tag{7}$$

Recall that $\Sigma_{\mathbf{N}}$ is the $\tau \times \tau$ covariance matrix of the multivariate Gaussian noise $\mathbf{N} = \{N_0, \cdots, N_{\tau-1}\}$.

It should be noted that by taking the expectation of the SNR of the output leakage over all traces, we get the 'global' SNR of the output leakage as the ratio of the variance of its deterministic part (signal) and the variance of noise – which is equivalent to the definition of SNR given in Sect. 4.3.2 of [2]. We need to select $\mathbf{h}$ such that it maximizes the SNR of every traces, thus the global SNR. The global SNR, in turn, increases the success rate of the DPA attacks [2].

Since without the correct key, one cannot separate the deterministic leakage from noise, the proper estimation of $\Sigma_{\mathbf{N}}$ is not possible in non-profiling DPA. Thus, we define *Signal Ratio* (SR) of the output leakage as the ratio of the power of the deterministic part and the average power of the centered output leakage $\tilde{l}_o$:

$$SR = \frac{|\tilde{i}\mathbf{h}'\mathbf{a}|^2}{E[|\tilde{l}_o|^2]}$$

We simplify the above definition as:

$$SR = \frac{\tilde{i}^2 |\mathbf{h}'\mathbf{a}|^2}{E[|\mathbf{h}'(1 - E[\mathbf{L}])|^2]}, \qquad \text{using Eq. (5)}$$

$$= \tilde{i}^2 \times \frac{|\mathbf{h}'\mathbf{a}|^2}{\mathbf{h}'E[(1 - E[\mathbf{L}])'(1 - E[\mathbf{L}])]\mathbf{h}}$$

$$= \tilde{i}^2 \times \frac{|\mathbf{h}'\mathbf{a}|^2}{\mathbf{h}'\mathbf{\Sigma_L}\mathbf{h}} \tag{8}$$

$$= \tilde{i}^2 \times \frac{|\mathbf{h}'\mathbf{a}|^2}{\mathbf{h}'\mathbf{\Sigma_D}\mathbf{h} + \mathbf{h}'\mathbf{\Sigma_N}\mathbf{h}}$$

$$= \tilde{i}^2 \times \frac{|\mathbf{h}'\mathbf{a}|^2}{Var(I)|\mathbf{h}'\mathbf{a}|^2 + \mathbf{h}'\mathbf{\Sigma_N}\mathbf{h}} \tag{9}$$

where $\mathbf{\Sigma_L}$ and $\mathbf{\Sigma_D}$ are the covariance matrices of the total leakage and the deterministic leakage respectively. The last step follows because $Cov(a_{t_1}(I + c), a_{t_2}(I + c)) = a_{t_1} a_{t_2} Var(I)$. Our objective is to find $\mathbf{h}$ such that SNR of the output leakage is maximum. Interestingly, both the SNR and the SR reaches their maximum simultaneously. It is stated in the following lemma.

Lemma 1. *The SNR of the output leakage l_o reaches its maximum value if and only if the SR of the leakage also reaches its maximum.*

Proof. If $\tilde{i} = 0$, the statement is trivially true. Let us assume $\tilde{i} \neq 0$. From Eq. (9),

$$SR = \frac{1}{\frac{Var(I)}{\tilde{i}^2} + \frac{\mathbf{h}'\mathbf{\Sigma_N}\mathbf{h}}{\tilde{i}^2|\mathbf{h}'\mathbf{a}|^2}} = \frac{1}{c_1 + \frac{1}{SNR}}$$

where $c_1 = \frac{Var(I)}{\tilde{i}^2}$. We can rewrite the above equation as, $\frac{1}{SR} = c_1 + \frac{1}{SNR}$. Since c_1 is constant for a given trace, the conclusion follows.

We now maximize the SR of the output signal l_o instead of the SNR. Lemma 2 provides an expression for the impulse response of a filter which maximizes the SR of l_o.

Lemma 2. *The impulse response of the linear filter which maximizes the SR of the output leakage l_o can be given by $\mathbf{\Sigma_L}^{-1}\mathbf{a}$.*

The proof of Lemma 2 is given in Appendix C. We now state and prove our final result in Theorem 1. Before that let us denote by $\mu_\mathbf{L}$ the mean leakage vector $E[\mathbf{L}] = \{E[L_0], \cdots, E[L_{\tau-1}]\}$.

Theorem 1. *Let the leakage $\mathbf{L}$ follows Eq. (2). The linear FIR filter with impulse response $\mathbf{h}_{opt} = \mathbf{\Sigma_L}^{-1}\mu_\mathbf{L}$ maximizes the SNR of the output signal $l_o = \mathbf{h}'_{opt}\mathbf{l}$.*

Proof. If we let $\mathbf{h}_{opt} = \mathbf{\Sigma_L}^{-1}\mathbf{a}$, according to Lemma 2, $\mathbf{h}_{opt}$ optimizes the SR of l_o. Thus, according to Lemma 1, $\mathbf{h}_{opt}$ also optimizes the SNR of l_o. Taking the expectation on both sides of Eq. (2) we get,

$$\mu_\mathbf{L} = (E[I] + c)\,\mathbf{a},$$

$$\text{or,} \quad \mathbf{a} = \mu_\mathbf{L}/(E[I] + c).$$

Putting this value of $\mathbf{a}$ into $\mathbf{h}_{opt} = \boldsymbol{\Sigma}_{\mathbf{L}}^{-1}\mathbf{a}$, we get $\mathbf{h}_{opt} = \boldsymbol{\Sigma}_{\mathbf{L}}^{-1}\mu_{\mathbf{L}}/(E[I]+c)$. Since a constant factor in the impulse response of a filter does not have any affect on the SNR of the output, by neglecting the constant factor, we get $\mathbf{h}_{opt} = \boldsymbol{\Sigma}_{\mathbf{L}}^{-1}\mu_{\mathbf{L}}$.

Thus, the impulse response of an optimum linear filter can be computed using the expression $\boldsymbol{\Sigma}_{\mathbf{L}}^{-1}\mu_{\mathbf{L}}$. It should be noted that neither $\boldsymbol{\Sigma}_{\mathbf{L}}$ nor $\mu_{\mathbf{L}}$ requires the knowledge of the correct key to estimate. Hence, the filter can be useful in non-profiling DPA also.

Elimination of the Matrix Inversion. Computation of $\boldsymbol{\Sigma}_{\mathbf{L}}^{-1}\mu_{\mathbf{L}}$ involves the computation of the inverse of a $\tau \times \tau$ matrix which has a computational complexity $\mathcal{O}(\tau^3)$. Moreover, the inverse operation is highly susceptible to the error in the estimation of the covariance matrix. To avoid this operation, we note that the diagonal elements $c_{t,t}$ of the matrix $\boldsymbol{\Sigma}_{\mathbf{L}} = (c_{t_1,t_2})$ are the variance of the leakage L_t and the off-diagonal elements c_{t_1,t_2}, where $t_1 \neq t_2$, are the covariance between L_{t_1} and L_{t_2}. Let us approximate the leakage covariance matrix $\boldsymbol{\Sigma}_{\mathbf{L}}$ by setting all of its off-diagonal elements to zero. Then, the approximated covariance $\tilde{\boldsymbol{\Sigma}}_{\mathbf{L}}$ will be a diagonal matrix having the diagonal elements $\{c_{0,0}, \cdots, c_{\tau-1,\tau-1}\} = \{\sigma_{L_0}^2, \cdots, \sigma_{L_{\tau-1}}^2\}$. Thus the impulse response of an approximate optimum linear filter can be given by

$$\mathbf{h}_{appr} = \tilde{\boldsymbol{\Sigma}}_{\mathbf{L}}^{-1}\mu_{\mathbf{L}} = \{\frac{\mu_{L_0}}{\sigma_{L_0}^2}, \cdots, \frac{\mu_{L_{\tau-1}}}{\sigma_{L_{\tau-1}}^2}\} \tag{10}$$

Estimation of $\mathbf{h}_{appr}$ is also computationally more efficient. The estimation of the mean and the variance of the leakages of τ sample points requires $O(q\tau)$ operation which is the lower bound for any pre-processing technique.

Computing in a New Basis. When the leakages of different sample points are significantly correlated, the approximation of Eq. (10) becomes less accurate. To avoid this, the leakage $L = \{L_0, \cdots, L_{\tau-1}\}$ can be transformed into a new basis system $\tilde{L} = \{\tilde{L}_0, \cdots, \tilde{L}_{\tau-1}\}$ by some linear transformation such that leakage components along two different axes $\tilde{L}_{t_1}$ and $\tilde{L}_{t_2}$ become uncorrelated. The basis of eigenvectors of the covariance matrix is the best choice for this as the components along different eigenvectors are independent to each other. The standard way of converting a data sample into the basis of eigenvectors (referred to as Principal Components) is known as Principal Component Analysis which has been studied in several side channel context such as in [10,11,22]. However, it is a computationally intensive process.

Other alternative is to use Discrete Fourier Transform (DFT) to convert the leakage samples to a new orthonormal basis (frequency domain). DFT of the trace l is given by the complex coefficient vector $\tilde{l} = \{\tilde{l}_0, \cdots, \tilde{l}_{\tau-1}\}$ where

$$\tilde{l}_j = \sum_{t=0}^{\tau-1} l_t \cdot e^{-i2\pi jt/\tau} = \sum_{t=0}^{\tau-1} l_t \cdot (cos\frac{2\pi jt}{\tau} - i \cdot sin\frac{2\pi jt}{\tau})$$

Here i represents the imaginary unit. DFT of a trace of size τ can be achieved using $O(\tau log\tau)$ operation. In frequency domain, the distinguisher is applied on

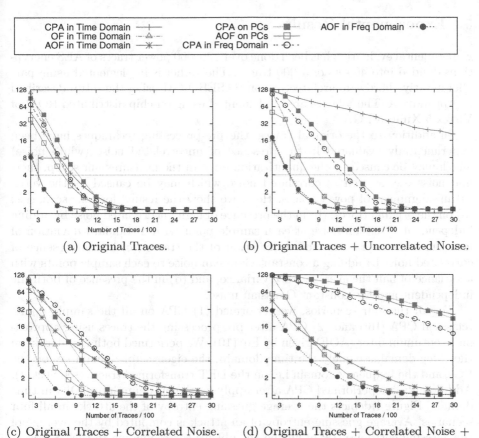

Fig. 4. Plots of the average guessing entropy with respect to increasing number of power traces. The double arrow depicts the difference between the number of required traces for CPA on the output of frequency domain AOF and the CPA on unfiltered traces to bring the average guessing entropy below 4.

the absolute value of the complex coefficients $\tilde{l}_j$ [6, 12]. We do not use it since the absolute operation is not a linear operation. Rather, we keep both the real part (cosine coefficient) and the imaginary part (sine coefficient) as separate sample points. Since, both the real and the imaginary part are obtained using linear transformations and the linear transformation does not destroy the statistical property of the power traces, the resulting DFT traces also follow Eq. (2). Moreover, even if there exist significant correlations among sample points in time dimension, we can assume that the covariance matrix of the sample points in frequency domain as a sparse matrix. Hence, we can apply the approximate optimum filter given by Eq. (10) in this domain to optimally pre process the power traces.

5   Experimental Results

Experimental evaluation has been done over 120, 000 power traces of AES encryptions divided into 40 sets of 3, 000 traces. The cipher is implemented using parallel iterative hardware architecture on SASEBO-GII using the setup described in Appendix A. The S-boxes are implemented using on-chip distributed ROM of Virtex-5 Xilinx FPGA.

In addition to the original traces, the pre-processing techniques have been experimentally evaluated in the presence of uncorrelated noise (white noise) which may be caused by the quantization error of the measurement setup, thermal noise etc. as well as correlated noise which may be caused by the vertical misalignment of power traces. Here, we show the results for four scenarios: (a) on the original traces, (b) in the presence of high uncorrelated noise by adding independent Gaussian noise at each sample point with a standard deviation of four times the average standard deviation of the traces, (c) in the presence of correlated noise by adding a constant Gaussian noise to each sample points with a variance of half the average trace variance, and (d) in the presence of both the independent and the constant Gaussian noise.

For all the four scenarios, we performed (1) CPA on all the sample points (classical CPA [16]) and (2) CPA after pre-processing the traces using approximate optimum filter (AOF) given by Eq. (10). We performed both the attacks in the three domains namely the time domain, the eigenvector domain i.e. on the PCs, and the frequency domain i.e. on the DFT transformed traces (see Sect. 4). Additionally, we performed CPA after applying the optimum filter (OF) in time domain. Figure 4 depicts the average guessing entropy of the attacks in all four scenarios. Average guessing entropy of an attack is computed by the average of the guessing entropies [14] of all the 16 subkeys corresponding to each S-box.

From Fig. 4, we note the following points:

1. CPA on all sample points performs badly compared to its performance on the filtered traces with an exception in scenario (c) where it performs slightly better on PCs than on the output of AOF in time domain.
2. AOF in time domain performs better in the scenarios where there is no added correlated noise i.e. in scenarios (a) and (b), but performs worse in scenarios (c) and (d) where leakages of different sample points have significant positive correlation.
3. The above inefficiency of AOF in the presence of correlated noise is circumvented by transforming the traces into frequency domain where the correlations among the leakages in different sample points get sparsed making the approximation in Eq. (10) more accurate. Thus, AOF in frequency domain performs better in all the four scenarios.
4. OF in time domain performs badly for lesser number of traces which is mainly due to the erroneous estimation of the covariance matrix Σ_L. However as the trace size increases, its performance improves rapidly. The performance of AOF on PCs are quite similar to the performance of OF in time domain.

In summary, the observations indicate that the best attack methodology reduces the number of power traces significantly which are required to decrease the average guessing entropy. For the various noise characteristics experimented, the reduction varies from 59 % to more than 75 % compared to CPA on unfiltered traces to reduce the guessing entropy below a constant value, say 4. These observations further substantiates better utilization of information contained in the multiple time instants of the power traces by the proposed pre-processing techniques. Comparisons with some more attacks are given in Appendix B.

6   Optimality of the Pre-processing Techniques

In this section, our objective is to verify how close the performance of CPA using AOF in frequency domain to the performance of an optimal multivariate attack. As an optimal attack, we choose profiling Stochastic attack since it can "learn" quickly using relatively smaller number of traces [23]. Profiling Stochastic attack [24] is a three step process: (1) the deterministic part of the leakage is approximated in a chosen vector space, (2) the multivariate density of the noise is estimated, and (3) the key is extracted from a different set of power traces.

In the first step, the vector space is chosen to capture the relation between the deterministic leakage and the bits of the target S. A lower dimensional vector space can only capture a simplified relation, thus performs worse in the key extraction step. However, it requires less number of traces and less computational effort to estimate the relation. On the other hand, a higher dimensional model can capture the relation between the deterministic leakage and the bits of the target S in more details at the cost of more computational effort and more number of traces in step (1) [24]. However, in this work, we do not try to evaluate how much efficiency can be increased by perfecting the model. Rather, our objective is to find how much information gain is possible by combining the leakages of multiple sample points. Thus, we have chosen the 2-dimensional vector space of Hamming distance model (see Sect. 3.3 of [24]). In step (3), two alternative ways for extracting the correct key have been discussed in [24] namely maximum likelihood principal and minimum principal. However, we have chosen the maximum likelihood principal since it yields better result [24].

For performing the Stochastic attack, we have chosen the same set of 120, 000 power traces for all the three steps. It should be noted that it is common in literature to use different sets of traces for profiling steps i.e. for steps (1) & (2) and key extraction step i.e. for step (3). Use of the same set of traces in the key extraction step as in the profiling steps and the knowledge of the correct key gives a slightly optimistic view of the results. Figure 5 depicts the results of Stochastic attack applied on the time domain traces along with the results of CPA on the output of AOF in frequency domain. The figure shows that the performances of CPA on the output of AOF in frequency domain are very close to that of Stochastic attack in all the four scenarios (see Sect. 5).

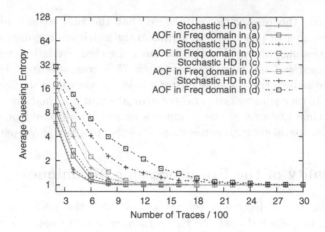

Fig. 5. Average guessing entropy of Stochastic attack with HD model and CPA on the output of AOF in frequency domain in all the four scenarios.

7 Conclusion

In this paper, we have derived the impulse response of the optimum linear filter which optimizes the SNR of the power traces for non-profiling DPA attacks. The derivation is based on recently introduced multivariate leakage model for Virtex-5 FPGA device. The proposed filter has been further approximated to improve the computational complexity and robustness against estimation error for lesser number of power traces. The experimental results reveal significant improvements of CPA using the proposed pre-processing techniques over the existing techniques in various noisy scenarios. We have further evaluated the optimality of the one proposed method by comparing it with profiling Stochastic attack.

Acknowledgements. We thank Shivam Bhasin of TELECOM-ParisTech, France for pointing out the window selection methods using NICV. This research work is partially funded by Department of Information Technology, India.

A   Experimental Setup and Pre-processing

For all the experiments, we have used standard side-channel evaluation board SASEBO-GII [25] which consists of a cryptographic FPGA device: Virtex-5 XC5VLX50. The cryptographic FPGA is driven by a clock frequency of 2 MHz. During the encryption process, voltage drops across VCC and GND of Virtex-5 are captured by Tektronix MSO 4034B Oscilloscope at the rate of 2.5 GS/s i.e. 1, 250 samples per clock period.

The traces acquired using the above setup are already horizontally aligned. However, they are not vertically aligned. The vertical alignment of the traces are

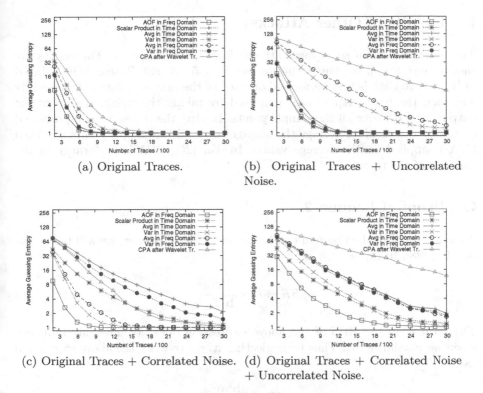

(a) Original Traces.

(b) Original Traces + Uncorrelated Noise.

(c) Original Traces + Correlated Noise.

(d) Original Traces + Correlated Noise + Uncorrelated Noise.

Fig. 6. Plots of the average guessing entropy of some more attacks in the four noisy scenarios.

performed by subtracting the DC bias from each sample point of the traces. The DC bias of each trace is computed by averaging the leakages of a window taken from a region when no computation is going on. This step is also necessary since the derived impulse response of the proposed filters is sensitive to the absolute value of mean leakages.

For mounting the attacks, we selected a window of 300 sample points around the last round register update. After transforming into a different domain, variance of some of the sample points may become very close to zero in the new domain. As a result, while applying AOF in this new domain, the weights (which are mean/variance of the sample points) of those sample points may become very high even if their mean leakages are very less. In other words, due to very low variance, some low SNR sample points may get very high weight. We solved this problem by setting the weight of a sample point having variance less than a fraction of 1/2000 of the maximum variance to zero.

B   Results of Other Attacks

The performances of some more attacks have been compared. The results are shown Fig. 6 for all the four scenarios (see Sect. 5). *Scalar Product* is introduced in [13] where CPA is first performed on each of the sample points independently and then the final outputs are computed by taking the weighted sum of the outputs of CPA over all the sample points. In *Avg*, the traces are pre-processed by taking the absolute average the leakages over all the sample points and then CPA is applied on the average values. In *Var* [26], CPA is performed on the variance of the traces.

C   Proof of Lemma 2

A formal proof of the theorem can be found in [27]. However, we will follow the proof of [28]. In Eq. (8), SR is given as,

$$SR = \tilde{i}^2 \times \frac{|\mathbf{h}'\mathbf{a}|^2}{\mathbf{h}'\mathbf{\Sigma_L}\mathbf{h}}$$

The term $\tilde{i}^2$ in the RHS of the above expression does not have any influence when we maximize SR. Thus by neglecting it, we re-write the above expression as

$$SR = \frac{|\mathbf{h}'\mathbf{a}|^2}{\mathbf{h}'\mathbf{\Sigma_L}\mathbf{h}}$$

Now, if $\mathbf{\Sigma_L}$ is not invertible, a subset of the τ sample points of size $rank(\mathbf{\Sigma_L})$ can be chosen such that the covariance matrix of the chosen sample points is invertible and all the computations can be carried out in this lower dimension. Thus, without loss of generality, we assume $\mathbf{\Sigma_L}$ is positive definite. Thus, the above expression of SR can be written as

$$SR = \frac{|(\mathbf{\Sigma_L}^{1/2}\mathbf{h})'(\mathbf{\Sigma_L}^{-1/2}\mathbf{a})|^2}{(\mathbf{\Sigma_L}^{1/2}\mathbf{h})'(\mathbf{\Sigma_L}^{1/2}\mathbf{h})}$$

Using the Cauchy-Schwarz inequality on the numerator of the RHS of the above expression, the SR is upper bounded by

$$SR \leq \frac{[(\mathbf{\Sigma_L}^{1/2}\mathbf{h})'(\mathbf{\Sigma_L}^{1/2}\mathbf{h})][(\mathbf{\Sigma_L}^{-1/2}\mathbf{a})'(\mathbf{\Sigma_L}^{-1/2}\mathbf{a})]}{(\mathbf{\Sigma_L}^{1/2}\mathbf{h})'(\mathbf{\Sigma_L}^{1/2}\mathbf{h})}$$
$$= \mathbf{a}'\mathbf{\Sigma_L}^{-1}\mathbf{a}$$

And, this upper bound is achieved when $\mathbf{\Sigma_L}^{1/2}\mathbf{h} = \alpha\mathbf{\Sigma_L}^{-1/2}\mathbf{a}$ or $\mathbf{h} = \alpha\mathbf{\Sigma_L}^{-1}\mathbf{a}$ for some normalization factor α. Setting the value of α to one, we complete the proof.

References

1. Kocher, P.C., Jaffe, J., Jun, B.: Differential power analysis. In: Wiener, M. (ed.) CRYPTO 1999. LNCS, vol. 1666, pp. 388–397. Springer, Heidelberg (1999)
2. Mangard, S., Oswald, E., Popp, T.: Power Analysis Attacks - Revealing the Secrets of Smart Cards. Springer, New York (2007)
3. Messerges, T.S., Dabbish, E.A., Sloan, R.H.: Investigations of power analysis attacks on smartcards. In: USENIX Workshop on Smartcard Technology, pp. 151–162 (1999)
4. Clavier, C., Coron, J.-S., Dabbous, N.: Differential power analysis in the presence of hardware countermeasures. In: Koç, Ç.K., Paar, C. (eds.) CHES 2000. LNCS, vol. 1965, pp. 252–263. Springer, Heidelberg (2000)
5. Rechberger, C., Oswald, E.: Practical template attacks. In: Lim, C.H., Yung, M. (eds.) WISA 2004. LNCS, vol. 3325, pp. 440–456. Springer, Heidelberg (2005)
6. Gebotys, C.H., Ho, S., Tiu, C.C.: EM analysis of Rijndael and ECC on a Wireless Java-based PDA. In: Rao, J.R., Sunar, B. (eds.) CHES 2005. LNCS, vol. 3659, pp. 250–264. Springer, Heidelberg (2005)
7. Plos, T., Hutter, M., Feldhofer, M.: On comparing side-channel preprocessing techniques for attacking RFID devices. In: Youm, H.Y., Yung, M. (eds.) WISA 2009. LNCS, vol. 5932, pp. 163–177. Springer, Heidelberg (2009)
8. Barenghi, A., Pelosi, G., Teglia, Y.: Improving first order differential power attacks through digital signal processing. In: Makarevich, O.B., Elçi, A., Orgun, M.A., Huss, S.A., Babenko, L.K., Chefranov, A.G., Varadharajan, V. (eds.) SIN, pp. 124–133. ACM, New York (2010)
9. Kasper, T., Oswald, D., Paar, C.: Side-channel analysis of cryptographic RFIDs with analog demodulation. In: Juels, A., Paar, C. (eds.) RFIDSec 2011. LNCS, vol. 7055, pp. 61–77. Springer, Heidelberg (2012)
10. Souissi, Y., Nassar, M., Guilley, S., Danger, J.-L., Flament, F.: First principal components analysis: a new side channel distinguisher. In: Rhee, K.-H., Nyang, D.H. (eds.) ICISC 2010. LNCS, vol. 6829, pp. 407–419. Springer, Heidelberg (2011)
11. Batina, L., Hogenboom, J., van Woudenberg, J.G.J.: Getting more from PCA: first results of using principal component analysis for extensive power analysis. In: Dunkelman, O. (ed.) CT-RSA 2012. LNCS, vol. 7178, pp. 383–397. Springer, Heidelberg (2012)
12. Oswald, D., Paar, C.: Improving side-channel analysis with optimal linear transforms. In: Mangard, S. (ed.) CARDIS 2012. LNCS, vol. 7771, pp. 219–233. Springer, Heidelberg (2013)
13. Hajra, S., Mukhopadhyay, D.: Pushing the limit of non-profiling DPA using multivariate leakage model. Cryptology ePrint Archive, Report 2013/849 (2013). http://eprint.iacr.org/
14. Standaert, F.-X., Malkin, T.G., Yung, M.: A unified framework for the analysis of side-channel key recovery attacks. In: Joux, A. (ed.) EUROCRYPT 2009. LNCS, vol. 5479, pp. 443–461. Springer, Heidelberg (2009)
15. Le, T.-H., Clédière, J., Canovas, C., Robisson, B., Servière, C., Lacoume, J.-L.: A proposition for correlation power analysis enhancement. In: Goubin, L., Matsui, M. (eds.) CHES 2006. LNCS, vol. 4249, pp. 174–186. Springer, Heidelberg (2006)
16. Brier, E., Clavier, C., Olivier, F.: Correlation power analysis with a leakage model. In: Joye, M., Quisquater, J.-J. (eds.) CHES 2004. LNCS, vol. 3156, pp. 16–29. Springer, Heidelberg (2004)

17. Doget, J., Prouff, E., Rivain, M., Standaert, F.-X.: Univariate side channel attacks and leakage modeling. J. Cryptogr. Eng. **1**(2), 123–144 (2011)
18. Akkar, M.-L., Bévan, R., Dischamp, P., Moyart, D.: Power analysis, what is now possible. In: Okamoto, T. (ed.) ASIACRYPT 2000. LNCS, vol. 1976, p. 489. Springer, Heidelberg (2000)
19. Coron, J.-S., Naccache, D., Kocher, P.C.: Statistics and secret leakage. ACM Trans. Embed. Comput. Syst. **3**(3), 492–508 (2004)
20. Moradi, A., Mischke, O., Eisenbarth, T.: Correlation-enhanced power analysis collision attack. In: Mangard, S., Standaert, F.-X. (eds.) CHES 2010. LNCS, vol. 6225, pp. 125–139. Springer, Heidelberg (2010)
21. Bhasin, S., Danger, J.-L., Guilley, S., Najm, Z.: NICV: normalized inter-class variance for detection of side-channel leakage. Cryptology ePrint Archive, Report 2013/717 (2013). http://eprint.iacr.org/
22. Archambeau, C., Peeters, E., Standaert, F.-X., Quisquater, J.-J.: Template attacks in principal subspaces. In: Goubin, L., Matsui, M. (eds.) CHES 2006. LNCS, vol. 4249, pp. 1–14. Springer, Heidelberg (2006)
23. Gierlichs, B., Lemke-Rust, K., Paar, C.: Templates vs. stochastic methods. In: Goubin, L., Matsui, M. (eds.) CHES 2006. LNCS, vol. 4249, pp. 15–29. Springer, Heidelberg (2006)
24. Schindler, W., Lemke, K., Paar, C.: A stochastic model for differential side channel cryptanalysis. In: Rao, J.R., Sunar, B. (eds.) CHES 2005. LNCS, vol. 3659, pp. 30–46. Springer, Heidelberg (2005)
25. Katashita, T., Satoh, A., Sugawara, T., Homma, N., Aoki, T.: Development of side-channel attack standard evaluation environment. In: European Conference on Circuit Theory and Design 2009, ECCTD 2009, pp. 403–408 (2009)
26. Tian, Q., Huss, S.A.: Power amount analysis: an efficient means to reveal the secrets in cryptosystems. Int. J. Cyber-Secur. Digit. Forensics **1**(2), 99–114 (2012)
27. Sills, J., Kamen, E.: Time-varying matched filters. Circuits Syst. Sign. Process. **15**(5), 609–630 (1996). http://dx.doi.org/10.1007/BF01188985 [Online]
28. Wikipedia: Matched filter – Wikipedia, The Free Encyclopedia (2013). http://en. wikipedia.org/wiki/. Accessed 20 December 2013 [Online]

Template Attacks on Different Devices

Omar Choudary and Markus G. Kuhn[✉]

Computer Laboratory, University of Cambridge, Cambridge, UK
{omar.choudary,markus.kuhn}@cl.cam.ac.uk

Abstract. Template attacks remain a most powerful side-channel technique to eavesdrop on tamper-resistant hardware. They use a profiling step to compute the parameters of a multivariate normal distribution from a training device and an attack step in which the parameters obtained during profiling are used to infer some secret value (e.g. cryptographic key) on a target device. Evaluations using the same device for both profiling and attack can miss practical problems that appear when using different devices. Recent studies showed that variability caused by the use of either different devices or different acquisition campaigns on the same device can have a strong impact on the performance of template attacks. In this paper, we explore further the effects that lead to this decrease of performance, using four different Atmel XMEGA 256 A3U 8-bit devices. We show that a main difference between devices is a DC offset and we show that this appears even if we use the same device in different acquisition campaigns. We then explore several variants of the template attack to compensate for these differences. Our results show that a careful choice of compression method and parameters is the key to improving the performance of these attacks across different devices. In particular we show how to maximise the performance of template attacks when using Fisher's Linear Discriminant Analysis or Principal Component Analysis. Overall, we can reduce the entropy of an unknown 8-bit value below 1.5 bits even when using different devices.

Keywords: Side-channel attacks · Template attacks · Multivariate analysis

1 Introduction

Side-channel attacks are powerful tools for inferring secret algorithms or data (passwords, cryptographic keys, etc.) processed inside tamper-resistant hardware, if an attacker can monitor a channel leaking such information, most notably the power-supply current and unintended electromagnetic emissions.

One of the most powerful side-channel attacks is the template attack [2], which consists of a profiling step to compute some parameters (the templates) on a training device and an attack step in which the templates are used to infer some secret data on a target device (Sect. 2). However, most previous studies [2,5,8,10,17] used the same device (and possibly acquisition campaign) for the

© Springer International Publishing Switzerland 2014
E. Prouff (Ed.): COSADE 2014, LNCS 8622, pp. 179–198, 2014.
DOI: 10.1007/978-3-319-10175-0_13

profiling and attack phases. Only recently, Renauld et al. [12] performed an extensive study on 20 different devices, showing that the template attack may not work at all when the profiling and attack steps are performed on different devices; Elaabid et al. [14] showed that acquisition campaigns on the same device, but conducted at different times, also lead to worse template-attack results; and Lomné et al. [16] evaluated this scenario using electromagnetic leakage.

In this paper, we explore further the causes that make template attacks perform worse across different devices. For this purpose, we evaluate the template attacks with four different Atmel XMEGA 256 A3U 8-bit devices, using different compression methods and parameters.

We show that, for our experiments, a main difference across devices and acquisition campaigns is a DC offset, and this difference decreases very much the performance of template attacks (Sect. 4). To compensate for differences between devices or campaigns we evaluate several variants of the template attack (Sect. 5). One of them needs multiple profiling devices, but can improve significantly the performance of template attacks when using sample selection as the compression method (Sect. 5.3). However, based on detailed analysis of Fisher's Linear Discriminant Analysis (LDA) and Principal Component Analysis (PCA), we explain how to use these compression techniques to maximise the performance of template attacks on different devices, even when profiling on a single device (Sect. 5.4).

Overall, our results show that a good choice of compression method and parameters can dramatically improve template attacks across different devices or acquisition campaigns. Previous studies [12,14] may have missed this by evaluating only one compression method.

2   Template Attacks

To implement a template attack, we need physical access to a pair of devices of the same model, which we refer to as the *profiling* and the *attacked* device. We wish to infer some secret value $k\star \in \mathcal{S}$, processed by the attacked device at some point. For an 8-bit microcontroller, $\mathcal{S} = \{0, \ldots, 255\}$ might be the set of possible byte values manipulated by a particular machine instruction.

We assume that we determined the approximate moments of time when the secret value $k\star$ is manipulated and we are able to record signal traces (e.g., supply current or electromagnetic waveforms) around these moments. We refer to these traces as *leakage vectors*. Let $\{t_1, \ldots, t_{m^r}\}$ be the set of time *samples* and $\mathbf{x}^r \in \mathbb{R}^{m^r}$ be the random vector from which leakage traces are drawn.

During the *profiling* phase we record n_p leakage vectors $\mathbf{x}^r_{ki} \in \mathbb{R}^{m^r}$ from the profiling device for each possible value $k \in \mathcal{S}$, and combine these as row vectors $\mathbf{x}^r_{ki}{}'$ in the leakage matrix $\mathbf{X}^r_k \in \mathbb{R}^{n_p \times m^r}$.[1]

Typically, the *raw* leakage vectors $\mathbf{x}^r_{ki}$ provided by the data acquisition device contain a very large number m^r of samples (random variables), due to high sampling rates used. Therefore, we might *compress* them before further processing,

---

[1] Throughout this paper $\mathbf{x}'$ is the transpose of $\mathbf{x}$.

either by selecting only a subset of $m \ll m^r$ of those samples, or by applying some other data-dimensionality reduction method, such as Principal Component Analysis (PCA) or Fisher's Linear Discriminant Analysis (LDA).

We refer to such compressed leakage vectors as $\mathbf{x}_{ki} \in \mathbb{R}^m$ and combine all of these as rows into the compressed leakage matrix $\mathbf{X}_k \in \mathbb{R}^{n_p \times m}$. (Without any such compression step, we would have $\mathbf{X}_k = \mathbf{X}_k^r$ and $m = m^r$.)

Using $\mathbf{X}_k$ we can compute the template parameters $\bar{\mathbf{x}}_k \in \mathbb{R}^m$ and $\mathbf{S}_k \in \mathbb{R}^{m \times m}$ for each possible value $k \in \mathcal{S}$ as

$$\bar{\mathbf{x}}_k = \frac{1}{n_p} \sum_{i=1}^{n_p} \mathbf{x}_{ki}, \qquad \mathbf{S}_k = \frac{1}{n_p - 1} \sum_{i=1}^{n_p} (\mathbf{x}_{ki} - \bar{\mathbf{x}}_k)(\mathbf{x}_{ki} - \bar{\mathbf{x}}_k)', \qquad (1)$$

where the sample mean $\bar{\mathbf{x}}_k$ and the sample covariance matrix $\mathbf{S}_k$ are the estimates of the true mean μ_k and true covariance Σ_k. Note that

$$\sum_{i=1}^{n_p} (\mathbf{x}_{ki} - \bar{\mathbf{x}}_k)(\mathbf{x}_{ki} - \bar{\mathbf{x}}_k)' = \widetilde{\mathbf{X}}_k' \widetilde{\mathbf{X}}_k, \qquad (2)$$

where $\widetilde{\mathbf{X}}_k$ is $\mathbf{X}_k$ with $\bar{\mathbf{x}}_k'$ subtracted from each row, and the latter form allows fast vectorised computation of the covariance matrices in (1).

In our experiments we observed that the particular covariance matrices $\mathbf{S}_k$ are very similar and seem to be independent of the candidate k. In this case, as explained in a previous paper [17], we can use a pooled covariance matrix

$$\mathbf{S}_{\text{pooled}} = \frac{1}{|\mathcal{S}|(n_p - 1)} \sum_{k \in \mathcal{S}} \sum_{i=1}^{n_p} (\mathbf{x}_{ki} - \bar{\mathbf{x}}_k)(\mathbf{x}_{ki} - \bar{\mathbf{x}}_k)', \qquad (3)$$

to obtain a much better estimate of the true covariance matrix Σ.

In the *attack* phase, we try to infer the secret value $k\star \in \mathcal{S}$ processed by the attacked device. We obtain n_a leakage vectors $\mathbf{x}_i \in \mathbb{R}^m$ from the attacked device, using the same recording technique and compression method as in the profiling phase, resulting in the leakage matrix $\mathbf{X}_{k\star} \in \mathbb{R}^{n_a \times m}$. Then, using $\mathbf{S}_{\text{pooled}}$, we can compute a linear discriminant score [17], namely

$$d_{\text{LINEAR}}^{\text{joint}}(k \mid \mathbf{X}_{k\star}) = \bar{\mathbf{x}}_k' \mathbf{S}_{\text{pooled}}^{-1} \left(\sum_{\mathbf{x}_i \in \mathbf{X}_{k\star}} \mathbf{x}_i \right) - \frac{n_a}{2} \bar{\mathbf{x}}_k' \mathbf{S}_{\text{pooled}}^{-1} \bar{\mathbf{x}}_k, \qquad (4)$$

for each $k \in \mathcal{S}$, and try all $k \in \mathcal{S}$ on the attacked device, in order of decreasing score (optimized brute-force search, e.g. for a password or cryptographic key), until we find the correct $k\star$.

2.1   Guessing Entropy

In this work we are interested in evaluating the overall practical success of the template attacks when using different devices. For this purpose we use the *guessing entropy*, which estimates the (logarithmic) average cost of an optimized brute-force search. The guessing entropy gives the expected number of bits of uncertainty remaining about the target value $k\star$, by averaging the results of the attack over all $k\star \in \mathcal{S}$. The lower the guessing entropy, the more successful the attack has been and the less effort remains to search for the correct $k\star$. We compute the guessing entropy g as shown in our previous work [17]. For all the results shown in this paper, we compute the guessing entropy on 10 random selections of traces $\mathbf{X}_{k\star}$ and plot the average guessing entropy over these 10 iterations.

2.2   Compression Methods

Previously [17], we provided a detailed comparison of the most common compression methods: sample selection (1ppc, 3ppc, 20ppc, allap), Principal Component Analysis (PCA) and Fisher's Linear Discriminant Analysis (LDA), which we summarise here. For the sample selection methods 1ppc, 3ppc, 20ppc and allap, we first compute a signal-strength estimate $\mathbf{s}(t)$ for each sample $j \in \{1, \ldots, m^r\}$, by summing the absolute differences[2] between the mean vectors $\bar{\mathbf{x}}_k^r$, and then select the 1 sample per clock cycle (1ppc, $6 \leq m \leq 10$), 3 samples per clock cycle (3ppc , $18 \leq m \leq 30$), 20 samples per clock cycle (20ppc, $75 \leq m \leq 79$) or the 5 % samples (allap, $m = 125$) having the largest $\mathbf{s}(t)$. For PCA, we first combine the first m eigenvectors $\mathbf{u}_j \in \mathbb{R}^{m^r}$ of the *between-groups* matrix $\mathbf{B} = \sum_{k \in \mathcal{S}}(\bar{\mathbf{x}}_k^r - \bar{\mathbf{x}}^r)(\bar{\mathbf{x}}_k^r - \bar{\mathbf{x}}^r)'$, where $\bar{\mathbf{x}}^r = \frac{1}{|\mathcal{S}|}\sum_{k \in \mathcal{S}} \bar{\mathbf{x}}_k^r$, into the matrix of eigenvectors $\mathbf{U} = [\mathbf{u}_1, \ldots, \mathbf{u}_m]$, and then we project the raw leakage matrices $\mathbf{X}_k^r$ into a lower-dimensional space as $\mathbf{X}_k = \mathbf{X}_k^r \mathbf{U}$. For LDA, we use the matrix $\mathbf{B}$ and the pooled covariance $\mathbf{S}_{\text{pooled}}$ from (3), computed from the uncompressed traces $\mathbf{x}_i^r$, and combine the eigenvectors $\mathbf{a}_j \in \mathbb{R}^{m^r}$ of $\mathbf{S}_{\text{pooled}}^{-1}\mathbf{B}$ into the matrix $\mathbf{A} = [\mathbf{a}_1, \ldots, \mathbf{a}_m]$. Then, we use the diagonal matrix $\mathbf{Q} \in \mathbb{R}^{m \times m}$, with $\mathbf{Q}_{jj} = (\mathbf{a}_j' \mathbf{S}_{\text{pooled}} \mathbf{a}_j)^{-\frac{1}{2}}$, to scale the matrix of eigenvectors $\mathbf{A}$ and use $\mathbf{U} = \mathbf{A}\mathbf{Q}$ to project the raw leakage matrices as $\mathbf{X}_k = \mathbf{X}_k^r \mathbf{U}$. In this case, the compressed covariances $\mathbf{S}_k \in \mathbb{R}^{m \times m}$ and $\mathbf{S}_{\text{pooled}} \in \mathbb{R}^{m \times m}$ reduce to the identity matrix $\mathbf{I}$, resulting in more efficient template attacks.

For most of the results shown in Sects. 4 and 5, we used PCA and LDA with $m = 4$, based on the elbow rule (visual inspection of eigenvalues) derived from a standard implementation of PCA and LDA. However, as we will then show in Sect. 5.4, a careful choice of m is the key to good results.

2.3   Standard Method

Using the definitions from the previous sections, we can define the following *standard* method for implementing template attacks.

Method 1 *(Standard)*

1. *Obtain the n_p leakage traces in $\mathbf{X}_k$ from the profiling device, for each k.*
2. *Compute the template parameters $(\bar{\mathbf{x}}_k, \mathbf{S}_{\text{pooled}})$ using (1) and (3).*
3. *Obtain the leakage traces $\mathbf{X}_{k\star}$ from the attacked device.*
4. *Compute the guessing entropy as described in Sect. 2.1.*

---

[2] The SNR signal-strength estimate generally provided similar results (omitted here).

3   Evaluation Setup

For our experimental research we produced four custom PCBs (named *Alpha, Beta, Gamma* and *Delta*) for the unprotected 8-bit Atmel XMEGA 256 A3U microcontroller. The current consumption across all CPU ground pins is measured through a single 10-ohm resistor. We powered the devices from a battery via a 3.3 V linear regulator and supplied a 1 MHz sine wave clock signal. We used a Tektronix TDS 7054 8-bit oscilloscope with P6243 active probe, at 250 MS/s, with 500 MHz bandwidth in SAMPLE mode. Devices Alpha and Beta used a CPU with week batch ID 1145, while Gamma and Delta had 1230.

For the analysis presented in this paper we run five acquisition campaigns: one for each of the devices, which we call *Alpha, Beta, Gamma* and *Delta* (i.e. the same name as the device), and another one at a later time for Beta, which we call *Beta Bis*. For all the acquisition campaigns we used the settings described above. Then, for each campaign and each candidate value $k \in \{0, \ldots, 255\}$ we recorded 3072 traces $\mathbf{x}_{ki}^{r}$ (i.e., 786 432 traces per acquisition campaign), which we randomly divided into a *training* set (for the profiling phase) and an *evaluation* set (for the attack phase). Each acquisition campaign took about 2 h. We note a very important detail for our experiments: instead of acquiring all the traces per k sequentially (i.e. first the 3072 traces for $k = 0$, then 3072 traces for $k = 1$, and so on), we used random permutations of all the 256 values k and acquired 256 traces at a time (corresponding to a random permutation of all the 256 values k), for a total of 3072 iterations. This method distributes equally any external noise (e.g. due to temperature variation) across the traces of all the values k. As a result, the covariances $\mathbf{S}_k$ will be similar and the mean vectors $\bar{\mathbf{x}}_k$ will be affected in the same manner so they will not be dependent on factors such as low-frequency temperature variation.

For all the results shown in this paper we used $n_p = 1000$ traces $\mathbf{x}_{ki}^{r}$ per candidate k during the profiling phase. Each trace contains $m^r = 2500$ samples, recorded while the target microcontroller executed the same sequence of instructions loaded from the same addresses: a MOV instruction, followed by several LOAD instructions. All the LOAD instructions require two clock cycles to transfer a value from RAM into a register, using indirect addressing. In all the experiments our goal was to determine the success of the template attacks in recovering the byte k processed by the second LOAD instruction. All the other instructions were processing the value zero, meaning that in our traces none of the variability should be caused by variable data in other nearby instructions that may be processed concurrently in various pipeline stages. This approach, also used in other studies [8,13,17], provides a general setting for the evaluation of the template attacks. Specific algorithm attacks (e.g. on the S-box output of a block cipher such as AES) may be mounted on top of this.

4   Ideal vs Real Scenario

Most publications on template attacks [2,5,8,10,17] used the same device (and most probably the same acquisition campaign) for the profiling and attack phase

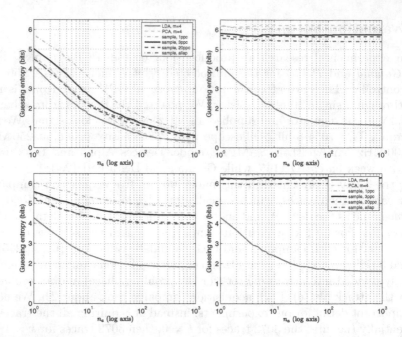

Fig. 1. Template attacks using Method 1 in different scenarios. Top-left (ideal): using same device and acquisition campaign (*Beta*) for profiling and attack. Top-right: using *Alpha* for profiling and *Beta* for attack. Bottom-left: arithmetic average of guessing entropy over all combinations of different pairs of devices for profile and attack. Bottom-right: using same device (Beta) but different acquisition campaigns for profile (*Beta*) and attack (*Beta Bis*).

in their evaluation. The results of the standard Method 1 in this ideal case, where we used the same acquisition data for profiling and attack (but disjoint sets of traces), are shown in Fig. 1 (top-left). We can see that most compression methods perform very well for large n_a, while for smaller n_a LDA is generally the best. This is in line with our previous results [17].

However, in a more realistic scenario, an attacker who wants to infer some secret data from a target device may be forced to use a different device for profiling. Indeed, there are situations where we could use non-profiled attacks, such as DPA [1], CPA [3], or MIA [9], to infer secret data using a single device (e.g. by targeting values that represent a known relationship between key and plaintext). But these methods cannot be used in more general situations where we want to infer a single secret data value that does not depend on any other values, which is the setting of our experiments. In such cases the template attacks or the stochastic approach [4] might be the only viable side-channel attack.[3] Moreover, the template attacks are expected to perform better than the other

---

[3] In our setting we cannot use the non-profiled stochastic method (termed *on-the-fly* attacks by Renauld et al. [12]) either, because our attacker only has data dependent on the target secret value.

attacks when provided with enough profiling data [11]. Therefore, we would like to use template attacks also with different devices for profiling and attack.

As we show in Fig. 1 (top-right), the efficacy of template attacks using the standard Method 1 drops dramatically when using different devices for the profiling and attack steps. This was also observed by Renauld et al. [12], by testing the success of template attacks on 20 different devices with 65 nm CMOS transistor technology. Moreover, Elaabid et al. [14] mentioned that even if the profiling and attack steps are performed on the same device but on different acquisition campaigns we will also observe weak success of the template attacks. In Fig. 1 (bottom-right) we confirm that indeed, even when using the same device but different acquisition campaigns (same acquisition settings), we get results as bad or even worse as when using different devices. In Sect. 5, we offer an explanation for why LDA can perform well across different devices.

4.1 Causes of Trouble

In order to explore the causes that lead to worse attack performance on different acquisition campaigns, we start by looking at two measures of standard deviation (std), that we call *std devices* and *std data*.

Let $\bar{x}_{kj}^{(i)}$ be the mean value of sample $j \in \{1, \ldots, m\}$ for the candidate $k \in \mathcal{S}$ on the campaign $i \in \{1, \ldots, n_c\}$, $\bar{x}_j^{(i)} = \frac{1}{|\mathcal{S}|} \sum_{k \in \mathcal{S}} \bar{x}_{kj}^{(i)}$, $\mathbf{z}_k(j) = [(\bar{x}_{kj}^{(1)} - \bar{x}_j^{(1)}), \ldots, (\bar{x}_{kj}^{(n_c)} - \bar{x}_j^{(n_c)})] = [z_k^{(1)}(j), \ldots, z_k^{(n_c)}(j)]$ and $\bar{z}_k(j) = \frac{1}{n_c} \sum_{i=1}^{n_c} z_k^{(i)}(j)$. Then,

$$\text{std devices}(j) = \frac{1}{|\mathcal{S}|} \sum_{k \in \mathcal{S}} \sqrt{\frac{1}{n_c - 1} \sum_{i=1}^{n_c} \left(z_k^{(i)}(j) - \bar{z}_k(j) \right)^2}, \tag{5}$$

and

$$\text{std data}(j) = \frac{1}{n_c} \sum_{i=1}^{n_c} \sqrt{\frac{1}{|\mathcal{S}| - 1} \sum_{k \in \mathcal{S}} \left(\bar{x}_{kj}^{(i)} - \bar{x}_j^{(i)} \right)^2}. \tag{6}$$

We show these values in Fig. 2. The results on the left plot are from the four campaigns on different devices, while the results on the right plot are from the two campaigns on the device Beta. We can observe that both plots are very similar, which suggests that the differences between campaigns are not entirely due to different devices being used, but largely due to different sources of noise (e.g., temperature, interference, etc.) that may affect in a particular manner each acquisition campaign. Using a similar type of plots, Renauld et al. [12, Fig. 1] observed a much stronger difference, attributed to physical variability. Their observed differences are not evident in our experiments, possibly because our devices use a larger transistor size (around $0.12\,\mu\text{m}$)[4].

---

[4] See http://www.avrfreaks.net/?name=PNphpBB2&file=viewtopic&p=976590

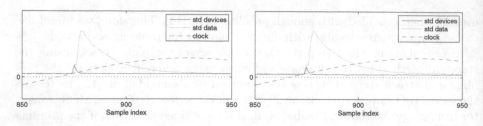

Fig. 2. *std devices*(j) and *std data*(j), along with clock signal for a selection of samples around the first clock cycle of our target LOAD instruction. Left: using the 4 campaigns on different devices. Right: using Beta and Beta Bis.

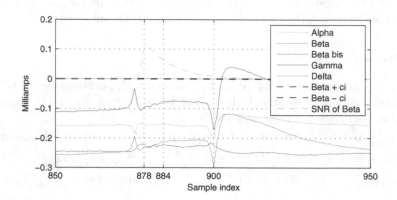

Fig. 3. Overall mean vectors $\bar{\mathbf{x}}$ for all campaigns, from which the overall mean vector of Beta was subtracted. *Beta+ci* and *Beta−ci* represent the confidence region ($\alpha = 0.05$) for the overall mean vector of Beta. *SNR of Beta* is the Signal-to-Noise signal strength estimate of Beta (rescaled). Samples at first clock cycle of target LOAD instruction.

4.2 How It Differs

Next we look at how the overall power consumption differs between acquisition campaigns. In Fig. 3, we show the overall mean vectors $\bar{\mathbf{x}} = \frac{1}{|\mathcal{S}|}\sum_{k \in \mathcal{S}} \bar{\mathbf{x}}_k$ for each campaign, from which we removed the overall mean vector of Beta (hence the vector for Beta is 0). From this figure we see that all overall mean vectors $\bar{\mathbf{x}}$ (except the one for Beta) are far outside the confidence region of Beta ($\alpha = 0.05$). Moreover, we see that the overall mean vector $\bar{\mathbf{x}}$ for Beta Bis is the most distant from the overall mean vector of Beta. This confirms our previous assumption that the main difference between acquisition campaigns is caused by campaign-dependent factors, such as temperature drift, environmental noise, etc. and not necessarily by the use of different devices. A similar observation was made by Elaabid et al. [14], however they used different setups for the different campaigns on the same devices. In our study we have used the exact same setup for the acquisition of data, while replacing only the tested device (evaluation board).

It is clear from Fig. 3 that a main difference between the different campaigns is an overall offset. We see that this is also the case over the samples corresponding to the highest SNR. If we now look at the distributions of our data, as shown in Fig. 4 for Alpha and Beta, we observe that the distributions are very similar (in particular the ordering of the different candidates k is generally the same) but differ mainly by an overall offset. This suggests that, for our experiments, this offset is the main reason why template attacks perform badly when using different campaigns for the profiling and attack steps.

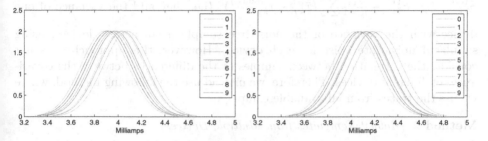

Fig. 4. Normal distribution at sample index $j = 884$ based on the template parameters $(\bar{\mathbf{x}}_k, \mathbf{S}_{\text{pooled}})$ for $k \in \{0, 1, \dots, 9\}$. Left: on Alpha. Right: on Beta.

4.3 Misalignment

We also mention that in some circumstances the recorded traces might be misaligned, e.g. due to lack of a good trigger signal, or random delays introduced by some countermeasure. In such cases, we should first apply a resynchronisation method, such as those proposed by Homma et al. [7]. In our experiments we used a very stable trigger, as shown by the exact alignments of sharp peaks in Fig. 3.

5   Improved Attacks on Different Devices

In this section, we explore ways to improve the success of template attacks when using different devices (or different campaigns), in particular by dealing with the campaign-specific offset noted in Sect. 4. We assume that the attacker can profile well a particular device or set of devices, i.e. can get a large number n_{p} of traces for each candidate k, but needs to attack a different device for which he only has access to a set of n_{a} traces for a particular unknown target value $k\star$. Unless otherwise mentioned, in the following evaluations we considered all possible combinations of the campaigns Alpha, Beta, Gamma and Delta, always ensuring that the campaign of one device is only used in either the profiling or attack phases, but not in both.

5.1   Profiling on Multiple Devices

Renauld et al. [12] proposed to accumulate the sample means $\bar{\mathbf{x}}_k$ and variances S_{jj} (where $\mathbf{S}$ can be either $\mathbf{S}_k$ or $\mathbf{S}_{\text{pooled}}$) of each sample x_j across multiple devices in order to make the templates more robust against differences between different devices. That is, for each candidate k and sample j, and given the sample means $\bar{\mathbf{x}}_k$ and covariances $\mathbf{S}$ from n_c training devices, they compute the robust sample means $\bar{x}_{kj}^{(\text{robust})} = \frac{1}{n_c}(\bar{x}_{kj}^{(1)} + \ldots + \bar{x}_{kj}^{(n_c)})$ (i.e. an average over the sample means of each device), and the robust variance as

$$S_{jj}^{(\text{robust})} = S_{jj}^{(1)} + \frac{1}{n_c-1} \sum_{i=1}^{n_c} \left(\bar{x}_{kj}^{(i)} - \bar{x}_{kj}^{(\text{robust})} \right)^2$$ (i.e. they add the variance of one

device with the variance of the noise-free sample mean across devices, using simulated univariate noise for each device). However, this approach does not consider the correlation between samples or the differences between the covariances of different devices. Therefore, we instead use the following method, where we use the traces from all available campaigns.

Method 2 *(Robust Templates from Multiple Devices)*

1. *Obtain the leakage traces $\mathbf{X}_k^{(i)}$ from each profiling device $i \in \{1, \ldots, n_c\}$, for each k.*
2. *Pull together the leakage traces of each candidate k from all n_c devices into an overall leakage matrix $\mathbf{X}_k^{(\text{robust})} \in \mathbb{R}^{n_p n_c \times m}$ composed as*

$$\mathbf{X}_k^{(\text{robust})'} = [\mathbf{X}_k^{(1)'}, \ldots, \mathbf{X}_k^{(n_c)'}].$$ (7)

3. *Compute the template parameters $(\bar{\mathbf{x}}_k, \mathbf{S}_{\text{pooled}})$ using (1) and (3) on $\mathbf{X}_k^{(\text{robust})}$.*
4. *Obtain the leakage traces $\mathbf{X}_{k\star}$ from the attacked device.*
5. *Compute the guessing entropy as described in Sect. 2.1.*

In our evaluation of Method 2, we used the data from the campaigns on the four devices (Alpha, Beta, Gamma, Delta), by profiling on three devices and attacking the fourth. The results are shown in Fig. 5. We can see that, on average, all the compression methods perform better than using Method 1 (Figs. 1 and 5, bottom-left). This is because, with Method 2, the pooled covariance $\mathbf{S}_{\text{pooled}}$ captures noise from many different devices, allowing more variability in the attack traces. However, the additional noise from different devices also has the negative effect of increasing the variability of each leakage sample [12, Fig. 4]. As a result, we can see that for the attacks on Beta, LDA performs better when we profile on a single device (Alpha) than when we use three devices (Figs. 1 and 5, top-right).

5.2   Compensating for the Offset

In Sect. 4.2 we showed that a main difference between acquisition campaigns (and devices) is a constant offset between the overall mean vector $\bar{\mathbf{x}}$. Therefore, we expect that a template attack that removes this offset should provide better

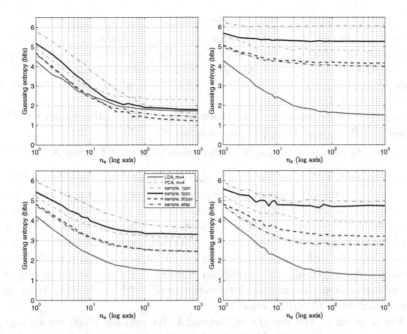

Fig. 5. Results of Method 2, profiling on three devices and attacking the fourth one. Top-left: attack on Alpha; top-right: attack on Beta; bottom-left: arithmetic average of guessing entropy over all four combinations; bottom-right: attack on Delta.

results. Elaabid et al. [14] have shown that, indeed, if we replace each trace from each campaign by the difference between itself and the overall mean $\bar{\mathbf{x}}$ of that campaign (they refer to this process as *normalisation*, and this process may also include division by the overall standard deviation), we can obtain results very similar to those in the ideal case (profiling and attack on the same campaign). However, this approach does not work straight away in a more realistic scenario in which the attacker only has access to a limited number of traces from the target device for a particular target value $k\star$, and hence he cannot compute the overall mean $\bar{\mathbf{x}}$ of the campaign. Nevertheless, if the difference between campaigns is mainly a constant overall offset (as we showed in Sect. 4.2), then an attacker may still use the subset of available attack traces $\mathbf{X}_{k\star}$ to improve the template attack. The method we propose is the following.

Method 3 *(Adapt for the Offset)*

1. Obtain the raw leakage traces $\mathbf{X}_k^r$ from the profiling device, for each k.
2. Compress the raw leakage traces $\mathbf{X}_k^r$ to obtain $\mathbf{X}_k$, for each k.
3. Compute the template parameters $(\bar{\mathbf{x}}_k, \mathbf{S}_{\text{pooled}})$ using (1) and (3) on $\mathbf{X}_k$.
4. Compute the overall mean vector $\bar{\mathbf{x}}^{r(\text{profile})} = \frac{1}{|\mathcal{S}|} \sum_k \bar{\mathbf{x}}_k^r$ from $\mathbf{X}_k^r$.

5. *Compute the constant offset* $c^{(\text{profile})} = \text{offset}(\bar{\mathbf{x}}^{r(\text{profile})}) \in \mathbb{R}$.[5]
6. *Obtain the leakage traces* $\mathbf{X}_{k\star}$ *from the attacked device.*
7. *Compute the offset* $c^{(\text{attack})} = \text{offset}(\mathbf{x}^r) \in \mathbb{R}$ *from each raw attack trace* $\mathbf{x}^r$ *(row of* $\mathbf{X}^r_{k\star}$*). As in step 5, for our data we used the median of* $\mathbf{x}^r$.
8. *Replace each trace* $\mathbf{x}^r$ *(row of* $\mathbf{X}^r_{k\star}$*) by* $\mathbf{x}^{r(\text{robust})} = \mathbf{x}^r - \mathbf{1}^r \cdot (c^{(\text{attack})} - c^{(\text{profile})})$, *where* $\mathbf{1}^r = [1, 1, \ldots, 1] \in \mathbb{R}^{m^r}$.
9. *Apply the compression method to each of the modified attack traces* $\mathbf{x}^{r(\text{robust})}$, *obtaining the robust attack leakage matrix* $\mathbf{X}^{(\text{robust})}_{k\star}$.
10. *Compute the guessing entropy as described in Sect. 2.1 using* $\mathbf{X}^{(\text{robust})}_{k\star}$.

Note that instead of Method 3 we could also compensate for the offset ($c^{(\text{attack})} - c^{(\text{profile})}$) in the template parameters ($\bar{\mathbf{x}}_k, \mathbf{S}_{\text{pooled}}$), but that would require much more computation, especially if we want to evaluate the expected success of an attacker using this method with an arbitrary number of attack traces, as we do in this paper. Note also that in our evaluation, each additional attack trace improves the offset difference estimation of the attacker: the use of the linear discriminant from (4) in our evaluation implies that, as we get more attack traces, we are basically averaging the differences ($c^{(\text{attack})} - c^{(\text{profile})}$), thus getting a better estimate of this difference.

In Fig. 6 we show the results of Method 3. We can see that, on average, we get a similar pattern as with Method 2, but slightly worse results. For the best case (top-right), LDA is now achieving less than 1 bit of entropy at $n_a = 1000$, thus approaching the results on the ideal scenario. On the other hand, we also see that for the worst case (top-left) we get very bad results, where even using LDA with $n_a = 1000$ doesn't provide any real improvement. This large difference between the best and worst cases can be explained by looking at Fig. 3. There we see that the difference between the overall means $\bar{\mathbf{x}}$ of Alpha and Beta is constant across the regions of high SNR (e.g. around samples 878 and 884), while the difference between Beta and Delta varies around these samples. This suggests that, in general, there is more than a simple DC offset involved between different campaigns and therefore this offset compensation method alone is not likely to be helpful.

We could also try to use a high-pass filter, but note that a simple DC block has a non-local effect, i.e. a far-away bump in the trace not related to k can affect the leakage samples that matter most. Another possibility, to deal with the low-frequency offset, might be to use electromagnetic leakage, as this leakage is not affected by low-frequency components, so it may provide better results [16].

5.3 Profiling on Multiple Devices and Compensating for the Offset

If an attacker can use multiple devices during profiling, and since compensating for the offset may help where this offset is the main difference between campaigns, a possible option is to combine the previous methods. This leads to the following.

---

[5] We used the median value of $\bar{\mathbf{x}}^{r(\text{profile})}$ as the offset, since it provides a very good approximation with our data. However, when using a higher clock frequency, the median can become very noisy, so we might have to find more robust methods.

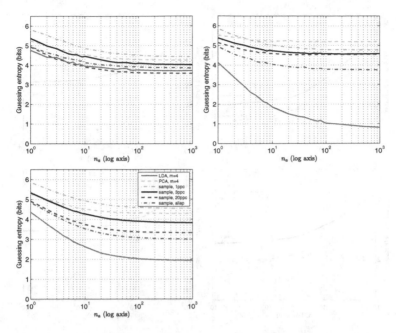

Fig. 6. Results of Method 3, profiling on one device and attacking a different device. Top-left: worst case (profiling on Beta, attack on Delta); top-right: best case (profiling on Alpha, attack on Beta); bottom-left: average over all possible 12 combinations using campaigns Alpha, Beta, Gamma, Delta.

Method 4 *(Robust Templates and Adapt for the Offset)*

1. *Obtain the overall raw leakage matrix* $\mathbf{X}_k^{r(\text{robust})}$ *using Steps (1, 2) of Method 2.*
2. *Use Method 3 with* $\mathbf{X}_k^{r(\text{robust})}$ *instead of* $\mathbf{X}_k^r$.

The results from Method 4 are shown in Fig. 7. We can see that using this method the sample selections (in particular 20ppc, allap) perform much better than using the previous methods, and in most cases even better than LDA. This can be explained as follows: the profiling on multiple devices allows the estimation of a more robust covariance matrix (which helps both the sample selection methods and LDA), while the offset compensation helps more the sample selection methods than LDA. We also notice that PCA still performs poorly, which was somewhat expected since the standard PCA compression method does not take advantage of the robust covariance matrix. In the following sections, we show how to improve template attacks when using LDA or PCA.

5.4   Efficient Use of LDA and PCA

In the previous sections, we showed that LDA did not benefit much from profiling on different devices or adapting the attack traces for a DC offset. In fact,

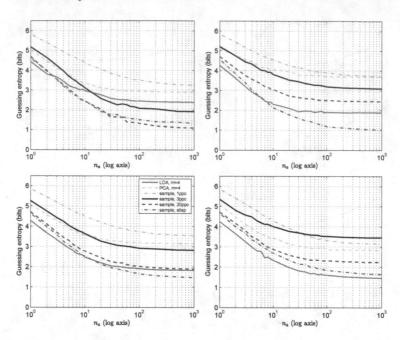

Fig. 7. Results of Method 4, profiling three devices and attacking the fourth one. Top-left: attack on Alpha; top-right: attack on Beta; bottom-left: average over all 4 combinations; bottom-right: attack on Delta.

using the standard Method 1, LDA was already able to provide good results across different devices (see Fig. 1). To understand why this happens, we need to look at the implementation of LDA, summarised in Sect. 2.2. There we can see that LDA takes into consideration the *raw* pooled covariance S_{pooled}. Also, as we explained in Sect. 3, we acquired traces for random permutations of all values k at a time and our acquisition campaigns took a few hours to complete. Therefore, the pooled covariance S_{pooled} of a given campaign contains information about the different noise sources that have influenced the current consumption of our microcontrollers over the acquisition period. But one of the major sources of low-frequency noise is temperature variation (which can affect the CPU, the voltage regulator of our boards, the voltage reference of the oscilloscope, our measurement resistor; see also the study by Heuser et al. [15]), and we expect this temperature variation to be similar within a campaign as it is across campaigns, if each acquisition campaign takes several hours. As a result, the temperature variation captured by the covariance matrix S_{pooled} of one campaign should be similar across different campaigns. However, the mean vectors $\bar{x}_k$ across different campaigns can be different due to different DC offsets (even if the overall temperature variation is similar), and this is why the sample selection methods (e.g. 20ppc, allap) perform poorly across different campaigns. Nevertheless, the LDA algorithm is able to remove the DC component and use only the rest of the trace for the attack. This, combined with the fact that with

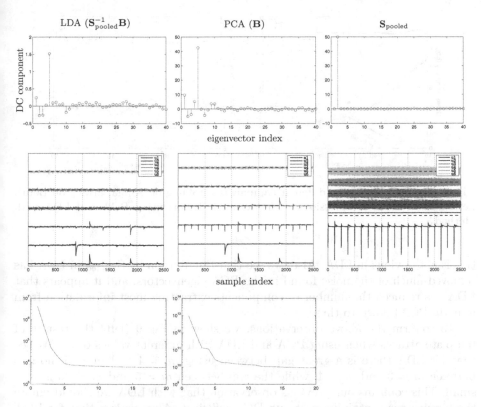

Fig. 8. Top: DC components of eigenvectors of LDA ($\mathbf{S}_{pooled}^{-1}\mathbf{B}$), PCA ($\mathbf{B}$) and $\mathbf{S}_{pooled}$. Middle: First six eigenvectors of LDA ($\mathbf{S}_{pooled}^{-1}\mathbf{B}$), PCA ($\mathbf{B}$) and $\mathbf{S}_{pooled}$. Bottom: eigenvalues (log y axis) of LDA and PCA.

LDA we no longer need a covariance matrix after compression, allows LDA to filter out temperature variations and other noise sources that are similar across campaigns, and provide good results even across different devices.

In order to show how LDA and PCA deal with the DC offset, we show in Fig. 8 (top) the DC components (mean) of the LDA and PCA eigenvectors. For LDA we can see that there is a peak at the fifth DC component, which shows that our choice of $m = 4$ avoided the component with largest DC offset by chance. For PCA we can see a similar peak, also for the fifth component, and again our choice $m = 4$ avoided this component. However, for PCA this turned out to be bad, because PCA does use a covariance matrix after projection and therefore it would benefit from getting knowledge of the temperature variation from the samples. This temperature variation will be given by the eigenvector with a high DC offset and therefore we expect that adding this eigenvector may provide better results. We also show in Fig. 8 the first six eigenvectors of LDA ($\mathbf{S}_{pooled}^{-1}\mathbf{B}$), PCA ($\mathbf{B}$) and $\mathbf{S}_{pooled}$, along with the first 20 eigenvalues of LDA and PCA. The fifth eigenvector of PCA clearly contains a DC offset, while

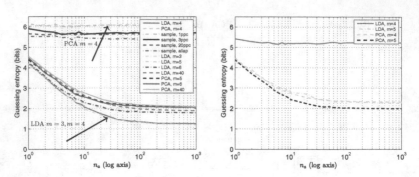

Fig. 9. Template attack on different campaigns (profiling on Alpha, attack on Beta). Left: using various compressions with Method 1. Right: using PCA and LDA with Method 5.

this is not obvious in LDA. Also, we see that the division by $\mathbf{S}_{\text{pooled}}$ in LDA has removed much of the noise found in the PCA eigenvectors, and it appears that LDA has reduced the number of components extracting most information from four (in PCA) down to three.

To confirm the above observations, we show in Fig. 9 (left) the results of template attacks when using PCA and LDA with different values of m. We see that for LDA there is a great gap between using $m = 4$ and $m = 5$, no gap between $m = 3$ and $m = 4$, while the gap between $m = 5$ and $m = 40$ is very small. This confirms our previous observation that with LDA we should ignore the eigenvector containing a strong DC coefficient. Also, we see that for PCA there is a huge gap between using $m = 4$ and $m = 5$ (in the opposite sense as with LDA), but the gap between $m = 5$ and $m = 40$ is negligible. Therefore, PCA can work well across devices if we include the eigenvectors containing the DC offset information. These results provide an important lesson for implementing template attacks across different devices or campaigns: the choice of components should consider the DC offset contribution of each eigenvector. This suggests that previous studies may have missed important information, by using only sample selections with one to three samples [12] or only the first PCA component [14].

5.5   Add DC Offset Variation to PCA

Renauld et al. [12] mentioned that *"physical variability makes the application of PCA irrelevant, as it cannot distinguish between inter-plaintext and inter-chip variances"*. While it is true that the standard PCA approach [6] is not aimed at distinguishing between the two types of variance, we showed in Sect. 5.4 that PCA can actually provide good results if we select the eigenvectors carefully. Starting from this observation, we can try to enhance the PCA algorithm by deliberately adding DC noise, in the hope of concentrating the DC sensitivity in one of the first eigenvectors, thereby making the other eigenvectors less DC sensitive (as all eigenvectors are orthogonal).

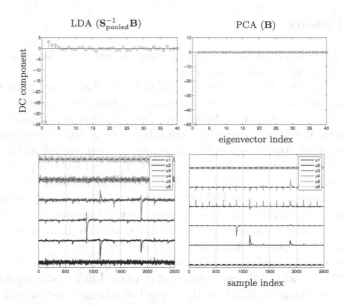

Fig. 10. Top: DC components of eigenvectors of LDA $(\mathbf{S}_{pooled}^{-1}\mathbf{B})$ and PCA $(\mathbf{B})$ after using Method 5. Bottom: First six eigenvectors of LDA $(\mathbf{S}_{pooled}^{-1}\mathbf{B})$ and PCA $(\mathbf{B})$.

Method 5 *(Add Random Offsets to the Matrix* $\mathbf{B}$ *– PCA and LDA only)*

1. *Obtain the* raw leakage traces $\mathbf{X}_k^r$ *from the profiling device, for each* k.
2. *Obtain the* raw pooled covariance matrix $\mathbf{S}_{pooled} \in \mathbb{R}^{m^r \times m^r}$.
3. *Pick a random offset* c_k *for each mean vector* $\bar{\mathbf{x}}_k$.[6]
4. *Compute the between-groups matrix as*
   $$\mathbf{B} = \sum_{k \in \mathcal{S}} (\bar{\mathbf{x}}_k^r - \bar{\mathbf{x}}^r + \mathbf{1}^r \cdot c_k)(\bar{\mathbf{x}}_k^r - \bar{\mathbf{x}}^r + \mathbf{1}^r \cdot c_k)'.$$
5. *Use PCA (uses* $\mathbf{B}$ *only) or LDA (uses both* $\mathbf{B}$ *and* $\mathbf{S}_{pooled}$*) to compress the* raw leakage traces and obtain $\mathbf{X}_k$ for each k.
6. *Compute the template parameters* $(\bar{\mathbf{x}}_k, \mathbf{S}_{pooled})$ *using (1) and (3).*
7. *Obtain the compressed leakage traces* $\mathbf{X}_{k\star}$ *from the attacked device.*
8. *Compute the guessing entropy as described in Sect. 2.1.*

The results of this method are shown in Fig. 9 (right). We see that now PCA provides good results even with $m = 4$. However, in this case LDA gives bad results with $m = 4$. In Fig. 10 we show the eigenvectors from LDA and PCA, along with their DC component. We can see that, by using this method, we managed to push the eigenvector having the strongest DC component first, and this was useful for PCA. However, LDA does not benefit from including a noise eigenvector into $\mathbf{B}$, so we propose this method only for use with PCA.

---

[6] We have chosen c_k uniformly from the interval $[-u, u]$, where u is the absolute average offset between the overall mean vectors shown in Fig. 3.

6   Conclusions

In this paper, we explored the efficacy of template attacks when using different devices for the profiling and attack steps.

We observed that, for our Atmel XMEGA 256 A3U 8-bit microcontroller and particular setup, the campaign-dependent parameters (temperature, environmental noise, etc.) appear to be the dominant factors in differences between campaign data, not the inter-device variability. These differences rendered the standard template attack useless for all common compression methods except Fisher's Linear Discriminant Analysis (LDA). To improve the performance of the attack across different devices, we explored several variants of the template attack, that compensate for a DC offset in the attack phase, or profile across multiple devices. By combining these options, we can improve the results of template attacks. However, these methods did not provide a great advantage when using Principal Component Analysis (PCA) or LDA.

Based on detailed analysis of LDA, we offered an explanation why this compression method works well across different devices: LDA is able to compensate temperature variation captured by the pooled covariance matrix and this temperature variation is similar across campaigns. From this analysis, we were able to provide guidance for an efficient use of both LDA and PCA across different devices or campaigns: for LDA we should ignore the eigenvectors starting with the one having the strongest DC contribution, while for PCA we should choose enough components to include at least the one with the strongest DC contribution. Based on these observations we also proposed a method to enhance the PCA algorithm such that the eigenvector with the strongest DC contribution corresponds to the largest eigenvalue and this allows PCA to provide good results across different devices even when using a small number of eigenvectors.

Our results show that the choice of compression method and parameters (e.g. choice of eigenvectors for PCA and LDA) has a strong impact on the success of template attacks across different devices, a fact that was not evidenced in previous studies. As a guideline, when using sample selection we should use a large number of samples, profile on multiple devices and adapt for a DC offset, but with LDA and PCA we may use the standard template attack and perform the profiling on a single device, if we select the eigenvectors according to their DC component. Overall, LDA seems the best compression method when using template attacks across different devices, but it requires to invert a possibly large covariance matrix, which might not be possible with a small number of profiling traces. In such cases, PCA might be a better alternative.

We conclude that with a careful choice of compression method we can obtain template attacks that are efficient also across different devices, reducing the guessing entropy of an unknown 8-bit value below 1.5 bits.

Data and Code Availability: In the interest of reproducible research we make available our data and related MATLAB scripts at:

http://www.cl.cam.ac.uk/research/security/datasets/grizzly/

Acknowledgement. Omar Choudary is a recipient of the Google Europe Fellowship in Mobile Security, and this research is supported in part by this Google Fellowship. The opinions expressed in this paper do not represent the views of Google unless otherwise explicitly stated.

References

1. Kocher, P.C., Jaffe, J., Jun, B.: Differential power analysis. In: Wiener, M. (ed.) CRYPTO 1999. LNCS, vol. 1666, pp. 388–397. Springer, Heidelberg (1999)
2. Chari, S., Rao, J., Rohatgi, P.: Template attacks. In: Kaliski, B.S., Koç, K., Paar, C. (eds.) CHES 2002. LNCS, vol. 2523, pp. 13–28. Springer, Heidelberg (2003)
3. Brier, E., Clavier, C., Olivier, F.: Correlation power analysis with a leakage model. In: Joye, M., Quisquater, J.-J. (eds.) CHES 2004. LNCS, vol. 3156, pp. 16–29. Springer, Heidelberg (2004)
4. Schindler, W., Lemke, K., Paar, C.: A stochastic model for differential side channel cryptanalysis. In: Rao, J.R., Sunar, B. (eds.) CHES 2005. LNCS, vol. 3659, pp. 30–46. Springer, Heidelberg (2005)
5. Gierlichs, B., Lemke-Rust, K., Paar, C.: Templates vs. stochastic methods. In: Goubin, L., Matsui, M. (eds.) CHES 2006. LNCS, vol. 4249, pp. 15–29. Springer, Heidelberg (2006)
6. Archambeau, C., Peeters, E., Standaert, F.-X., Quisquater, J.-J.: Template attacks in principal subspaces. In: Goubin, L., Matsui, M. (eds.) CHES 2006. LNCS, vol. 4249, pp. 1–14. Springer, Heidelberg (2006)
7. Homma, N., Nagashima, S., Imai, Y., Aoki, T., Satoh, A.: High-resolution side-channel attack using phase-based waveform matching. In: Goubin, L., Matsui, M. (eds.) CHES 2006. LNCS, vol. 4249, pp. 187–200. Springer, Heidelberg (2006)
8. Standaert, F.-X., Archambeau, C.: Using subspace-based template attacks to compare and combine power and electromagnetic information leakages. In: Oswald, E., Rohatgi, P. (eds.) CHES 2008. LNCS, vol. 5154, pp. 411–425. Springer, Heidelberg (2008)
9. Gierlichs, B., Batina, L., Tuyls, P., Preneel, B.: Mutual information analysis. In: Oswald, E., Rohatgi, P. (eds.) CHES 2008. LNCS, vol. 5154, pp. 426–442. Springer, Heidelberg (2008)
10. Standaert, F.-X., Malkin, T.G., Yung, M.: A unified framework for the analysis of side-channel key recovery attacks. In: Joux, A. (ed.) EUROCRYPT 2009. LNCS, vol. 5479, pp. 443–461. Springer, Heidelberg (2009)
11. Standaert, F.-X., Koeune, F., Schindler, W.: How to compare profiled side-channel attacks? In: Abdalla, M., Pointcheval, D., Fouque, P.-A., Vergnaud, D. (eds.) ACNS 2009. LNCS, vol. 5536, pp. 485–498. Springer, Heidelberg (2009)
12. Renauld, M., Standaert, F.-X., Veyrat-Charvillon, N., Kamel, D., Flandre, D.: A formal study of power variability issues and side-channel attacks for nanoscale devices. In: Paterson, K.G. (ed.) EUROCRYPT 2011. LNCS, vol. 6632, pp. 109–128. Springer, Heidelberg (2011)
13. Oswald, D., Paar, C.: Breaking Mifare DESFire MF3ICD40: Power analysis and templates in the real world. In: Preneel, B., Takagi, T. (eds.) CHES 2011. LNCS, vol. 6917, pp. 207–222. Springer, Heidelberg (2011)
14. Elaabid, M.A., Guilley, S.: Portability of templates. J. Crypt. Eng. 2(1), 63–74 (2012)

15. Heuser, A., Kasper, M., Schindler, W., Stöttinger, M.: A new difference method for side-channel analysis with high-dimensional leakage models. In: Dunkelman, O. (ed.) CT-RSA 2012. LNCS, vol. 7178, pp. 365–382. Springer, Heidelberg (2012)
16. Lomné, V., Prouff, E., Roche, T.: Behind the scene of side channel attacks. In: Sako, K., Sarkar, P. (eds.) ASIACRYPT 2013, Part I. LNCS, vol. 8269, pp. 506–525. Springer, Heidelberg (2013)
17. Choudary, O., Kuhn, M.G.: Efficient template attacks. In: Francillon, A., Rohatgi, P. (eds.) CARDIS 2013. LNCS, vol. 8419, pp. 253–270. Springer, Zürich (2014)

Using the Joint Distributions of a Cryptographic Function in Side Channel Analysis

Yanis Linge[1,2]([✉]), Cécile Dumas[1], and Sophie Lambert-Lacroix[2]

[1] CEA-LETI/MINATEC, 17 Rue des Martyrs,
38054 Grenoble Cedex 9, France
yanis.linge@st.com, cecile.dumas@cea.fr
[2] UJF-Grenoble 1/CNRS/UPMF/TIMC-IMAG UMR 5525,
38041 Grenoble, France
Sophie.Lambert@imag.fr

Abstract. The Side Channel Analysis is now a classic way to retrieve a secret key in the smart-card world. Unfortunately, most of the ensuing attacks require the plaintext or the ciphertext used by the embedded algorithm. In this article, we present a new method for exploiting the leakage of a device without this constraint. Our attack is based on a study of the leakage distribution of internal data of a cryptographic function and can be performed not only at the beginning or the end of the algorithm, but also at every instant that involves the secret key. This paper focuses on the distribution study and the resulting attack. We also propose a way to proceed in a noisy context using smart distances. We validate our proposition by practical results on an AES128 software implemented on a ATMega2561 and on the DPAContest v4 [32].

Keywords: AES software · Power analysis · Side-channel attacks · Smart-card · Statistical attack · DPAContest V4

1 Introduction

The original work on Side Channel Analysis was done by Kocher in the early 90s [14]. He introduced two new attacks: the Simple Power Analysis (SPA) and the Differential Power Analysis (DPA). In 2004, Brier et al. [4] formalized the DPA and provided a statistical way to compare the leakage model and the power traces thanks to the Pearson correlation factor. Today, side channel attacks gather many methods to attack a device from its power consumption or electromagnetic radiations, such as high order techniques in presence of a masking countermeasure [13,17–19], collision attacks [3,7,29], Algebraic Side Channel Attacks [21,22,26–28], etc.

Side Channel Attacks are generally based on statistical properties and tend to compare two random variable groups. The first one is represented by all the points of the acquired traces, while the second one depends on the underlying cryptographic function. For example, the Correlation Power Analysis (CPA) [4]

© Springer International Publishing Switzerland 2014
E. Prouff (Ed.): COSADE 2014, LNCS 8622, pp. 199–213, 2014.
DOI: 10.1007/978-3-319-10175-0_14

consists in the correlation between the device leakage at one instant and the possible value of one intermediate data. For the attack achievement, this value must be computable, *i.e.* it only depends on some few key bits and it is obtained from the plaintext (or the ciphertext). When neither is known, the acquired trace can not be connected to any cryptographic algorithm data.

The two random variable groups may only be studied independently. It was interesting to us to assume that we do not have any prior knowledge of the plaintext and the ciphertext. In fact, many smart-card applications use cryptographic functions without outputting the plaintext and ciphertext. In this case no internal data can be guessed, even partially, and a classic attack like CPA is not conceivable. Today, a cryptographic algorithm is implemented on a smart-card in a secure way. Many methods exist for masking the data and restricting the leakage [1,9,12,20,25]. However, it may happen for speed reason that countermeasures are only present at the beginning and the end of the implementation, but not in the middle. It is also possible that no protection is positioned precisely because the plaintext and the ciphertext are not outputted by the chip. For example, the GENERATE AC command of the EMV application [33] computes an Application Cryptogram using the algorithm CBC-MAC. A usual way for ensuring the security of this cryptographic scheme against Side Channel Analysis is to protect the first DES of the first block and the last DES of the final Triple-DES.

Nevertheless, the acquired traces contain some leakage information and we presume that it is correlated to the data computed by the device. A trace comprises many instants that reflect the chip activity during the algorithm execution. Each instant may be considered as a real random variable. The variance of these variables tells us that some instants are noisier or linked to the variation of the input data.

Failing to associate one trace to its corresponding algorithm guessing value, we can still study separately the various instants and the different algorithm values that involve a part of the key. This forms the main idea of our proposition. We propose to extract some properties from the algorithm and from the trace and to compare them.

Section 2 presents theoretical aspects by considering the data variations in the cryptographic algorithm. Section 3 discusses how to relate them to the acquired signals and Sect. 4 provides the last needed tools. In Sect. 5, we develop the complete attack. Experiments illustrate the attack's efficiency and its interest in Sect. 6 before the conclusion.

2   Study of the Variations in a Cryptographic Algorithm

An algorithm may be decomposed in small functions that mostly use a part of the secret key.

We will denote by g one of these functions and by k^* the involved part of the secret key, named subkey.

$$g : A \times K \longrightarrow B$$
$$(a, k) \longmapsto b = g(a, k)$$

We propose to study how the output b varies when the input a is uniformly distributed in A. More precisely, we are interested in the leakage caused by a and b. Let's denote by $L(z)$ the leakage induced by the handling of the data z, as Rivain did in his thesis [23]. $L(z)$ is comprised of the *leakage function* φ and the *leakage noise* B.

We consider the random variables $\varphi(a)$ and $\{\varphi(g(a, k))\}_{k \in K}$ and the joint probability distributions $\{(\varphi(a), \varphi(g(a, k)))\}_{k \in K}$. We denote for each subkey k the joint probability distribution by $S(g, k) = \{p_{i,j} | i \in \{0, \dots, n\}, j \in \{0, \dots, m\}\}$ where $p_{i,j}$ is the probability that $\varphi(a) = i$ and $\varphi(g(a, k)) = j$.

For calculating the distribution of the subkey k, we compute $\varphi(a)$ and $\varphi(g(a, k))$ for each a in A. Then by counting the occurrence of the values $i = \varphi(a)$ and $j = \varphi(g(a, k))$, we obtain the probability for $(\varphi(a), \varphi(g(a, k)))$ to be equal to (i, j).

As $\varphi(g(a, k))$ depends on k, each distribution also depends on the subkey value k. If we get the distribution for an unknown subkey k^* and if each subkey k matches with a unique distribution[1], we are able to guess the value of k^* by comparing the distributions; for example, if we consider that g is defined by:

$$g : \{0, 1\} \times \{0, 1\} \longrightarrow \{0, 1\}$$
$$(a, k) \longmapsto b = a \oplus k$$

and φ by:

$$\varphi : \{0, 1\} \longrightarrow \{0, 1\}$$
$$a \longmapsto a$$

If $k = 0$, $\varphi(a) = \varphi(g(a, k))$. If $k = 1$, $\varphi(a) = 1 - \varphi(g(a, k))$ mod 2.

The distributions $S(g, 0)$ and $S(g, 1)$ are drawn in Table 1. These two distributions are definitely different. So given any distribution, we are able to determine what subkey k was used to produce it.

Table 1. Joint distribution of $(a, b = a \oplus k)$ in $\mathbb{Z}/2\mathbb{Z}$

$k = 0$				$k = 1$		
$\varphi(b)$ \ $\varphi(a)$	0	1		$\varphi(b)$ \ $\varphi(a)$	0	1
0	1/2	0		0	0	1/2
1	0	1/2		1	1/2	0

---

[1] This property is true for most cryptographic functions like DES S-boxes or AES SubBytes.

We have computed the theoretical distributions for several functions that involve a part of the key, like the *exclusive-or* between bytes, the DES S-boxes [31] and the AES SubBytes function [8]. All present some differences, even if the non linear functions present more differences. As the distributions of a function do not depend on a device, they may be pre-computed for different targeted functions (g) and for different leakage functions (φ).

If the distributions are easily distinguished, that means the function g could be a good choice for an attack. However, an attacker will face two problems.

First, he must be able to get a distribution that will be compared to the theoretical ones, knowing he has access only to some traces. We suppose that he can acquire many traces he wants and that the trace number is sufficient for a uniform distribution of the input g function. This assumption is not restrictive because the cryptographic functions generally try to achieve this property. For obtaining a relevant distribution, the attacker needs also to locate the instants corresponding to the handling of the variables a and b. As the traces contain some information but also noise, he will only be able to *estimate* the frequency of the couple $(\varphi(a) = i, \varphi(b) = j)$ denoted $f_{i,j}$. We name $S_d = \{f_{i,j} | i \in \{0, \ldots, n\}, j \in \{0, \ldots, m\}\}$ the estimated distribution of the device. A solution for getting it is proposed in the next section.

The second problem the attacker faces is the need for a method to compare two distributions:

- $S(g, k)$, which is theoretical. It is issued from the preliminary study and depends on the function g and a key guess k.
- S_d, which is estimated. It is computed from the traces and related to the device.

Section 4 examines the existing distances and selects the most promising ones for comparing $S(g, k)$ and S_d.

For the rest of this article, we consider that the function $\varphi(z)$ represents the Hamming weight of z, *i.e.* the number of 1 in binary representation. The function g is composed of the AES operations: AddRoundKey followed by SubBytes, *i.e.* the data a represents a state byte before the AddRoundKey and the data b a state byte after the SubBytes. Notice that other φ models and other g functions could be studied.

3   How to Estimate the Distribution of the Device

We suggest here a method to first identify the suitable instants and then estimate the Hamming weight values that they represent. These instants, named points of interest, are denoted by *PoI*.

To determine the most interesting instants of our traces, we used the variance. The higher the variance, the more favorable the instant, because it represents either the maximal variability of the noise or the maximal variability of some data spend by the algorithm. Determining the *PoI* is an important part of our proposal. In some other cases, the attacker may need more advanced techniques like in [2, 10, 11], but this simple way is initially sufficient and does not requiert any prior knowledge on the leakage.

After selecting some *PoI*, we have to decide from their amplitude value what the corresponding Hamming weight value is.

In [26], Renauld and Standaert used a Bayesian template described in [6] to retrieve the Hamming weight of the targeted variables. Template attacks are very efficient at obtaining a good approximation of the Hamming weight of the data. However, they require complete access to a device similar to the targeted one.

We suggest here a method that does not recognize the exact Hamming weight value, but allows a reasonable estimation for a low time and memory complexity by using the only traces of the targeted device. The estimation we present is close to the value of the Hamming weight of the targeted data.

Let $Y(t)$ be a set of M measured values corresponding to the same instant t of M traces. We sort this set in an ascending order. As we suppose that the data values of the cryptographic algorithm are uniform, this implies a particular distribution of the Hamming weight values. If n is the maximal Hamming weight value, among the M elements, $\dfrac{M \times C_n^p}{2^n}$ elements have a Hamming weight p. The elements of $Y(t)$ are classified knowing this distribution. The maximal Hamming weight value is assigned to the highest elements of the set $Y(t)$ and the minimal Hamming weight value to the smallest one.

For example, if 100 values represent the leakage of two bits, we associate the Hamming weight of:

- 2 for the $\dfrac{100 \times C_2^2}{2^2} = 25$ greater elements
- 1 for the $\dfrac{100 \times C_2^1}{2^2} = 50$ following elements
- 0 to the $\dfrac{100 \times C_2^0}{2^2} = 25$ smaller elements

Indeed, the way to classify the elements depends on the leakage quality. This method is effective if the noise is low. So by reducing the noise, for example thanks to the cumulant of order 4 [15], the estimation will be better. Using this simple method, we obtain an approximation of the Hamming weight of the targeted variable. Further, one error in the ranking generally gives a Hamming weight close to the real one. Some random mistakes may occur and perturb the estimated distribution. In this case, more traces will be necessary for obtaining an estimated distribution close to the theoretical distribution corresponding to the true key. We also can choose to sort the M elements in fewer groups by reducing φ. For example, φ may represent the most significant bit, *i.e.* $\varphi(z) = 0$ if the higher significant bit is zero, 1 otherwise. This implies fewer errors, but the function φ is less precise and the theoretical distributions will be more similar. This technique has a low complexity in time and memory but only gives an estimation. This method can be easily replaced by method based on clustering and machine learning [16].

Since we have a way to approximate the Hamming weight of the input and the output of the AES SubBytes, we can compute an estimated distribution S_d. We need now explain how to compare two distributions.

4   How to Compare Two Distributions

To confront the theoretical distribution $S(g, k)$ and an estimated distribution S_d, the first idea is to use the well-known χ^2 distance between them defined as:

$$\chi^2(S(g, k), S_d) = \sum_{i=0}^{i=n} \sum_{j=0}^{j=m} \delta(p_{i,j}, f_{i,j}) \tag{1}$$

The distance between $p_{i,j}$ and $f_{i,j}$ is defined by:

$$\delta(p_{i,j}, f_{i,j}) = \begin{cases} \frac{(p_{i,j} - f_{i,j})^2}{p_{i,j}}, & p_{i,j} \neq 0 \\ 0, & p_{i,j} = f_{i,j} \\ \infty, & p_{i,j} = 0 \neq f_{i,j} \end{cases} \tag{2}$$

Unfortunately, this distance does not allow errors in the estimated distribution S_d. Indeed, a theoretical distribution generally presents a lot of zero values $p_{i,j}$, so a small mistake in the estimated Hamming weight can cause a non-zero value for the corresponding $f_{i,j}$. Thus the distance between S_d and $S(g, k^\star)$ will be infinite with only one error.

So we need to find another distance. In [5], Cha proposes a comprehensive study of different distances between two distributions. We have tested all the 65 distances presented in this article by using the theoretical distributions based on the Hamming weight leakage and the AES SubBytes function.

When trying to match a distribution that is well estimated to the theoretical ones, most distances give similar results and return the good subkey with few samples. But if the device distribution is not well estimated because of the presence of errors for some samples, some distances give better results than others. We simulated 50 % erroneous samples[2] to obtain biased device distributions and tried all the distances to compare each estimated distribution to the theoretical ones. We kept the four following best distances, that are those that on average lead to a successful attack.

– The distance based on the Inner Product defined by:

$$d_{IP}(S(g, k), S_d) = 1 - \sum_{i=0}^{i=n} \sum_{j=0}^{j=m} p_{i,j} \cdot f_{i,j} \tag{3}$$

– The distance based on the Harmonic Mean defined by:

$$d_{HM}(S(g, k), S_d) = \begin{cases} 1 - 2 \cdot \sum_{i=0}^{i=n} \sum_{j=0}^{j=m} \frac{p_{i,j} \cdot f_{i,j}}{p_{i,j} + f_{i,j}}, & p_{i,j} + f_{i,j} \neq 0 \\ 0, & p_{i,j} + f_{i,j} = 0 \end{cases} \tag{4}$$

---

[2] An erroneous sample is obtained by adding a white noise to the true value.

– The χ^2 Pearson distance

$$d_{\chi_P^2}(S(g,k), S_d) = \begin{cases} \sum_{i=0}^{i=n} \sum_{j=0}^{j=m} \frac{(p_{i,j} - f_{i,j})^2}{f_{i,j}}, & f_{i,j} \neq 0 \\ 0, & f_{i,j} = p_{i,j} \\ \infty, & f_{i,j} = 0 \neq p_{i,j} \end{cases} \quad (5)$$

– The distance of Kullback-Leiber

$$d_{KL}(S(g,k), S_d) = \begin{cases} \sum_{i=0}^{i=n} \sum_{j=0}^{j=m} p_{i,j}.ln(\frac{p_{i,j}}{f_{i,j}}), & f_{i,j} \neq 0 \\ 0, & f_{i,j} = 0 \end{cases} \quad (6)$$

With the study of the distributions of two variables related to the cryptographic algorithm, the method presented in Sect. 3 for estimating an equivalent distribution related to the device and the distances introduced here, we are now able to establish an attack in order to retrieve the subkey $k^\star$.

5   The Proposed Attack

Our attack consists of four phases. **First**, we get the pre-computed theoretical distributions that are not device dependent. This part is described in Algorithm 1.

Algorithm 1. Computation of the theoretical distributions.

1: **procedure** COMPUTATION OF $S(g,k)(g : K \times A \rightarrow B$, $N = |K|)$
2:     **for** $k \in K$ **do**
3:         $S(g,k) \leftarrow 0$ ▷ $S(g,k) \in \{0 \ldots n\} \times \{0 \ldots m\}$
4:         **for** $a \in A$ **do**
5:             $S(g,k)(\varphi(a), \varphi(g(a,k))) \leftarrow S(g,k)(\varphi(a), \varphi(g(a,k))) + \frac{1}{|A|}$
6:         **end for**
7:     **end for**
8: **return** $S(g,k)$
9: **end procedure**

In the second step, we detect some *PoI* thanks to the variance criteria. We denote the found *PoI* by $t_a \in T_a$ for the input of our function g and by $t_b \in T_b$ for the output. **The third step** consists of extracting the estimated Hamming weights of each $Y(t_a)$ and each $Y(t_b)$ and computing several estimated distributions $S_d(t_a, t_b)$ for each $t_a \in T_a$ and $t_b \in T_b$ with the method described in Sect. 3. **Finally**, we compute all the distances between the theoretical distributions and the different estimated distributions. The secret subkey for the couple of *PoI* (t_a, t_b) will be given by:

$$k^\star = \underset{k \subset K}{\text{argmin}}(d(S(g,k), S_d(t_a, t_b)))$$

We name the number of samples M, the number of possible keys $N = |K|$. We describe our attack in Algorithm 2.

Algorithm 2. Our proposal Attack

1: **procedure** ATTACK(M estimated Hamming weight pairs (a_i, b_i))
2:   $g : K \times A \rightarrow B$, $N = |K|$
3:   **for** $k \in K$ **do**
4:     $S(g,k) \leftarrow 0$ ▷ $S(g,k) \in \{0\ldots n\} \times \{0\ldots m\}$
5:     **for** $a \in A$ **do**   ▷ Compute the theoretical distributions
6:       $S(g,k)(\varphi(a), \varphi(g(a,k))) \leftarrow S(g,k)(\varphi(a), \varphi(g(a,k))) + \frac{1}{|A|}$
7:     **end for**
8:   **end for**
9:   $S_d \leftarrow 0$ ▷ $S_d \in \{0\ldots n\}$ x $\{0\ldots m\}$
10:   **for** i from 0 to $M - 1$ **do**   ▷ Compute the estimated distribution
11:     $S_d(a_i, b_i) \leftarrow S_d(a_i, b_i) + \frac{1}{M}$
12:   **end for**
13:   $key \leftarrow 0$
14:   **for** $k \in K$ **do**   ▷ Compare the estimated distribution to the theoretical distributions
15:     **if** $d(S(g,k), S_d) < d(S(g, key), S_d)$ **then**
16:       $key \leftarrow k$
17:     **end if**
18:   **end for**
19: **return** key
20: **end procedure**

Our algorithm complexity is:

- First step: one multiplication and $N \cdot |A|$ additions for the computation of the theoretical distributions.
- Second step: one multiplication and M additions for the computation of the estimated distribution.
- Third step: $N \cdot n \cdot m$ multiplications and $1 + N \cdot n \cdot m$ additions to compute N distances based on the Inner Product.

We notice that the complexity in time and memory of the attack is low. The first step is performed once and for all. The cost of the attack depends on the sample number for the second step and on the key number for the last step.

6 Experimentations

6.1 Unprotected Software Implementation on ATMega2561

To validate our Hamming weight estimation and our attack, we have targeted a software AES on an ATMega2561. For this implementation, the internal representation of the data is based on eight bits. The system is not very vulnerable and the acquired traces are a bit noisy.

First, we need to ensure that our methodology for estimating the Hamming weight gives good results. We have acquired 1,000 samples on our device. The different AES steps can be distinguished on the traces (see Fig. 1). We consider

Table 2. Percentage of good Hamming weight estimations for the input of the targeted function for all the state bytes.

PoI	0	1	2	3	4	5	6	7	8	9	10	11	12	13	14	15
SB region : 0	24%	21%	28%	18%	78%	22%	24%	29%	23%	24%	29%	24%	23%	21%	24%	25%
SB region : 1	21%	19%	20%	27%	24%	21%	25%	24%	26%	21%	29%	22%	24%	24%	28%	23%
SB region : 2	25%	24%	21%	27%	22%	29%	81%	26%	31%	21%	24%	28%	27%	29%	26%	24%
SB region : 3	22%	23%	24%	68%	21%	27%	23%	25%	23%	31%	25%	21%	23%	25%	21%	22%

the nine instants with a variance greater than 10 times the average variance (see Fig. 2 that is synchronized with Fig. 1.).

As some *PoI* are poorly located regarding the region of the trace identified as the function AddRoundKey followed by SubBytes, we are able to identify some unusable *PoI*. For example, one of the *PoI* is localized at the beginning of the trace. Four *PoI* are situated in the SubBytes (SB) region and may therefore correspond to the input of the targeted function. The four remaining *PoI* are positioned in the MixColumn (MC) region and may be associated with the output of the SubBytes function.

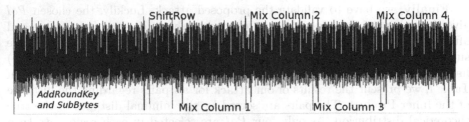

Fig. 1. Electromagnetic emanation signal from an ATMega2561 during the execution of the first round of an AES128 software implementation.

Fig. 2. Variance obtained for 1,000 electromagnetic emanation signals from an ATMega2561 during the execution of the first round of an AES128 software implementation.

For validating the Hamming weight estimation method we compare the estimated values to the theoretical ones. Table 2 (resp. Table 3) presents the percentage of good Hamming weight estimations for the four *PoI* in the SubBytes region (resp. in the MixColumn region) for all the state bytes.

As the implementation handles byte by byte, one *PoI* corresponds to, at most, one state byte. So the estimator shall associate many correct Hamming weight values to, at most, one state byte. For the other state bytes, the number

Table 3. Percentage of good Hamming weight estimations for the output of the targeted function for all the state bytes.

PoI	0	1	2	3	4	5	6	7	8	9	10	11	12	13	14	15
MC region : 0	18%	21%	25%	27%	22%	24%	27%	29%	23%	22%	28%	20%	23%	21%	28%	29%
MC region : 1	25%	24%	21%	27%	22%	29%	73%	26%	31%	21%	24%	28%	27%	29%	26%	24%
MC region : 2	23%	25%	28%	75%	25%	25%	24%	28%	21%	24%	21%	24%	22%	24%	29%	23%
MC region : 3	24%	21%	28%	18%	64%	22%	24%	29%	23%	24%	29%	24%	23%	21%	24%	25%

of correct Hamming weight values is close to a random estimation. For example, we can remark that the first *PoI* in SubBytes region shall represent the state byte 4 before AddroundKey. Thus the estimator gives us a good approximation of six bytes, each one corresponding to one *PoI*.

We conclude that our estimator gives good results, at least for the trace instants where the variance is high. Thus an attacker could directly use the variance criteria and the identification of the trace blocks to choose the *PoI*. Of course, he does not have the means to verify the estimation method because he does not know the key value.

Finally, we have to validate the proposed attack. Luckily, the chosen *PoI* give Hamming weight values that correspond to the same state byte before and after the targeted function. So we expect to find the bytes 3, 4 and 6 of the subkey. Four *PoI* have been considered by region, so $4 \times 4 = 16$ pairs (t_a, t_b) have to be tested. The whole attack has been performed in a few seconds. In Table 4, we present the results of our attack for all pairs regarding the distance of the Inner Product. The pairs are sorted by the minimal distance to the true theoretical distribution. As only four *PoI* are selected in each region, we keep the four subkeys with a lower distance. As expected, we retrieve three bytes of the key and a wrong one.

It is important to notice that every recorded key byte reduces the cryptographic security. Here an attacker must still guess the position of the recovered bytes and the missing bytes, knowing that he may get a wrong byte. So he would like to retrieve more key bytes. For that we propose to get more *PoI* by considering for each region the 50 instants with the highest variance. As the *PoI* number rises, the time required for the attack increases too. We need a few minutes to obtain the results showed in Table 5 where the 16 first ones are ranked regarding the distance based on the Inner Product. Ten key bytes are the real ones so we have still $10! \cdot 2^{6.8} \approx 2^{70}$ keys to test. This number may seem huge, but it is possible to perform again our attack at another round and then combine the results. More, we can attribute some probability to each possible key bytes and then use the algorithm proposed in [30] to retrieve the most probable key.

Notice that if we consider an *ineffective PoI* the minimal distance between the theoretical distributions and the distribution of the device will be huge. So *PoI* can easily be discriminated by this way.

We have also performed the attack by using the other distances of Cha's article [5]. This leads to worse results and validates the choice of the Inner Product distance.

Table 4. Attack results for the 4 × 4 chosen *PoI*.

PoI in SB region	*PoI* in MC region	Byte value	Distance	True?
2	1	54	0.0036051	✓
3	2	31	0.0036711	✓
0	3	61	0.0037023	✓
3	3	224	0.0037423	X
0	0	200	0.0037556	X
2	3	234	0.0037823	X
2	0	39	0.0037883	X
1	3	154	0.0037976	X
3	0	55	0.0037986	X
0	2	216	0.0038011	X
1	1	159	0.0038514	X
2	2	206	0.0038786	X
1	2	21	0.0038983	X
3	1	218	0.0039113	X
0	1	257	0.0039115	X
1	0	197	0.0039612	X

Table 5. The top 16 attack results for the 50 *PoI* with the higher variance for each region.

PoI in SB region	*PoI* in MC region	Byte value	Distance	True?
8	23	31	0.035180	✓
42	18	23	0.035773	✓
33	45	54	0.035813	✓
1	8	228	0.035867	✓
16	49	191	0.035941	✓
12	38	138	0.035977	X
11	21	61	0.035996	✓
48	20	224	0.036023	X
5	19	61	0.036023	✓
28	12	207	0.036051	✓
13	33	25	0.036094	X
21	42	39	0.036121	X
9	34	197	0.036137	X
25	47	198	0.036137	✓
38	15	109	0.030187	X
17	31	145	0.036203	✓

The targeted implementation is eight bits, but it is also possible to attack a 16-bit implementation. This implies computing more distributions that are larger, but their computation can be performed in less than a half hour.

More, if the implementation provides a data masking countermeasure, our proposal can still be effective by targeting the several AddRoundKey operations.

6.2   DPAContest V4 [32]

In the 2013 summer, the DPAContest version 4 [32] has been released. It provides 100,000 samples corresponding to the first round and the beginning of the second round of an AES-256 software. As only the beginning of the second round is available, we will focus only on the subkey used in the first round.

The proposed implementation is protected by using a countermeasure called RSM [24]. The RSM is a masking countermeasure that uses an unique 16-byte mask that is randomly rotated by an offset between 0 and 15 at each execution. So the AES is computed with 16 different random masks. First we have classed the traces obtained by the same mask offset by using the redundancy of the offset thanks to a pattern detection by autocorrelation. This classification does not need to be very accurate because our methodology is resilient to distribution errors. Then we only consider one class of traces: about six thousand samples corresponding to the computation with a same, but unknown, mask offset j.

The SubBytes function in the AES is replaced by sixteen masked sboxes:

$$SB(X \oplus M_{i+j \text{ mod } 16} \oplus K) \oplus M_{i+1+j \text{ mod } 16}$$

where $M_0 \ldots M_{15}$ are the bytes of the mask and i is the sbox number. As the value of the 16-byte mask is known, this function contains two unknowns values: the secret byte subkey K and also the value $i + j$.

We decide to retrieve these two values together by using our method. If the offset j is fixed, the knowledge of $i + j$ is an advantage as it gives the relative position between the finding bytes. This hugely reduces the number of remaining keys in the exhaustive search.

As previously we have selected 1,000 PoI by using the variance. But this time we use four distances:

- Inner Product
- Harmonic mean
- Pearson χ^2
- Kullback-Leiber

These four distances will give different results, but we expect that the good key byte will has a good rank for each distance. The idea is to compute the top 16 attack results for each distance and each pair of PoI. Then we keep only the results for each pair that appear for all distances. Finally the first 16 most frequent values are proposed for the subkey. We found 7 ordered bytes of the secret subkey. It is important to notice that here we only have $7 \cdot 2^{9.8} \approx 2^{75}$ remaining subkeys.

We have applied the same attack on another class of traces by considering the other offset values and compared the different results. The same bytes of the subkey have been obtained. More secret key bytes could be retrieved with the acquisition of the AES next rounds.

7 Conclusion

We propose a promising Side Channel Attack based on the joint distributions of a cryptographic function. The great advantage is that it is not necessary to know the plaintext or the ciphertext. First, we have investigated the way the internal data varies between them and noticed that the joint distribution of two data sets highly depends on the secret key used by the algorithm. In parallel, we have proposed to deduce the real joint distribution from the acquired traces thanks to a simple Hamming weight estimator based on the statistical variance and the particular repartition of random variables. In order to compare this estimated distribution with the theoretical ones, we have tried several distances and chosen the more favorable to build an attack. In the ideal case where the Hamming weight estimation is always correct, our proposed attack is very effective and the true key is found with fewer than 30 samples. In the real world, the acquired signals are noisy and the estimator is not perfect. But, with more samples the attack still remains successful, even with 50 % of estimation error.

Indeed, we have validated both the estimation method and the key recovery by applying our attack on two sets of acquisition. The first one contains 1,000 traces issued from an AES128 software implementation into an ATMega2561. The results show that 10 disordered key bytes can be retrieved without any knowledge of the plaintext or the ciphertext. The second one comes from the DPAContest v4. Here we found 7 ordered bytes of the key.

The software context is well adapted to estimate the joint distribution of two internal data sets because few bits are processed at the same time. Attacking a hardware implementation in this manner remains a challenge, as it involves a huge bit number. This represents an easy way to protect a cryptographic algorithm. However, our attack may be also relevant for non-cryptographic operations like masking or reverse engineering.

Acknowledgements. We would like to thank Victor Lomné for providing us traces and suggestions. We are also grateful to Thomas Roche and Christophe Giraud for their reviews and helpful comments.

References

1. Akkar, M.-L., Giraud, C.: An implementation of DES and AES, secure against some attacks. In: Koç, Ç.K., Naccache, D., Paar, C. (eds.) CHES 2001. LNCS, vol. 2162, pp. 309–318. Springer, Heidelberg (2001)
2. Archambeau, C., Peeters, E., Standaert, F.-X., Quisquater, J.-J.: Template attacks in principal subspaces. In: Goubin, L., Matsui, M. (eds.) CHES 2006. LNCS, vol. 4249, pp. 1–14. Springer, Heidelberg (2006)

3. Bogdanov, A.: Improved side-channel collision attacks on AES. In: Adams, C., Miri, A., Wiener, M. (eds.) SAC 2007. LNCS, vol. 4876, pp. 84–95. Springer, Heidelberg (2007)

4. Brier, E., Clavier, C., Olivier, F.: Correlation power analysis with a leakage model. In: Joye, M., Quisquater, J.-J. (eds.) CHES 2004. LNCS, vol. 3156, pp. 16–29. Springer, Heidelberg (2004)

5. Cha, S.-H.: Comprehensive survey on distance/similarity measures between probability density functions. Int. J. Math. Models Methods Appl. Sci. 1(4), 300–307 (2007)

6. Chari, S., Rao, J., Rohatgi, P.: Template attack. In: Kaliski Jr., B.S., Koç, Ç.K., Paar, C. (eds.) CHES 2002. LNCS, vol. 2523, pp. 13–28. Springer, Heidelberg (2003)

7. Clavier, C., Feix, B., Gagnerot, G., Roussellet, M., Verneuil, V.: Improved collision-correlation power analysis on first order protected AES. In: Preneel, B., Takagi, T. (eds.) CHES 2011. LNCS, vol. 6917, pp. 49–62. Springer, Heidelberg (2011)

8. Daemen, J., Rijmen, V.: AES proposal: Rijndael (1998)

9. Debraize, B.: Efficient and provably secure methods for switching from arithmetic to boolean masking. In: Prouff, E., Schaumont, P. (eds.) CHES 2012. LNCS, vol. 7428, pp. 107–121. Springer, Heidelberg (2012)

10. Gierlichs, B., Batina, L., Tuyls, P., Preneel, B.: Mutual information analysis - a generic side-channel distinguisher. In: Oswald, E., Rohatgi, P. (eds.) CHES 2008. LNCS, vol. 5154, pp. 426–442. Springer, Heidelberg (2008)

11. Gierlichs, B., Lemke-Rust, K., Paar, C.: Templates vs. stochastic methods. In: Goubin, L., Matsui, M. (eds.) CHES 2006. LNCS, vol. 4249, pp. 15–29. Springer, Heidelberg (2006)

12. Goubin, L., Patarin, J.: DES and differential power analysis - The duplication method. In: Koç, Ç.K., Paar, C. (eds.) CHES 1999. LNCS, vol. 1717, pp. 158–172. Springer, Heidelberg (1999)

13. Joye, M., Paillier, P., Schoenmakers, B.: On second-order differential power analysis. In: Rao, J.R., Sunar, B. (eds.) CHES 2005. LNCS, vol. 3659, pp. 293–308. Springer, Heidelberg (2005)

14. Kocher, P.C., Jaffe, J., Jun, B.: Differential power analysis. In: Wiener, M. (ed.) CRYPTO 1999. LNCS, vol. 1666, pp. 388–397. Springer, Heidelberg (1999)

15. Le, T.-H., Clédière, J., Servière, C., Lacoume, J.-L.: Noise reduction in side channel attack using fourth-order cumulant. IEEE Trans. Inf. Forensics Secur. 2(4), 710–720 (2007)

16. Lerman, L., Medeiros, S.F., Veshchikov, N., Meuter, C., Bontempi, G., Markowitch, O.: Semi-supervised template attack. In: Prouff, E. (ed.) COSADE 2013. LNCS, vol. 7864, pp. 184–199. Springer, Heidelberg (2013)

17. Mangard, S., Oswald, E., Popp, T.: Power Analysis Attack - Revealing the Secret of Smart Cards. Springer, Heidelberg (2007)

18. Messerges, T.S.: Using second-order power analysis to attack DPA resistant software. In: Koç, Ç.K., Paar, C. (eds.) CHES 2000. LNCS, vol. 1965, pp. 238–251. Springer, Heidelberg (2000)

19. Oswald, E., Mangard, S., Herbst, C., Tillich, S.: Practical second-order DPA attacks for masked smart card implementations of block ciphers. In: Pointcheval, D. (ed.) CT-RSA 2006. LNCS, vol. 3860, pp. 192–207. Springer, Heidelberg (2006)

20. Oswald, E., Mangard, S., Pramstaller, N.: Secure and efficient masking of AES - A mission impossible? Cryptology ePrint Archive, Report 2004/134. http://eprint.iacr.org/2004/134

21. Oren, Y., Kirschbaum, M., Popp, T., Wool, A.: Algebraic side-channel analysis in the presence of errors. In: Mangard, S., Standaert, F.-X. (eds.) CHES 2010. LNCS, vol. 6225, pp. 428–442. Springer, Heidelberg (2010)
22. Oren, Y., Wool, A.: Tolerant algebraic side-channel analysis of AES. Cryptology ePrint Archive, report 2012/092. http://eprint.iacr.org/2012/092
23. Rivain, M.: On the physical security of cryptographic implementations. Ph.D. thesis, University of Luxembourg (2009)
24. Nassar, M., Souissi, Y., Guilley, S., Danger, J.-L.: RSM: a small and fast countermeasure for AES, secure against 1st and 2nd-order zero-offset SCAs. In: DATE 2012, 1173–1178 (2012)
25. Rivain, M., Prouff, E., Doget, J.: Higher-order masking and shuffling for software implementations of block ciphers. In: Clavier, C., Gaj, K. (eds.) CHES 2009. LNCS, vol. 5747, pp. 171–188. Springer, Heidelberg (2009)
26. Renauld, M., Standaert. F-X.: Algebraic side-channel attacks. Cryptology ePrint Archive, report 2009/279. http://eprint.iacr.org/2009/279
27. Renauld, M., Standaert, F.-X., Veyrat-Charvillon, N.: Algebraic side-channel attacks on the AES: why time also matters in DPA. In: Clavier, C., Gaj, K. (eds.) CHES 2009. LNCS, vol. 5747, pp. 97–111. Springer, Heidelberg (2009)
28. Saied Emam Mohamed, M., Bulygin, S., Zohner, M., Heuser, A., Walter, M.: Improved algebraic side-channel attack on AES. Cryptology ePrint Archive, report 2012/084. http://eprint.iacr.org/2012/084
29. Schramm, K., Wollinger, T., Paar, C.: A new class of collision attacks and its application to DES. In: Johansson, T. (ed.) FSE 2003. LNCS, vol. 2887, pp. 206–222. Springer, Heidelberg (2003)
30. Veyrat-Charvillon, N., Gérard, B., Renauld, M., Standaert, F.-X.: An optimal key enumeration algorithm and its application to side-channel attacks. In: Knudsen, L.R., Wu, H. (eds.) SAC 2012. LNCS, vol. 7707, pp. 390–406. Springer, Heidelberg (2013)
31. Federal Information Processing. Data Encryption Standard. Standards Publication 46-1 National Technical Information Service, U.S. Dept. of Commerce (1977)
32. DPA contest v4. http://www.dpacontest.org/v4/
33. EMVCo EMV Integrated Circuit Card Specifications for Payment Systems, Book 2, Security and Key Management, Version 4.3, November 2011

A Multiple-Fault Injection Attack by Adaptive Timing Control Under Black-Box Conditions and a Countermeasure

Sho Endo[1]($\boxtimes$), Naofumi Homma[1], Yu-ichi Hayashi[1], Junko Takahashi[2], Hitoshi Fuji[2], and Takafumi Aoki[1]

[1] Graduate School of Information Sciences, Tohoku University,
6-6-05, Aramaki Aza Aoba, Aoba-ku, Sendai-shi 980-8579, Japan
endo@aoki.ecei.tohoku.ac.jp
[2] NTT Secure Platform Laboratories, Nippon Telegraph and Telephone Corporation,
3-9-11, Midori-cho, Musashino-shi, Tokyo 180-8585, Japan

Abstract. This paper proposes a multiple-fault injection attack based on adaptive control of fault injection timing in embedded microprocessors. The proposed method can be conducted under the black-box condition that the detailed cryptographic software running on the target device is not known to attackers. In addition, the proposed method is non-invasive, without the depackaging required in previous works, since such adaptive fault injection is performed by precisely generating a clock glitch. In this paper, we demonstrate the validity of the proposed method through an experiment on Advanced Encryption Standard (AES) software with a typical recalculation-based countermeasure on an 8-bit microprocessor. We first describe the proposed method to inject two kinds of faults, designed to obtain a faulty output available for differential fault analysis and to avoid a conditional branch for the countermeasure, respectively. We then show an experimental result that the faulty output can be obtained by circumventing countermeasure without using information from the detailed instruction sequence. Furthermore, we proposed a countermeasure against our attack, which prevents the attackers from calling the output routine through skipping the branch or branch test instruction.

Keywords: Embedded processors · Cryptographic software · Fault injection attacks

1 Introduction

Fault injection attacks are attracting much attention in the field of cryptographic hardware and embedded systems. The attackers first inject faults into cryptographic operations to obtain faulty ciphertexts and then estimate a secret key from several faulty ciphertexts. After the first publication focusing on public-key cryptosystems [5], fault injection attacks were extended to symmetric-key cryptosystems [4]. Since then, many variations of fault attacks and countermeasures

© Springer International Publishing Switzerland 2014
E. Prouff (Ed.): COSADE 2014, LNCS 8622, pp. 214–228, 2014.
DOI: 10.1007/978-3-319-10175-0_15

have been presented, and new variants are still being proposed [2,7,15]. Differential fault analysis (DFA) [4] extracts the secret key from the difference between correct and faulty outputs. In DFA, we assume that temporal faults are injected into some bits (or bytes) during a short time and the faulty values are propagated through subsequent operations or hardware logics without any additional faults. Ineffective fault analysis (IFA) [7] injects faults into specific operations and deduces the secret key from the observation whether the output changes or not.

A typical countermeasure against such fault injection attacks is to cancel the output (i.e., the ciphertext) when faults are detected because many fault injection attacks require faulty ciphertexts. Recalculation is commonly used in fault detection methods. The recalculation methods include duplicate or redundant calculations [2,17], which repeat the same cryptographic operation several times, and error-detection calculations, which calculate an inverse, error-detection code, or checksum after the cryptographic operation [6,12]. Such countermeasures with recalculation often assume that the attacker can inject faults once during the target cryptographic process. Hence, these countermeasures are potentially vulnerable to multiple-fault injection attacks, which can inject several faults during the cryptographic process. Indeed, such multiple-fault injection attacks have been successfully applied to RSA-CRT software in [11,19]. The attackers defeated the recalculation-based countermeasure and obtained the faulty ciphertexts, as described in the literature.

However, previous multiple-fault injection attacks have assumed that the attackers know the details of the target software. More precisely, the attackers must know the execution timing of the assembler instruction sequence for the target software. In [11], the attacker injects faults by inducing a decreased voltage twice, at the times of encryption and recalculation, to obtain a faulty ciphertext. That method assumes that the attacker knows in advance how to time both injections. In [19], the attacker injects faults by laser pulses at the times of encryption and conditional branching following recalculation. The attack also assumes that the attacker can modify the software running on the microcontroller to generate a trigger signal that will precisely indicate the execution timing of the branch instruction. As described above, the previous attacks can be applied only when the attacker knows the target instruction sequence in some way. To the best of our knowledge, the possibility of multiple-fault instruction attacks under black-box conditions, in which the attackers do not know the execution timing of the target software (i.e., the assembler instruction sequence), are not well studied in literature.

In this paper, we propose multiple-fault injection attacks based on adaptive control of fault injection timing. The attackers can adapt the fault-injection timings from just the output of the cryptographic software. Such adaptation requires a precise and brief fault injection into a specific clock cycle without disturbing any other clock cycles. In this paper, we implement such fault injections by introducing clock glitches for our attack. These clock glitches can induce faults with higher reproducibility in a non-invasive manner than can other fault injection methods such as introducing a power glitch. The proposed method is a combination of simple search algorithms, but the total number of fault injection trials required for the attack c is at most $3c_p$, where c_p is the cycle counts of the cryptographic operations. This paper also demonstrates, through an experiment on Advanced Encryption Standard (AES) software with a recalculation-based countermeasure, that the proposed attack can obtain faulty ciphertexts available for DFA in a black-box setting. The rest of this paper is organized as follows. Section 2 describes related works. Section 3 presents the concept of the proposed attack and its application to cryptographic software with a recalculation-based countermeasure. Section 4 shows an experiment of the proposed attack on a specific piece of AES software. Section 5 shows a software countermeasure against the proposed attack. Section 6 concludes our paper.

2   Related Works

Many papers have reported that an instruction skip was observed when a fault was injected during a cryptographic process in experiments on various microcontrollers [3,9,14,18]. In previous works, such instruction skips were observed on 8-bit AVR microprocessors when a fault was injected by a power glitch [18] or by an electromagnetic pulse [9]. Such instruction skips were also observed on 32-bit ARM processors, induced by a laser pulse [2,19] or an electromagnetic pulse [14]. The attackers obtain faults caused by these instruction skips and exploit them for fault injection attacks, such as DFA.

The effects of multiple fault injections have also been studied in DFA proposals. A previous work [16] presented the effect of multiple faults in the DFA on AES. Another work [13] described a generic fault model that covers all the faults that could happen on the AES execution. Note that these papers do not cover the effect of multiple faults in a program flow, which is exploited to defeat countermeasures in the proposed attack.

Many countermeasures have also been presented [2] to thwart the fault injection attacks described above. In particular, software countermeasures are usually applied to embedded microcontrollers because hardware countermeasures are often unavailable on low-cost microcontrollers. Among such software countermeasures, recalculation is one of the most typical. The countermeasure is roughly classified into two types: those that perform the same cryptographic operations repeatedly [3], and those that perform a different operation, such as an inverse or checksum operation, after the cryptographic operation [6,17]. Both types ultimately compare or check two or more computation results to detect faults. The former countermeasures can be defeated when the same fault is injected into all repeated operations. However, the latter countermeasures are resistant to the above attack because it is hard to inject two or more faults that will pass the final check. However, these countermeasures can be defeated if a fault is injected into the final check.

There are some recalculation schemes for the above countermeasures. A typical scheme is to perform recalculation after the cryptographic process to be

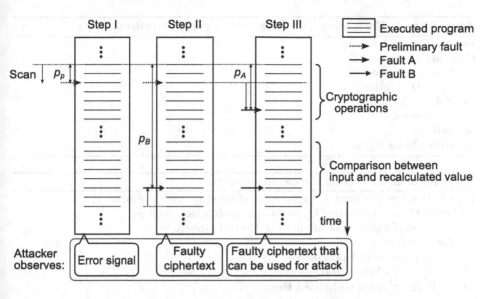

Fig. 1. Basic procedure of proposed attack.

protected [2]. We focus on countermeasures based on the recalculation scheme as follows. Duplication of instructions is also presented in [3]. That scheme is immune to any single fault injection attack because of the duplicated instructions. However, this kind of countermeasure is defeated if a multiple-fault injection attack skips all duplicated instructions.

Another countermeasure [8] is to insert a random delay time before and after the cryptographic operation. This prevents attackers from determining the timing of a specific cryptographic operation needed for fault injections. The application of our attack to such countermeasures is discussed in the following section.

3   A Multiple-Fault Injection Attack Based on Adaptive Fault Injection

This section presents a multiple-fault injection attack that can be applied to cryptographic software with a typical recalculation-based countermeasure, such as in [2], under a black-box condition. In the proposed attack, we change the injection timing cycle by cycle and determine the appropriate timing from the resulting outputs. We start injecting faults when the cryptographic process starts.

3.1   Proposed Attack

The black-box condition considered here is that we do not know the details of cryptographic software implemented in an embedded processor. On the other

Algorithm 1. Encryption with Recalculation (EncWithRecal)

Input: Plaintext P
Output: Ciphertext C
 1: $C \leftarrow \text{Encryption}(P)$
 2: $P_2 \leftarrow \text{Decryption}(C)$
 3: **if** $P = P_2$ **then**
 4:     return C
 5: **end if**
 6: return Error signal

Algorithm 2. Activating the countermeasure

Input: Random plaintext P, cycle count of cryptographic operation c_p
Output: Correct ciphertext C, position of preliminary fault p_p
 1: $C \leftarrow \text{EncWithErrorDetection}(P)$ # Correct ciphertext
 2: **for** $p_p = 0$ to c_p **do**
 3:     SetPreliminaryFaultPosition(p_p)
 4:     $C_f \leftarrow \text{EncWithErrorDetection}(P)$
 5:     **if** Error signal is observed **then**
 6:         return p_p
 7:     **end if**
 8: **end for**

---

hand, our attack assumes that we know the following information: (i) cryptographic algorithm, (ii) the fact that the cryptographic algorithm is implemented in software, and (iii) presence of a countermeasure based on recalculation. Also, we assume that we can observe the execution timing of the cryptographic operation in some way (e.g., from a communication signal). Note here that we do not need the detailed information about the cryptographic operation such as the execution timing of a specific cryptographic operation.

Figure 1 shows the basic concept of the proposed attack, which consists of three steps. Let Fault A and Fault B be the faults to be injected into the software (i.e., the assembly instruction sequence) for the ciphertext production and the countermeasure, respectively. Step I searches for the injection timing for the preliminary fault, which will activate the countermeasure. We first set the injection timing of preliminary fault p_p to be zero and then inject a fault at time p_p. The value of p_p is incremented after each injection.

We assume here that the countermeasure returns an error signal when the fault is detected [19]. Step I is ended when the error signal is obtained. Step II looks for an appropriate injection timing for Fault B, namely p_B, while continuing to inject the preliminary fault. We can obtain a faulty ciphertext when a fault skips a critical instruction (e.g., a conditional branch instruction). Step II is ended when p_B is obtained. Step III looks for an appropriate injection timing for Fault A, namely p_A, while continuing to inject Fault B. We use the timing of the preliminary fault as a starting point for examining the injection timing for Fault A. Note that the original timing for the preliminary fault does not always

---

Algorithm 3. Injecting a fault to circumvent the countermeasure

---

Input: Random plaintext P, correct ciphertext C, cycle count of cryptographic operation c_p, position of preliminary fault p_p
Output: Position of Fault B p_B
1: SetPreliminaryFaultPosition(p_p)
2: **for** $p_B = c_p$ to p_p **do**
3:     SetFaultBPosition(p_B)
4:     $C_f \leftarrow$ EncWithErrorDetection(P)
5:     **if** $C_f \neq C$ and Error signal is not observed **then**
6:         return p_B
7:     **end if**
8: **end for**

Algorithm 4. Obtaining an faulty ciphertext for attacks

Input: Random plaintext P, correct ciphertext C, cycle count of cryptographic operation c_p, position of preliminary fault p_p
Output: Position of Fault B p_B, faulty ciphertext for attacks C_f
1: SetFaultBPosition(p_B)
2: **for** $p_A = p_p$ to c_p **do** # Glitch position
3:     SetFaultAPosition(p_A)
4:     $C_f \leftarrow$ EncWithErrorDetection(P)
5:     $d \leftarrow C_f \oplus C$
6:     **if** d has four non-zero bytes **then**
7:         return C_f
8:     **end if**
9: **end for**

---

provide a faulty ciphertext suitable for attacks such as DFA. Step III ends when a suitable faulty ciphertext is obtained.

Typical algorithms for Steps I, II, and III are shown below. In this paper, we focus on a recalculation-based countermeasure, such as the one shown in Algorithm 1. Steps I, II, and III are implemented in Algorithms 2, 3, and 4, respectively. c_p is the cycle count of the entire cryptographic process. First, we use Algorithm 2 to discern the injection timing for the preliminary fault. The timing p_p is examined in the range of $0 \leq p_p \leq c_p$. Algorithm 2 ends when an error signal is obtained.

Next, we run Algorithm 3 to determine the timing for Fault B p_B. We examine the timing of p_B from the end of the instruction sequence while injecting the preliminary fault at the timing p_p. Algorithm 3 ends when a faulty ciphertext is obtained. Note again that the faulty ciphertext obtained after Step II is not always suitable for attacks because the preliminary fault is not always injected at the timing that is specified by the attack algorithms the attacker use.

Finally, we run Algorithm 4 to obtain a faulty ciphertext that can be used for DFA. We examine the timing of p_A for Fault A in the range from p_p to c_p. Algorithm 4 ends when a suitable faulty ciphertext is obtained. For example, Piret's DFA [15] requires a single-byte fault at the output of the 8th round of

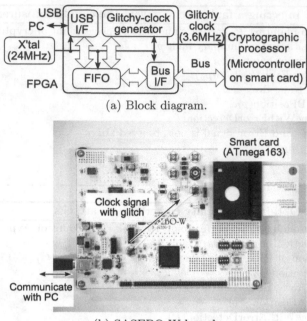

(a) Block diagram.

(b) SASEBO-W board.

Fig. 2. Experimental environment.

the AES process. In this case, the output ciphertexts include a four-byte error. Therefore, Step III can end when any faulty ciphertext containing a four-byte error is obtained. In an 8-bit processor, we can inject one-byte fault easily by skipping a instruction such as XOR in AddRoundKey.

The cost of the proposed attack depends on the number of fault injections c that is required for the observation of a faulty ciphertext available for DFA. c is described as $c = p_p + (p_B - c_p) + p_A$. $c < 3c_p$ since all of p_A, p_B, and p_p are smaller than c_p. In modern microprocessors, c_p would be at most 100000 cycles, therefore c would be less than 300000 cycles. The trial number is much smaller than that of a brute force search for a 128-bit key. Note that the proposed method can be conducted automatically without any reverse engineering.

The timing of fault injection is independent of input data. Therefore, once we find the appropriate timings of fault injections, we can obtain any number of faulty ciphertexts using different plaintexts. Also, c is constant for any input data.

4   Experiment

4.1   Overview

This section describes an experiment in which the proposed attack was used against a piece of AES software with a recalculation-based countermeasure.

Table 1. Experimental conditions

Cryptographic algorithm	128-bit AES with re-calculation-based countermeasure (Written from scratch)
Microcontroller	ATmega163 (8-bit)
Compiler	GCC 4.3.3 (optimized by -Os)
FPGA	Xilinx XC6SLX150
Glitch width	54 ns
Plaintext	$(00112233445566778899aabbccddeeff)_{16}$
Secret key	$(000102030405060708090a0b0c0d0e0f)_{16}$

Algorithm 5. AES Encryption with Recalculation(AESEncWithRecal)

Input: Plaintext P
Output: Ciphertext C
1: $C \leftarrow \text{AESEncryption}(P)$
2: $P_2 \leftarrow \text{AESDecryption}(C)$
3: $r1 \leftarrow 1$
4: **if** $P = P_2$ **then**
5:     $r1 \leftarrow 0$
6: **end if**
7: return r1

Figure 2 shows the experimental environment implemented on the Side-channel Attack Standard Evaluation Board SASEBO-W. An on-chip glitchy-clock generator [10], shown in Fig. 2(a), was implemented on the FPGA, and the clock signals with glitches were fed into the smart card. Table 1 shows the experimental conditions. The microcontroller ATmega163 on the smart card ran a 128-bit AES program equipped with the recalculation shown in Algorithm 1. This program was written by the authors from scratch. The program was written in the C language and compiled with the GCC 4.3.3 compiler. In this experiment, we used Algorithms 2, 3, and 4 for Steps I, II, and III, respectively, of the proposed method. Algorithm 4 ended when a faulty ciphertext with a four-byte error, suitable for Piret's DFA, was obtained.

4.2 Fault Injection with Glitchy-Clock Generator

Figure 3 shows an image of the clock signal generated by the glitchy-clock generator. The glitchy clock cycle is inserted in the clock signal with the aim of causing a setup time violation fault. The glitch width w represents the width between the first and the second rising edges in the glitchy clock cycle. The resulting fault varies with w because the number of affected paths increases as w decreases. The glitch setup time s represents the width between the first rising and falling edge in the cycle, which does not affect the type of injected fault but should be configured to be shorter than w.

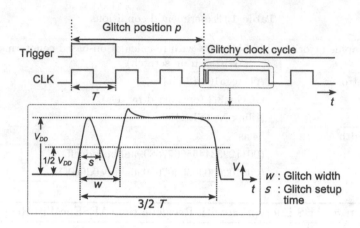

Fig. 3. Glitchy-clock signal.

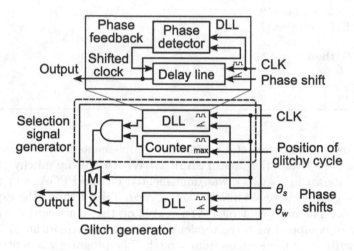

Fig. 4. Block diagram of glitchy-clock generator.

Figure 4 shows a block diagram of the glitch generator. It consists of a counter and two delay locked loop (DLL) circuits in the digital clock managers (DCMs) available on Xilinx FPGAs. In Fig. 4, the selection signal is given by the counter output and the clock signal with different phases. We can program the DCMs and control the phase-shift parameters θ_w and θ_s, which correspond to w and s, respectively. Phase-shift parameters for DLLs can be controlled from an external PC through a series of communication interfaces (a FIFO interface and a USB I/F device) on Fig. 2. We can adjust the parameters of the glitch in increments of about 0.020 ns on the SASEBO-W. Also, we can generate clock glitches with high reproducibility. The jitter of w was below 0.2 ns, with the specific value depending on the specifications of the DLLs.

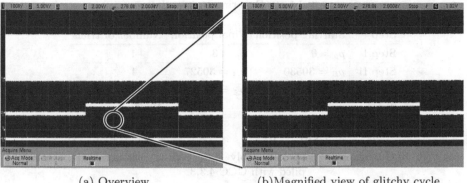

(a) Overview.   (b)Magnified view of glitchy cycle.

Fig. 5. Waveform of the clock signal.

Code 1: Main function.
```
1: LBL_MAIN:
2: CALL AESEncWithRecal
3: TST r1      ;Stores 1 in Z when r1=0
4: BRNE LBL_FAIL  ;Jumps when Z=0
5: CALL SendData
6: JMP LBL_FINISH
7: LBL_FAIL:
8: CALL SendError
9: LBL_FINISH:
```

In this experiment, w was adjusted to 54 ns so that an instruction would be affected by the clock glitch. Figure 5 shows the screenshot from the oscilloscope during the experiment. In Fig. 5(a), the bottom signal is the trigger signal of the fault injection. Figure 5(b) shows the magnified view of the glitchy clock cycle. Thus, the glitchy clock generator is satisfied with the condition that the proposed method requires a precise fault injection clock by clock. According to the above generator specification, the proposed attack can be applied to targets with clock frequency of more than 100 MHz.

4.3   Experimental Results

Code 1 shows the **main** function of the program used in this experiment. AESEncWithRecal, SendData, and SendError indicate respectively (i) the functions to perform encryption, recalculation, and comparison between the ciphertext and the recalculated value; (ii) to output a ciphertext; and (iii) to output an error signal. Algorithm 5 shows the AESEncWithRecal function. This function corresponds to Algorithm 1 in lines 1 to 3, but it returns the ciphertext and the result of comparison between P and P_2. In AESEncWithRecal, the value '0' is stored on the register r1 when the plaintext and the results of the recalculation

Table 2. Experimental results

Step	Starting position	Final position	Number of trials
Step I	$p_p = 0$	$p_p = 3$	4
Step II	$p_B = 30530$	$p_B = 30527$	4
Step III	$p_A = 3$	$p_A = 9996$	9994
Total			10002

Code 2: AddRoundKey.

(a) Code in C language.   (b) Assembly code compiled with GCC 4.3.3.

Code 3: Example of instruction duplication.

```
add_round_key(void)
{
  u8_t i;
  for (i=0; i<16;i++){
    s[i] ^= k[i];
  }
}
```

```
 1: LDS   r26, 0x0000
 2: LDS   r27, 0x0000
 3: LDI   r30, 0x00
 4: LDI   r31, 0x00
 5: LD    r24, X
 6: LD    r25, Z+
 7: EOR   r24, r25
 8: ST    X+, r24
 9: LDI   r24, 0x00
10: CPI   r30, 0x00
11: CPC   r31, r24
12: BRNE  .+0
13: RET
```

```
 1: LBL_MAIN:
 2: CALL AESEncWithRecal
 3: TST r1
 4: BRNE LBL_FAIL
 5: BRNE LBL_FAIL
 6: CALL SendData
 7: JMP LBL_FINISH
 8: LBL_FAIL:
 9: CALL SendError
10: LBL_FINISH:
```

are consistent, and '1' is stored otherwise. Next, the test (TST) instruction in line 3 examines register r1. Test instruction stores '1' in the register Z (called Zero Flag) when the register r1 has '0' and '1' otherwise. Then, the branch (BRNE) instruction is executed. If Z holds 1 (so r1 holds 0) the instruction "CALL SendData" in line 5 is executed because the program does not jump to LBL_FAIL. In contrast, if Z holds 0 (so r1 holds 1), which means that a fault has been detected, the program jumps to LBL_FAIL and an error signal is sent. However, when a fault is injected during the execution of the BRNE instruction in line 4, the instruction "CALL SendData" is executed regardless of the value of register r1 because the BRNE instruction is skipped.

Table 2 shows the number of trials needed to complete the proposed attack. Here, we observed in advance that the cycle count of cryptographic operation c_p was 30527. We performed 10002 fault injection trials in total and obtained a ciphertext with a four-byte error, suitable for Piret's attack. In this experiment, Fault A was injected into the AddRoundKey function at the 8th round. Code 2(a) presents the AddRoundKey code used in this experiment, where the variables k and s denote the round key and the intermediate value, respectively. Code 2(b) shows the assembly code obtained by compiling Code 2(a). The fault was injected into the load (LD) instruction in line 5. Fault B was injected into the branch instruction in line 4 of Code 1.

4.4 Applications of Proposed Attack

The proposed attack has the potential to defeat various countermeasures in addition to the countermeasure shown in Algorithm 1. First, we describe the application of our attack to another recalculation-based countermeasure that performs the same cryptographic operation twice. We assume that two cryptographic operations are performed by the same function in the program. In this case, the same algorithms as above can be applied to the countermeasure without any change. In addition, we can obtain a faulty ciphertext in a different manner. After finding the timing p_p for the preliminary fault by Algorithm 2, we search for the timing for Fault B by Algorithm 3 from p_p. We can obtain a faulty ciphertext when Fault B is injected into the instruction corresponding to the instruction providing the preliminary fault. Let c_i be the elapsed time between the preliminary fault and Fault B. To obtain a faulty ciphertext for DFA, we change the timings of two fault injections while keeping the interval c_i.

The proposed attack also has the potential to defeat countermeasures based on instruction duplication. Code 3 shows an example of Code 2 equipped with this kind of countermeasure. The attacker cannot inject a fault even when the branch instruction in line 4 is skipped because the same instruction in line 5 is executed instead of the skipped instruction [14]. However, the countermeasure is defeated when both instructions in lines 4 and 5 are skipped. This is feasible if we search for the timing for the preliminary fault and the interval between the preliminary fault and Fault B at the same time. Note that the number of fault injection trials is $O(n^2)$, where n is the length of code. We finally obtain a faulty ciphertext when we chose a correct timing and interval.

A random delay countermeasure [8] is also potentially vulnerable to the proposed attack. This countermeasure generates a random number and feeds it to a loop counter. In this case, the attacker can target the branch instruction at the end of the loop. If the branch instruction is skipped, the delay time becomes constant. The attacker can find that the countermeasure was disabled by measuring the execution time. After the countermeasure has been disabled, we can apply the proposed method shown above.

The proposed attack can also be combined with side-channel attacks, such as power analysis attacks. For example, a masking countermeasure can be disabled when a fault is injected into the generation or addition of a random number.

5   Countermeasure

This section describes a software countermeasure against the proposed attack. First, we consider a countermeasure against the skipping of branch instructions. Code 4 shows code immune to the skipping of branch instructions. In this code, the program counter moves to the error handling routine when the

Code 4: Countermeasure by default fail.

```
1:  JMP LBL_MAIN
2:  LBL_SUCCESS:
3:  CALL SendData
4:  JMP LBL_FINISH
5:  LBL_MAIN:
6:  CALL AESEncWithRecal
7:  TST r1
8:  BREQ LBL_SUCCESS
9:  LBL_FAIL:
10: CALL SendError
11: LBL_FINISH:
```

Code 5: Proposed countermeasure.

```
1:  JMP LBL_MAIN
2:  LBL_SUCCESS:
3:  CALL SendData
4:  JMP LBL_FINISH
5:  LBL_TEST:
6:  TST r1
7:  BREQ LBL_SUCCESS;jumps when Z=1
8:  JMP LBL_FAIL
9:  LBL_MAIN:
10: CALL AESEncWithRecal
11: CLZ      ;Stores 0 in Z
12: BRNE LBL_TEST  ;Go to LBL_TEST when Z=0
13: LBL_FAIL:
14: CALL SendError
15: LBL_FINISH:
```

branch instruction in line 8 is skipped. Such a scheme is called "default fail" [20]. In addition, in Code 4, the call of the output routine ("CALL SendData" in line 3) is located before the encryption, which prevents the attacker from skipping all the instructions between the encryption and the output routine.

However, another piece of vulnerability still remains in Code 4. The Zero Flag (Z) is not updated when the TST instruction in line 7 is skipped. In this case, the branch instruction might jump to the label LBL_SUCCESS regardless of the value of r1 because the value of Z depends on the last instruction to update the value of Z. To prevent this attack, we should initialize Z and check whether Z is the correct value before executing the test instruction. Code 5 presents the proposed countermeasure. After the encryption, we first set Z to be the value that does not satisfy the branch condition in line 7. In Code 5, Z is initialized as 0. Then, the program checks Z and jumps only when the value of Z is 0. The branch instruction at line 11 does not jump to the label LBL_TEST if Z is 1. Therefore, the value of Z (i.e., 0) is guaranteed at line 6. The program does not jump to LBL_SUCCESS when the test instruction is skipped or when the value of Z is 0. The proposed countermeasure can be implemented in many processor architectures, because many architectures have branch and flag manipulation instructions. Furthermore, if the architectures support some specific instructions, a more efficient countermeasure might be possible. For example, the CBZ instruction is available on the ARM architecture [1]. The instruction performs atomic testing and branching. In Code 4, by replacing the test instruction and the branch instruction with the CBZ instruction, we can prevent the attacker from skipping the test instruction by itself.

6 Conclusion

This paper proposed a multiple-fault injection attack based on adaptive control of fault injection timing in embedded microprocessors. The proposed method can be conducted under the black-box condition that the details of the cryptographic software running on the target device are not known to attackers. In addition, the proposed method is non-invasive, without the depackaging required in previous works, since such adaptive fault injection is performed by precisely generating a clock glitch. In this paper, we demonstrated the validity of the proposed method through an experiment on AES software with a typical recalculation-based countermeasure on an 8-bit microprocessor. We first described the proposed method to inject two kinds of faults, designed to obtain a faulty output suitable for differential fault analysis and to avoid a conditional branch for the countermeasure. We then showed experimentally that a faulty output can be obtained from the software without using information on the detailed instruction sequence. Furthermore, we proposed a countermeasure against our attack. This countermeasure prevents the attackers calling the output routine by skipping a branch or branch test instruction.

Future work should include further applications of the proposed attack to other processors that have larger and different instruction sets, such as ARM. Also, a more sophisticated searching method would reduce the cost of the proposed attack. As a countermeasure for the proposed attack, we are developing a compiler that implements the proposed countermeasure automatically.

References

1. ARMv8 instruction set overview (2012). https://silver.arm.com/download/ARM_and_AMBA_Architecture/AR100-DA-70501-r0p0-00eac5/ARMv8_ISA_PRD03-GENC-010197-30-0.pdf
2. Bar-El, H., Choukri, H., Naccache, D., Tunstall, M., Whelan, C.: The sorcerer's apprentice guide to fault attacks. Proc. IEEE **94**(2), 370–382 (2006)
3. Barenghi, A., Breveglieri, L., Koren, I., Pelosi, G., Regazzoni, F.: Countermeasures against fault attacks on software implemented AES: effectiveness and cost. In: Proceedings of the 5th Workshop on Embedded Systems Security (WESS), pp. 7:1–7:10, October 2010
4. Biham, E., Shamir, A.: Differential fault analysis of secret key cryptosystems. In: Kaliski Jr., B.S. (ed.) CRYPTO 1997. LNCS, vol. 1294, pp. 513–525. Springer, Heidelberg (1997)
5. Boneh, D., DeMillo, R.A., Lipton, R.J.: On the importance of checking cryptographic protocols for faults. In: Fumy, W. (ed.) EUROCRYPT 1997. LNCS, vol. 1233, pp. 37–51. Springer, Heidelberg (1997)
6. Ciet, M., Joye, M.: Practical fault countermeasures for Chinese remaindering based RSA. In: FDTC 2005, pp. 124–131, September 2005
7. Clavier, C.: Secret external encodings do not prevent transient fault analysis. In: Paillier, P., Verbauwhede, I. (eds.) CHES 2007. LNCS, vol. 4727, pp. 181–194. Springer, Heidelberg (2007)

8. Coron, J.-S., Kizhvatov, I.: Analysis and improvement of the random delay countermeasure of CHES 2009. In: Mangard, S., Standaert, F.-X. (eds.) CHES 2010. LNCS, vol. 6225, pp. 95–109. Springer, Heidelberg (2010)

9. Dehbaoui, A., Dutertre, J.M., Robisson, B., Tria, A.: Electromagnetic transient faults injection on a hardware and a software implementations of AES. In: FDTC 2012, pp. 7–15, September 2012

10. Endo, S., Hayashi, Y.i., Homma, N., Aoki, T., Katashita, T., Hori, Y., Sakiyama, K., Nagata, M., Danger, J.L., Le, T.H., Bazargan-Sabet, P.: Measurement of side-channel information from cryptographic devices on security evaluation platform: demonstration of SPACES project. In: Proceedings of SICE Annual Conference, pp. 313–316, August 2012

11. Kim, C.H., Quisquater, J.-J.: Fault attacks for CRT based RSA: new attacks, new results, and new countermeasures. In: Sauveron, D., Markantonakis, K., Bilas, A., Quisquater, J.-J. (eds.) WISTP 2007. LNCS, vol. 4462, pp. 215–228. Springer, Heidelberg (2007)

12. Medwed, M., Schmidt, J.M.: A continuous fault countermeasure for AES providing a constant error detection rate. In: FDTC 2010, pp. 66–71, August 2010

13. Moradi, A., Shalmani, M.T.M., Salmasizadeh, M.: A generalized method of differential fault attack against AES cryptosystem. In: Goubin, L., Matsui, M. (eds.) CHES 2006. LNCS, vol. 4249, pp. 91–100. Springer, Heidelberg (2006)

14. Moro, N., Dehbaoui, A., Heydemann, K., Robisson, B., Encrenaz, E.: Electromagnetic fault injection: towards a fault model on a 32-bit microcontroller. In: FDTC 2013, pp. 77–88, August 2013

15. Piret, G., Quisquater, J.-J.: A differential fault attack technique against SPN structures, with application to the AES and KHAZAD. In: Walter, C.D., Koç, Ç.K., Paar, C. (eds.) CHES 2003. LNCS, vol. 2779, pp. 77–88. Springer, Heidelberg (2003)

16. Saha, D., Mukhopadhyay, D., RoyChowdhury, D.: A diagonal fault attack on the advanced encryption standard. Cryptology ePrint Archive, Report 2009/581, November 2009

17. Satoh, A., Sugawara, T., Homma, N., Aoki, T.: High-performance concurrent error detection scheme for AES hardware. In: Oswald, E., Rohatgi, P. (eds.) CHES 2008. LNCS, vol. 5154, pp. 100–112. Springer, Heidelberg (2008)

18. Schmidt, J.M., Christoph, H.: A practical fault attack on square and multiply. In: FDTC 2008, pp. 53–58, October 2008

19. Trichina, E., Korkikyan, R.: Multi fault laser attacks on protected CRT-RSA. In: FDTC 2010, pp. 75–86, August 2010

20. Witteman, M.: Secure application programming in the presence of side channel attacks (2013). https://www.riscure.com/benzine/documents/Paper_Side_Channel_Patterns.pdf

Adjusting Laser Injections for Fully Controlled Faults

Franck Courbon[1,2](✉), Philippe Loubet-Moundi[1], Jacques J.A. Fournier[3], and Assia Tria[3]

[1] GEMALTO, Security Labs, La Ciotat, France
{franck.courbon,philippe.loubet-moundi}@gemalto.com
[2] Ecole des Mines de Saint-Etienne, CMP-GC/LSAS, Gardanne, France
franck.courbon@mines-stetienne.fr
[3] CEA, CEA Tech Region, DPACA/LSAS, Gardanne, France
{jacques.j.a.fournier,assia.tria}@cea.fr

Abstract. Hardware characterizations of integrated circuits have been evolving rapidly with the advent of more precise, sophisticated and cost-efficient tools. In this paper we describe how the fine tuning of a laser source has been used to characterize, set and reset the state of registers in a 90 nm chip. By adjusting the incident laser beam's location, it is possible to choose to switch any register value from '0' to '1' or vice-versa by targeting the PMOS side or the NMOS side. Plus, we show how to clear a register by selecting a laser beam's power. With the help of imaging techniques, we are able to explain the underlying phenomenon and provide a direct link between the laser mapping and the physical gate structure. Thus, we correlate the localization of laser fault injections with implementations of the PMOS and NMOS areas in the silicon substrate. This illustrates to what extent laser beams can be used to monitor the bits stored within registers, with adverse consequences in terms of security evaluation of integrated circuits.

Keywords: Laser fault injection · Registers attacks · Bit set and reset · Fault model

1 Introduction

Several attacks can be performed on integrated circuits to bypass security mechanisms or access sensitive data. Those attacks are usually classified into four categories: logical attacks where the attacker exploits a weak software implementation [3]; side-channel attacks where power or electromagnetic or timing based information are used to learn about the data manipulated by a given device (SPA [16], DPA [12] and CPA [4]); invasive attacks where the device is physically and irreversibly modified [1]; and fault attacks where external perturbations are used to induce faults during the execution of a given sensitive program or on the sensitive data being manipulated [2,20]. This last kind of

© Springer International Publishing Switzerland 2014
E. Prouff (Ed.): COSADE 2014, LNCS 8622, pp. 229–242, 2014.
DOI: 10.1007/978-3-319-10175-0_16

attack can be performed using several means like a flash light, laser beam, electromagnetic pulse [5], voltage or clock glitches.

In this paper we focus on the use of a laser beam as a security characterization tool for Integrated Circuits (IC): with such means, precise and localized effects can be induced into the device without damaging the latter (usually a simple decapsulation of the chip is enough) at relatively low costs ($\approx 20Keuros$), thanks to the decreasing costs of laser sources. We describe how the precise use of a laser beam can be used to characterize, set and reset the state of registers in a 90 nm IC. We correlate laser faults injection results with physical implementations of the PMOS and NMOS. The explanation for the observed phenomenon is obtained by the use of imaging techniques.

The paper is organized as follows. We first introduce some of the hardware design concepts used in the paper as well as some background information on laser-based fault injection techniques. Then we describe the experimental set-up used, the device under test (DUT) and the methodology applied. The monitoring of registers using laser-based fault injections is then depicted: we describe the tests performed and show the overlay between the laser fault-based mapping and the register's physical implementation. We then discuss about our findings relative to recent publications, we describe limitations and future work before concluding on how such techniques can have adverse consequences in terms of security.

2 Hardware Design Aspects

2.1 IC Physical Layers

Integrated circuits are made out of silicon wafers. The different manufacturing steps are performed on only one side of the wafer usually called the active side, top side or front side. For our laser fault injections, we will use the other side, called the backside, which can be thinned and polished. Either way, the final wafer thickness is relatively high - 100 times - compared to the active layer. This parameter must be considered for setting up the laser.

The active layer is made, from bottom to top, of P or N doped silicon regions to constitute a transistor's drain and source. A polysilicon layer is used to make transistor gates with minimal dimensioning. Then, the first metal layer is used to connect the different transistors to build a logic gate. Those gates are linked together by interconnection or supplied by power routing lines. All metal layers are separated by insulation layers. Finally, a passive layer protects the chip from corrosion or packaging or handling stresses.

2.2 Logic Gate Consideration

Integrated circuits are made up of elementary functional gate structures also called standard cells. During the place and route phase of the circuit's design the arrangement of standard cells is optimized to reach the best compromise between area, timing and power constraints. In a typical secure product, basic blocks - i.e. CPU, coprocessors, logic functions - are scrambled and are part of the synthesized logic. Depending on the chip complexity, several thousands to millions of logic gates are implemented. The smallest gate is the inverter which is composed of two transistors (as we are in Complementary MOS circuit design). The number of transistors used in other, more complex, logic gates can be ten times larger. Basic gates function are NOT, AND, NOR, XOR, NAND and few others like flip-flops or latches. Even if the number of logic functions provided is relatively small, the number of basic gates available in the standard cell library could be more than 10 times larger, depending on the number of inputs (i.e. NAND2, NAND3), the amount of current driven or on the presence of optional reset or clock signals. It is possible to temporarily store a single bit of data in a register which can be either a latch or a flip-flop. A latch output is constantly affected by its input as long as the enable signal is set. On the other hand, a flip-flop updates its value only at a rising or falling edge of the enable signal which usually is the clock signal. This article only deals with flip-flops even if it could be extended to any CMOS based logic gate or to volatile storage structures.

2.3   Register Hardware Structure

Storing bits within the synthesized logic requires several transistors: about 20 to 30 transistors are needed to build a single flip-flop. We focus in this paper on bistable flip-flops that are standard cells implemented within the synthesized logic in order to store temporary values or to speed up the data access. They are widely used in core processor unit or in cryptographic coprocessors.

The structure of flip-flops depends on their types; i.e. D type or E type (enable) and if there is a synchronous reset input or an asynchronous one. Typically, for a 90 nm technology a flip-flop size is of the order of $15\,\mu m^2$ and becomes bigger when an enable and a reset signal are implemented. Flip-flops such as other memory elements require specific timing requirements including set up and hold times on data and minimum pulse widths on clock inputs [11].

The flip-flop considered here is of D-type with an asynchronous reset from which any edge-triggered type storage element can be designed with a few extra gates. For performance, layout density and energy efficiency, gates are always designed and optimized at the transistor level. Their implementation requires several stages: inverting input buffer, two types of latches, possibly an output multiplexer, output buffers, clock preparation and asynchronous reset signal.

A basic D flip-flop layout is given in Fig. 1; we acknowledge that this type of gate is more complex that those studied in previous works [17]. This flip-flop contains 24 transistors and a theoretical study of a laser beam's effect over such a gate would require dedicated and custom tools to be able to run significant simulations.

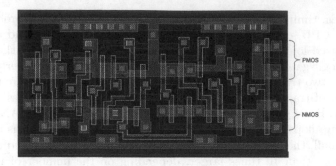

Fig. 1. A flip-flop layout

3   Laser Beam Injection

3.1   Laser/Matter Interaction in CMOS Circuits

Within a single flip-flop logic gate, several pairs of NMOS and PMOS transistors are implemented. Implanting P-type dopants into some N-type base material, or vice versa, create PN junctions. Those junctions are sensitive to a photoelectric effect when exposed to a laser beam [8]. This induced photocurrent may switch a transistor's state thus affecting the output of a logic gate. Hériveaux et al. [9] gave an attempt to try to simulate and analyze the behaviour of an inverter gate under the stress of a laser beam. Moreover, previous practical works based on an inverter [17] showed that when the input is '1', the drain of the NMOS 'becomes the sensitive' part and when the input is '0' the drain of the PMOS 'becomes the sensitive' one. Moreover, depending on the type of targeted MOS transistors the required power to switch a transistor is more or less important [18]. Measurements made by Sarafianos *et al.* [18] give a difference of photocurrent 6 times higher for a specific NMOS junction (N+/P-sub, large ellipse) than for a PMOS one (P+/N-well, small ellipse) in 90 nm technology and for a given process.

In [19], the author also notes that the N-well/P-sub junction (present only for PMOS transistors as seen in Fig. 2) despite having the largest surface, creates

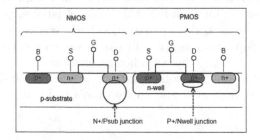

Fig. 2. NMOS, PMOS and generated photocurrent

a small photocurrent. Furthermore, as our shoot duration is superior to tens of ns, we use the model given for a shoot duration over $8ns$ and in this model, even if pnp associations are present, currents created with parasite bipolar junction transistors are neglected. Without any knowledge of our flip-flop layout, based on these previous works, we can guess that a bit initialized at '1' would be more sensitive to a laser beam. Indeed, as PMOS transistors are connected to the upper rail voltage and NMOS ones to the lower rail voltage, reaching a '0' value might be performed through the switching of the state of one or several NMOS transistors.

3.2 Laser Based Fault Attacks

The laser bench used to perform faults in integrated circuits evaluation is characterized by:

- High spatial precision
- Local effect area
- Accurate timing
- High fault repeatability
- Multiple faults capability

Thus, using laser fault injections, several types of attacks are feasible against cryptographic operations: such as safe error attacks where the attacker can guess for example key value by observing the output after a single bit modification [14,15]; algorithm modification attacks [6] where the attacker can change a single bit of a register and reduce, for instance, the number of rounds performed in a cryptographic algorithm; and differential fault attacks [7] where an attacker can exploit fault injections to guess a key. This paper deals with the laser effect over a complex logic gate.

4 Experimental Set-up

4.1 Device Under Test and Methodology

In our experiments, we use a recent IC microcontroller with a technology node of 90 nm. We focus our investigations onto the synthesized logic of the sample covering about a fourth of the global integrated circuit's size. Due to dense metal routing on the top side of the chip, we decided to use backside analysis in order to ensure that a uniform laser power reaches the active layer. Thus, the DUT's backside is opened and then placed under the microscope which focuses the laser beam through the substrate. The DUT is monitored and we perform the following experimental operations:

- A. Load data register.
- B. Perform laser shoot.
- C. Read back register value.
- D. Move XY stage and perform A/B/C repeatedly.

Using an open sample, we only read a unique register value. The resulting output file is a matrix of the faulted XY positions which displays only the faults injected into this single register.

4.2 Laser Platform

The laser test platform is composed of a microscope with different focusing capabilities, a laser cavity, an electrically controlled XYZ stage, an oscilloscope, a device under test (DUT) and electronic boards to drive the different equipments and to precisely synchronize them together. The set up must be well defined in terms of:

- Pulse shape and characteristics such as wavelength, energy, duration.
- Pulse repeatability.
- Spatial localization on the chip.
- Temporal localization in the process (not really applicable for static registers approach though).

Our platform enables us to measure the power reaching the integrated circuit's backside. We measured this for each input command value applied to our laser source. This output power can vary from few mW to $800mW$ peak and we can set the pulse duration as short as tens of ns. According to power measurements and oscilloscope signal observations, we can measure the energy reaching the backside surface of the die.

$$E = P_{peak} * \Delta T$$
$$E(Joules) = P_{peak}(W) * \Delta T(s)$$

We use a 1064 nm laser wavelength that enables us to obtain a trade-off in terms of photoelectric effect and substrate absorption [10]. The optical absorption of a laser beam in the silicon depends on the substrate doping concentration and the wavelength used. Our set up has a spatial precision of the order of the μm.

5   Monitoring Register Bits Using a Laser Beam

In the rest of this paper, we assume that timing constraints are not an issue as we perturb a static register which stores the programmed data during the entire execution of our process. The hardware design of those registers does not include a dynamic return to the previous value so we can fault a register at any time, and then read the value back. Within the following subsections we describe how to find a register location over the entire DUT (Sect. 5.1), how a localized laser beam can control the bit value (Sect. 5.2), how the bit value can be obtained with a laser mapping (Sect. 5.3) and how a power controlled laser beam can clear a register value (Sect. 5.4).

5.1   Finding the Area of Interest

The entire synthesized logic block is scanned with a large step (around $25\,\mu m$) and a large beam spot (around $10\,\mu m$). This allows finding the bits of interest over the entire chip. Some bits are missing as we attack with a large scanning step. We also obtain multiple-bit faults with such energy and spot sizes. However, once a register bit is found, chances are high of finding all the others nearby, even if the synthesized logic scrambles the structure. The precision of our experimental set-up is the key point for the success of our experiments. After empirical tests, we found a set up for a hundred percent faults injection success rate by applying an energy of tens of nJ on the backside of the circuit. With these laser parameters, no particular alarm is triggered by the chip.

For the rest of our experiments, we limit the area of interest to the area where some bits of the register have been revealed. This area becomes the new region to scan. Thus, the next figures only display a small part of the integrated circuit. This is less time consuming, more attacks can be performed with different sets of parameters. After finding this area of interest, we then use a smaller step (around $1\,\mu m$) and a smaller laser spot size (around $2\,\mu m$). We increase the magnification with a $50\times$ objective and we target an area of $30 \times 38\,\mu m^2$. The laser scans are performed with an X and Y step of $1\,\mu m$. We hence have $30 \times 38 = 1140$ positions to analyze.

5.2   Controlling the Modification of a Register by Localization

A flip-flop is usually implemented using a large number of transistors and there are only two values that can be stored in a flip-flop logic gate, a '1' or a '0'.

Over the reduced scan area defined in (Sect. 5.1), only 8 bits are implemented, and for the first scan on the left of Fig. 3, we set the register value with '00000000' before scanning the $30 \times 38\,\mu m^2$. As the registers are all programmed with a '0' value, we are only able to detect when the laser shoot switches the output value to '1'. As naming convention we talk about 'reset' or 'bit reset' when the

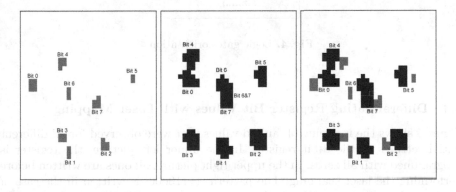

Fig. 3. '0' to '1' bits faults, '1' to '0' bits faults, '1' to '0' and '0' to '1'

value switches from '1' to '0' and 'set' or 'bit set' when the value switches from
'0' to '1'. In the figures to come, the grey or black squares represent a bit switch
whereas white pixels are used when no error is recorded. For the middle part
of Fig. 3, inversely we set the initial register bits with '1's. It gives us another
mapping on which we see the positions where the laser beam switches a bit to
'0'. Both mappings put together give the "superposed representation" on the
rightmost picture of the figure.

We thus localize characteristic patterns: for each bit set in Fig. 3 for instance,
we get a specific location where the laser could be applied to change the bit value.
8 distinguishable locations are found, one for each of the 8 register bits. With
the second mapping we get the same status to have bit reset. However with the
third part of the image we can say that bit set or bit reset sensitive areas are
distinct areas. As another result, if we assume that the same logic gate is used for
all the bits, we also get some information about pattern rotation. For instance
if bit number 1 has a reference rotation, then bit number 3 is mirrored. We thus
suppose the flip-flop gate physical implantation to be mirrored. For each of those
eight logic gates, using one laser shoot targeting the right sensitive positions, we
can exactly control the stored value at the logic gate output.

In Fig. 4, we show that half of the bits present over this area have their bit
set sensitive part on the left side of the reset sensitive part. This gives some
information about the orientation of each logic gate.

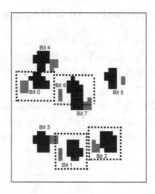

Fig. 4. Logic gates orientation

5.3   Differentiating Register Bit Values with Laser Mapping

Figure 5 shows the mapping of faulted values that were observed for '4' different
initial settings of the 8-bit register. In the upper left picture, the register is
programmed with all zeros. In the upper right picture, all ones are written before
performing the laser scanning. The pattern '11110000' is written in the case of
the lower left picture and in the lower right one, '00001111' is programmed in
the register.

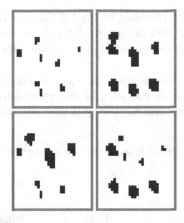

Fig. 5. Laser fault injection mappings at $39nJ$ with different initial values; top-left: '00000000', top-right: '11111111', bottom-left: '11110000', bottom-right: '00001111'

We observe that the bit set and bit reset have different sensitivities. The observation of the location where the faults occurred gives direct information about the initial value of the bit. In our tests the "larger" sensitive areas correspond to an initial state at '0' and the "smaller ones" are representative of an initial state of '1'.

5.4 Controlled Register Clearing with Energy Selection

We observed that the laser location can be tuned to change in a controlled way the stored value in a register flip-flop. So, another test campaign was conducted to find if other laser parameters can be used to increase our capabilities to change registers' contents in a controlled way. Therefore, we set the initial register value to '00001111' and consecutively change the laser exposure time and the laser beam power, resulting in a successively decreasing the energy. If we look at the pictures from the left to the right in Fig. 6, the energy hitting the chip's backside is successively $32nJ$, $13nJ$ and $10nJ$.

Figure 6 shows that a careful control (an energy high enough to perturb a type of transistors without perturbing the other type of transistors) of the injected

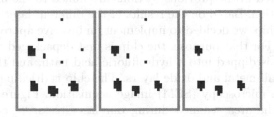

Fig. 6. Pertubation of the register initialized at '00001111' with different energies; left: $32nJ$, middle: $13nJ$, right: $10nJ$

energy only allows to reset bits and to let bit initialized at '0' unchanged. The contents can be controlled very precisely with this set up. Using a large spot size and adequate energy, an attacker could clear all the bits of the flip-flops present under the laser beam.

A sensitivity map is drawn from the experiments done, it well illustrates obtained effects depending on the level of energy applied. Obviously, Table 1 is valid over this given circuit and for the spot size and wavelength used.

Table 1. Observed effect depending on level of energy hitting the circuit backside

Case number	1	2	3	4	5
Energy level	Few nJ	10nJ	13nJ	32nJ	Over several tens of nJ
Bit reset	Not all bits switched	All bits switched at a given location	All bits switched at a given location	All bits switched at a given location, different of bit set zone	All bits switched but no more sub-gate spatial resolution
Bit set	No bit set	No bit set	Not all bits switched	All bits switched at a given location, different of bit reset zone	All bits switched but no more sub-gate spatial resolution

6   Correlating Fault Attacks and Transistors Implementation

The effects depicted in the previous sections are linked to the underlying hardware implementation. Based on the results of the different laser injection effects obtained on the chip, we decided to implement an invasive approach on a second identical sample. For that purpose, the chip is first depackaged with nitric acid. Then, the device is dipped into a hydrofluoric acid bath, and then rinsed with water to remove all metal and oxide layers. The chip is dried before performing scanning electron microscopy (SEM) image acquisition. Figure 7 is the "bulk" level picture of the area scanned during our laser tests. '8' columns of logic gates are visible and the P-well or N-well active areas - representative of CMOS process - of each column can be easily distinguished. In the same picture, a logic gate is highlighted by a black rectangle whereas the white circle gives an idea of the size of the laser spot used ($\approx 2\,\mu$m). In CMOS circuits the output current of PMOS or NMOS transistors can be approximated by $I \approx \mu_{p,n} * W/L$ where μ is the mobility of the carriers, W and L respectively the width and length of the transistor gate. L is fixed by the technology node. This output current must be balanced. So, this is partially realized by adjusting the W parameter. The mobility μp of the hole carriers is smaller than that of the electrons μn. So, the width of the gate of PMOS transistors must be larger. On the SEM image, this property is used to clearly identify PMOS or NMOS location.

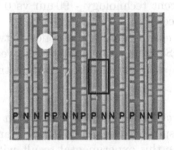

Fig. 7. N and P-well implementation, single gate and spot size representation

If the laser fail map is overlaid with the SEM image (Fig. 8), we can directly see that the relative locations of the bit set (white squares) or bit reset areas (black squares) within a gate are respectively over the PMOS area and the NMOS area. In addition, for the energy of laser shoot, the sensitive area is larger when the bit is initially programmed at '1' (bit reset, black squares). For the flip-flop gate used in the analyzed register, shooting with the laser on the NMOS will reset the bit whereas shooting on the PMOS will set the bit from '0' to '1'.

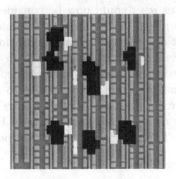

Fig. 8. Laser faults mapping overlaid on Scanning Electron Microscope image

7   Discussion and Future Work

Comparison to SRAM fault model and generated junction photocurrent: The work of Roscian *et al.* [17] targeted a SRAM memory element with a valid bit set and bit reset model. In their work the experimental results are in line with the electrical simulations performed. In our work we target a more complex gate where the layout of the flip-flop and the logic gate transistors schematic were not available. Moreover, we showed a strong dependency between laser fault injection behavior and PMOS or NMOS areas. In addition, we also validated this model on a more recent technology - 90 nm vs 0.25 μm - used in current standard smart card devices.

In [18], Sarafianos *et al.* observed a difference between the generated photocurrents over an NMOS pn junction and those over a PMOS pn junction. This result is also confirmed by our results as NMOS transistors reveal a higher sensitivity.

Limitations and future works: As the internal design of the gate studied was unknown and as our laser spot size was not capable of targeting a single transistor it is impossible to validate this experimental result with electrical simulations. For example, the number of transistors disturbed by the laser effect is unknown. The contribution of each disturbed transistor to the final flip-flop switching is missing. This knowledge is very significant for a designer who wants to make a standard cell more resistant against laser attacks. The future work will be to reproduce the same experiments on a device where all the data of the standard cell used for bit storage registers are available. Simulations and deeper fault modeling at transistor and gate level would also be possible.

Threats and countermeasures: Our experiments reveal a threat introduced by the capability of controlling the values of registers bits with a proper laser set up. As an evolution of the work of Leveugle *et al.* [13], and from an attackers point of view, bit set, bit reset or register reset could now be considered as really practicable fault models, even on very recent semiconductor technologies. We can reasonably think that state of the art cryptographic implementations are protected against safe errors or DFA but vulnerabilities introduced on other sensitive registers must be carefully analyzed. If no existing hardware countermeasures - such as hardware redundancy - are provided by the device to protect against registers modifications, the software must monitor those registers' integrity frequently. For example, randomly check of register coherence could be performed before and after sensitive operations. This may imply significant performances loss though.

8   Conclusion

We present in this paper the realization of practical laser tests performed on a 90 nm device. Our initial target was to analyze the effect of the laser beam on flip-flops of a register and to reach the limits provided by our equipment.

We highlight that a reliable fault injection requires to perfectly monitor the laser beam positioning, the laser beam size and the laser pulse parameters. With the correct set up, it is possible to control with a 100 % success rate the fault injection effect on a single bit: '0' to '1' or '1' to '0'. We also succeed in tuning our laser parameters to only reset the register bits initialized at '1' whereas register bits with initial value at '0' are left unchanged. Finally, we correlate the laser fault mapping with the physical image of the area under test. With this observation, we are able to explain that the difference of sensitivity is due to the nature of the active area (PMOS or NMOS) exposed within the standard cell. This latest result shows the interest for security characterization to use laser beam sizes smaller than the logical gate's width. The fault models usually used in cryptographic attacks - e.g. safe errors, register reset - are validated by the present study. High injection rates with fine tuned laser beam increase the requirements of strong software or hardware counter measures against fully controlled faults.

Acknowledgment. We gratefully acknowledge technical support and knowledge sharing of Pascal Moitrel. We also would like to thank Francis Olivier for proofreading this paper.

References

1. Anderson, R., Kuhn, M.: Low cost attacks on tamper resistant devices (1997)
2. Bar-El, H., Choukri, H., Naccache, D., Tunstall, M., Whelan, C.: The sorcerer's apprentice guide to fault attacks. IACR Cryptology ePrint Archive, p. 100 (2004)
3. Bond, M., Choudary, O., Murdoch, S.J., Skorobogatov, S.P., Anderson, R.J.: Chip and skim: cloning emv cards with the pre-play attack. CoRR (2012)
4. Brier, E., Clavier, C., Olivier, F.: Correlation power analysis with a leakage model. In: Joye, M., Quisquater, J.-J. (eds.) CHES 2004. LNCS, vol. 3156, pp. 16–29. Springer, Heidelberg (2004)
5. Dehbaoui, A., Dutertre, J.M., Robisson, B., Tria, A.: Electromagnetic transient faults injection on a hardware and a software implementations of aes. In: FDTC, pp. 7–15 (2012)
6. Dutertre, J.M., Mirbaha, A.P., Naccache, D., Ribotta, A.L., Tria, A., Vaschalde, T.: Fault round modification analysis of the advanced encryption standard. In: 2012 IEEE International Symposium on Hardware-Oriented Security and Trust (HOST), pp. 140–145 (2012)
7. Giraud, C.: DFA on AES. In: Dobbertin, H., Rijmen, V., Sowa, A. (eds.) AES 2005. LNCS, vol. 3373, pp. 27–41. Springer, Heidelberg (2005)
8. Habing, D.: The use of lasers to simulate radiation-induced transients in semiconductor devices and circuits. IEEE Trans. Nucl. Sci. **12**(5), 91–100 (1965)
9. Hériveaux, L., Clédière, J., Anceau, S.: Electrical modeling of the effect of photo-electric laser fault injection on bulk cmos design. In: ISTFA 2013 (2013)
10. Johnston, A.: Charge generation and collection in p-n junctions excited with pulsed infrared lasers. IEEE Trans. Nucl. Sci. **40**(6), 1694–1702 (1993)
11. Kaeslin, H.: Digital Integrated Circuit Design: From VLSI Architectures to CMOS Fabrication, 1st edn. Cambridge University Press, New York (2008)
12. Kocher, P.C., Jaffe, J., Jun, B.: Differential power analysis. In: Wiener, M. (ed.) CRYPTO 1999. LNCS, vol. 1666, pp. 388–397. Springer, Heidelberg (1999)

13. Leveugle, R., Ammari, A., Maingot, V., Teyssou, E., Moitrel, P., Mourtel, C., Feyt, N., Rigaud, J.B., Tria, A.: Experimental evaluation of protections against laser-induced faults and consequences on fault modeling. In: Proceedings of the Conference on Design, Automation and Test in Europe, DATE 2007, pp. 1587–1592. EDA Consortium, San Jose (2007)

14. Loubet-Moundi, P., Vigilant, D., Olivier, F.: Static fault attacks on hardware des registers. IACR Cryptology ePrint Archive 2011, 531 (2011)

15. Marc Joye, P.P., Yen, S.M.: Secure evaluation of modular functions (2001)

16. Mayer-Sommer, R.: Smartly analyzing the simplicity and the power of simple power analysis on smartcards. In: Paar, C., Koç, Ç.K. (eds.) CHES 2000. LNCS, vol. 1965, pp. 78–92. Springer, Heidelberg (2000)

17. Roscian, C., Sarafianos, A., Dutertre, J.M., Tria, A.: Fault model analysis of laser-induced faults in sram memory cells. In: 2013 Workshop on Fault Diagnosis and Tolerance in Cryptography (FDTC), pp. 89–98 (2013)

18. Sarafianos, A., Roscian, C., Dutertre, J.M., Lisart, M., Tria, A.: Electrical modeling of the photoelectric effect induced by a pulsed laser applied to an SRAM cell. Microelectronics Reliability 53(9–11), 1300–1305 (2013). (european Symposium on Reliability of Electron Devices, Failure Physics and Analysis)

19. Sarafianos, A.: Injection de fautes par impulsion laser dans des circuits sécurisés. These, Ecole Nationale Supérieure des Mines de Saint-Etienne (2013)

20. Skorobogatov, S.P., Anderson, R.J.: Optical fault induction attacks. In: Kaliski Jr., B.S., Koç, Ç.K., Paar, C. (eds.) CHES 2002. LNCS, vol. 2523, pp. 2–12. Springer, Heidelberg (2003)

ChipWhisperer: An Open-Source Platform for Hardware Embedded Security Research

Colin O'Flynn[(✉)] and Zhizhang (David) Chen

Dalhousie University, Halifax, Canada
{coflynn,z.chen}@dal.ca

Abstract. This paper introduces a complete side channel analysis toolbox, inclusive of the analog capture hardware, target device, capture software, and analysis software. The highly modular design allows use of the hardware and software with a variety of existing systems. The hardware uses a synchronous capture method which greatly reduces the required sample rate, while also reducing the data storage requirement, and improving synchronization of traces. The synchronous nature of the hardware lends itself to fault injection, and a module to generate glitches of programmable width is also provided. The entire design (hardware and software) is open-source, and maintained in a publicly available repository. Several long example capture traces are provided for researchers looking to evaluate standard cryptographic implementations.

Keywords: Side-channel analysis · Acquisition · Synchronization · FPGA

1 Introduction

The introduction of Differential Power Analysis (DPA) [1] spurred interest in the vulnerabilities of embedded systems previously thought to be secure. The difficulty in comparing results of attacks on different platforms was realized early on, and the SASEBO board aimed to provide a standard platform for attacking [2]. Likewise it was realized that for new entrants into the world of side-channel attacks, having available code and algorithms was a useful starting point such as the OpenSCA toolbox [3], and the DPA Book [4]. Despite this, there is still considerable progress to be made. A researcher looking to replicate existing work, even if that work uses a board such as the SASEBO/SAKURA board, needs to purchase an oscilloscope, interface the oscilloscope to the computer, and (re)implement the attack.

Work into making a complete platform has already been presented, for example the GIAnT system, which even uses the same FPGA board as this work [5,6] (and with additional details in [7]). This work was developed in parallel to these systems, and the two systems use different architectures and design languages. The ChipWhisperer system presented in this work is a more modular design, and has more extensive publicly available code for the computer control. Certain features do differ between them: the GIAnT system has a high-speed

© Springer International Publishing Switzerland 2014
E. Prouff (Ed.): COSADE 2014, LNCS 8622, pp. 243–260, 2014.
DOI: 10.1007/978-3-319-10175-0_17

Digital-to-Analog Converter (DAC) for fault injections of adjustable magnitude, something missing on the current ChipWhisperer hardware.

This work presents a side-channel attack platform which integrates all required elements: target device, measurement equipment, capture software, and attack software. This work has benefits for almost any user: students have a low-cost laboratory, researchers have an environment which can be duplicated around the world, and embedded engineers have a method of easily testing published research on their own systems. The entire design (both hardware and software) is open-source, encouraging future development from users. Versions of the project are designed to work with existing hardware, such as the SAKURA-G and SASEBO-W board which researchers may already have access to. Modules to control standard oscilloscopes such as PicScopes and VISA-connected devices are also present, encouraging the use of the ChipWhisperer software with existing measurement labs.

Beyond side-channel attacks, the hardware lends itself to glitch and fault attacks. The device runs synchronous to the device under test (DUT), greatly simplifying the introduction of faults on certain clock cycles. A simple glitch generation module is included for inserting glitches at specific offsets from the clock edge.

2   Hardware

The hardware consists of both the hardware design and the FPGA code. The system is designed to work with several different FPGA boards, all based on the Spartan 6 FPGA. A 'reference' FPGA board is also provided based on a commercially-available FPGA module, shown in Fig. 1. This has a ZTEX FPGA Module with a Spartan 6 LX25 FPGA, however these modules are available in sizes from the LX9 – LX150. Researchers interested in implementing more logic inside the control FPGA may simply switch the ZTEX module for a larger one.

This board provides several features specific to side-channel analysis: two headers for mounting ADC or DAC boards, an AVR programmer, voltage-level translators for the target device, clock inputs, power for a differential probe and Low Noise Amplifier (LNA), external Phase Locked Loop (PLL) for clock recovery, and extension connectors for future improvements such as fault injection hardware. This board will be referred to as the *ChipWhisperer Capture Rev2*.

2.1   Modular FPGA Design

The blocks within the FPGA are designed around a central 'register control' module, as shown in Fig. 3. The design greatly simplifies the addition of new modules: only one small section of the design needs to be modified to insert the bus connections, otherwise the new module can live independently of the rest of the system.

The modular design allows customizing of which modules to include of interest to the researcher; including for example only the clock glitching module if it is desired to work with fault attacks and use a smaller FPGA.

Fig. 1. The reference implementation runs on a ZTEX Spartan 6 LX25 FPGA Module, with an OpenADC as the analog front-end. The completed board is referred to as the ChipWhisperer Capture Rev2.

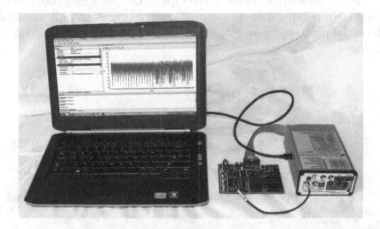

Fig. 2. The complete system, including the FPGA board from Fig. 1 which is mounted in an enclosure, a laptop computer, and the example capture board from Fig. 8. The system can also use a breakout board to connect other embedded hardware targets.

2.2 Capture and Clock Control

If the underlying objective is to measure data on the clock edges of the system clock, sampling at the clock rate of the system is sufficient, provided such samples occur at the correct moment (i.e. on the clock edge). This sampling technique is called synchronous sampling, where the sample clock is synchronized to the device clock; the application of synchronous sampling to side-channel analysis was first described in Sect. 5.2 of [8]. Hardware to perform synchronous sampling called the OpenADC was described in [9], where the SASEBO-GII board was attacked, and this demonstrated how sampling at 96 MS/s synchronously achieved similar results to sampling at 2 GS/s asynchronously. The OpenADC is used as the basis for this work.

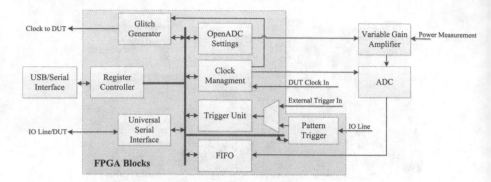

Fig. 3. The base design consists of several blocks connected via a internal bus in the FPGA, shown in the blue box (Color figure online).

The analog front-end used here is the OpenADC [9], which provides a −5 dB to 55 dB gain, simplifying measurement of low-level signals. Additionally designs for a differential probe and Low Noise Amplifier (LNA) are provided, an example shown in Fig. 4.

Fig. 4. Beyond capture hardware, design for a differential probe and H–Field probe with LNA are available.

For the synchronous sampling to work, the device must be able to lock onto the system clock. If the clock is readily available as a digital signal (e.g. from the crystal oscillator on the DUT), it can be fed into the FPGA directly, where internally it can be multiplied if desired. If the clock is not available, such as in the case of internal RC oscillators, an external PLL can be used with clock recovery logic to recover the clock [10]. Finally an asynchronous clock is available, although due to the limited sample-rate in this platform will have very poor performance compared to synchronous capture [9] (Fig. 5).

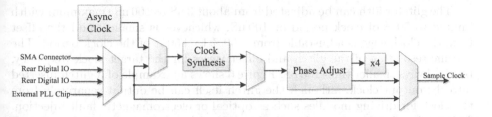

Fig. 5. Clock Routing in ChipWhisperer capture hardware.

2.3   Target Control and Triggering

The FPGA provides some basic IO blocks for driving standard devices. This includes a UART, a Smart Card interface, and Universal Serial IO device, which can be controlled from the computer. Note the target device can be driven by an existing connection instead; the FPGA-based IO blocks are provided simply as a convenience to allow a single USB connection to provide both communications and target control.

Several triggering options are provided. The most basic allows standard triggering: triggering on the rising edge of a digital line for example. This is suitable when analyzing devices which the researcher has programmed, and is able to insert a suitable trigger event into. For more realistic examples, two additional triggering blocks are provided. The first is a digital pattern match, which looks for a specific sequence of transitions on an IO line. This is implemented as a state machine, where it moves through to the next state only if the IO line remains in the expected state for the 'allowed' amount of time. If the IO line fails to match the expected state transition, the state machine resets. This system is specifically designed for triggering on communications protocols, for example by waiting on a response byte. The final triggering system looks for an analog pattern in the waveform, using a Sum of Absolute Difference (SAD) criteria, which is frequently used in video compression, and fast FPGA implementions exist for [11]. Here the system continuously compares the incoming waveform to a known pattern: when the SAD criteria falls below some threshold, the system triggers the capture.

All of these triggering options feature a pretrigger ability. The capture buffer is continuously filled, meaning that the trigger can occur after the actual cryptographic operation has occurred. The limit is simply the size of the capture buffer, which is primarily dependent on the size of the chosen FPGA.

The trigger out signal can be dynamically routed to an external pin. This allows triggering of external equipment with this advanced trigger source.

2.4   Glitch Generation

A clock glitch module is also present in the system. Using two adjustable delay lines built into the FPGA, it can insert glitches into a 'target clock': the 'target clock' either coming from the device under test or generated by the FPGA itself.

The glitch width can be adjusted from about 3 nS to 100 nS (maximum width limited to 50 % of clock period or 100 nS, whichever is smaller) and the offset from the clock edge is adjustable from −50 % to +50 % of the clock period. The specific resolution of the glitch and offset varies for the target clock frequency, but is always smaller than 100 pS. Figure 6 shows an example of a glitch inserted into the output clock, although the glitch itself can be output separately from the clock for driving modules such as optical or electromagnetic fault injection. This method is the same as described in [12], although with improved resolution on the glitch width and location. The minimum glitch width is limited by the FPGA IO-pin speed: using a faster IO-standard (e.g. LVDS) allows a smaller minimum glitch width if required.

The use of the special Digital Clock Manager (DCM) blocks along with partial reconfiguration (discussed next) allow this extremely fine-grained control over glitch width. This is an improvement on previously proposed glitch generation methods where the 'coarse' width control comes from a higher-speed clock, which generally limits glitch 'coarse' control to a multiple of this clock speed (often 4–10 nS) [7].

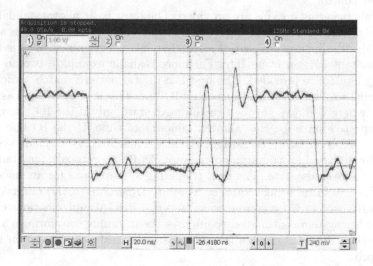

Fig. 6. Inserting a glitch into a 7.37 MHz clock coming from a target device.

2.5 Partial Reconfiguration

The clock generation and glitch generation modules both use the Digital Clock Manager (DCM) blocks within the FPGA. These blocks have limited support for run-time configuration of parameters such as phase delay and frequency generation, and for maximum performance the configuration must be fixed at design time. The Xilinx-provided *run-time* adjustment can shift the phase only by about ±5 nS in 30 pS increments (exact values vary with operating conditions).

To allow adjustments over a wider phase range, a partial reconfiguration interface is provided. This interface allows changes to the FPGA configuration while the system is operating. This is specifically used to reconfigure the DCM blocks for a variety of parameters which are fixed at the implementation stage. This partial reconfiguration requires that appropriate 'bitstream difference' files are generated by the FPGA tools for every possible setting of the desired parameter, e.g. the DCM phase delay attribute. Due to the opaque nature of the FPGA tools there is no simple mapping between parameter changes and a specific portion of the bitstream.

To generate these bitstream difference files, Xilinx's *FPGA Editor* tool is used to modify the Native Circuit Description (NCD) file for the design. A script generates versions of the NCD file with every possible setting of the desired attribute, e.g. for the DCM block with a fixed phase value of −255 to +255. These NCD files are converted into bitstream difference files with the Xilinx *bitgen* utility. Setting the desired DCM fixed phase offset means loading the appropriate bitstream difference file[1].

2.6   Implementation on Other Boards

This entire system is implemented as generic FPGA blocks. Whilst a reference platform is provided, it can be used on any FPGA platform. For example this system can be programmed into the control FPGA provided in the SAKURA-G or SASEBO-W platform. Figure 7 shows a photo of the SAKURA-G board with

Fig. 7. The modular design allows easy implementation on other hardware, such as the SAKURA-G board. A Spartan 6 LX75 FPGA is used for a cryptographic algorithm, and the LX9 FPGA is used for control of the FPGA along with capturing of power traces. This replaces both the 'ChipWhisperer Capture Rev2' hardware box and the 'Target Device', meaning the entire side-channel analysis system is present on the SAKURA-G board

---

[1] See the ChipWhisperer sources for details, with additional information in the June 2014 issue of Circuit Cellar and at programmablelogicinpractice.com/?p=143.

an OpenADC mounted. This system allows implementation of a cryptographic algorithm in the main FPGA on the SAKURA-G, while the control FPGA serves to actually perform the measurements. Any of the available blocks can be inserted into this system, for example adding clock glitch generation into the control FPGA for the SASEBO-W.

2.7   Generic Device Under Test Board

For demonstration of basic attacks, a generic target board is provided. This board provides several target options: a 28-pin AVR socket, an XMEGA device, and a Smart Card socket. The board also has two LNAs built onto it, along with several clock options. Jumpers can select which target is connected, measurement mode (high-side or low-side shunt), connect the AVR programmer from the ChipWhisperer Capture Rev2, and allows an external Smart Card reader to be connected to the smart card socket by way of a feed-through smart card PCB. The target board is shown in Fig. 8.

The choice of a 28-pin AVR socket allows the board to accept many similar AVR devices. Attacks targeting recent processes can use the AtMega328P or AtMega48A. Attacks looking to test older devices may use an older Mega8 device[2]. Note that many 'Smart Card' attacks are tested on a AtMega163 card,

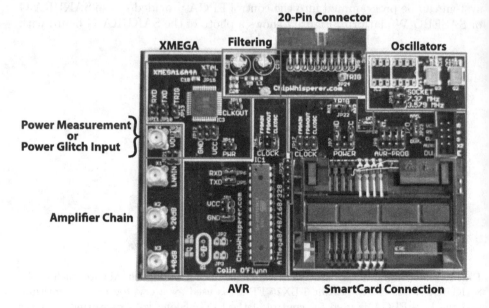

Fig. 8. The Multi-Target board provides a simple platform for testing various attacks and cryptographic implementations.

---

[2] While the Mega8 is an older device, recently bought ones may be produced on newer processes. If looking for a device produced on older IC process, one will need to confirm the production date via the date code.

which contains an AtMega163 die from Atmel. Existing code targeting the AtMega163 can be ported to work on a 28-pin AVR, avoiding the need to find outdated Mega163 cards, and also using a more recent semiconductor process.

3 Software Architecture

The software is implemented in entirely in Python. Python was chosen for a variety of reasons: it is natively cross-platform, provides a simple GUI through PySide, can easily interface to other languages including C/C++ and MATLAB, provides high performance using Cython, and has a large collection of modules which provide functionality such as cryptographic functions, plotting, numeric computations, low-level IO, and smart card interfaces. In addition the choice of an interpreted language such as Python enables considerably more advanced scripting options. This section will only briefly outline the software architecture, full documentation is kept using the Sphinx system[3], which combines documentation built into the Python source with additional files. This documentation is linked from www.ChipWhisperer.com, or available directly at www.newae.com/sidechannel/cwdocs/.

The project is split into two programs. One program captures the power traces and saves them, the other perform side-channel analysis algorithms (e.g. CPA). The decision to split the project into two programs was done to allow use of only part of this project by other researchers. For example researchers with existing attack code can still use the capture program, for example saving the data to a MATLAB workspace. Or researchers with existing traces can load them into the analysis program without using the capture portion.

Both capture and analysis software share a common base class; this class defines methods of modifying parameters, saving and restoring projects, using trace files, and plotting data. In addition support for a special 'scripting' system is provided. This 'scripting' language allows execution of either the capture or analysis software from another Python application, which forms the 'script'. This design is especially powerful since it allows the script to call any function within the entire program, and does not require the definition of specific scripting commands. As an example, when adding a new FPGA module, it requires the addition of the appropriate driver module to the capture software. However by using the scripting interface, it is possible to simply send raw commands to this module, which allow testing and debugging it before the complete driver has been written. When options are changed using the GUI, the GUI also shows how to accomplish the same operation with a script. Thus a user can simply setup appropriate options from the GUI, and then save these script commands to recreate the configuration. Listing 1.1 in Appendix A shows an example of such a script.

The graph windows allow transformations to be performed on the data, such as switching from time-domain to frequency-domain through an FFT, filtering and smoothing, and exporting data in the graph.

---

[3] sphinx-doc.org

3.1 Trace Management

The trace management module is common to both the capture and analysis software, which provides a method of mapping traces from different formats into a continuous block of trace data. The default storage method used by the software uses the Python NumPY library's native save and load commands. Alternatives which store the traces to a MySQL server, and saving the traces to the same format used by the DPAContestv3 tools are also provided.

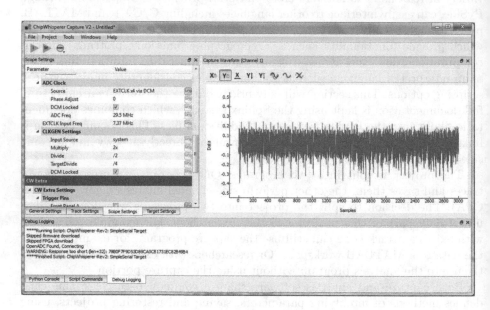

Fig. 9. The Capture GUI provides an interface to the capture hardware, target device, and storage media.

4 Capture Software

The capture GUI (Fig. 9) is ideal for initial experimentations with a new system, such as trying different ADC settings or different trigger settings. For repeatable captures it is desirable to instead script the setup, which sets appropriate values to various parameters. In addition this script can perform actions such as saving the target data to a different format (e.g. a MATLAB workspace), or used for automatically performing captures under different target conditions (e.g. selecting an algorithm with and without countermeasures).

The script can either run the entire capture program, or simply configure part of the window. Several example scripts are provided, which can be loaded in an already-running ChipWhisperer-Capture application. See Listing 1.1 in Appendix A for an example script.

For debug purposes, a monitor window shows the input and output results of the cryptographic operation being performed on the target. This window also displays what the expected result would be for a known key. This can be quickly used to confirm a device under test is operating as expected, and the encryption key was correctly loaded into the device.

4.1 Capture Performance

The capture performance demonstrates how quickly traces can be captured with the default system. The measurements are taken on two different computers: a Windows 7 based Intel i5-2540M laptop, and a Linux based AMD A10-5800K desktop. Captures are averaged over 10,000 traces. The 'Target Connection' indicates how the device under test (e.g. the cryptographic target, *not* the Chip-Whisperer capture) connects to the computer. The 'FPGA-x' mode means one of the ChipWhisperer IO blocks are being used.

For high-speed USB targets (ChipWhisperer Rev2, SAKURA-G, SASEBO-W) the capture speed is primarily limited by USB latency in the host computer stack. Note the AVR target shows both 3000 and 20000 points per trace; the resulting speed change is much less than the 6x increase in data size would suggest. Targets connected to the computer directly run much faster, as the IO blocks in the ChipWhisperer tend to required several USB transactions, each transaction adding latency from the USB stack. This suggests that there is considerable room for speed improvements by streamlining transactions to reduce this latency.

In addition to the OpenADC capture hardware, three standard oscilloscopes are shown for comparison. The capture software can be programmed to support other oscilloscopes with minimal changes (Table 1).

5 Analysis Software

The analysis software uses the same project and trace management system used by the capture software. Moving a project over simply means saving the project in the capture software, and opening it in the analysis software. Alternatively, traces can be manually imported, either if they come from an external source or if you wish to combine traces from several different captures into a single analysis run. In addition this manual mode is used for configuring database operation; in this mode the analysis software can read traces from a MySQL database, which allows analysis to occur while the capture is still ongoing.

When traces are loaded, a single trace is plotted in time. A number of traces can be overlaid on each other, which is useful to confirm the synchronization of traces. If traces are incorrectly synchronized, one of the preprocessing modules (described next) can be used to resynchronize the traces.

5.1 Preprocessing

Several basic preprocessing modules are provided, which operate on the data before passing through to the attack. Three types of resynchronization are implemented: a sum-of-errors minimizer, peak detect, and cross-correlation. These

Table 1. Traces/Second for various targets and capture hardware. Points/Trace varies by target, and indicates number of points stored in each trace to attack the target. The '—' indicates lack of supported driver for the host OS.

Capture hardware	Attack target	Target connection	Points/ Trace	Traces/Second	
				Win7	Linux
ChipWhisperer Rev2	SASEBO-GII	USB	100	14.8	28.3
ChipWhisperer Rev2	AVR, 38400 Baud	FPGA-Serial	3000	11.3	3.91
ChipWhisperer Rev2	AVR, 38400 Baud	FPGA-Serial	20000	7.04	3.78
ChipWhisperer Rev2	AVR, 38400 Baud	USB-Serial	3000	18.2	18.9
ChipWhisperer Rev2	SmartCard	PS/SC Reader	3000	7.40	6.62
SAKURA-G	SAKURA-G	Integrated	400	6.67	7.18
SASEBO-W	SmartCard	FPGA-USI	3000	0.271	0.279
SASEBO-W	SmartCard	FPGA-SmartCard	3000	1.49	1.52
Agilent MSO54831D	SASEBO-GII	USB	1500	8.01	—
PicoScope 6403D	SASEBO-GII	USB	1500	12.1	43.6
PicoScope 6403D	SAKURA-G	USB	1500	15.4	29.6
PicoScope 5444B	AVR, 38400 Baud	USB-Serial	12000	16.4	5.63

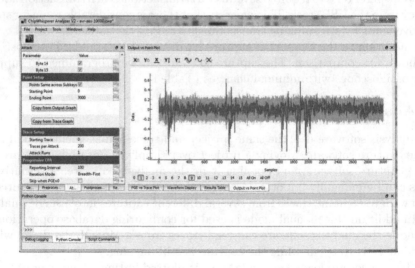

Fig. 10. The Analyzer GUI runs a given attack on the stored traces.

methods provide very simple sliding resynchronization, which works well with the synchronous capture methodology of the ChipWhisperer Capture hardware. In addition a simple low-pass filter is also provided. Any of the preprocessing modules can be chained together in an arbitrary order, and additional modules can trivially be added to the system.

The waveform display window shows the results after the preprocessing chain. This could be used to confirm that traces are properly resynchronized in the time domain before continuing on to the attack.

5.2   Attack Implementation

The attack module is designed to simplify how new attacks are added to the system. The cryptographic model, leakage model, and attack algorithm are all separate modules. This greatly simplifies changes and increases reuse: if a new attack is added, it can pull in the existing cryptographic model and leakage model modules to automatically work with both software and hardware AES implementations. If a new cryptographic model is added such as DES for example, it should work with the existing CPA attack.

The main attack implemented currently is a CPA attack. Figure 11 shows the data flow within the attack system. Data coming from the 'Trace Container' may also have had preprocessing applied, or a certain window of data may be selected instead of the entire trace range. The correlation calculation has several modules that can be loaded, for example selecting between a version that takes advantage of the fast NumPy library, and a version compiled in C using Cython. The 'correlation calculation' may actually implement more advanced algorithms, an example is the Bayesian calculation given in [13] is also implemented. The results are stored in the 'Attack Statistics', which stores results after a given number of traces, and also calculates metrics such as Partial Guessing Entropy (PGE) at the current state [14].

The number of traces to use in the attack is also configurable, and allows for looping the attack several times over different sections of the traces. If 100,000 traces are present in the project for example, one could perform the attack with

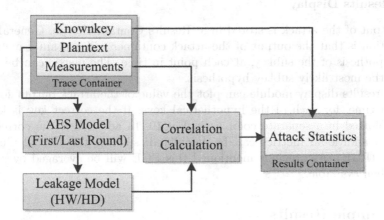

Fig. 11. In the CPA attack module, the cryptographic model, hardware model, and statistics update are all separate. This allows simple selecting of Hamming-Weight (HW) or Hamming-Distance (HD) models for example, or selecting the AES round to attack.

1000 traces, and repeat it 100 times. When final metrics are calculated, the system can average the results of all 100 attacks.

Correlation Power Analysis. The basic equation for a Correlation Power Analysis (CPA) attack, where $r_{i,j}$ is the correlation coefficient at point j for hypothesis i, $t_{d,j}$ is power measurement of trace number d at point j, and $h_{d,i}$ is the hypothetical power consumption of hypothesis i for trace number d, with a total of D traces is given in Eq. 1. This basic formula does not allow online calculation, where new traces are easily added without recalculation of the entire sum. Instead the form shown in Eq. 2 is used [15]. This form lends itself to online calculation, where when a new trace is added the sums are updated and the new correlation coefficient calculated.

The online update is used during calculation of attack statistics, where it is desired to track the attack results as new traces are added. As a practical matter, note the denominator of either Eq. 1 or 2 may have numeric stability problems due to cancellation in either of the two terms. Forms given in [16] may result in more stable calculations, however experimental results shown that for measurements of real systems the numerical stability is not an issue.

$$r_{i,j} = \frac{\sum_{d=1}^{D} \left[\left(h_{d,i} - \overline{h_i} \right) \left(t_{d,j} - \overline{t_j} \right) \right]}{\sqrt{\sum_{d=1}^{D} \left(h_{d,i} - \overline{h_i} \right)^2 \sum_{d=1}^{D} \left(t_{d,j} - \overline{t_j} \right)^2}} \tag{1}$$

$$r_{i,j} = \frac{D \sum_{d=1}^{D} h_{d,i} t_{d,j} - \sum_{d=1}^{D} h_{d,i} \sum_{d=1}^{D} t_{d,j}}{\sqrt{\left(\left(\sum_{d=1}^{D} h_{d,i} \right)^2 - D \sum_{d=1}^{D} h_{d,i}^2 \right) \left(\left(\sum_{d=1}^{D} t_{d,j} \right)^2 - D \sum_{d=1}^{D} t_{d,j}^2 \right)}} \tag{2}$$

5.3   Results Display

The output of the attack is stored in a 'Results Container' type. Generally the assumption is that the output of the attack container will contain a metric for each hypothesis of the subkey, at each point in time. The metric can be sorted to give the most likely subkey hypothesis.

The results display module can plot the value of the attack output for each point in time, for each of the hypothetical keys. If the correct key is known, this is plotted in a separate color as in Fig. 10. In addition if the correct key is known additional metrics can be calculated, such as the Partial Guessing Entropy (PGE). As previous mentioned this PGE will be averaged over many trials when available.

6   Example Results

This section demonstrates some example results of the platform. Two example devices will be tested: the first is the AtMega328P microcontroller, which is a reasonably recent AVR microcontroller from Atmel. The system is loaded with

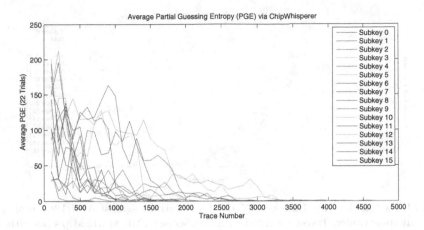

Fig. 12. Partial Guessing Entropy (PGE) of SASEBO-GII running at 24 MHz. No smoothing has been applied.

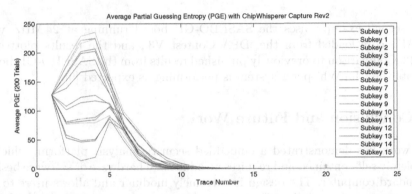

Fig. 13. Partial Guessing Entropy (PGE) of CPA attack against AES-128 running on AVR Microcontroller. Traces recorded with ChipWhisperer Capture Rev2 hardware at 29.5 MS/s synchronous to device clock. No smoothing has been applied, graph comes from ChipWhisperer Analyzer software.

basic code which performs encryptions when requested over a serial protocol, and returns the encryption result. The Partial Guessing Entropy (PGE) of the CPA attack is shown in Fig. 13 using the *ChipWhisperer Capture Rev2* hardware (i.e. as in Fig. 2). As a comparison Fig. 14 shows the PGE of the same attack where traces have been recorded with a normal oscilloscope.

This device can also be targeted for glitch attacks. When the AVR was running at 7.3728 MHz, glitches were inserted into the clock with the following specifications: glitch width of 15.2 % (20.6 nS), glitch offset of −17.0 % (−23.1 nS). The glitch was XOR'd with the clock, and repeated on 200 consecutive clock edges. The objective was simply to cause the embedded system to skip authentication code, which was successfully accomplished.

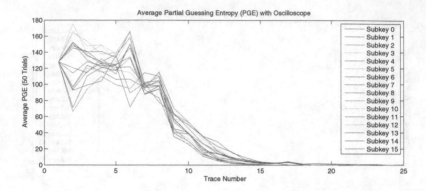

Fig. 14. Partial Guessing Entropy (PGE) of CPA attack against AES-128 running on AVR Microcontroller. Traces recorded with PicoScope 6403D at 312 MS/s (as with any oscilloscope, this sampling is done asynchronous to device clock). No smoothing has been applied, graph comes from ChipWhisperer Analyzer software.

A second example uses the SASEBO-GII board running at 24 MHz, with the AES core loaded from the 'DPA Contest V3', and the results plotted in Fig. 12. Comparison to previously published results from the SASEBO-GII board indicate the ChipWhisperer system is performing as expected [9].

7   Conclusion and Future Work

This work has demonstrated a embedded security analysis platform, which is completely self-contained and requires no additional hardware or software besides a standard computer. The design is extremely modular and allows users to use only a portion of the design; for example using a normal oscilloscope with this system, taking advantage of the advanced triggering mechanisms or the clock glitching capability without using the analog capture hardware.

All design material including source code and hardware design files are maintained in a GIT repository at www.ChipWhisperer.com. A wiki is used to maintain documentation, and contributions to either documentation or design are welcome. For users interested in the analysis algorithms, large example captures are available as well: a set of 500,000 traces of AES-128 executed on an AtMega328P microcontroller along with 500,000 traces from the SASEBO-GII. Example traces from other hardware is also available, and community submissions are welcomed.

Acknowledgments. Thanks to Akashi Satoh for donation of the SAKURA-G used in this work, and Akashi Satoh and Pankaj Rohatgi for donation of the SASEBO-GII and SASEBO-W also used in this work. Thanks to COSADE 2014 reviewers for many insightful comments on initial revision of this papers.

Appendix A: Script Example

Listing 1.1. Example user script for running automated capture and saving traces to MATLAB file

```
1  lst = [
2  # Clock Routing Setup
3    ['CW Extra', 'CW Extra Settings', 'Clock Source',
4                                      'Target IO-IN'],
5    ['OpenADC', 'Clock Setup', 'ADC Clock', 'Source',
6                                      'EXTCLK x4 via DCM'],
7  # Sample Length/Offset Setup
8    ['OpenADC', 'Trigger Setup', 'Total Samples', 3000],
9    ['OpenADC', 'Trigger Setup', 'Offset'        , 1500],
10 # Low Noise Amplifier Gain Setting
11   ['OpenADC', 'Gain Setting', 'Setting'        , 45],
12 # Rising Edge Trigger
13   ['OpenADC', 'Trigger Setup', 'Mode'          , 'rising edge'],
14 # Final step: make DCMs relock in case they lost sync
15   ['OpenADC', 'Clock Setup'  , 'Relock DCMs'  , None], ]
16
17 # cap variable contains instance of ChipWhispererCapture()
18
19 # Download all hardware setup parameters
20 for cmd in lstexample: cap.setParameter(cmd)
21
22 # Set number of traces
23 cap.setParameter(['Generic Settings', 'Acquisition Settings',
24                   'Number of Traces', 75])
25
26 # Capture a few traces initially (not saved)
27 cap.capture1()
28 # pe() is a macro which processes any queued events it must
29 # be called when interacting with the low-level API directly.
30 pe()
31 cap.capture1()
32 pe()
33
34 # Start capture process of 75 traces, save to memory
35 writer = cap.captureM()
36
37 # Save files to MATLAB workspace file instead of native format
38 sio.savemat('sca_data.mat', {'powertrace': writer.traces,
39                   'textin'    : writer.textins,
40                   'textout'   : writer.textouts,
41                   'knownkey'  : writer.knownkey})
```

References

1. Kocher, P.C., Jaffe, J., Jun, B.: Differential power analysis. In: Wiener, M. (ed.) CRYPTO 1999. LNCS, vol. 1666, pp. 388–397. Springer, Heidelberg (1999)
2. Satoh, A.: Side-channel Attack Standard Evaluation Board (SASEBO) (2011). http://www.morita-tech.co.jp/SASEBO/en/index.html
3. Oswald, E.: OpenSCA: a matlab-based open source framework for side-channel attacks (2009). http://opensca.sourceforge.net/
4. Mangard, S., Oswald, E., Popp, T.: Power Analysis Attacks: Revealing the Secrets of Smart Cards. Advances in information security. Springer, New York (2008)
5. Oswald, D., Kasper, T., Markhoff, S., Paar, C.: FPGA-based Implementation Attacks with GIAnT. In: 9th CrypArchi Workschop, Bochum, November 2011
6. Oswald, D.: Implementation attacks: from theory to practice. Ph.D. thesis, Ruhr University Bochum, September 2013
7. Kasper, T., Oswald, D., Paar, C.: A versatile framework for implementation attacks on cryptographic RFIDs and embedded devices. In: Gavrilova, M.L., Tan, C.J.K., Moreno, E.D. (eds.) Transactions on Computational Science X. LNCS, vol. 6340, pp. 100–130. Springer, Heidelberg (2010)
8. Messerges, T.: Power analysis attacks and countermeasures for cryptographic algorithms. Ph.D. thesis, University of Illinois at Chicago (2000)
9. O'Flynn, C., Chen, Z.: A case study of side-channel analysis using decoupling capacitor power measurement with the OpenADC. In: Garcia-Alfaro, J., Cuppens, F., Cuppens-Boulahia, N., Miri, A., Tawbi, N. (eds.) FPS 2012. LNCS, vol. 7743, pp. 341–356. Springer, Heidelberg (2013)
10. O'Flynn, C., Chen, Z.D.: Synchronous Sampling and Clock Recovery of Internal Oscillators for Side Channel Analysis. Cryptology ePrint Archive, Report 2013/294.
11. Olivares, J., Hormigo, J., Villalba, J., Benavides, I.: Minimum sum of absolute differences implementation in a single FPGA device. In: Becker, J., Platzner, M., Vernalde, S. (eds.) FPL 2004. LNCS, vol. 3203, pp. 986–990. Springer, Heidelberg (2004)
12. Balasch, J., Gierlichs, B., Verbauwhede, I.: An in-depth and black-box characterization of the effects of clock glitches on 8-bit MCUs. In: Proceedings of the 2011 Workshop on Fault Diagnosis and Tolerance in Cryptography, FDTC '11, pp. 105–114. IEEE Computer Society, Washington, DC (2011)
13. Veyrat-Charvillon, N., Gérard, B., Renauld, M., Standaert, F.-X.: An optimal key enumeration algorithm and its application to side-channel attacks. In: Knudsen, L.R., Wu, H. (eds.) SAC 2012. LNCS, vol. 7707, pp. 390–406. Springer, Heidelberg (2013)
14. Standaert, F.-X., Malkin, T.G., Yung, M.: A unified framework for the analysis of side-channel key recovery attacks. In: Joux, A. (ed.) EUROCRYPT 2009. LNCS, vol. 5479, pp. 443–461. Springer, Heidelberg (2009)
15. Brier, E., Clavier, C., Olivier, F.: Correlation Power analysis with a leakage model. In: Joye, M., Quisquater, J.-J. (eds.) CHES 2004. LNCS, vol. 3156, pp. 16–29. Springer, Heidelberg (2004)
16. Chan, T.F., Golub, G.H., Leveque, R.J.: Algorithms for computing the sample variance: analysis and recommendations. Am. Stat. **37**(3), 242–247 (1983)

Verifying Software Integrity in Embedded Systems: A Side Channel Approach

Mehari Msgna[1](✉), Konstantinos Markantonakis[1], David Naccache[2], and Keith Mayes[1]

[1] Smart Card Centre, Information Security Group, Royal Holloway, University of London, Egham TW20 0EX, UK
{mehari.msgna.2011,k.markantonakis,k.mayes}@rhul.ac.uk
[2] Département D'informatique, École Normale Supérieure, 45 Rue D'Ulm, 75230 Paris Cedex 05, France
david.naccache@ens.fr

Abstract. In the last few decades embedded processors have invaded the modern lifestyle. Embedded systems have hardware and software components. Assuring the integrity of the software is very important as it is the component that controls what the hardware does through its instructions. Although there exist a number of software integrity verification techniques, they often fail to work in embedded environment. One main reason is, the memory read protection, frequently implemented in today's microprocessors, that prevent the verifier from reading out the necessary software parts. In this paper we show that side channel leakage (power consumption) can be used to verify the integrity of the software component without prior knowledge of the software code. Our approach uses instruction-level power consumption templates to extract information about executed instructions by the processor. Then this information together with pre-computed signatures are used to verify the integrity of the executed application using RSA signature screening algorithm. The instruction-level templates are constructed ahead of time using few authentic reference processors.

Keywords: Side channel leakage · Power analysis · Templates · Principal components analysis · RSA signature screening · Application integrity

1 Introduction

Commercial and economic conditions have forced electronic device manufacturers to outsource their components production to countries with cheaper infrastructure cost. While this significantly reduces the total production cost, it also makes it much easier for an attacker to compromise the supply chain for components used in critical business and military applications, and replace them with defective components. This threat to the electronic components supply chain is already a cause for alarm in some countries [1,2]. For this reason,

© Springer International Publishing Switzerland 2014
E. Prouff (Ed.): COSADE 2014, LNCS 8622, pp. 261–280, 2014.
DOI: 10.1007/978-3-319-10175-0_18

some governments have been subsidizing few high-cost local foundries for producing components used in military applications [3]. However, this is not affordable solution for most of the developing countries.

According to [4], defective components incident has increased from 3,868 in 2005 to 9,356 in 2008. Such electronic components have at least the following ramifications; (a) original component providers incur an irrecoverable loss due to the sale of often cheaper counterfeit components, (b) low performance of defective products (that are often of lower quality and/or cheaper older generations of a chip family) affects the overall efficiency of the integrated systems that unintentionally uses them; this could in turn harm the reputation of authentic providers, (c) unreliability of defective devices could render the integrated systems that unknowingly use the parts unreliable; this potentially affects the performance of weapons, airplanes, cars or other crucial applications [5], and (d) untrusted defective components may have intentional malware or some backdoor for spying information, remotely controlling critical objects and leaking secret information. These ramifications and their growing presence in the market makes them important problem to address.

So far many methods have been proposed to verify the integrity of desktop software. These methods often fail to work in embedded environment. The main reason being the memory read protection implemented by most of today's microcontrollers. However, in the real world these processors leak information about their internal state unintentionally. As an example, we can consider a game of poker, where everyone plays by the same functional rules and keeps their cards well concealed. If a novice player looks worried or excited when he receives his cards, then he leaks information about his hand to the other players. An experienced player may manipulate his reaction (block his emotions/expressions or fake them) to fool the other players. However, if other physiological reactions (such as heart beat, blood pressure, respiratory rate and electro-dermal activity) of the players are measured then even an expert player's deception can be detected. Of course, measuring such physiological reactions need more sophisticated instruments, like *Polygraph* [6], than reading someone's facial reaction.

Embedded processors do not have emotions or physiological reactions but as electronic devices they have a varying electric current flowing through them. This current may potentially give away information about the internal (data dependent) state in the form of variations in power consumption or electromagnetic emission which can be recorded and analysed. This leakage can be used to adequately detect changes in the underlying hardware or the applications. For instance in [7], a gate-level passive hardware characterisation of an IC was proposed to identify defective ICs. The authors use the negative bias temperature instability model proposed in [8] to calculate the original characteristics of aged ICs. In another proposal [9], power consumption of a device was proposed for detecting hardware Trojans implanted in electronic components. Process variation noise modeling (constructed using genuine ICs) is used for detecting Trojan circuits through statistical analysis. In this paper we present an approach that uses the power consumption of a processor to detect changes in the original design of the applications. The verifying device uses the processor's instruction-level power consumption templates to extract executed instructions from its power consumption waveform. Then verifies the application using *RSA signature screening algorithm* [10].

The rest of the paper is structured as follows. Section 2 briefly provides background information on side channel leakage and RSA signature screening algorithm. Section 3 presents our proposed methodology. Sections 4 and 5 discuss our experimental results and its practical application area. Finally, Sect. 6 concludes the paper.

2   Background

In this section we briefly discuss the background information on side channel leakage and RSA signature screening.

2.1   Side Channel Leakage

Side channel leakage is information revealed by a device about its internal processing state while running a certain task. In the context of cryptography, side channel leakage has been used to retrieve cryptographic secret information from target devices. Side channel leakage such as timing [11–13], power consumption [14,15] and electromagnetic emission [16–18] have been used to attack the implementations of cryptographic algorithms including AES [19], DES [20] and RSA [21].

Smart cards and other electronic devices have transistors that turn on and off causing current transients. The instantaneous electric current that the device consumes depends on how many transistors that the executed instructions and data turn on and off. This difference in the electric current is then reflected in the power consumption of the device. The power consumption can then be recorded and analysed to extract secret information from the target device [22]. Besides extracting cryptographic keys, side channel leakage has also been used to reverse engineer embedded device applications [23–25]. This is done by constructing a power consumption template of the target device using an identical reference device. Then the templates are used to recognise executed instructions from the target device's power consumption waveform.

Apart from key extraction and reverse engineering, side channel information can also be used by device manufacturers and application developers to counter attacks and design advanced applications. Instruction-level power consumption model of an embedded device has been used to design low-power consuming applications for mobile embedded devices where batteries are the main power source [26,27]. In [28], the authors discuss, theoretically, how side channel leakage can be used to fingerprint a smart card platform and then use it later to detect cloned cards. However, this paper is a high-level and do not discuss in detail how the platform fingerprint is constructed and how a cloned card is detected. George et al. [29], demonstrated the Hamming weight of executed instructions can create a unique power consumption fingerprint which may be enough to verify the originality of a software program.

2.2   RSA Signature Screening

Digital signatures are used to verify the authenticity and integrity of a block of message. RSA [21] is one of the popular digital signature algorithms. The verification of n RSA signatures involve the verification of n signatures sequentially. In a hash-and-sign scheme the process of verifying n signatures involves the generation of n hash values and n public key encryptions with respect to the issuer's public key. A known method of improving the performance of such a system is to verify a batch of signatures at the same time. In [10], the authors discuss a method that verifies if a batch of messages were signed by the correct authority without verifying the individual signatures. This process is called the *RSA signature screening*. The *RSA signature screening* works as follows: given a batch of message and signature pairs

$$\{\{M_1, S_1\}.....\{M_n, S_n\}\},$$

where S_i (computed as $S_i = M_i^d \bmod N$) is the signature of a message M_i with respect to some private key (N, d). We assume that the signatures were generated using the hash-and-sign scheme, then this batch of signatures is verified using the computation in the Eq. (1) with respect to the corresponding public key (N, e).

$$(\Pi_{i=1}^n S_i)^e = \Pi_{i=1}^n H(M_i) \bmod N \tag{1}$$

However, as discussed in [30], *RSA signature screening* can be bypassed if a message M_i appears more than $e - 1$ times even though it was never signed before. This can be an issue if the value of e is significantly small. The good news is that, the problem can be easily solved by choosing a large value of the public key component e.

3   Embedded Software Integrity Verification

An embedded system have hardware and software components. The software part controls what the hardware does by using the underlying hardware's (the processor's) executable instructions. Therefore, ensuring the integrity of the software is vital for the security of the entire system. Figure 1, elaborates the block diagram of our proposed software integrity verification method.

The first step in our verification is the construction of instruction-level side channel templates using few identical processors. During verification, the verifying device records the processor's power consumption waveform while executing the application and extracts the executed instructions by matching it against the pre-constructed templates (as described in Sect. 3.2). The extracted information together with the pre-computed signatures are then used to verify the

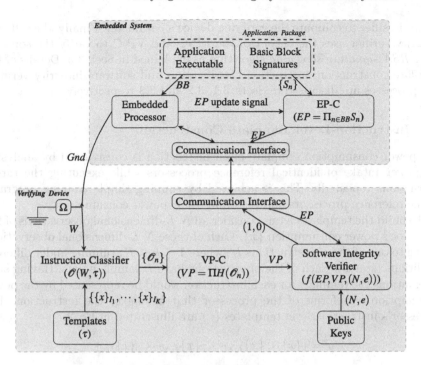

Fig. 1. Software integrity verification block diagram

integrity of the software component using *RSA signature screening* algorithm as explained in Sect. 3.3.

As shown in the diagram (Fig. 1), the embedded system has the embedded parameter calculator (EP-C), embedded processor and the application package which includes the application executable and the basic block signatures. The EP-C is a special module that calculates the product of two large numbers. It can be implemented in hardware or software; although, hardware would be preferable for performance reasons. The embedded processor is the core that executes the software component of the embedded system (application executable). After the execution of every basic block the EP-C updates its parameter (EP) by multiplying it with the basic block's signature. A basic block is a sequence of instructions with a single entry and a single exit point.

The verifying device has the templates, the instruction classifier, the verifier parameter calculator (VP-C) and the software integrity verifier. The templates are constructed ahead of time using identical processors and then installed into the verifying device's non-volatile memory. How these templates are installed into the verifying device is beyond the scope of this paper. The instruction classifier uses these templates to extract the executed instructions from the processor's power consumption waveform (W). The power consumption waveform is measured as a voltage drop across a shunt resistor connecting the embedded processor's ground and the verifying device's ground voltage. The VP-C uses the output of the classifier to compute the verifying device's parameter. Finally, the software integrity verifier uses the output of the EP-C and VP-C to verify the software using *RSA signature screening* algorithm as explained in Sect. 3.3. Details of the template construction, instruction classification and software integrity verification processes are discussed in Sects. 3.1, 3.2 and 3.3 respectively.

3.1   Instruction-Level Template Construction

The power consumption template of an instruction is constructed by analysing the power intake of identical reference processors while executing the target instructions repeatedly. This is achieved by running simple training programs on the reference processors and recording their power consumption.

To build the templates let us consider an N L-dimensional observations of the processor's power consumption $\{x\}$. Each of these N L-dimensional observations belong to one of the K instructions I_k, where $1 \le k \le K$, running under different conditions (states). Each of the observations have L sample points. Having such observations the template for each instruction would be represented by the power consumption waveforms of the processor that belong to the instruction. The processor's instruction-level templates (τ) are illustrated in Eq. 2.

$$\tau = \{\{x\}_{I_1}, \{x\}_{I_2}, \cdots, \{x\}_{I_k}, \cdots, \{x\}_{I_K}\} \tag{2}$$

Practically each observation x_n may have too many closely correlated sample points and the instruction classification may be too time consuming. This problem can be solved by projecting x_n onto a lower subspace vector. In such a case a smaller number of samples of x_n are chosen to create a well-conditioned template and make the instruction classification more reliable. In the standard literature and in the context of side channel analysis several methods have been proposed [31–33]. In this paper we have used the *Principal Components Analysis* to reduce the dimensionality of the observations.

Principal Components Analysis (PCA). PCA [34] is a technique that searches for vectors that best describes the underlying original data. This is achieved by projecting the data orthogonally onto a lower dimensional subspace. Now let us consider again the N L-dimensional observations $(\{x\})$ and their global covariance matrix (σ). The covariance matrix of the kth instruction (σ_k) is computed as shown Eq. 3.

$$\sigma_k = \frac{1}{N} \sum_{n=1, k \in \{1, \cdots, K\}}^{N} (x_n - \mu_k)(x_n - \mu_k)^T \tag{3}$$

where μ_k is the mean of the kth instruction's observations and is computed as shown in Eq. 4.

$$\mu_k = \frac{1}{N} \sum_{n=1, \{x\} \in I_k}^{N} x_n \tag{4}$$

A lower dimensional subspace in this Euclidean space can be defined by a D-dimensional unit vector $\vec{u_1}$. The projection of each observation, x_n, onto that subspace is given by $\vec{u_1}^T \cdot x_n$. Now if we stack up all the observations into a matrix we will have an observation matrix of $N \times L$, where L is the number of samples in each observation. The projection of each row of the matrix is represented as $U^T \cdot X$, where U is a matrix of *eigenvectors* of the covariance matrix σ. Now the projection of the observations into a D-dimensional subspace, where $D < L$, that maximises the projected variance is given by D *eigenvectors* [35] $\vec{u_1}, \ldots, \vec{u_d}$ with the D largest *eigenvalues* $\lambda_1, \ldots, \lambda_d$.

3.2   Instruction Classification

Once the templates are constructed, the next phase is recognising executed instructions from target processor's power consumption waveform. To do that the verifying device records the power consumption waveform of the processor while it executes the application at run-time and match it against the templates. Given the templates, τ, we will use k-Nearest Neighbors Algorithm (kNN) to classify the instructions.

The k-Nearest Neighbors Algorithm (kNN) is a non-parametric lazy supervised learning algorithm. The "non-parametric" means the learning algorithm does not make assumptions about the data and "lazy" means data generalization (training) is not needed. In a supervised learning the training data D is an ordered pair $\langle x, y \rangle$, where x is an instance and y is its class label. The goal of the classifier is to predict a class for a given instance x'. In kNN, the training phase simply stores the templates alongside with their class labels. During classification, the classifier computes the distance between the instance x' and all template observations $\{x\}_{I_k}, \forall k \in \{1, \cdots, K\}$. Then it keeps the k closest observations, where $k \geq 1$. The class that is most common among these observations is assigned to the instance x'. In this algorithm there are two major design choices to be made; (a) the value of k, for example, if only two classes exist $k = 3$ is used to avoid ties, and (b) the distance function. The most common distance function used in kNN is the *Euclidean distance function* [36,37]. Given two instances x and x' the Euclidean distance, d_e is computed as shown in Eq. (5).

$$d_e(x, x') = \|x - x'\| = \sqrt{(x_1 - x_1')^2 + \cdots + (x_m - x_m')^2} = \sqrt{\sum_{i=1}^{m}(x_i - x_i')^2} \quad (5)$$

where m is the number of points in the instances. Some of the other distance functions are *Correlation* and *Cosine* learning distance functions.

3.3   Software Integrity Verification

At this point we assume that we have (on the verifying device) the power consumption templates of the processor's instructions. We also assume that we have a function, $\mathcal{O}$, implemented on the verifying device that returns a list of the executed instructions from the power waveform W.

$$\mathcal{O}(W,\tau) = \{Ins_1, Ins_2, \cdots, Ins_n\} \tag{6}$$

During development, the application is divided into basic blocks and that each basic block is signed with the developer's RSA private key. Then these basic blocks together with their signatures are installed in the processor's non-volatile memory. Let S_n and $\mathcal{O}_n$ be the signature and the list of instructions of the nth basic block respectively. During runtime, when the application execution starts, the processor and the verifying device create their own screening parameter and initialise them to the value "1". As the execution commences the processor updates its parameter by multiplying it with the signature of the executed basic block. At the same time the verifying device updates its parameter by multiplying it with the hash of the executed basic block's instructions. At the end of the execution the processor's parameter, EP, and verifying device's parameter, VP, will look like as shown in Eq. (7).

$$EP = \Pi_{n \in BB} S_n \quad and \quad VP = \Pi_{n \in BB} H(\mathcal{O}_n) \tag{7}$$

where BB is a list of the application's basic blocks. Once the execution ends, the processor sends its updated screening parameter to the verifying device. Then the verifying device verifies the integrity of the executed application using the RSA Signature Screening algorithm as shown in Eq. (8) with respect to the developer's public key (N, e).

$$f(EP, VP, (N, e)) = \begin{cases} 1, & if \ (EP)^e = VP \ mod \ N \\ 0, & otherwise \end{cases} \tag{8}$$

If the result of Eq. (8) is "1", the integrity of the software part that is executed is still intact. Otherwise, the software is regarded as compromised (modified by an unauthorised entity).

4   Experimental Results

To implement the techniques discussed above we selected *ATMega163* processor. The *ATMega163* is a Complementary Metal-Oxide-Silicon (CMOS) 8-bit microcontroller based on an AVR architecture, and it has 130 instructions. These instructions are used to transfer data from one location to another, perform arithmetic or logic operations and interface the processor with the external environment. Since our main objective here is to provide a proof-of-concept implementation of the proposed method we selected 39 instructions to simplify our experiment. During the instruction selection process we considered the following criteria; redundancy and usage of instructions. The redundancy refers to more than one instruction performing similar operation; for example in ATMega163 the instructions LD R_d, Z and LDD R_d, Z+q perform indirect load operation.

So, in our experiment we only use LD. Besides the redundancy, we also tried to choose the most commonly used instructions by analyzing several source codes. We created a source code base by using publicly available source codes from various web sites [38, 39]. We have also included our own implementation of cryptographic algorithms and general purpose applications in the analysis. The selected instructions are listed in Appendix A.

To construct a reliable template for each instruction we attempted to remove all other factors that influence the power consumption apart from the instruction itself. Such factors can be the initial values of source and destination registers/memory cells, data processed by the instruction and, intrinsic or ambient noise introduced by the measurement setup. To remove the influence of the source and destination registers/memory cells we selected a random source and destination before we executed the selected instructions and we initialised them with random values. As per the data processed, we have generated random data for each execution of the target instruction. To minimise the influence of the ambient noise introduced in the measurement, all equipments are properly warmed up beforehand so that it is all running at a uniform temperature throughout the power trace collection phase. This requires keeping the environment in the laboratory at constant temperature for few hours beforehand and running few test measurements to be discarded before the actual power trace collection begins. To minimise the effect of noise introduced by the reference card on the templates we used 5, the same model, reference cards throughout the experiment.

The power consumption is captured via a voltage drop across a shunt resistor connecting the ground pin of the ATMega163 processor and the ground pin of the voltage source. The processor is running at a 4 MHz clock cycle and is powered by a +5 V supply from the reader. The measurements are performed using a *LeCroy WaveRunner 6100A* [40] oscilloscope capable of measuring traces at a rate of 5 billion samples per second (5 GS/s). The samples have 8-bit accuracy within a pre-selected range. The shunt resistor is connected with the oscilloscope using a special cable, a *probe*, which was a *Pomona 6069A* [41], a 1.2 m co-axial cable with a 250 MHz bandwidth, 10 MΩ input resistance and 10 pf input capacitance. All measurements are sampled at a rate of 500 MS/s. The same measurement setup is used throughout the experiment.

4.1   Instruction-Level Template Construction

To build templates for the selected instructions, we generated several training code snippets for the selected device. We executed these specifically generated training codes while varying the data processed, registers/memory cells used by the instructions and their initial values. For each instruction executed the data processed is randomly generated and sent to the processor at runtime. If the target instruction operates on registers, they are randomly selected and their initial values are also randomly generated. The registers are then initialised to these random values prior to being accessed. On the other hand if the instruction operates on memory cells, their location is randomly generated and initialised to random values.

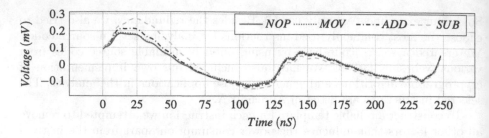

Fig. 2. Power consumption waveform of selected ATmega163's one clock cycle instructions (NOP, MOV, ADD and SUB).

For instructions that need multiple clock cycles, each clock cycle is treated as consecutive instructions. Hence, more than one template is created for these instructions. For each of the conditional branching instructions, templates are created for both conditions. When the condition is false the branching instructions only need one clock cycle; however, when it is true they need two clock cycles. Therefore, for each conditional branching instruction we created three templates. As mentioned earlier the processor is driven by a 4 MHz clock signal. That means each clock cycle lasts for 250 ns and the power consumption trace is represented by 125 sample points.

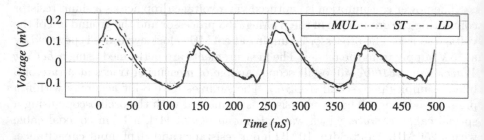

Fig. 3. Power consumption waveform of selected ATmega163's two clock cycle instructions (MUL, ST and LD).

In Figs. 2 and 3 we have shown plots of the power consumption waveforms generated by one and two clock cycle instructions respectively for selected instructions. As shown in both the plots, some instructions (for instance NOP and SUB) generate sufficiently different waveforms to recognise them successfully. However, others generate similar waveforms which makes it more difficult to recognise them from their power waveform. So, in order to recognise each instruction from a given waveform we have to create a well-conditioned template. This means that we have to maximise the variance across templates as much as possible. For each of the instructions we collected 3000 observations (traces) and 2500 of them are used in constructing the templates. The remaining 500 are used in the classification phase. Including the multiple templates for the multi-clock cycle instructions and the conditional branching instructions we generated a total of 76 templates.

Principal Components Analysis (PCA). When performing PCA, the new dimensionality D of the subspace has to be chosen carefully. On the one hand, if D is too small, too much of variance of the original data may get lost and with it important information about the observation. On the other hand, if D is too large, the templates may contain cross-correlated samples and becomes less reliable. In Fig. 4, we plotted the variance accounted for each principal components of instructions NOP, MOV, CLR and ADD.

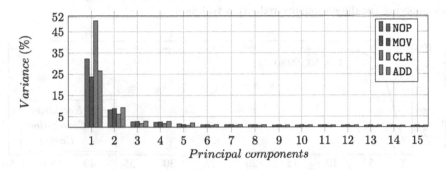

Fig. 4. Overall variance of the original data accounted for the first 15 principal components of the instructions NOP, MOV, CLR and ADD.

As shown in Fig. 4, for the instruction MOV, the first 4 components accounted for 37.598 %, the first 10 for 44.163 % and the first 15 for 48.3387 % of the overall variance of the original data. For the instruction CLR 59.796 %, 64.089 % and 66.648 % of the original variance is accounted for the first 4, 10 and 15 components respectively. So, when choosing the new dimensionality, D, we have to decide how much variance of the original data that we are willing to lose.

4.2   Instruction Classification

As discussed in Sect. 3.2, k-Nearest Neighbor have two major design decision criteria that need to be made. The first criteria is the number of neighbor observations, k, participating in the decision making. To understand the effect of k in our work, we started with $k = 1$ and the classification rate result is presented in Fig. 5. In this work the original observations are reduced by using PCA. Using the reduced dimensions we achieved a 100 % classification rate after only using the first 13 dimensions.

In order to see the effect of k on the classification rate, we repeated the experiment for $k = \{5, 10, 15, 20\}$ and the result was exactly the same. The second criteria is the distance function used to compute the closeness between the test observation and the template observations. In our work we tested the

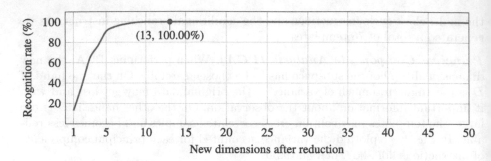

Fig. 5. Instruction recognition rate using *K-Nearest Neighbours Algorithm* for k = 1 after applying the dimensionality reduction techniques.

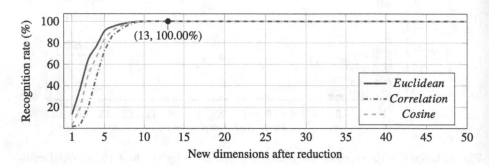

Fig. 6. Recognition rate result of *K-Nearest Neighbors Algorithm* with different distance functions for $k = 1$ after applying the PCA.

classification using three different distance functions. These are the *Euclidean*, *Correlation* and *Cosine* distance function. The result is plotted in Fig. 6.

As shown in the graph, the classification result is exactly the same for all three distance functions apart from the minor differences for dimensions $1 \leq D \leq 12$. After the 13th dimension , that is $D \geq 13$, they all reached a 100 % of classification rate. Finally, it may be worth mentioning that apart from the kNN, we have also experimented with several other classifiers. These algorithms include Self-Organizing Maps [42], Support Vector Machines [43], Linear Vector Quantization [44], Naive Bayes Classifiers [45] and Multivariate Gaussian Distribution [46]. However, their results were not satisfactory and we stopped pursuing them.

4.3   Software Integrity Verification

To test the verification technique explained in Sect. 3.3, we generated a pair of RSA keys. Normally it is recommended to use large prime numbers in order to be secure against factorization attacks. However, our aim here is to show that side channel leakage can be used to verify the integrity of embedded applications. Therefore, we generated the key pairs using small prime numbers. We selected the prime numbers to be $q = 23$ and $p = 59$. Using CrypTool [47] we generated the public and private key to be $(N = 1357, e = 3)$ and $(N = 1357, d = 851)$ respectively. For this experiment we also implemented an application that verifies a four digit PIN value. The reference PIN is stored in the non-volatile memory of the processor and the PIN that needs to be verified is sent from a terminal (PC). Once the processor receives the PIN, it compares it with the reference PIN digit by digit.

Before signing the basic blocks of our application we generated a hash (fixed) value on the immutable part of the basic block instructions. For example, in *ATMega163* instructions have two parts the *Opcode* and the *Operand*. The *Opcode* is always static and the *Operand* depends on the arguments (parameters). In the RSA hash-and-sign scheme, standard hash algorithms such as SHA-1 [48] and MD5 [49] are used to generate the hash value. However, since our experiment was not about attacking hash algorithms we used a simple XOR of the immutable parts for simplicity.

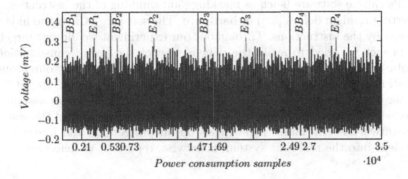

Fig. 7. Power consumption of the processor when executing PIN checking application with embedded processor parameter update in between the basic blocks.

In Fig. 7, the plot sections labelled as "BB" are when the processor executes the basic blocks and the sections labelled as "EP" belong to the processor's parameter update operation. To test our technique, we changed some of the instructions of the application after the signatures were generated and ran it. In our first trial we replaced two consecutive MOV instructions with MOVW. They both accomplish the same task, but generate different waveforms. Secondly we changed the compare instruction CP to CPC in the first two basic blocks. The PIN still gets verified correctly, but the waveform was not quite the same and we detected that using our proposed method. Finally we replaced the branching statement BRNE with BREQ and ran it. As expected Eq. (8) returned "0", which means the integrity of the application is violated, for all three cases. We have also implemented the same function in PIC16F876 microcontroller and run the verification process using the templates built for ATMega163. Again as we expected it, the instruction classification function did not produce the correct instructions. As a result the verification function returned "0".

5   Practical Application Area

Embedded system developers buy different components from different countries and put them together before deploying them in operation. In a big system, each component is designed to perform certain function. In such a system it is vital to verify the integrity of each component before putting them together as one defective component can jeopardise the entire system. In this kind of situation our proposed technique can be used to verify the integrity embedded applications.

At the heart of our technique is the construction of reliable templates and successful classification of executed instructions. However, manufacturers of embedded processors will protect their products from side channel attacks by using side channel protection (SCP) techniques. The SCP techniques tend to obscure the leakage of the target device. So, the obvious question here is, how would the proposed method work against processors with side channel attack protection?

SCPs can be software (such as masking [50], shuffling of the instructions [51] or inserting random delays [52]) or hardware. The software SCP try to hide data processed by the instructions. Throughout our experiment we did not target the data, in fact we tried to avoid the dependency of the power consumption on the data processed. Therefore, the software SCPs will not affect our proposed verification method. As for the hardware protection, we assume the SCP has two operational modes; switched on and off. Based on the above assumption, the verifier switches off all protections and verifies the integrity of the software. If the software is still intact he switches on all protections and integrates the component into the real-time system; otherwise, reports it as defective.

6   Conclusion

This paper has explored the unconventional idea of permitting side channel leakage from an electronic component, before it is deployed in real-time operation, for the purposes of useful analysis and application code integrity verification. We conducted an experiment on an AVR architecture microcontroller, *ATMega163*. In our work we acheived a 100 % of classification rate using k nearest neighbors algorithm for executed instructions. As the verification process is only performed once after acquiring the components (but before deploying them in operation) our method will not affect the performance of the chip once deployed into operation. Furthermore, special equipments are not required to support the components in real-time operation. Therefore, the technique can be used for forensic analysis of electronic components, application integrity verification and counterfeit components detection purposes.

Appendix

A Selected AVR Instructions

Out of the 130 instructions supported by ATMega163 microcontroller we have
selected 39 instructions for our experiment. In Table 1 we present the notations
use in Table 2.

Table 1. Notations used in Table 2

Notation	Description	Notation	Description
R_d	Destination register	C	Carry flag
R_r	Source register	K	Constant data
X, Y, Z	Indirect address registers $(X = R_{27} : R_{26},\ Y = R_{29} : R_{28},\ Z = R_{31} : R_{30})$	k	Constant address
		Pt	I/O Port address

In Table 2, the first column is the list of selected instructions followed by their
description. The third column is the operation that the instructions accomplish
when executed. The forth column is the number of clock cycles that the instructions take to be executed.

Table 2. AVR's 39 instructions selected for the experiment.

Instruction	Description	Operation	Clock cycles
mov R_d, R_r	Move a byte between registers	$R_d \leftarrow R_r$	1
movw R_d, R_r	Move a word between registers	$R_{d+1} : R_d \leftarrow R_{r+1} : R_r$	1
ldi R_d, K	Load immediate into register	$R_d \leftarrow K, 0 \leq d \leq 31,$	1
ld R_d, P	Load indirect	$R_d \leftarrow (P)$ $P \in \{X, Y, Z\}, 0 \leq d \leq 31$	2
ld $R_d, P+$	Load indirect with post-increment	$R_d \leftarrow (P),\ P \leftarrow P + 1$ $P \in \{X, Y, Z\}, 0 \leq d \leq 31$	2
ld $R_d, -P$	Load indirect with pre-decrement	$P \leftarrow P - 1,\ R_d \leftarrow (P)$ $P \in \{X, Y, Z\}, 0 \leq d \leq 31$	2
lds R_d, k	Load direct from SRAM	$R_d \leftarrow (k)$ $0 \leq d \leq 31, 0 \leq k \leq 65535$	2

Table 2. (*Continued*)

Instruction	Description	Operation	Clock cycles
st P, R_r	Store indirect	$(P) \leftarrow R_r$ $P \in \{X, Y, Z\}, 0 \leq r \leq 31$	2
st $P+, R_r$	Store indirect with post-increment	$(P) \leftarrow R_r, P \leftarrow P + 1$ $P \in \{X, Y, Z\}, 0 \leq r \leq 31$	2
st $-P, R_r$	Store indirect with pre-decrement	$P \leftarrow P - 1, (P) \leftarrow R_r$ $P \in \{X, Y, Z\}, 0 \leq r \leq 31$	2
sts k, R_r	Store direct into SRAM	$(k) \leftarrow R_d$ $0 \leq r \leq 31, 0 \leq k \leq 65535$	2
lpm R_d, P	Load program memory	$R_d \leftarrow (P)$ $0 \leq d \leq 31, P \in \{Z, Z+\}$	3
spm	Store program memory		4
in R_d, P_t	In port	$(P_t) \leftarrow R_d$	1
out P_t, R_r	Out port	$R_r \leftarrow (P_t)$	1
push R_r	Push register on stack	$STACK \leftarrow R_d$	2
pop R_d	Pop register from stack	$R_d \leftarrow STACK$	2
nop R_d, R_r	Do nothing		1
add R_d, R_r	Add two registers	$R_d \leftarrow R_d + R_r$	1
adc R_d, R_r	Add two registers with carry	$R_d \leftarrow R_d + R_r + C$	1
adiw R_d, K	Add register with immediate word	$R_{d+1} : R_d \leftarrow R_{d+1} : R_d + K$	2
sub R_d, R_r	Subtract two registers	$R_d \leftarrow R_d - R_r$	1
sbc R_d, R_r	Subtract two registers with carry	$R_d \leftarrow R_d - R_r - C$	1
sbiw R_d, K	Subtract immediate from a word stored in consecutive registers	$R_{d+1} : R_d \leftarrow R_{d+1} : R_d - K$	2
mul R_d, R_r	Multiply two registers	$R_d \leftarrow R_d \times R_r$	2
eor R_d, R_r	Exclusive or two registers	$R_d \leftarrow R_d \oplus R_r$	1
inc R_d	Increment a register	$R_d \leftarrow R_d + 1$	1
dec R_d	Decrement a register	$R_d \leftarrow R_d - 1$	1
clr R_d	Clear a register	$R_d \leftarrow R_d \oplus R_d$	1
cpi R_d, K	Compare immediate with a value stored in the given register	$R_d - K$	1

Table 2. (*Continued*)

Instruction	Description	Operation	Clock cycles
cp R_d, R_r	Compare two registers	$R_d - R_r$	1
cpc R_d, R_r	Compare two registers with carry	$R_d - R_r - C$	1
rjmp k	Relative jump	$PC \leftarrow PC + k + 1$	2
jmp k	Direct jump	$PC \leftarrow k$	3
rcall k	Relative subroutine call	$PC \leftarrow PC + k + 1$	3
call k	Direct subroutine call	$PC \leftarrow k$	4
ret k	Subroutine return	$PC \leftarrow STACK$	4
breq k	Branch if equal	if $(Z = 1)$ then $PC \leftarrow PC + k + 1$	1/2
brne k	Branch if not equal	if $(Z = 0)$ then $PC \leftarrow PC + k + 1$	1/2
brcs k	Branch if carry is set	if $(C = 1)$ then $PC \leftarrow PC + k + 1$	1/2
brcc k	Branch if carry is clear	if $(C = 0)$ then $PC \leftarrow PC + k + 1$	1/2
brbc b, k	Branch if flag is clear	if $(SREG(b) = 0)$ then $PC \leftarrow PC + k + 1$	1/2
brbs b, k	Branch if flag is set	if $(SREG(b) = 1)$ then $PC \leftarrow PC + k + 1$	1/2

References

1. Defense Advanced Research Projects Agency: Darpa baa06-40, a trust for integrated circuits, Visited, May 2013. https://www.fbo.gov/index?s—opportunity&mode=form&id=db4ea611cad3764814b6937fcab2180a&tab=core&_cview=1
2. Lieberman, J.I.: The national security aspects of the global migration of the U.S. semiconductor industry, Visited, May 2013. http://www.fas.org/irp/congress/2003_cr/s060503.html
3. Defense Science Board Task Force: High performance microchip supply, Visited, May 2013. http://www.acq.osd.mil/dsb/reports/ADA435563.pdf
4. U.S. Department of Commerce: Defense industrial base assessment: counterfeit electronics. Technical report, Bureau of Industry and Security, Office of Technology Evaluation, January 2010. http://www.bis.doc.gov/defenseindustrialbase-programs/osies/defmarketresearchrpts/final_counterfeit_electronics_report.pdf
5. Koushanfar, F., Sadeghi, A.-R., Seudie, H.: EDA for secure and dependable cybercars: challenges and opportunities. In: 2012 49th ACM/EDAC/IEEE Design Automation Conference (DAC), pp. 220–228 (2012)
6. Larson, J.: The Cardio-pneumo-psychogram in deception. J. Exp. Psychol. **6**(6), 420–454 (1923). http://books.google.co.uk/books?id=b6appwAACAAJ

7. Wei, S., Nahapetian, A., Potkonjak, M.: Robust passive hardware metering. In: International Conference on Computer-Aided Design (ICCAD), 7–10 November 2011, pp. 802–809. IEEE (2011)
8. Chakravarthi, S., Krishnan, A.T., Reddy, V., Machala, C.F., Krishnan, S.: A comprehensive framework for predictive modeling of negative bias temperature instability. In: 2004 IEEE International Reliability Physics Symposium Proceedings 42nd Annual, pp. 273–282 (2004)
9. Agrawal, D., Baktir, S., Karakoyunlu, D., Rohatgi, P., Sunar, B.: Trojan detection using IC fingerprinting. In: IEEE Symposium on Security and Privacy 2007, SP '07, pp. 296–310 (2007)
10. Bellare, M., Garay, J.A., Rabin, T.: Fast batch verification for modular exponentiation and digital signatures. In: Nyberg, K. (ed.) EUROCRYPT 1998. LNCS, vol. 1403, pp. 236–250. Springer, Heidelberg (1998)
11. Kocher, P.C.: Timing attacks on implementations of Diffie-Hellman, RSA, DSS, and other systems. In: Koblitz, N. (ed.) CRYPTO 1996. LNCS, vol. 1109, pp. 104–113. Springer, Heidelberg (1996)
12. Dhem, J.-F., Koeune, F., Leroux, P.-A., Mestré, P., Quisquater, J.-J., Willems, J.-L.: A practical implementation of the timing attack. In: Schneier, B., Quisquater, J.-J. (eds.) CARDIS 1998. LNCS, vol. 1820. Springer, Heidelberg (2000)
13. Arnaud, C., Fouque, P.-A.: Timing attack against protected RSA-CRT implementation used in PolarSSL. In: Dawson, E. (ed.) CT-RSA 2013. LNCS, vol. 7779, pp. 18–33. Springer, Heidelberg (2013)
14. Kocher, P.C., Jaffe, J., Jun, B.: Differential power analysis. In: Wiener, M. (ed.) CRYPTO 1999. LNCS, vol. 1666, p. 388. Springer, Heidelberg (1999)
15. Popp, T., Mangard, S., Oswald, E.: Power analysis attacks and countermeasures. IEEE Des. Test Comput. 24(6), 535–543 (2007)
16. Heyszl, J., Mangard, S., Heinz, B., Stumpf, F., Sigl, G.: Localized electromagnetic analysis of cryptographic implementations. In: Dunkelman, O. (ed.) CT-RSA 2012. LNCS, vol. 7178, pp. 231–244. Springer, Heidelberg (2012)
17. Gu, K., Wu, L., Li, X., Zhang, X.: Design and implementation of an electromagnetic analysis system for smart cards. In: Wang, Y., Cheung, Y., Guo, P., Wei, P., (eds) CIS, Sanya, Hainan, China, 3–4 December 2011, pp. 653–656. IEEE (2011)
18. Van Eck, W., Laborato, N.: Electromagnetic radiation from video display units: an eavesdropping risk? Comput. Secur. 4, 269–286 (1985)
19. Daemen, J., Rijmen, V.: The Design of Rijndael: AES - The Advanced Encryption Standard. Information Security and Cryptography. Springer, New York (2002)
20. Tuchman, W.: A brief history of the data encryption standard. In: Denning, D., Denning, P. (eds.) Internet Besieged, pp. 275–280. ACM Press, New York (1998)
21. Rivest, R.L., Shamir, A., Adleman, L.M.: A method for obtaining digital signatures and public-key cryptosystems. Commun. ACM 21(2), 120–126 (1978)
22. Oswald, D., Paar, C.: Breaking mifare DESFire MF3ICD40: power analysis and templates in the real world. In: Preneel, B., Takagi, T. (eds.) CHES 2011. LNCS, vol. 6917, pp. 207–222. Springer, Heidelberg (2011)
23. Vermoen, D., Witteman, M., Gaydadjiev, G.N.: Reverse engineering Java Card applets using power analysis. In: Sauveron, D., Markantonakis, K., Bilas, A., Quisquater, J.-J. (eds.) WISTP 2007. LNCS, vol. 4462, pp. 138–149. Springer, Heidelberg (2007)
24. Eisenbarth, T., Paar, C., Weghenkel, B.: Building a side channel based disassembler. Trans. Comput. Sci. 6340, 78–99 (2010)

25. Clavier, C.: Side channel analysis for reverse engineering (SCARE) - an improved attack against a secret A3/A8 GSM algorithm. IACR Cryptology ePrint Archive 2004:49 (2004)

26. Lee, S., Ermedahl, A., Min, S.L., Chang, N.: An accurate instruction-level energy consumption model for embedded RISC processors. In: Hong, S., Pande, S., (eds.) LCTES/OM, Snowbird, Utah, USA, 22–23 June 2001, pp. 1–10. ACM (2001)

27. Kavvadias, N., Neofotistos, P., Nikolaidis, S., Kosmatopoulos, C.A., Laopoulos, T.: Measurements analysis of the software-related power consumption in microprocessors. IEEE Trans. Instrum. Measur. 53(4), 1106–1112 (2004)

28. Mayes, K., Markantonakis, K., Chen, C.: Smart card platform-fingerprinting. Advanced Card Technology, pp. 78–82 (2006)

29. Becker, G.T., Strobel, D., Paar, C., Burleson, W.: Detecting software theft in embedded systems: a side-channel approach. IEEE Trans. Inf. Forensics Secur. 7(4), 1144–1154 (2012)

30. Coron, J.-S., Naccache, D.: On the security of RSA screening. In: Imai, H., Zheng, Y. (eds.) PKC 1999. LNCS, vol. 1560, p. 197. Springer, Heidelberg (1999)

31. Bishop, C.M., Nasrabadi, N.M.: Pattern recognition and machine learning. J. Electron. Imaging 16(4), 049901 (2007)

32. Rechberger, C., Oswald, E.: Practical template attacks. In: Lim, C.H., Yung, M. (eds.) WISA 2004. LNCS, vol. 3325, pp. 440–456. Springer, Heidelberg (2005)

33. Standaert, F.-X., Archambeau, C.: Using subspace-based template attacks to compare and combine power and electromagnetic information leakages. In: Oswald, E., Rohatgi, P. (eds.) CHES 2008. LNCS, vol. 5154, pp. 411–425. Springer, Heidelberg (2008)

34. Berrendero, J.R., Justel, A., Svarc, M.: Principal components for multivariate functional data. Comput. Stat. Data Anal. 55(9), 2619–2634 (2011)

35. Strang, G.: Introduction to Linear Algebra, vol. 3. Wellesley-Cambridge Press, Wellesley (2003)

36. Wang, L., Zhang, Y., Feng, J.: On the Euclidean distance of images. IEEE Trans. Pattern Anal. Mach. Intell. 27(8), 1334–1339 (2005)

37. Deza, M.M., Deza, E.: Encyclopedia of Distances. Springer, Heidelberg (2009)

38. Web site: Tutorial for learning assembly language for the AVR-Single-Chip-Processors, Visited, October 2013. http://www.avr-asm-tutorial.net/avr_en/

39. Web site: AVR freaks, Visited, October 2013. http://www.avrfreaks.net/

40. Teledyne LeCroy: Teledyne LeCroy website, Visited, February 2013. http://www.teledynelecroy.com

41. Pomona Electronics: 6069A scope probe, website, Visited, October 2012. www.pomonaelectronics.com/pdf/d4550b-sp150b_6_01.pdf

42. Kohenen, T.: Self-organized formation of topologically correct feature maps. Biol. Cybern. 43(1), 59–69 (1982)

43. Cortes, C., Vapnik, V.: Support-vector networks. Mach. Learn. 20(3), 273–297 (1995)

44. Kohenen, T.: Learning vector quantization. In: Self-Organizing Maps. Springer, Heidelberg (2001)

45. Rish, I.: An empirical study of the Naive Bayes classifier. IJCAI 2001 Workshop on Empirical Methods in Artificial Intelligence 3(22): 41–46 (2001)

46. Gut, A.: An Intermediate Course in Probability, 2nd edn. Springer, New York (2009). (Department of Mathematics, Uppsala University, Sweden)

47. Deutsche Bank AG and Contributors: Cryptool 1-4-31, Downloaded, May 2013. http://www.cryptool.org/en/jct-downloads-en

48. National Institute of Standards and Technology: FIPS 180–2, secure hash standard, federal information processing standard (FIPS), publication 180–2. Technical report, Department Of Commerce (1995)
49. Rivest, R.: RFC 1321: The MD5 message-digest algorithm, April 1992
50. Coron, J.-S., Goubin, L.: On Boolean and arithmetic masking against differential power analysis. In: Paar, C., Koç, Ç.K. (eds.) CHES 2000. LNCS, vol. 1965, p. 231. Springer, Heidelberg (2000)
51. Bo, Y., Xiangyu, L., Cong, C.: An AES chip with DPA resistance using hardware-based random order execution. J. Semicond. **33**(6), 065009-8 (2012)
52. Clavier, C., Coron, J.-S., Dabbous, N.: Differential power analysis in the presence of hardware countermeasures. In: Paar, C., Koç, Ç.K. (eds.) CHES 2000. LNCS, vol. 1965, p. 252. Springer, Heidelberg (2000)

Studying Leakages on an Embedded Biometric System Using Side Channel Analysis

Maël Berthier[1], Yves Bocktaels[1], Julien Bringer[1](✉), Hervé Chabanne[1,2],
Taoufik Chouta[2], Jean-Luc Danger[2], Mélanie Favre[1], and Tarik Graba[2]

[1] Morpho, Issy-les-Moulineaux, France
julien.bringer@morpho.com
[2] Télécom ParisTech Identity and Security Alliance
(The Morpho and Télécom ParisTech Research Center), Paris, France

Abstract. This paper addresses the potential information leakages of
a fingerprint comparison algorithm embedded as a hardware implementation. Such solution aims at comparing a reference fingerprint with a
freshly acquired one completely inside an embedded system (e.g. ASIC,
smart card, FPGA). The same way as for cryptographic operations
within a cryptoprocessor, we consider the reference fingerprint template
as a sensitive data that one may try to retrieve by attacking the chip. On
one hand, we show that we can find relevant information by the means
of Side Channel Analysis (SCA) that may help to retrieve the reference
fingerprint. On the other hand, we illustrate that reconstructing the fingerprint remains not trivial and we give some simple countermeasures to
protect further the comparison algorithm.

Keywords: Side channel analysis · Fingerprint · Hardware biometric
coprocessor · Biometric comparison · Hill climbing

1 Introduction

Biometric authentication, particularly using fingerprints, is commonly used to
uniquely identify individuals. Compared to the well know *What I know* (password) and *What I have* (token), the *Who I am* (biometrics) offers an inherent
security. However, biometric data are personal data and their usage in authentication systems requires to take care of privacy issues. Compared to a database,
the use of a personal device as a smart card to store the reference template
is a way to protect it and thus be compliant to user privacy. An even better
approach is the Match-On-Card (MOC) principle as it performs the comparison[1] inside the smart card [7,10,12,19]. The demand for such devices is growing.
At *Fingerprint Verification Competition* (FVC) of 2004 [3], a new competition
category was added to evaluate performances of authentications under resource
constraints: a 1.41 GHz working frequency, a maximum of 4 MB RAM usage

---

[1] The comparison algorithm is often also called a matching algorithm.

© Springer International Publishing Switzerland 2014
E. Prouff (Ed.): COSADE 2014, LNCS 8622, pp. 281–298, 2014.
DOI: 10.1007/978-3-319-10175-0_19

and matching execution time limited to 0.3 s. Even with this restrictions, the available resources on these platforms are far better than what we can find in a common smart card used for authentication (around 30 MHz frequency and 5 KB RAM in [7]). Recently, to overcome the limited resources of a smart card when a comparison algorithm is implemented in software, [9] introduced the design of a hardware implementation of a fingerprint comparison algorithm in order to define a biometric coprocessor, similarly to what had been done years ago for cryptographic coprocessors to speed up cryptographic operations. Note that some other embedded implementations for small devices have been proposed earlier (see for instance [21]), but we focus on the work presented in [9] as it is based on a classical fingerprint comparison algorithm.

A parallel to embedded cryptographic implementations on electronic chips can thus be done by evaluating the information leakages of the biometric comparison algorithm. The so called Side Channel Analysis (SCA) consists in passively exploiting leaked information. Since Kocher presented the first *timing analysis* to extract the private key of RSA asymmetric ciphering algorithm [14], a lot of other vulnerabilities were studied mainly related to power consumption [15] and electromagnetic emanations [17]. In this work we want to take advantage of leakages on something else than cryptographic operations, namely biometric comparison. These leakages have not the same consequences than for cryptography: while the knowledge of a secret is targeted in the latter, in biometrics it's authentication that is sought, like, for instance, in PIN comparison.

Concerning the security of biometric matching systems, authors of [18] identified 8 points of vulnerability that an attacker may exploit. In fact, a generic biometric system can be divided into four main modules (see Fig. 1): the *sensor* taking a raw image of the fingerprint, the *extractor* that performs pre-processing and features extraction, the *matcher* that calculates the similarity between two biometric templates, leading to a similarity *score*, and the *database* that contains the reference template. The embedded comparison approach, or Match-On-Card, only considers the matcher and the reference fingerprint template.

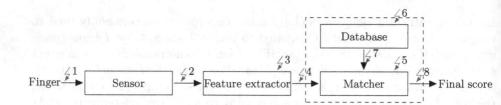

Fig. 1. Modules of a generic biometric system

Specific attention has also been paid to *Hill Climbing* attacks [16,22]. These algorithms produce synthetic templates iteratively adapted to the score they produce. We can as well cite a timing analysis on fingerprint matching [11] where authors show that there can be a correlation between execution time and score.

There is a mention of SCA on Match-On-Card in [6] but, to our knowledge, this has not been studied much further. The ThumbPod project [21] has designed an FPGA implementation (cf. for instance [20,23]) that resists to side channel leakage thanks to dual rail techniques but the biometric algorithm used [24] is not a standard one contrary to the one used in [9] and the study made was not specific to the biometric leakages. Note again that side-channel analysis on biometric comparison has been hardly studied in the literature and so have the countermeasures, that is why our analysis could rely on simpler ones compared to what is known today for attacking protected cryptographic implementations.

In this paper we present methods based on the simple analysis of power consumption during the matching process within an embedded system to recover some sensitive information. Then, we go further in our analysis of the leakage by presenting a template based attack that permits to retrieve, under some conditions, the hidden comparison score. All in one, this enables to launch an improved hill climbing algorithm to approach the reference fingerprint template. We illustrate our work on the hardware biometric comparison solution described in [9]. We present also some simple countermeasures to strengthen the embedded matcher against these information leakages. Our main goal is to highlight how hardware biometric solutions like [9], that rely on state-of-the-art minutiae-based fingerprint comparison techniques, could be improved to lead to a secure biometric coprocessor, thus avoiding sensitive leakages.

The article is structured as follows. In Sect. 2, we give some general information about fingerprint biometrics and the studied Match-On-Card algorithm and about its hardware implementation. Section 3 presents our observations coming from Side Channel Analysis while Sect. 4 presents a template attack on the matching score. Section 5 deals with the exploitation of the leakages mainly based on a hill climbing strategy. Finally, we give some countermeasures in Sect. 6.

2 Biometric Matching System

2.1 Fingerprint Biometrics

Fingerprints are one of the most used biometrics. The matching process is commonly based on the similarity analysis of some specific points called minutiae, extracted from a fingerprint image. Minutiae are discontinuity points on the ridge flows (ridge ending and ridge bifurcation). The INCITS 378 and the ISO 19794-2 [4] standards specify a compact template format based on minutiae for limited resource systems. Each fingerprint can be represented as a set of 3-dimensional minutiae points, where a single minutia point is described as an oriented 2D point $\{x(8\,\text{bits}), y(8\,\text{bits}), \theta(6\,\text{bits})\}$. The angle θ is the ridge ending or bifurcation orientation. Fingerprint comparison algorithms aim at best superimpose both minutiae sets and measure their similarity. In what follows we consider that the sensitive data that we are aiming to retrieve from the embedded system is a set of standard minutiae points $\mathbb{S} = (\{(x_0, y_0, \theta_0)\}, \ldots, \{x_n, y_n, \theta_n\})$.

2.2 The Studied Fingerprint Matching Module

In [9], the authors propose a hardware module to achieve an embedded biometric comparison (hardware MOC), with the goal to define a biometric coprocessor, the aim being to speed up operations as do cryptographic coprocessors. The corresponding algorithm has two main steps called registration and pairing. Registration phase aims at retrieving best rotation and translation that make overlap reference and input minutiae sets. After applying this affine transformation to the input set, pairing uses a Gaussian scoring method to evaluate more accurately the similarity between both sets.

The coprocessor is composed of three modules (*Transformation*, *Votes* and *Pairing*). It uses a Read Only Memory (ROM) to store the reference minutiae and has a private volatile memory for all the processing steps. For our study we have used a SASEBO GII board [1] that is specially designed for the study of side channels and that includes a Virtex-5 LX30 FPGA on which the coprocessor was embedded.

Compared to the main related works on biometric comparison with hardware implementations, two important properties of [9]'s implementation are that it relies on a biometric algorithm working simply with a standard compact fingerprint template [4] and that is very close to the best performing algorithms with respect to biometric error rates. For instance, with FVC2000 DB2 dataset (cf. [2]), it achieves 1.50 % of false reject rate at 10^{-3} of false acceptance rate. The speed of one comparison is also sufficiently good (less than 0.5 s) to enable efficient side channel captures.

First Phase of a Fingerprint Comparison: Registration. Registration (also called alignment) consists in the construction of a histogram of all possible affine transformations $(\Delta_x, \Delta_y, \Delta_\theta)$ by overlapping each input minutia with each reference minutia. The most voted parameter triplet is considered to be optimal. However, the number of possible transformations is too big to store the whole histogram in a smart card. Its construction is thus adapted by dividing the research space in many small subspaces and votes are only done with respect to the processed subspace. This allows to reduce the size of the embedded memory to the size of a subspace: the same memory is used for all subspace histograms. These sub-histograms are calculated in an increasing rotation angle (Δ_θ) from $\Delta_{\theta_{min}}$ to $\Delta_{\theta_{max}}$ and their memory is completely reset between each subset. The most voted $(\Delta_x, \Delta_y, \Delta_\theta)$ triplet is updated on the fly in an internal register.

The drawback of this optimization is the need to test all possible affine transformations for each subspace even if the result is not within the processed subspace borders. To improve the processing time, the sub-histogram construction is not done on the whole reference minutiae set. For each minutia of the input set, only minutiae of the reference set, such that the difference in orientation angles (Δ_θ) belongs to the subspace, are tested. To optimize the research of these particular reference minutiae, the reference set is sorted offline regarding the minutiae angle. A mapping array is added, called *set_access*, with the orientation angle as key, to point directly to the first and last minutiae (noted $F_{\theta i}$ and

$L_{\theta i}$) with this particular orientation angle. A special *NONE* value is used if no reference minutia has this orientation angle. Figure 2 and Algorithm 1 describe the iterative registration process. m_{ref} denotes a minutia of the reference fingerprint and m_{in} a minutia of the input fingerprint (the fingerprint that has been submitted to the embedded comparison module).

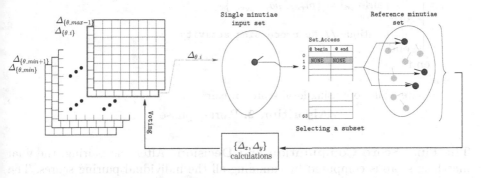

Fig. 2. Sub-histogram construction using a memory mapping array

> **foreach** $\Delta_{\theta i} \in [\Delta_{\theta_{min}}, \Delta_{\theta_{max}}]$ **do**
> > **foreach** *subspace* **do**
> > > **foreach** $m_{in} \in$ *input set* **do**
> > > > Read $(F_{\theta_i}, L_{\theta_i}) = set\_access(\Delta_{\theta_i} + \theta_{min})$
> > > > **if** $F_{\theta_i} \neq NONE$ **and** $L_{\theta i} \neq NONE$ **then**
> > > > > Calculate Δ_x and Δ_y parameters
> > > > > Fill subspace histogram memory with votes
> > > > > Update best $\{\Delta_\theta, \Delta_x, \Delta_y\}$ if greater triplet is voted
> > > >
> > > > **else**
> > > > > Continue // No processing activity
> > > >
> > > > **end**
> > >
> > > **end**
> >
> > **end**
> > Erase subspace memory
>
> **end**

Algorithm 1. Subspaces histogram built during registration phase

Second Phase of the Fingerprint Comparison: Pairing. In the pairing phase the affine transformation found during registration is applied on the input set. Then a similarity measure is used to associate pairs of input and reference minutiae: each input set point is iteratively compared to all the points of the reference set. If close enough, the reference minutia resulting in the highest pairing score is paired with the processed input minutia. Pairing phase is therefore data dependent, the number of input and reference minutiae is directly related to the duration of this step. Algorithm 2 illustrates the pairing process after the affine transformation has been applied.

```
foreach m_in ∈ input set do
    max_3D_score = 0
    pair[m_in] = {none,0}
    foreach m_ref ∈ reference set do
        pair_score = Gauss(Dist_θ, Dist_X, Dist_Y)
        if max_3D_score ≤ pair_score then
            max_3D_score = pair_score
            pair[m_in] = {m_ref, pair_score }
        else
            Continue // No processing activity
        end
    end
end
```
Compute final score using local scores in pair

Algorithm 2. Pairing phase

The Final Score Computation and Decision. After the pairing, the final matching score is computed by summing all the individual pairing scores. The final decision is then taken by comparing a normalized value of the score with a predefined threshold $Score_{Th}$.

The normalization of the score is necessary because the two minutiae sets could have very different sizes leading to erroneous results. In the studied implementation, the computation of the final score is done as follows:

$$finalScore = \frac{\sum_{i=0}^{size_{in}} pair[i]}{\text{Max}(size_{in}, size_{ref})} \qquad (1)$$

Where $size_{in}$ and $size_{ref}$ are respectively the number of minutiae in the input and reference sets.

Note that this approach in three steps for fingerprint comparison is quite classical. Consequently our side-channel analysis and associated results discussed in the remaining of the paper can probably be also adapted to other comparison algorithms that rely on the standard minutiae representation.

2.3   Assumptions on the Matching System

The studied biometric matching system structure is compliant to the one pictured in Fig. 1 but we can additionally make the following assumptions[2] on it, in order to simplify the study, as we aim to define recommendations for designing a secure biometric hardware coprocessor:

- We have full control of the inputs;
- There is no protection of the implementation:
  - There are no side channel countermeasures;
  - There is no retry counter (i.e. any number of attempts is possible).

---

[2] Note that the scope here is not to discuss the security of any existing Match-On-Card products.

All these points will greatly help us to study the information leakages of the design.

3   Information Leakage

The studied biometric hardware module behaves as follows. The private reference fingerprint template is stored in the module and the input fingerprint template is sent directly to the matcher. This means that the attacker has a complete control on the submitted fingerprint (the one sent as input to the module). During the matching execution, both reference and submitted fingerprint are manipulated, generating secret dependent variations on power consumption.

As an analogy with usual side channel analysis on cryptographic processes, we will study here the impact of manipulating a secret data (reference fingerprint is used here instead of the secret key for classical side channel analysis) and a chosen data (a chosen fingerprint sent to the comparison algorithm is used here instead of a plain text message for classical side channel analysis). However there are several differences:

The size of the secrets space, for example on an AES (Advanced Encryption Standard) is 2^{128}, with a 128-bit key. For our fingerprint comparison scenario, each minutia is represented on 22 bits (8 bits for x and y, and 6 bits for the angle), which means that with an average minutiae number of 20, the average secrets space size is upper bounded by 2^{440}.

On the other hand, a single bit difference on the secret key in cryptography directly leads to a rejection while an error on fingerprint acquisition is allowed (more or less minutiae, slight shift on position or angle of a minutia...). Thus the attacker may gain an interesting advantage by adapting the submitted fingerprints during an attack.

In the sequel we use Simple Power Analysis (SPA) in order to identify some patterns in power consumption which give information about what is executed on the target chip. As usual, this is made by measuring current that flows from the power supply to the attacked device.

3.1   SPA on Pairing Phase

In the second part of the matching execution, each minutia of the reference fingerprint is compared with all the transformed input fingerprint minutiae. On Fig. 3, we can see that the pairing phase is composed of $Size_{in}$ similar patterns that correspond to the iterations of the pairing loop. If we zoom on a single loop iteration, we can identify $Size_{ref} + 1$ steps. For each input minutia (the outer loop), there are $Size_{ref}$ accesses to reference minutiae plus one access to the input minutia access. A simple count gives the size of the reference minutiae set.

3.2   SPA on Registration Phase

As we can see from the Algorithm 1, there is a difference of process activity if the set_access value for a specific angle is $NONE$ or not.

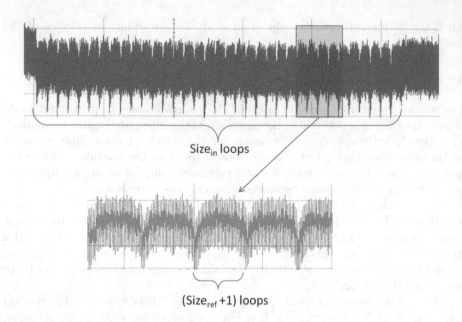

Fig. 3. Information leakage on pairing step

Since we have full control on the input fingerprint, we tried to submit a single minutia as a fingerprint input to reveal some activity which only depends on the reference fingerprint. The coordinates of the single minutia are not important, but we set the angle value at 0, to start from the first angle. For each computed transformation, if all the corresponding differences in orientation angles $\Delta_{\theta i}$ are out of bounds (i.e. $[\theta_{in} - 1, \theta_{in} + 1]$), there will be a noticeable difference in power consumption due to the process activity inequality. This difference can be seen on the power consumption trace of the registration part (Fig. 4). The angle values of the reference fingerprint minutiae were distributed as follows:

$$|19\ 20\ 20\ 20\ 22\ 23\ 23\ 24\ 25\ 26\ 26\ 27\ 27\ 27\ 28\ 28\ 28\ 30\ 30\ 31\ 31\ 32\ 32\ 34$$
$$|50\ 53\ 53\ 54\ 54\ 55|62 \tag{2}$$

We can see some drops in the power consumption which correspond to the angle area where there is no minutiae matching in the reference fingerprint (red lines in (2) vs. red markers in Fig. 4). This is due to the affine transformation of the input fingerprint (single minutia) that does not match with a reference one.

We then tried to analyze the dependence between the angle of the submitted fingerprint minutia and these drops on the trace. We processed several matchings with an increasing angle value and kept the trace for each match. Figure 5 shows the traces of 3 different matchings with an increasing angle value (not consecutive).

The drops are shifted to the left when we start the registration with a higher angle value. Increasing the angle of the input minutia from i to $i + 1$ will cause

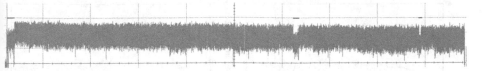

Fig. 4. Power consumption during registration with a single minutia input fingerprint (color figure online)

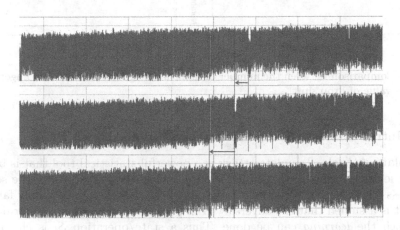

Fig. 5. Shifting drops in power consumption with 3 increasing input minutia angle values

a shift in the starting reference minutia from the angle $i - 1$ to i. This means that we can get the number of minutiae for each angle value by increasing the angle value of the input minutia.

As we can see in Fig. 6, there is a strong dependence between the number of minutiae for a chosen angle in the reference fingerprint and the drops shift in power consumption. By observing the drops delay between two consecutive angle values of input minutia for each possible angle value, we are able to get the distribution of the reference fingerprint minutiae angles (the number of minutiae concerned by the ith angle value among the total number of minutiae). There are only 64 matchings to perform.

4   Side Channel Attack on the Comparison Score

A traditional approach to enhance privacy is to hide the score that can be exploited by Hill Climbing attacks in favor of a boolean answer. Therefore, we investigate side channels in order to retrieve the score when not directly available and thus we are able to climb back to the reference minutiae set.

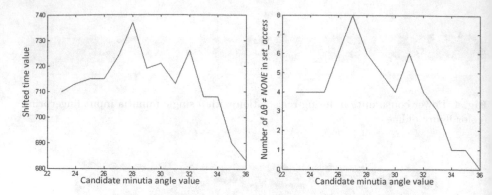

Fig. 6. Comparison between the number of minutiae neighbors in reference fingerprint and the value of drop shift

4.1   Introduction to Template Attack Combined with PCA

Template Attack. Template attack is a powerful statistical tool that is based on the leakage profiling of a similar device, which allows to retrieve the secret with less traces than differential attacks, or where these last ones simply fail [8]. Thus it is assumed that the adversary is in possession of an open similar device on which the *learning* can be done. Thus a state/operation S_i is characterized by computing its template $T_{S_i} = \{\mu_{S_i}, Cov_{S_i}\}$ consisting of the mean and the covariance matrix of the leakage traces respectively. In order to decrease the learning stage complexity, the computation is restricted to relevant leakage points as it will be discussed further in Sect. 4.2.

Therefrom, when another similar device is attacked, the adversary aims to reveal an unknown S_x by computing the maximum likelihood. Computation of the likelihood is done as the following:

$$p(\mathcal{L}|S = S_i) = \prod_{j=1}^{T} p(\mathcal{L}_j|\mu_{S_i}, Cov_{S_i}), \text{ where} \tag{3}$$

$$p(\mathcal{L}_j|\mu_{S_i}, Cov_{S_i}) = \frac{1}{\sqrt{(2\pi)^N |Cov|}} \times e^{-\frac{1}{2}(\mathcal{L}_j - \mu_{S_i})^T Cov^{-1}(\mathcal{L}_j - \mu_{S_i})}. \tag{4}$$

Where $i \in \{1, \ldots, \lambda\}$, with λ the total number of possible states. T is the set of leakage traces $\mathcal{L}$ each one of N samples.

Projection on Principal Components. Computation magnitude of the maximum likelihood increases according to the number of used samples in leakage traces, which may result in significant resources loads. Inversion of the covariance matrix can also be one of the barriers prohibiting a direct computation of the likelihood. This may be due to the potential linearity between neighbour samples. Therefrom the adversary can consider the Principal Component Analysis [13] in order to keep only relevant informations (i.e., with maximum variance). This operation is done by projecting templates and leakage traces into low dimensional subspaces. Computation of the principal components and projection matrices is out of the scope of this paper (see [5]). Thus, in our attack we use PCA to avoid covariance matrix issues.

4.2 Profiling and Attacking the Score Computation

The Hardware Implementation. For our analysis we focused on profiling the score register consumption. The score computation stated in Eq. 1 is processed as follows: first, the register that will hold the final score is used to accumulate all local scores. In fact, this accumulation requires a 22-bit register and consists of the computation of the division nominator. Second, the accumulated scores are normalized by the $maxPairs$ denominator (see Sect. 2.2) by using a restoring division. This technique is a naive Euclidean approach that processes successive subtractions and comparisons, and outputs one quotient bit at each clock cycle. The binary version of this approach relies on successive left shifts of the nominator register which allows to reuse this register to store the quotient bits successively in the LSB. Thus, at the first clock cycle of this computation the score MSB is output and so on. Interestingly, the restoring division is one of the standard implementation that is adopted by many processors and hardware designers.

The Learning Phase. To perform the learning phase $10k$ traces were used. As the target register is an LFSR, we assume the Hamming distance between two consecutively computed bits as the leakage model. This results in two classes for each of the 22 bits. In practice, in order to determine relevant leakage moments, we compute the correlation coefficient between the ith bit model over all samples. Figure 7a shows the correlation traces for the 16 LSB, in order of computation. In fact, it turns out that the first 6 MSBs of the acquisition campaign have an unbalanced parity of 0 and 1 (more than 90 % equal to 0). Hence, for a proof of concept, we consider that profiling and attacking remaining bits is sufficient.

The Attack Phase. The success rate metric is a simple statistical tool giving the average of successful attacks on different sets of traces of different sizes. In other words, it allows to determine the average of what an adversary can achieve or expect with a certain amount of traces. For our attack, the amount of traces to reach a success rate of 80 %, varies according to the targeted bit from a single trace to 34 traces (the LSB need less traces). This is due to the low SNR consequence of the intrinsic and ambient noise. Indeed, the activity leaked by one register bit is low relatively to the rest of the device activity. In Fig. 7b we plot the success rate with 100 attack retries on independent sets of traces.

5 Exploitation

We emphasized in the previous sections different information that are observed through side channel from the comparison algorithm execution. We will explain here an advanced strategy to exploit those information.

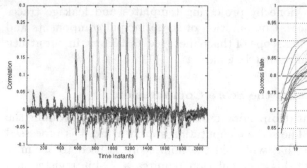

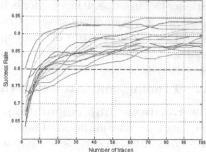

(a) Localization of relevant samples   (b) Success rate of the template attack

Fig. 7. The proling and the attack results

5.1   Hill Climbing Attack

One of the possible attacks on a biometric system is to reach a positive verification using synthetic input minutiae sets rather than using the genuine user
fingerprint. A brute-force attack is very hard unless the verification system has
a significant discrimination error rate (false acceptance rate). This is due to the
amount of minutiae points in a fingerprint template ($\approx$20–100) which results in
a possibility space of 2^{2200} $((2^{(8+8+6)})^{100})$ in the worst case. Note that, in this
rough estimation, we consider that the attacker has no knowledge on fingerprint
geometry and will take into account the whole possibility space. Fingerprints
with minutiae at the edges or with identical minutiae are hence considered.

A more efficient strategy exists: Authors of [22] used the Hill Climbing (HC)
heuristic to find modifications that increase the comparison score between synthetic minutiae sets and the targeted reference set. It considers a starting set
of minutiae points which is iteratively modified and sent back to the matcher
module for score evaluation. An applied modification is kept only when the score
increases. Possible modifications on a minutiae set are:

1. Randomly translate or rotate a randomly selected minutia;
2. Add a minutia;
3. Replace a randomly selected minutia;
4. Delete a randomly selected minutia.

The heuristic stops when the synthetic set reaches the matcher validation
score for which sets are considered as sufficiently close to reference data. Thus,
the attack on the matcher combined with this private reference fingerprint template is considered as a success.

Of course, the HC approach assumes that the attacker has a direct access
to the matcher input (i.e. the attacker is able to choose the input fingerprint)
and that the matching score is known (not only the binary OK/NOK result).
The first condition is verified in our case following the assumptions explained in

Sect. 2.3. And we explained in the previous section how to retrieve the matching score, thus we assume below that the score could be known.

5.2 Hill Climbing Improvement

In the previous description of Hill Climbing, the added and modified minutiae are randomly chosen. This means that there are $2^{22} = 256 \times 256 \times 64$ possibilities each time we have to add or modify a single minutia. Our study on power consumption, as discussed in Sect. 3, gave some interesting information about the reference fingerprint template: the number of minutiae per angle. The most important information here is to have the distribution of the minutiae among the 64 angles.

A simple way to use this knowledge is to pick a minutia according to a distribution table. This distribution table, containing an associated probability for each angle, is created thanks to the shift timings values from the previous study. For each angle (64 matching executions) we store the time shift value among the total of all the 64 time shifts (which correspond to the registration step time).

To evaluate the improvement, we compared 3 different levels of Hill Climbing:

- Without optimization: new minutiae are picked randomly (equivalent to the HC in [22] with a single initial guess).
- List mode: new minutiae are picked from a list of existing angles, but there is no associated probability.
- Distribution mode: new minutiae are picked from a distribution table, with probabilities deduced from side channel analysis and thus approximately corresponding to those of the reference fingerprint template.

Figure 8 shows the result of these 3 modes on 4 times averaged Hill Climbing. It describes the score (vertical scale) among the matching iterations (horizontal scale). The horizontal line depicts the score threshold above which the synthesized fingerprint is accepted as corresponding to the reference one.

The distribution mode reaches the threshold score with 4000 iterations instead of 8000 iterations for the two other modes. To achieve this improvement, only 64 matching executions are necessary.

It has to be recalled (see Sect. 4.2) that the extraction of the score using the profiled attack, needs roughly 34 traces at each iteration. This gives an idea of the total number of traces needed to construct an approximation of the reference fingerprint data.

Keeping the assumptions from Sect. 2.3 verified, we are able to succeed a Hill Climbing with half the matching iterations otherwise needed. This improvement is possible thanks to the information leaked via side channel while executing biometric comparisons. We bet that deeper analysis of the side channel leakage would probably lead to further improvement. This means that some specific countermeasures have to be implemented to protect the biometric comparison coprocessor from that kind of leakages.

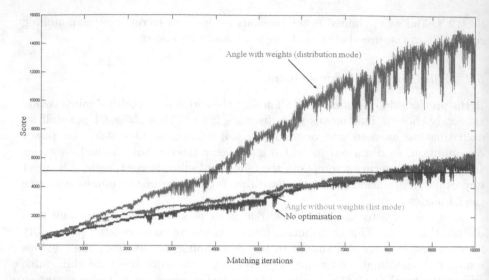

Fig. 8. Hill Climbing result for 3 modes, each replayed and averaged 4 times

6   Countermeasures

In previous sections we presented an approach that may allow an adversary to break through the simple countermeasure of hiding the score in order to perform the HC again. We also showed how it can be possible to reduce the HC needed iterations by a further exploitation of side channels. In this section, we will describe one countermeasure for each threat previously identified. Many of them require random numbers, which could be assumed coming from a random generator from the smart card in which the biometric coprocessor is attached to.

6.1   Protecting the Score Computation

Manipulation of the comparison score, whether by normalization (our case) or other approaches may leak sensitive information leading to its recovery. As stated in Sect. 2.2, in order to produce a binary answer, normalization of the accumulated score is followed by a comparison to acceptance threshold $Score_{Th}$. This operation can be expressed in a different way in manner to avoid normalization. Thus the accumulated score is compared to a dynamically adjusted threshold. This approach avoids the usage of a register which makes the combinatorial path the main source of leakage. The answer computation is thus:

Here, the number of minutiae in the reference set $size_{ref}$ is not considered as a sensitive information. Thus, even if the decision is made in two cycles (i.e. $DyScore_{Th}$ is stored in a register) and the adversary succeeds in retrieving $size_{ref}$, this last one is of a low entropy.

$AccuScore = \sum_{i=0}^{size_{in}} pair[i]$
$DyScore_{Th} = Score_{Th} \times \text{Max}(size_{in}, size_{ref})$
if $DyScore_{Th} \leqslant AccuScore$ **then**
 | Answer = 1
else
 | Answer = 0
end

Algorithm 3. Hiding score computation

6.2   Randomization of the Registration Phase by Masking

A first method to protect the information leakage during the registration part
is to start the registration from a randomly chosen rotation angle instead of
going systematically from $\Delta_{\theta min}$ to $\Delta_{\theta max}$. This random offset value has to be
different for each fingerprint comparison to avoid the correlation between the
processing order and the orientation of the input minutiae. The same result can
be obtained by applying on the reference fingerprint a randomly chosen pre-
translation-rotation. This countermeasure would solve the incremental minutia
angle parse threat, but would not be efficient enough because reference minutiae
are still parsed in a sorted angle order. On average, 400 attempts of matching
with a same single minutia will give the 64 angles distribution, with a 90 %
success rate. In this case, the probability of obtaining the original minutiae parse
sequence is 1/64.

A better countermeasure is to completely randomize the processing sequence
regarding the orientation angle. An efficient way to achieve this is to use a
randomly generated *mask* to change the sequence order. There are 64 rotation
angles to test, thus a $log_2(64)$-bit length vector *rot_a* is used to iterate through
the sequence $\Delta_{\theta min}..\Delta_{\theta max}$. *rot_a* $\oplus mask$ will give a random permutation of the
original sequence. As the angle parse order is changed (and not only the angle
start value), the drops on which we measure the time shift are split and other
may appear. In that way, the angles distribution of the reference fingerprint is
impossible to retrieve. The hardware cost of such a countermeasure is very small,
and the probability of obtaining the original minutiae parse sequence is increased
to 1/64!.

6.3   Input Fingerprint Requirements

The observation of the angles distribution of the reference minutiae is eased by
the fact that we are allowed to send and match a single minutia fingerprint, or
a fingerprint with several occurrences of the same minutia repeated. An either
simple countermeasure would be to disable matching if the submitted fingerprint
does not fulfill some basic requirements like:

– A minimum and maximum number of minutiae.
– No duplicated minutiae.

6.4   Random Additional Cycles During Pairing Phase

The pairing phase leaks some information about the reference fingerprint minutiae number. This information alone is not enough to improve a Hill Climbing attack, but it can still be protected with a low cost countermeasure.

As we have seen on Fig. 3, it is easy to count the number of cycles inside a reference minutia loop, and hence get the minutiae number of the reference fingerprint. Adding a random number of extra cycles per reference minutia loop would break this leakage and create a random delay effect on the whole pairing step. The idea is to choose a single random value Rng_FP which will be common to all reference minutiae loops, and an additional one Rng_minu_i, different for each loop.

For instance, if Rng_FP is chosen with a maximum of 20 % of the reference minutiae number ($Rng\_FP \in [0; 0.2 * size_{ref}]$), and Rng_minu_i are chosen with max of 10 %, the average global extra computation time on pairing step will be 15 %. This is a low cost countermeasure as the pairing step represents less than 10 % of the whole matching process.

7   Conclusion

In this paper, we analyzed, for the first time, the potential information leakages of a hardware biometric comparison module that relies on state of the art fingerprint comparison techniques. We pointed out that we can find out relevant information of the private reference fingerprint template by the means of side channel analysis. These informations, together with a template attack to retrieve the value of the comparison score, enable us to mount an improved hill climbing attack to approach the reference template. This shows the need to protect the implementation. Fortunately, there are some simple countermeasures that can be used to thwart the information leakages. Our future work will thus cover the design study of a secure biometric coprocessor by including such kind of countermeasures.

Acknowledgment. This work has been partially funded by the French ANR project BMOS and by the European FP7 BEAT project (SEC-2011-284989). The authors would like to thank the other BMOS partners, especially Thibault Porteboeuf from Secure-IC, for their help on the FPGA prototype.

References

1. http://www.rcis.aist.go.jp/special/SASEBO/SASEBO-GII-en.html
2. Fingerprint Verification Competition. http://biolab.csr.unibo.it/FVCOnGoing/
3. Fingerprint Verification Competition (2004). http://bias.csr.unibo.it/fvc2004/
4. Iso/iec 19794-2 information technology - biometric data interchange formats - part 2: Finger minutiae data

5. Archambeau, C., Peeters, E., Standaert, F.-X., Quisquater, J.-J.: Template attacks in principal subspaces. In: Goubin, L., Matsui, M. (eds.) CHES 2006. LNCS, vol. 4249, pp. 1–14. Springer, Heidelberg (2006)
6. Barral, C., Vaudenay, S.: A protection scheme for moc-enabled smart cards. In: 2006 Biometrics Symposium: Special Session on Research at the Biometric Consortium Conference, pp. 1–6. IEEE (2006)
7. Bistarelli, S., Santini, F., Vaccarelli, A.: An asymmetric fingerprint matching algorithm for java card ^{TM}. Pattern Anal. Appl. 9(4), 359–376 (2006)
8. Chari, S., Rao, J.R., Rohatgi, P.: Template attacks. In: Kaliski, B.S., Koç, K., Paar, C. (eds.) CHES 2002. LNCS, vol. 2523, pp. 13–28. Springer, Heidelberg (2003)
9. Chouta, T., Danger, J.-L., Sauvage, L., Graba, T.: A small and high-performance coprocessor for fingerprint match-on-card. In: DSD, pp. 915–922. IEEE (2012)
10. Cucinotta, T., Brigo, R., Di Natale, M.: Hybrid fingerprint matching on programmable smart cards. In: Katsikas, S.K., López, J., Pernul, G. (eds.) TrustBus 2004. LNCS, vol. 3184, pp. 232–241. Springer, Heidelberg (2004)
11. Galbally, J., Carballo, S., Fierrez, J., Ortega-Garcia, J.: Vulnerability assessment of fingerprint matching based on time analysis. In: Fierrez, J., Ortega-Garcia, J., Esposito, A., Drygajlo, A., Faundez-Zanuy, M. (eds.) BioID MultiComm2009. LNCS, vol. 5707, pp. 285–292. Springer, Heidelberg (2009)
12. Govan, M., Buggy, T.: A computationally efficient fingerprint matching algorithm for implementation on smartcards. In: First IEEE International Conference on Biometrics: Theory, Applications, and Systems, 2007, BTAS 2007, pp. 1–6. IEEE (2007)
13. Jolliffe, I.: Principal Component Analysis. Wiley Online Library, New York (2005)
14. Kocher, P.C.: Timing attacks on implementations of Diffie-Hellman, RSA, DSS, and other systems. In: Koblitz, N. (ed.) CRYPTO 1996. LNCS, vol. 1109, pp. 104–113. Springer, Heidelberg (1996)
15. Kocher, P.C., Jaffe, J., Jun, B.: Differential power analysis. In: Wiener, M. (ed.) CRYPTO 1999. LNCS, vol. 1666, pp. 388–397. Springer, Heidelberg (1999)
16. Martinez-Diaz, M., Fierrez-Aguilar, J., Alonso-Fernandez, F., Ortega-Garcia, V., Siguenza, J.: Hill-climbing and brute-force attacks on biometric systems: a case study in match-on-card fingerprint verification. In: Proceedings 2006 40th Annual IEEE International Carnahan Conferences Security Technology, pp. 151–159. IEEE (2006)
17. Quisquater, J.-J., Samyde, D.: ElectroMagnetic Analysis (EMA): measures and counter-measures for smart cards. In: Attali, S., Jensen, T. (eds.) E-smart 2001. LNCS, vol. 2140, pp. 200–210. Springer, Heidelberg (2001)
18. Ratha, N.K., Connell, J.H., Bolle, R.M.: An analysis of minutiae matching strength. In: Bigun, J., Smeraldi, F. (eds.) AVBPA 2001. LNCS, vol. 2091, pp. 223–228. Springer, Heidelberg (2001)
19. Reisman, J., Uludag, U., Ross, A.: Secure fingerprint matching with external registration. In: Kanade, T., Jain, A., Ratha, N.K. (eds.) AVBPA 2005. LNCS, vol. 3546, pp. 720–729. Springer, Heidelberg (2005)
20. Tiri, K., Hwang, D., Hodjat, A., Lai, B.-C., Yang, S., Schaumont, P., Verbauwhede, I.: AES-based cryptographic and biometric security coprocessor IC in 0.18- μm CMOS resistant to side-channel power analysis attacks. In: 2005 Symposium on VLSI Circuits 2005. Digest of Technical Papers, pp. 216–219 (2005)
21. UCLA. Thumbpod: a next generation biometrically secure wireless embedded system. http://www.emsec.ee.ucla.edu/thumbpod

22. Uludag, U., Jain, A.K.: Attacks on biometric systems: a case study in fingerprints. In: Delp, E.J., Wong, P.W. (eds.) Security, Steganography, and Watermarking of Multimedia Contents. Proceedings of SPIE, vol. 5306, pp. 622–633. SPIE (2004)
23. Yang, S., Sakiyama, K., Verbauwhede, I.: Efficient and secure fingerprint verification for embedded devices. EURASIP J. Adv. Signal Process. **2006**(1), 058263 (2006)
24. Yang, S., Verbauwhede, I.: Automatic secure fingerprint verification system based on fuzzy vault scheme. In: IEEE International Conference on Acoustics, Speech, and Signal Processing (ICASSP 2005), pp. 609–612 (2005)

On the Security of RSM - Presenting 5 First- and Second-Order Attacks

Sebastian Kutzner[1,2]($\boxtimes$) and Axel Poschmann[1,2]

[1] Physical Analysis and Cryptographic Engineering,
Temasek Laboratories@NTU, Singapore, Singapore
{skutzner,aposchmann}@ntu.edu.sg
[2] School of Physical and Mathematical Sciences, Division of Mathematical Sciences,
Nanyang Technological University, Singapore, Singapore

Abstract. Lightweight cryptography and efficient implementations, including efficient countermeasures against side-channel analysis, are of great importance for embedded devices, and, consequently, a lot of progress has been done in this area in recent years. In 2012, the RSM masking scheme [15] was introduced as an efficient countermeasure against side-channel attacks on AES. RSM has no time penalty, only reasonable area overhead, uses only 4 bit of entropy, and is deemed to be secure against univariate first- and second-order attacks. In this paper we first review the original practical security evaluation and discuss some shortcomings. We then reveal a weakness in the set of masks used in RSM, i.e., we found that certain pairs of masks have a constant difference. This weakness is subsequently exploited to mount five different side-channel attacks against RSM: a univariate first-order CPA enabled by simple pre-processing and a variant of a first-order correlation-enhanced collision attack, both on a smart card implementation, and a univariate second-order CPA as well as two first- and second-order collision attacks against an FPGA implementation. All five attacks show how such a vulnerability in the mask set can undermine the security of the scheme and therefore highlight the importance of carefully choosing the masks.

Keywords: Side-channel analysis · RSM · Smart card · FPGA · CPA · First-order attack · Second-order attack · Collision

1 Introduction

Embedded devices are already ubiquitous, and an ongoing trend is to interconnect them both to private as well as public networks, i.e., the Internet. At the same time, new services and revenue models are developed for the changed IT landscape, and one example is the so-called *industrial Internet*. Therefore, privacy, confidentiality and authenticity are of great concern, which can be effectively achieved by using modern cryptographic algorithms. However, even security-enabled devices implementing proper cryptographic algorithms can be easily broken by *power analysis attacks* [9]. Power analysis exploits the fact that

© Springer International Publishing Switzerland 2014
E. Prouff (Ed.): COSADE 2014, LNCS 8622, pp. 299–312, 2014.
DOI: 10.1007/978-3-319-10175-0_20

the power consumption of a device is correlated to the processed values, which enables an adversary to gain additional information about the inner workings of the cryptographic algorithms, and eventually leads to a security breach, e.g., extraction of the secret key.

Since the introduction of side-channel attacks, there is an ever ongoing arms race between attackers and defenders. A wide variety of different countermeasures have been proposed, e.g., hiding and masking, which aim at breaking the link between the observable side-channel and the processed data. The main problem usually is that most of the countermeasures cause a high overhead regarding memory and processing time, which are particularly scarce resources for embedded devices. Thus lightweight countermeasures are of particular interest for these devices and plenty of research was conducted in this field, e.g., [16].

At DATE 2012 the RSM [15] scheme was introduced as a very lightweight masking countermeasure against side-channel attacks targeting AES. It causes no timing overhead and only reasonable memory overhead, and is provably secure against first- and second-order univariate attacks. Furthermore, and probably more important, it only requires 4 bit of randomness for each encryption while other schemes require random bits equal to (or multiples of) their state size. It should be noted here that generating random numbers is very expensive and time consuming on embedded devices, thus recent research aims at reducing the randomness needed, e.g., [8].

RSM uses 4 bits of randomness to determine the initial *rotation* of 16 fixed and publicly known masks. It is noteworthy to point out that the security of the RSM scheme is solely based on the secrecy of this initial value. In our first attack we show how, with simple pre-processing, encryptions using the same initial value can be filtered which enables a subsequent first-order correlation power analysis (CPA) [3] attack. This attack is conducted on the RSM implementation taken from the DPA contest v4 [7]. Our remaining attacks exploit a weakness we found in the fixed masks, i.e., certain combinations of these masks have a constant difference. We show how this property can be exploited to mount different attacks on both smart card as well as FPGA implementations and undermine the security of the scheme.

The remainder of this paper is organized as follows. In Sect. 2 the RSM scheme is introduced and its original security evaluation and the selected masks (and their shortcomings) are discussed. Subsequently, in Sect. 3 our measurement setup is described. Then two attacks on smart card implementations of RSM (Sect. 4) and three attacks on FPGA implementations of RSM (Sect. 5) are presented. Finally, we conclude the paper in Sect. 6.

2   The RSM Countermeasure

This section briefly recalls the RSM countermeasure before we discuss the original security evaluation in more detail. Finally, we describe some important observations regarding several mask sets in RSM.

2.1   Introduction to RSM

Rotating S-box Masking (RSM) is a boolean masking scheme for AES and was introduced in [15]. It is very efficient since it does not introduce a timing overhead and only causes a small area overhead. Furthermore, it only needs 4 bit of entropy per encryption, which define the so-called *starting rotation offset*.

16 masked S-boxes have to be pre-calculated once, based on 16 8-bit *base masks* m_i (yielding a 128-bit mask $M = \{m_0, ..., m_{15}\}$), which are fixed throughout the lifetime of the device and are public information (see Sect. 2.3). The masked S-boxes fulfill the following property:

$$S_i(x_i \oplus k_i \oplus m_i) = S_{AES}(x_i \oplus k_i) \oplus m_{(i+1)\%16}, \ \forall i \in \{0, 15\} \qquad (1)$$

Furthermore, 16 128-bit constants $CSRMC_i$ are needed to *correct* the masked state after each linear layer, i.e., ShiftRows and MixColumns. The constants fulfill the following property:

$$CSRMC_i = (M >>> i) \oplus ShiftRows(MixColumns(M >>> i)), \ \forall i \in \{0, 15\} \qquad (2)$$

where $>>>$ means byte-wise rotation. Since the last round has no MixColumns, 16 more constants CSR_i have to be calculated as in Formula 2, but without the MixColumns operation.

The encryption works as follows:

1. Choose random starting rotation index $j \in_R \{0, 15\}$
2. Mask plaintext P with $M >>> j$ and perform AddRoundKey
3. Do ten times:
   (a) For every byte $i \in \{0, 15\}$ calculate $S_{j+i}(p_i \oplus m_{j+i} \oplus k_{i,r}) = S_{AES}(p_i \oplus k_{i,r}) \oplus m_{j+i+1}$, i.e., the output is now masked with $M >>> (j+1)$ meaning every output byte is masked with the mask byte m_{j+i+1} succeeding the input mask byte m_{j+i}[1].
   (b) Perform ShiftRows, MixColumns and AddRoundKey on the masked state.
   (c) Xor with $CSRMC_j$ to compensate for linear layer, such that the state is again masked with $M >>> (j+1)$.
   (d) $j = j + 1$.
4. Perform final SubBytes, ShiftRows and AddRoundKey.
5. Xor final constant CSR_j which automatically unmasks the state.

2.2   Discussion About Original Security Evaluation

In this section we discuss the original security evaluation of the RSM scheme presented in [15], which was implemented on an FPGA as described in [2]. It is well known that the number of traces required to successfully break any implementation by side-channel analysis depends on the Signal-to-Noise-Ratio (SNR)

---

[1] All operations are %16.

of the recorded power/EM traces. It is thus greatly dependent on both the leakage characteristics of the target device and the measurement setup. While the former part can be normalized to a certain degree –e.g. by using the same implementation on a similar target device– the latter is a particular challenge due to a great range of varying experimental parameters. Most notably are environmental conditions (temperature, humidity), cleanliness of the power supply, pre-processing techniques (alignment, low-pass filters) amongst others. All these factors can have a great influence on the SNR, and thus the number of traces required. As a consequence, it is common practice in security evaluations to take a worst-case scenario assumption, which means for the designer of a countermeasure to record many more times traces than one assumes (or better, shows) are required.

It was shown in e.g., [10,14], that a few million traces are needed to exploit remaining first-order or second-order leakage. Taking these numbers into consideration, it seems that the 150,000 measurements taken during the original security evaluation in [15] may be too few to reliably prove the security of RSM. Furthermore, the authors may have chosen a non-optimal model for their security evaluation. When conducting an attack with *known* masks and targeting the Hamming distance between subsequent S-box inputs as proposed in [15], we were not able to mount a successful attack. The reason might be that the BRAM address register, which is used as state register in this implementation [2], does not have enough load and hence does not cause enough leakage to be exploitable [1]. Instead, the output latch of the BRAM should be targeted.

Figure 1 shows the result of a CPA (with known masks) targeting the Hamming distance between the initial latch value of the BRAM after a reset and the S-box output of the first round. As one can see, the correct key hypothesis yields the highest correlation, therefore successfully verifying our updated attack model and our setup.

To re-verify the security of the RSM scheme, we repeated the original security analysis, i.e., a first- and second-order CPA on 10 million traces, targeting the output latch as described above. As expected, both attacks fail, see Fig. 2. We also performed a mutual information analysis, which in theory (and verified in simulations) is able to break RSM. Nevertheless, 10 million traces were not enough to identify the correct key which confirms the statement that RSM has very little leakage in general.

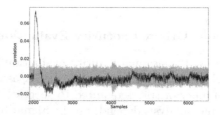

Fig. 1. CPA with known masks

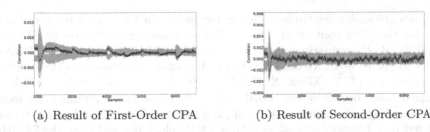

(a) Result of First-Order CPA   (b) Result of Second-Order CPA

Fig. 2. Results of CPA attacks

2.3 Mask Properties

The following are the base masks which are used in the DPA contest v4 and in the original FPGA implementation in [15].

$$[0x00, 0x0f, 0x36, 0x39, 0x53, 0x5c, 0x65, 0x6a, 0x95, 0x9a, 0xa3, 0xac, 0xc6, 0xc9, 0xf0, 0xff] \quad (3)$$

In the original paper a SAT solver was used to generate this mask set with the goal to minimize leakage. The authors do not mention if the mask set has to fulfill certain properties, but when looking at the 16 masks it can be seen that 14 of the 16 masks have a Hamming weight of 4 and the Hamming distance between them is 4 as well. We are guessing that these masks follow a so-called *binary constant weight code*, and it can be seen in [4] that it is indeed only possible to find 14 values which fulfill these properties for $n = 8$, $d = 4$ and $w = 4$. However, looking at other masks provided by the authors and [5], we were not able to find a corresponding code or special properties. Hence, the question remains what general properties a mask set has to fulfill to minimize leakage, in particular second-order leakage.

In this paper we focus on the original mask set. By calculating the pair-wise differences between each base mask, we found the following special property which is true for all mask values ($0 \leq i \leq 7$):

$$m_i = m_{i+8} \oplus 0x95 \quad (4)$$

This constant difference may have been overlooked, and we will show in the next sections how to exploit this property to mount successful attacks against the RSM scheme. We also analyzed three other mask sets, two of which also showed a constant difference of $0x8d$ and $0xff$, respectively. The third did not show this weakness but certain distances between mask pairs showed a clear bias towards certain mask differences. These biases might be exploitable as well, but will not be the topic of this paper.

3 Experimental Setup

We used two measurement setups for our analyses. Our smart card measurements were obtained using an Infineon raw SC reader and an AVR FunCard hosting an ATmega163 microcontroller. This is the same platform used to record the traces for the DPA contest v4. Our FPGA measurements were obtained from a SASEBO G-II evaluation platform. The SASEBO G-II hosts two FPGAs, i.e., a control FPGA (Xilinx XC3S400A-4FTG256, Spartan-3A series) and a cryptographic FPGA (Xilinx XC5VLX50-1FFG324, Virtex-5 series) which is decoupled from the rest of the board in order to minimize electronic noise from the surrounding components. It was supplied with a voltage of 1 V by an external stabilized power supply as well as with a 2 MHz clock derived from the 24 MHz on-board clock oscillator. The power consumption is measured in the VDD line by using a current probe. All power traces are collected with a LeCroy WR610Zi-s-32 oscilloscope at a sampling rate of 1 GS/s. Figure 3 shows two sample traces of the smart card and FPGA implementation, respectively.

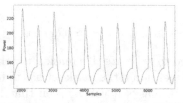
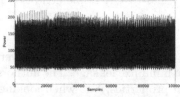

(a) Whole encryption on an FPGA   (b) First round on a smart card

Fig. 3. Sample side-channel traces of RSM

4   Attacking a Smart Card Implementation of RSM

In this section we present two attacks on the smart card implementation of RSM. We used the smart card implementation of RSM which can be downloaded from the DPA contest v4 homepage [7]. We programmed the unmodified hex-file on a FunCard with an Atmel ATmega 163 micro-processor, which is the suggested platform. We repeated the measurements with our own setup since the publicly available traces omitted the index update $j = (j + 1)\%16$, although it belongs to the round function (see step 3d in previous section) and is the target of one of our attacks.

4.1   Univariate First-Order CPA Attack Using Pre-processing

Our first (profiled) attack targets the smart card implementation and actually does not yet exploit the constant mask difference we presented before. Instead, this attack uses simple pre-processing to filter out traces using the same initial rotation offset, which, as explained before, is key for the security and must be random in every encryption and kept secret.

As explained in Sect. 2.3 the masks are rotated by one position after every round, therefore the rotation index must be updated to keep track of the rotation. This is done in the software implementation by the following line of code:

$$j[0] = (j[0] + 1)\%16; \tag{5}$$

where j[0] is the current rotation index.

We know that in CMOS logic the power consumption is highly dependent on the Hamming weight of the processed value [13], i.e., processing a value with Hamming weight 0 will have a distinguishable power consumption from processing Hamming weight 4. Furthermore, Hamming weight 0 and 4 uniquely determine the processed values, i.e., 0 and 15 (since the rotation index is only 4 bit). For our attack we tried to identify if the Hamming weight of the updated rotation index after the first round equals 0, which in return means that the initial rotation index was j[0]=15. Note that if the initial rotation index is known, all masks are uniquely determined.

Figure 4 shows two average traces of the first encryption round recorded during profiling (i.e., we know all j[0]), one representing the group of traces when the starting index j[0]=15 and the other j[0]!=15. The bottom trace shows the difference and one can clearly identify a peak around sample 98,000, where we assume the index update takes place. For all measurements we integrated over all samples in this particular clock cycle and applied the k-means clustering algorithm [12]. The k-means clustering algorithm takes n measurements, tries to group them into k groups and returns the best thresholds to distinguish between these groups. Since we have five Hamming weights here, i.e., $0 - 4$, we chose $k = 5$.

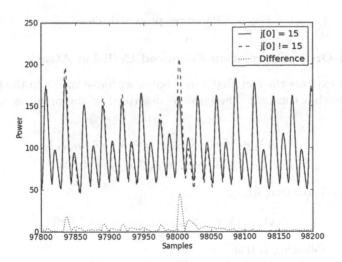

Fig. 4. Two average traces and their difference

To filter out traces we used the threshold given by the k-means clustering algorithm to identify the processing of Hamming weight 0, i.e., j[0]=15. All filtered traces were then used in a standard first-order CPA attack targeting the Hamming weight of the S-box output. Although some false-positives were included in the CPA, only 90 traces were needed for the key recovery, c.f. Fig. 5. As we can see, there are two clear correlation peaks which correspond to the S-box calculation itself and loading the S-box output from memory again to perform the following ShiftRows operation. Note that since we only use roughly every 16th trace because of the filtering process, we need approximately 1,500 measurements in total to mount this attack.

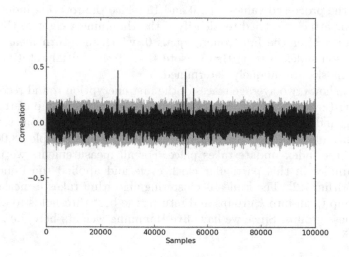

Fig. 5. CPA on pre-processed traces

4.2   First-Order Correlation-Enhanced Collision Attack

This attack exploits the fact that two S-boxes with distance 8 in the first round use masks with a constant difference, as described in the previous section. We know that

$$S_i(x_i \oplus k_i \oplus m_i) \oplus S_{i+8}(x_{i+8} \oplus k_{i+8} \oplus m_{i+8}) = \qquad (6)$$
$$S_{AES}(x_i \oplus k_i) \oplus S_{AES}(x_{i+8} \oplus k_{i+8}) \oplus 0x95 \qquad (7)$$

Therefore we know that if

$$S_{AES}(x_i \oplus k_i) = S_{AES}(x_{i+8} \oplus k_{i+8}) \oplus 0x95 \qquad (8)$$

then also the following is true

$$S_i(x_i \oplus k_i \oplus m_i) = S_{i+8}(x_{i+8} \oplus k_{i+8} \oplus m_{i+8}) \qquad (9)$$

and hence we know we have a collision regarding the S-box output.

In a standard correlation-enhanced collision attack [14] one averages multiple traces corresponding to the same plaintext byte. Here we cannot do this since the masks are different in every measurement and averaging would actually destroy all information. Therefore, all measurements have to be compared individually. The attack is similar to [6] and works as follows:

1. For every measurement n and key hypotheses k_i and k_{i+8} check if $S_{AES}(x_{i,n} \oplus k_i) = S_{AES}(x_{i+8,n} \oplus k_{i+8}) \oplus 0x95$ and save the measurement in a group corresponding to its key hypotheses, resulting in 2^{16} different groups.
2. Then, for every group, calculate the correlation between the power consumptions of two time instances over all measurements. Note that we know the distance between these time instances corresponding to the calculation of S_i and S_{i+8} since single S-box look-ups are clearly identifiable in the power trace. Therefore, we only have to compare every sample s with sample $s +$ distance.
3. If the key hypotheses are correct and the two time instances correspond to the time instances where S_i and S_{i+8} were processed, we will get a high correlation.

Analyzing some averaged power traces (by visual inspection) we determined the distance between the calculation of two S-boxes with distance 8, i.e., 11287 samples. Figure 6 shows the result of our attack targeting S_0 and S_8, and we can clearly identify a correlation peak for the correct key hypothesis (plotted in black) at sample 53841. We used the same traces as in the last section, i.e., taken with the implementation from the DPA contest v4. Note that this attack is deemed to be a first-order attack, since we neither combine samples from our measurements (we only compare) nor pre-process them in any way, e.g., by squaring.

5   Attacking an FPGA Implementation of RSM

In this section we present three attacks on the FPGA implementation of RSM. The FPGA implementation is the original implementation of the RSM scheme taken from [15] and implemented following the idea of [2].[2]

5.1   Univariate Second-Order CPA Attack

In this attack we will show how to exploit the constant mask difference to mount a univariate second-order attack.

Based on our findings in Sect. 2.3 we know the following holds true for some intermediate value $I(k_i, k_{i+8})$:

$$I(k_i, k_{i+8}) = S_i(x_i \oplus k_i \oplus m_i) \oplus S_{i+8}(x_{i+8} \oplus k_{i+8} \oplus m_{i+8})$$
$$= S_{AES}(x_i \oplus k_i) \oplus m_{i+1} \oplus S_{AES}(x_{i+8} \oplus k_{i+8}) \oplus m_{i+8+1}$$
$$= S_{AES}(x_i \oplus k_i) \oplus S_{AES}(x_{i+8} \oplus k_{i+8}) \oplus 0x95$$

---

[2] We would like to thank the authors for providing the implementation.

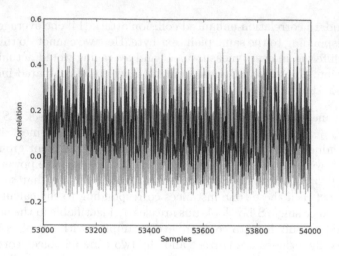

Fig. 6. Correlation-enhanced collision attack on the first round

which an attacker can calculate without knowing the masks. Hence, as power model, the attacker calculates the Hamming distance between the S-box outputs (with the distance of the two S-boxes being 8) and the previous register values and XORs them together with the constant $0x95$. Using this model an attacker has to test 2^{16} key hypotheses. Since the two S-boxes are processed in parallel the power consumption can be estimated by the sum of their individual power consumptions. However, the XOR between two variables does not correlate with the sum of their power consumptions, but as shown in [17], it is possible to mount a CPA on the XOR of two in parallel processed variables if the power traces are squared beforehand, i.e., by exploiting the variances.

Figure 7 depicts the results of the univariate second-order attack exploiting the constant mask difference analyzing 10,000,000 traces. The correct key hypothesis can be clearly distinguished around sampling point 2000. Approximately 1,500,000 traces are needed until the correct key hypothesis yields the highest correlation.

5.2   Two More Collision Attacks

In this section we present two different collision attacks. In contrary to the other attacks we were only able to verify them in simulations and simplified measurements so far, due to their complexity. Nevertheless, we believe that both attacks are interesting and might be applied in real-world scenarios in the future.

The first collision attack exploits the fact that we are able to force collision between two S-boxes in the first round. We know that if

$$p_{i+8} = S_{AES}^{-1}(S_{AES}(p_i \oplus k_i) \oplus 0x95) \oplus k_{i+8} \tag{10}$$

this will result in a collision between S_i and S_{i+8}. We observed that the power consumption over multiple measurements shows a higher variance if two

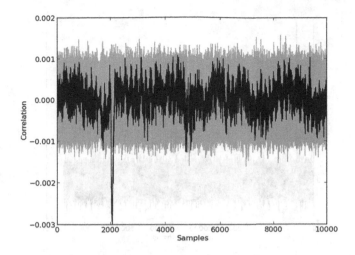

Fig. 7. Univariate second-order CPA exploiting constant mask difference

S-boxes always collide than if they have random outputs. A similar observation was made in [11]. Based on key hypotheses for k_i and k_{i+8} an attacker can build groups of traces which (supposedly) collide (verifying Eq. 10) in every measurement and calculate the variances of these groups for every point in time. The highest variance indicates the correct key. Figure 8 shows the result of a simulated attack with the keys $k_i = 0x12$ and $k_{i+8} = 0x24$. For the simulation we estimated the power consumption of in parallel processed masked S-boxes by calculating the sum of the individual Hamming weights of the S-box outputs (Hamming distance can be used accordingly), and added Gaussian noise. As one can see the variance of the measurements corresponding to the correct key hypotheses ($0x1224 = 4644$) is clearly the highest.

In our last attack we try to exploit collisions between the first and last round. We know that the masks are rotated by one in every round, hence, for example, S_0 in the first round uses the same output mask as S_7 in the last round. Given a plaintext p and a ciphertext c, where p_i and c_i are the ith nibble of the plaintext and ciphertext, respectively, and $k_{i,j}$ is the ith nibble of the subkey in the jth round, we need to check if

$$S_{AES}(p_0 \oplus k_{0,0}) = c_{11} \oplus k_{11,10} \tag{11}$$

For the correct key hypotheses the side-channel measurements of the S-box outputs of round 1 and round 10 will always collide, and hence will have a similar power consumption. Note that for this attack an adversary has to know input and output of an encryption while for classical attacks either input or output is sufficient.

However, such collisions do not happen very often with random plaintexts. Therefore, an adversary has to precompute sets of plaintexts, given a hypothesis for $k_{0,0}$ and $k_{11,10}$, which fulfill Eq. 11, and perform side-channel measurements

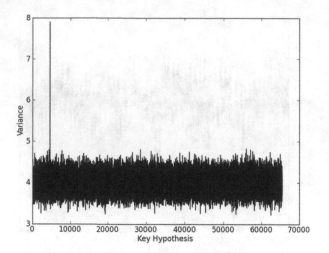

Fig. 8. Forced collisions attack on first round

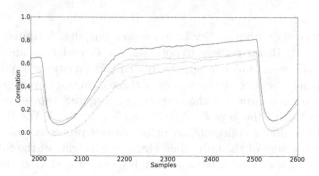

Fig. 9. Collision attack between first and last round

with every one of these precomputed sets. Since this process takes a lot of time, we were only able to build 4 different sets, one with the correct hypothesis and three with wrong hypotheses (instead of 2^{16} sets), and measured 1,000,000 traces for each set. As before, since the masks are chosen randomly and therefore every S-box has a different output mask in every measurement, we are not able to average multiple traces with the same plaintext or ciphertext as it is done in a classical correlation-enhanced collision attack. Instead, we have to compare the S-box outputs for every trace individually, similar to [6].

Figure 9 shows the result of our (shortened) attack. The 4 plots represent the correlation between the power consumptions of the two clock cycles where the S-box outputs in round 1 and round 10 are calculated, with the black plot representing the set taken with the correct key. The correct key should yield the highest correlation since then the S-boxes always collide, and as can be seen, this is indeed the case. It should be noted that although the (here simplified) attack works, it might be too costly to generate 2^{16} sets of plaintexts and take 1,000,000 measurements for every set.

6 Conclusion

In this paper we re-evaluated the security analysis of the RSM scheme presented in [15]. We showed that the attack model used in the original evaluation was not optimal, therefore presented an updated model, repeated the security analysis and confirmed that RSM is indeed secure against classical univariate first- and second-order attacks.

Second, we found a constant difference between base masks with certain distance. Based on this vulnerability we presented five different attacks, two on the smart card implementation used in the DPA contest v4 and three on the original FPGA implementation, which can undermine the security of RSM. These attacks have shown that the base masks have to be very carefully chosen. Two of three other analyzed sets showed the same vulnerability, while the third showed a clear bias towards certain differences.

Future research will investigate if this bias can be exploited as well. Another interesting task will be the definition of special properties to minimize leakage while circumventing constant differences or biases, i.e., the generation of secure mask sets.

Acknowledgments. The authors would like to thank Thomas Peyrin and Ivica Nikolic for the fruitful discussions and Marc Stöttinger for the pointer to the k-means algorithm. We would also like to thank the reviewers for their valuable comments which greatly helped to improve this paper.

References

1. Bhasin, S., Guilley, S., Heuser, A., Danger, J.L.: From cryptography to hardware: analyzing and protecting embedded xilinx bram for cryptographic applications. J. Cryptographic Eng., 1–13 (2013)
2. Bhasin, S., He, W., Guilley, S., Danger, J.L.: Exploiting fpga block memories for protected cryptographic implementations. In: 2013 8th International Workshop on Reconfigurable and Communication-Centric Systems-on-Chip (ReCoSoC), pp. 1–8. IEEE (2013)
3. Brier, E., Clavier, C., Olivier, F.: Correlation power analysis with a leakage model. In: Joye, M., Quisquater, J.-J. (eds.) CHES 2004. LNCS, vol. 3156, pp. 16–29. Springer, Heidelberg (2004)
4. Brouwer, A.E., Shearer, J.B., Sloane, N.J., Smith, W.D.: A new table of constant weight codes. IEEE Trans. Inf. Theor. **36**(6), 1334–1380 (1990)
5. Carlet, C., Guilley, S.: Side-channel indistinguishability. In: Proceedings of the 2nd International Workshop on Hardware and Architectural Support for Security and Privacy, p. 9. ACM (2013)
6. Clavier, C., Feix, B., Gagnerot, G., Roussellet, M., Verneuil, V.: Improved collision-correlation power analysis on first order protected AES. In: Preneel, B., Takagi, T. (eds.) CHES 2011. LNCS, vol. 6917, pp. 49–62. Springer, Heidelberg (2011)

7. Digital Electronic Systems research group: DPA Contest v4 (2013). http://www. dpacontest.org/v4/

8. Guilley, S., Bhasin, S., Najm, Z., Danger, J.L.: A low-entropy first-degree secure provable masking scheme for resource-constrained devices (2013)

9. Kocher, P.C., Jaffe, J., Jun, B.: Differential power analysis. In: Wiener, M. (ed.) CRYPTO 1999. LNCS, vol. 1666, pp. 388–397. Springer, Heidelberg (1999)

10. Kutzner, S., Nguyen, P.H., Poschmann, A., Wang, H.: On 3-share threshold implementations for 4-bit s-boxes. IACR Cryptology ePrint Archive 2012, 509 (2012)

11. Li, Y., Sakiyama, K., Batina, L., Nakatsu, D., Ohta, K.: Power variance analysis breaks a masked asic implementation of AES. In: Proceedings of the Conference on Design, Automation and Test in Europe, pp. 1059–1064. European Design and Automation Association (2010)

12. MacQueen, J., et al.: Some methods for classification and analysis of multivariate observations. In: Proceedings of the Fifth Berkeley Symposium on Mathematical Statistics and Probability, California, USA, vol. 1, p. 14 (1967)

13. Mangard, S., Oswald, E., Popp, T.: Power analysis attacks: Revealing the secrets of smart cards, vol. 31. Springer (2007)

14. Moradi, A., Mischke, O., Eisenbarth, T.: Correlation-enhanced power analysis collision attack. In: Mangard, S., Standaert, F.-X. (eds.) CHES 2010. LNCS, vol. 6225, pp. 125–139. Springer, Heidelberg (2010)

15. Nassar, M., Souissi, Y., Guilley, S., Danger, J.L.: RSM: a small and fast countermeasure for AES, secure against 1st and 2nd-order Zero-Offset SCAs. In: Design, Automation & Test in Europe Conference & Exhibition (DATE) 2012, pp. 1173–1178. IEEE (2012)

16. Poschmann, A., Moradi, A., Khoo, K., Lim, C.W., Wang, H., Ling, S.: Side-channel resistant crypto for less than 2,300 ge. J. Cryptology 24(2), 322–345 (2011)

17. Waddle, J., Wagner, D.: Towards efficient second-order power analysis. In: Joye, M., Quisquater, J.-J. (eds.) CHES 2004. LNCS, vol. 3156, pp. 1–15. Springer, Heidelberg (2004)

Author Index